A POPULAR SCIENCE BOOK

WOODWORKING PROJECTS FOR THE HOME

118 PRACTICAL AND USEFUL PROJECTS FROM POPULAR SCIENCE MONTHLY

POPULAR SCIENCE BOOKS

HARPER & ROW, PUBLISHERS

NEW YORK, SAN FRANCISCO, HAGERSTOWN, LONDON

Library of Congress Catalog Number: 73-86629
SBN: 06-013394-5

Eighth Printing, 1980

Designed by Jeff Fitschen

Manufactured in the United States of America

FOREWORD

The projects in this book range wide in usefulness and complexity. Some are simple trays and plate holders that a novice woodworker can make in an evening or two; others are highly developed, intricate pieces of furniture that will delight and challenge the expert craftsman. There are tables, chairs, chests, desks, storage units, planters, children's furniture, bars, projection tables and other projects ranging in style from conservative-traditional to ultra-mod. Most can be constructed with simple hand tools or power tools, whichever the reader prefers to use.

These pieces were planned, built and described with great care by many of the finest craftsmen-writers, designers and architects. Most are full-time authors who originate and build useful objects for the home, often with the latest innovative techniques and materials. Others are now-and-then contributors who have occupations in other fields, but whose favorite avocation is to build and write about woodworking projects. All photograph and describe their projects with clarity and precision.

The Book Division of Popular Science Publishing Company is grateful to Hubert Luckett, Editor-in-Chief of Popular Science Monthly, for permission to use the articles that are reprinted in these pages, and thanks go also to the editors of the magazine for their care and expertise in the original preparation of the articles.

CONTENTS

A DINING TABLE YOU'LL BE PROUD OF   1

A MOVABLE PENINSULA FOR YOUR KITCHEN   4

PROVINCIAL-STYLE DESK   6

FLOATING TABLES   11

HUTCH-STYLE PLANTER FOR THE WALL   12

SEVEN-IN-ONE GAME TABLE   14

DESK CADDY   18

TELESCOPING WOOD RINGS TURN INTO LAMP   19

ALL-IN-ONE "TURNITURE"   23

BUFFET OR DINING TABLE: HERE ARE BOTH IN ONE   27

HOW TO ADD A TYPEWRITER TABLE TO A DESK   32

BOX SHELVES ARE IN STYLE   33

DOUBLE-DUTY CENTERPIECE FOR YOUR HOME   34

CLASSIC PICTURE FRAME   35

ADJUSTABLE SHELF SYSTEM FOR A SHOW-OFF WALL   36

GROOMING TRAY   38

A FINE MARBLE-TOPPED TABLE   39

PUT THAT CRAWL SPACE TO WORK   47

BOOKSHELVES   48

SHALLOW CABINET FOR A HALLWAY   49

CONTENTS (Continued)

SCULPTURED END TABLE	51
SLICING PLATFORM	54
RECLINING CHAIR ADJUSTS FOR COMFORT	55
KEEP THE DIRECTORY NEAR YOUR KITCHEN PHONE	60
ONE-SHEET PARTY KNOCKDOWNS	61
PLYWOOD ROCKER-TABLE FOR 4-IN-1 PATIO FUN	66
A SLATE-TOPPED BUFFET	70
COFFEE MUG HOUSE	72
WESTERN-STYLE TRESTLE DESK AND BENCH	73
AIR FORCE ACADEMY DESK	74
SWIVEL-TOP PROJECTION CABINET	80
SPANISH-STYLE TILE TABLE	84
CORIAN-TOPPED SERVER IN THE CLASSIC STYLE	88
BALCONY SHELVES FOR APARTMENT DWELLERS	93
HOW TO REPRODUCE A PEMBROKE TABLE	94
LOW-COST, HIGH-STYLE OTTOMAN	98
SHAKER SETTEE	99
EARLY AMERICAN DOLL CRIB	103
LOCKUP GUN CABINET	104
CHILD'S WARDROBE: A "HOUSEKEEPER" YOU CAN BUILD	106
COFFEE TABLE THAT SOLVES A PROBLEM	107
KITCHEN-TOWEL HOLDER	110
MOBILE PLANTER FOR HEAVY HOUSEPLANTS	111
OUTDOOR-INDOOR FURNITURE	112
SHELVES THAT MOVE WITH YOU	113
FLIP-TOP TABLE: TWO GAMES IN ONE	118
AIR CONDITIONER SHELF	123
TWO-FACED COUCH IS A REAL SLEEPER	124
A MAKE-UP STAND	125
THE FURNITURE THAT SERVES YOU FOUR WAYS	126
GLASS-TOPPED COFFEE TABLE	131
HOW TO BUILD A TABLE THE CHINESE WAY	132
SPACE-SAVING SPICE RACK	136
STORAGE CABINETS MADE EASY	137
YOUR CHOICE: TWO PHONE BENCHES FOR YOUR HOME	138
A LOG HAMPER	140

HOW TO BUILD THE MICRODORM 141
DUAL-PURPOSE HAMPER 146
NO-TOOL KNOCKDOWN PUZZLE BOOKCASE 147
GUEST ROOM IN A TEN-INCH SPACE 148
A TILT-TOP TABLE 155
SMART FISH BOWL UNDER THE TABLE 161
ADJUSTABLE BOOK RACK FOR DESK 165
MODERN VANITY FOR A SPARE CORNER 166
NO-CLUTTER SHOE RACK 167
EASY-TO-BUILD DESK:
  EVERYTHING AT YOUR FINGERTIPS 168
A DROP-LEAF TABLE WITH A NEW TWIST 172
KNOCKDOWN DESK IS A KNOCKOUT 173
SLAW-BOARD TABLE 176
SAILMAKER'S BENCH 178
BUFFET WITH WOVEN PANELS 180
LUGGAGE RACK FOLDS COMPACTLY FOR STORAGE 185
A ROOMFUL OF 2 x 2s 186
AN "I" TABLE AND A SET OF CUBE CHAIRS 191
A STURDY TYPEWRITER STAND 195
SHAKER CANDLESTAND . . . AND CANDLESTICK, TOO 196
DESK . . . HOBBY BENCH . . . AND IT'S ALSO A BAR 198
COFFEE-TABLE MUSIC CENTER 201
TV DINNER TRAY 206
MOD MINI-CANDELABRA 207
NO ATTIC? SHELVES WILL DO THE JOB 208
TABLETOP WITH RECESSED TILE PATTERN 210
DELTA DESK 215
WALL-MOUNTED DESK 218
PHOTO COASTERS 219
STORAGE WALL FOR FAMILY ROOM 220
NONSKID CUTTING BOARD 224
EARLY AMERICAN HUTCH 225
BUILD A CLOSET ORGANIZER 226
FOOTSTOOL FROM ABE LINCOLN'S HOME 228
COUNTER-TOP CUTOUTS 234
PARTICLEBOARD COFFEE TABLE 238

xi

CONTENTS (Continued)

HOME HOBBY CENTER   242
CHILD'S SLEEP-PLAY UNIT   245
STURDY STACK TABLES—TRIO   250
CANDLESTICK PLATE HOLDER   251
DESKS YOU CAN SIZE TO SUIT YOUR HOME   252
ROTATING BOOKSHELF   255
CORNER-HUNG BAR   256
AN EASY CHAIR JUST FOR YOURSELF   257
SAW BOOKENDS   262
DRY-SINK RECIPE HOLDER   263
CARVING BOARD   264
FANCY PARSONS TABLE   266
FRAME A CLOCK   269
ADD A MODERN VANITY TO YOUR BATH   270
SNACK BAR FOR THE KITCHEN   272
BEVERAGE SERVER   273
FIVE-DOOR PHONE BOOTH FOR YOUR FAMILY ROOM   274
MAGAZINE RACK   275
HOME-SHOW STAND SETS UP FAST, STORES FLAT   276
REFRIGERATOR SHELF   279
TWO ROOMS FROM ONE   280
MODULAR PLANTER   284
HEADBOARD FOR NIGHT OWLS   286
UNDER-CABINET SPICE RACK   289
STORAGE-ALL TABLE WITH HIGH-STYLE HINGES   290
PANTRY STORAGE BEHIND KITCHEN DOOR   294

WOODWORKING PROJECTS FOR THE HOME

A DINING TABLE YOU'LL BE PROUD OF

BY DARRELL HUFF

A slab of handsome green marble between two slabs of polished wood. That's the top of a distinguished dining table that has three major virtues:

- It's unusually simple to build.
- It's highly functional.
- It's a handsome addition to any dining room.

The three-piece top eliminates any need to edge-glue lumber or put trim around plywood, often the hardest part of building a table. The legs are simple four-by-four lumber columns, bolted on. Much of the assembly is with copper nails. These, their heads sanded flush with the wood, give the effect of metal dowels or heavy pins.

Besides being handsome, the marble provides a place to put hot pots and dishes, right off the stove or out of the oven. When the marble is removed and the legs are unbolted, the table is easy to handle for storing or on moving day.

In 76″ length, without leaves, the table seats six generously. With drop leaves up you can squeeze in as many as a dozen. For a small family or limited space, a half-length version may be more suitable. I built both versions for members of my family—and know that both have been useful.

Buy your marble first. Let the size in which you find it most conveniently available determine dimensions of the wood parts. These are easily varied from those I used. The size of my table, for instance, was influenced by my find of a fine piece of marble measuring 22¾″ by 38″. Cut in half lengthwise, it made two strips of fine proportions.

Corian is another choice—if you prefer, or if you have any trouble finding real marble. DuPont's man-made marble, Corian, comes in slabs ¾″ thick, up to 30″ wide, and 96″ long. Buy it from a DuPont dealer; some lumberyards have it. Work it with woodworking tools.

With drop leaves up, table seats eight. With the leaves down, it takes six. Center strip of marble is highly functional, stays in place between wood strips without any fastenings.

1

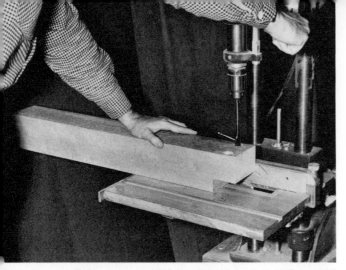

Table legs are 29″ lengths of lumber 3¾″ by 3¾″ square. Cut 1¼″-by-2½″ notch at one end, drill, and counterbore to take two ⅜″-by-4″ carriage bolts.

Clamp on legs, bore holes through frame. Bolt in place, nuts inside (no glue), so legs can be removed. Note notches in cross rails for drop-leaf support.

Make two U-shaped drop-leaf supports from 1″-by-1″ hardwood strips (left). For each, assemble a 14¾″ strip across ends of two strips, each about 34½″ long, using copper nails and glue. Photo at right shows how drop-leaf support fits and works. A snug fit in slots is desirable. Apply wax to the long strips for easy sliding.

Drop leaf for each end is 13½″-by-38¼″ piece of same material as top. Ends of hinges shown had to be recessed a bit into frame. Position and screw them into place with leaf folded.

Cut four cleats and two trim pieces from 1¼″ stock as in sketches. Bevel-rip trim pieces from stock 3½″ wide, 74½″ long. Glue two cleats across each leaf to discourage warping, aligning with side rail. Glue edge trim on each side of table. Plane and sand table edge and trim to a continuous taper to look like one piece.

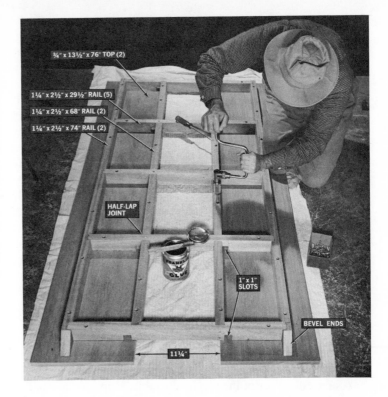

¾" x 13½" x 76" TOP (2)

1¼" x 2½" x 29½" RAIL (5)

1¼" x 2½" x 68" RAIL (2)

1¼" x 2½" x 74" RAIL (2)

HALF-LAP JOINT

1" x 1" SLOTS

BEVEL ENDS

11¼"

Underside view (right) shows parts. Notch and assemble frame with glue and copper nails, fasten to top pieces with glue and screws. Space center rails so marble can rest on them. Counterbore for screws as shown, then plug holes.

MATERIALS LIST

¾" Philippine mahogany to make:
- 2 tops 13½" x 76"
- 2 drop leaves 13½" x 38¼"

1¼" Philippine mahogany to make:
- 2 outside rails 2½" x 74½"
- 2 center rails 2½" x 68"
- 5 cross rails 2½" x 29½"
- 4 cleats (from 2½" x 29" piece)
- 2 edge trimmers (from 3½" x 74½")

3¾" x 3¾" hardwood (apitong or similar) to make:
- 4 legs 29" long

1" x 1" hardwood (oak) to make:
- 4 pieces 34½" long
- 2 pieces 14¾" long (for drop-leaf supports)

Marble or Corian to suit
2 pr. drop-leaf hinges with screws
34 2½"-12 F.H. wood screws
8 ¾"-4" carriage bolts
Copper nails 2" to 2½" long
Finish: Danish teak oil

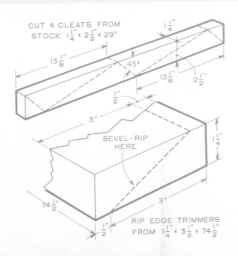

CUT 4 CLEATS FROM STOCK 1¼" x 2½" x 29"

1¼"

13⅛"

45°

13⅛"

2½"

½"

3"

BEVEL-RIP HERE

1¼"

74½"

3"

1¼"

½"

RIP EDGE TRIMMERS FROM 1¼" x 3½" x 74½"

Lumber can be anything that goes well with your marble or Corian. Because it is richly colored, available in wide boards and remarkably inexpensive, I used Philippine mahogany for everything but the legs. Since I couldn't find Philippine in thick enough stock I switched to apitong, a tropical hardwood of similar color and grain.

For finish I rubbed on Danish teak oil. This shows scratches far less than varnish does and is easily renewed when necessary.

A MOVABLE PENINSULA FOR YOUR KITCHEN

Three kitchen essentials are provided by this unique rolling unit—an eating counter, handy storage for odd-shaped slim items such as trays and place mats, and a work surface the housewife can move wherever it's needed.

The movable peninsula is of standard table height, and takes conventional chairs instead of stools. Part of the top is hinged to drop out of the way when not needed, and lockable casters keep the unit fixed when desired.

The peninsula is part of a custom kitchen designed by Armstrong Cork to display their new Valargo design in the Coronelle Vinyl Corlon flooring. Since the unit moves, floor cleaning is easier.

The same prefinished paneling that's on the wall was used for the vertical cabinet surfaces, inside and outside.

To complement the floor covering, the drawer fronts are painted a soft blue.

The legs and rails are of two-by-two stock ripped to 1½" square. Since they will be painted, fir can be used but the wood first requires thorough sanding and sealing. Use glue for all assembly, together with dowels, screws, or brads as indicated on the drawing.

Construction hints. If the plywood panels are cut accurately, you can eliminate the ¼" quarter-round. And to keep the frame square during the steps that follow, brace it with several diagonals after it has been assembled. Also, if you paint the frame before the paneling goes on, you'll save time and avoid the risk of spattering. Tip: Since you need only a small amount of the black-plastic laminate for the self-edge, try to buy the strips from a local cabinet shop.

The drawer pulls on the unit shown are custom-made and unavailable. Anyway, hardware should be chosen to tie in with existing pulls in your kitchen.

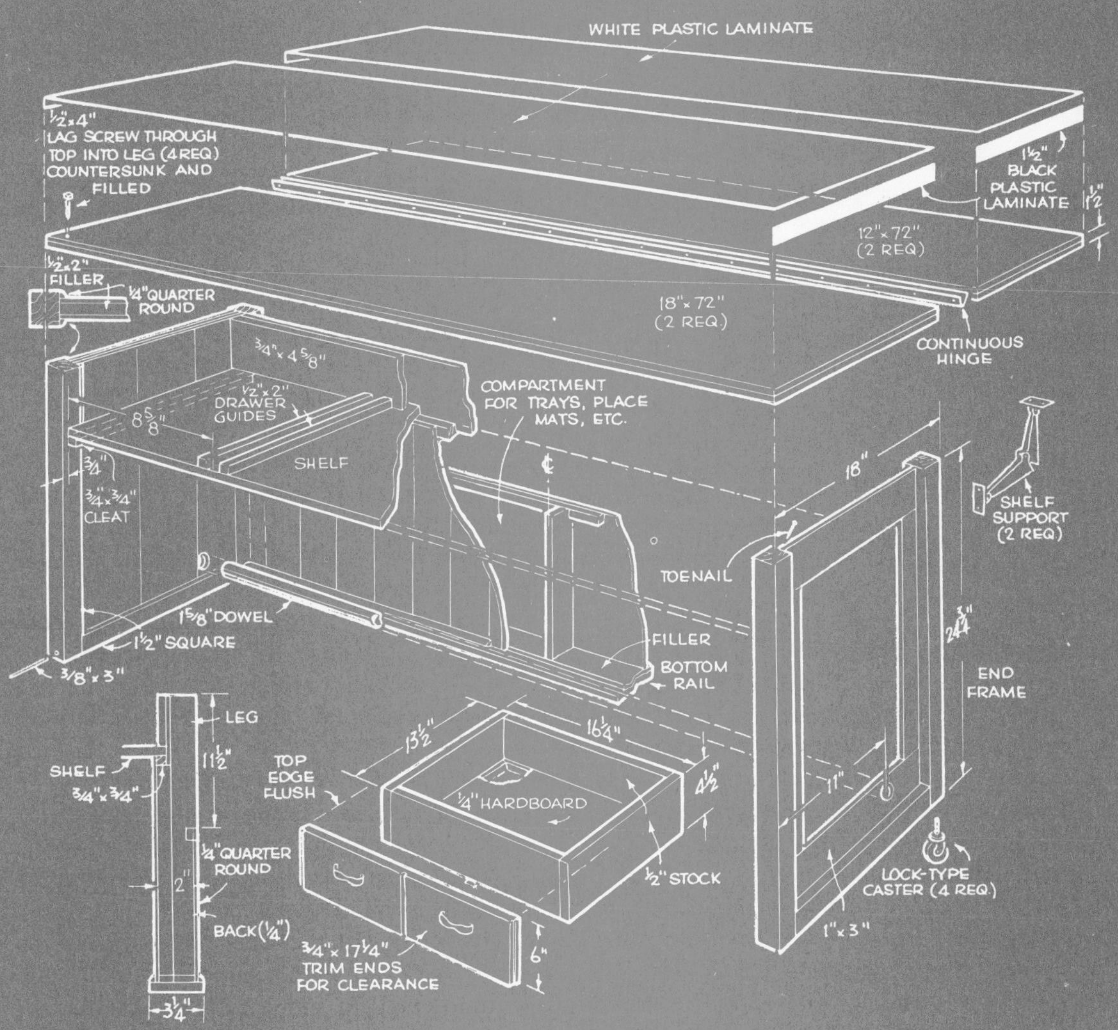

WHITE PLASTIC LAMINATE
½"x4" LAG SCREW THROUGH TOP INTO LEG (4 REQ) COUNTERSUNK AND FILLED
1½" BLACK PLASTIC LAMINATE
1½"
12"x72" (2 REQ)
½"x2" FILLER
¼" QUARTER ROUND
18"x72" (2 REQ)
CONTINUOUS HINGE
¾"x4⅝"
½"x2" DRAWER GUIDES
8⅝"
COMPARTMENT FOR TRAYS, PLACE MATS, ETC.
SHELF
¾"
¾"x¾" CLEAT
18"
SHELF SUPPORT (2 REQ)
TOENAIL
1⅝" DOWEL
1½" SQUARE
⅜"x3"
FILLER
BOTTOM RAIL
24¾"
END FRAME
LEG
SHELF
11½"
¾"x¾"
TOP EDGE FLUSH
13½"
16¼"
¼" HARDBOARD
4½"
11"
¼" QUARTER ROUND
2"
BACK (¼")
½" STOCK
LOCK-TYPE CASTER (4 REQ)
¾"x17¼" TRIM ENDS FOR CLEARANCE
6"
1"x3"
3¼"

MATERIALS LIST

White plastic laminate
- 1 pc. 12″ x 72″ (hinged top)
- 1 pc. 18″ x 72″ (fixed top)

Black plastic laminate (all 1½″ wide)
- 2 pcs. 18″, 1 pc. 72″ (fixed top)
- 2 pcs. 12″, 1 pc. 72″ (hinged top)

Particleboard
- 2 pcs. 18″ x 72″, (top)
- 2 pcs. 12″ x 72″, (top)

Lumber
- 2″ x 2″—4 pcs. 25″, 2 pcs. 18″ (frame)
- ½″ x 3″—1 pc. 3′ (dowel supports)
- ½″ x 2″—30′ (fillers)
- 1″ x 5″—6′ (back of drawer cabinet)
- 1″ x 4″—6′ (bottom rail, back)
- ½″ x 3″—6′ (compartment-base filler)
- ¾″ x ¾″—2 pcs. 6′ (compartment rails)
- 1⅝″ dowel—6′
- ¼″ quarter-round molding—42′

Plywood
- ¾″—14¾″ x 69″ (shelf)
- ¼″ prefinished paneling—1 pc. 4′ x 8′ and 1 pc. 4′ x 4′ (facing)

Miscellaneous

6′ pc. 3″ continuous hinge, 2 locking shelf supports, 4 lock-type casters, screws, brads, ⅜″ wood dowels, white glue, and contact cement.

PROVINCIAL-STYLE DESK

BY CHESTER DAVIS

This desk was designed to meet two specific challenges. First, it had to blend in with the provincial furniture in my daughter's room; and second, I wanted to use fir plywood wherever possible, due to its low cost. By using one of the commercially marketed antiquing kits for finishing, both design and material requirements were met.

Pine was used for framing members and the legs were made from fir. The desk top is ¾" ply, and is plastic laminated; all other plywood is ¼".

To speed up the decorative molding work, all the pieces that required shaping were done at the same time. Craftsman mono-head cutters were used here, and the catalogue number for each one is shown on the blueprint. The numbers given are for a mono head; if you own a three-bit cutter, drop the last digit (3) from the number when ordering.

Start with the legs. Cut them to length and trim them to 1½" square. The decorative molding work is required on the three front legs only. To assure uniformity of groove length, clamp start and stop blocks as shown.

The two ⅛" grooves at top and bottom were done with a router and template. When measuring the router shoe to determine the distance at which the template is set, measure from the outside of the cutter to shoe edge. When grooving, the router cutter should be on the inside of the mark on the leg. It's best to test both of these steps on scrap before proceeding with the legs.

The ¾" groove above the foot can be made using dado heads, or by making repeated passes through the combination blade. Taper the bottom 3" on the bandsaw or by hand.

The panels for the sides and back can be cut next. The molded rails, at top and bottom, are cut to length and attached to the panels. The rails on the back panels are not shaped, but are grooved to receive the ply panels.

Cut the stiles and rails for the front frames next. After grooving, assemble both of the frames temporarily and check the outside measurements. Each frame should be exactly the same as its opposite back panel.

Assembling the desk. If you are limited in the number of bar clamps you own, the best method for desk assembly is to preassemble subsections. Start by gluing each side panel to its mating legs. Check with a square before and after clamping. After the glue has dried you can go to work on the left side of the desk.

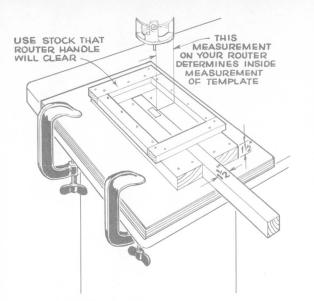

USE STOCK THAT ROUTER HANDLE WILL CLEAR

THIS MEASUREMENT ON YOUR ROUTER DETERMINES INSIDE MEASUREMENT OF TEMPLATE

1½

½

To make the ⅛" grooves on the legs, use 1½" stock and a clamp to hold the leg, ¼" ply for the template. Each side of the template is set parallel to its corresponding groove line a distance equal to the measurement from router bit to shoe edge. Start the plunge in a corner and keep the shoe in constant contact with template. Do three rectangles; then, using same ply, remake templates to do squares.

To flute the legs, make up a jig with the starting block set 21¼" back from the point where the molding head starts to cut. Place the stop block 22¾" beyond that point. Dimensions can vary, so test with scrap, and adjust if necessary. With the leg against starting block, and fence, lower it onto the turning cutter. Make the same pass on all three legs, move the fence for the next two. Drawing shows details of the jig.

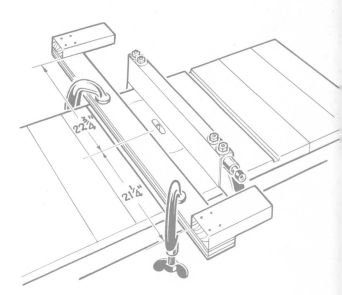

22¾"

21¼"

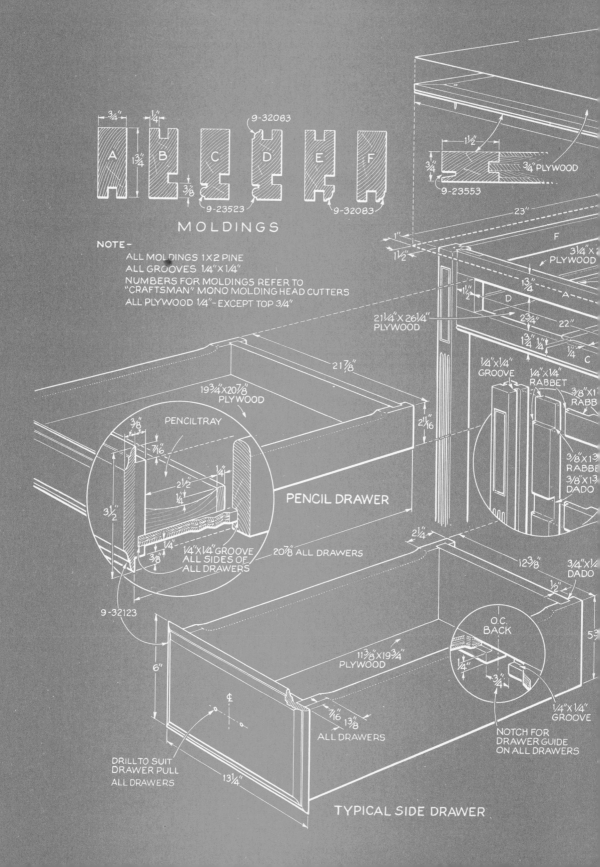

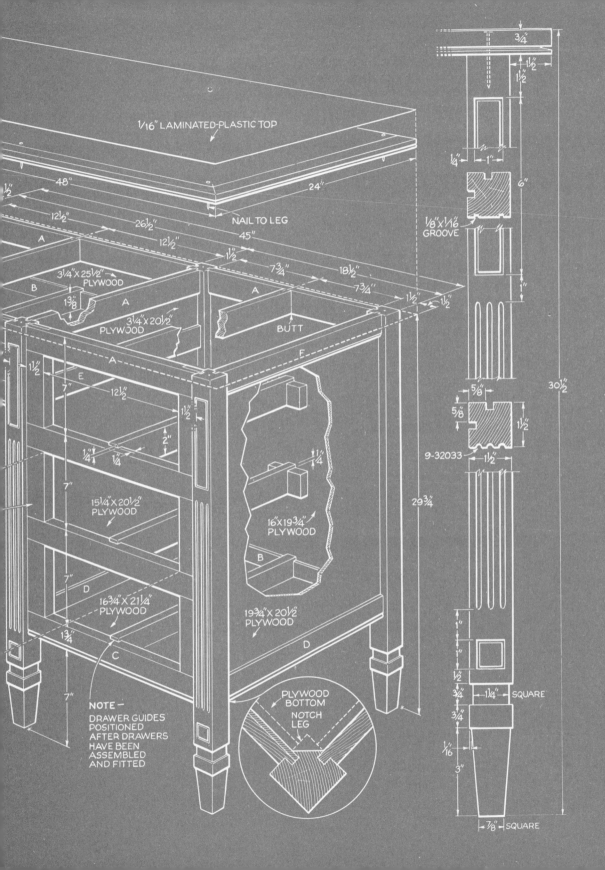

1/16" LAMINATED-PLASTIC TOP

NAIL TO LEG

1/2"
48"
12 1/2"
26 1/2"
12 1/2"
45"
1 1/2"
7 3/4"
18 1/2"
7 3/4"
1 1/2"
1 1/2"
24"

A

B
3 1/4" X 25 1/2"
PLYWOOD
1 3/8"
A
3 1/4" X 20 1/2"
PLYWOOD

A
BUTT

E

A
1 1/2"
E
7"
12 1/2"
1 1/2"
2"
1/4"
1/4"

15 1/4" X 20 1/2"
PLYWOOD

16" X 19 3/4"
PLYWOOD

7"

7"

D
16 3/4" X 21 1/4"
PLYWOOD

1 3/4"

C

7"

B

19 3/4" X 20 1/2"
PLYWOOD

D

1/4"

29 3/4"

NOTE—
DRAWER GUIDES
POSITIONED
AFTER DRAWERS
HAVE BEEN
ASSEMBLED
AND FITTED

PLYWOOD
BOTTOM

NOTCH
LEG

3/4"
1 1/2"
1 1/2"
1/4"
1"
6"
1/8" X 1/16"
GROOVE
1"

5/8"
5/8"
1 1/2"
9-32033
1 1/2"

30 1/2"

1"
1"
1/2"
3/4"
1 1/4" SQUARE
3/4"
1/16"
3"

7/8" SQUARE

Insert the back panel and front frame into the left side. Slide the bottom into the grooves and attach the center section. Next attach the front frame and back for the right side. Install the ply bottom and attach the final side.

Making the drawers. Build the four drawers as shown. Adjust the dimensions if necessary to insure that they slide freely in the desk. Each drawer should be a minimum of 1/8″ less in width, and 1/16″ less in height, than its corresponding opening. The drawer guide is simply a notch cut in the drawer back. Locate the cleat position by working from the front with a framing square. Use a couple of brads and glue to attach the cleats. Cut the drawer guides to length and install them starting with the lowest drawer and working up. Place the guide in its approximate location and slide the drawer in. After positioning the drawer, slide it out carefully, and mark the guide location.

The top can now be assembled and positioned on the desk. Check the overhang to be sure it is set square; glue, and put an 8d nail into each leg.

Laminating the desk top. Follow the manufacturer's instructions to apply the contact cement. When the glue has dried, carefully drop the plastic onto the desk top. To assure a good bond, slide a block of wood over the entire surface, tapping it with a hammer as you go. Trim any overhang with a file.

The pencil tray is simply a piece of crown molding glued to the bottom of the drawer. Make sure there is enough space for the drawer pull screws before inserting the tray. A strip of 1/4″ lattice can be attached to the tray edge to keep pencils from rolling out.

Sand the desk and apply a coat of sanding sealer before antiquing. The color choice for the desk shown was antique white with gold striping. Attach the hardware, and you can catch up on those letters you've been promising to write for such a long time.

MATERIALS LIST
1 plywood panel 3/4″ x 2′ x 4′
1 plywood panel 1/4″ x 4′ x 8′
1 pc. 1/16″ x 2′ x 4′, plastic laminate
3 pcs. 1″ x 2″ x 6′ pine
5 pcs. 1″ x 2″ x 8′ pine
1 pc. 2″ x 2″ x 10′ pine or fir
1 pc. 2″ x 2″ x 5′ pine or fir
2 pcs. 1″ x 3″ x 8′ pine
1 pc. 1″ x 4″ x 2′ pine
1 pc. 1″ x 6″ x 10′ pine
1 pc. 1″ x 6″ x 8′ pine
1 pc. 2⅝″ x 2′ crown molding
Misc: 4 drawer pulls, 1 qt. contact cement, antiquing kit, assorted nails, flathead screws, glue

The gold striping on antique white gives added period accent to the desk. It goes on just before the final clear finish.

FLOATING TABLES

BY JOHN GRAVES

Here's a concept that can be adapted to making handsome contemporary tables of many sizes and shapes—end tables, bedside tables, occasional tables. Acrylic plastic sheets serve as legs and make the solid-wood top seem to float in the air. The well-sanded wood has an oil finish.

The table above was made from a teak two-by-eight. The plank was cut into three lengths, each 42″ long, and then doweled and edge-glued together. Two-by-two teak cleats were attached across the underside, each with three screws. If you make the middle screw hole slightly larger than the screw, the wood can expand and contract with humidity changes.

Cut the plastic to dimensions to suit the intended use of the table. Finish the cut edges by rubbing them with pumice. Drill holes on one edge for legs.

Tops could be made of plywood and the edges veneered, if solid wood is unavailable.

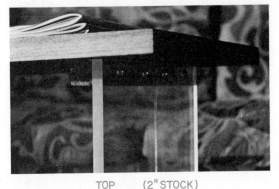

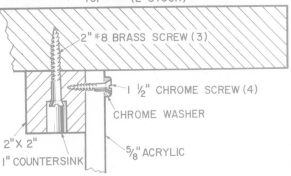

TOP   (2″STOCK)

2″ #8 BRASS SCREW (3)

I ½″ CHROME SCREW (4)

CHROME WASHER

2″X 2″

I″ COUNTERSINK

⅝″ ACRYLIC

HUTCH-STYLE PLANTER FOR THE WALL

BY JOHN E. REPPERT

The hutch-cabinet design of this planter lets it double as a wall display case. Glass doors keep dust from a treasured collection inside. You can make the planter out of any wood you choose, perhaps ½″ hardwood plywood.

Cut the sides first. Dado the grooves for the shelves, cut the shelves, and glue and brad them in place. Make the mask (parts C and D) and glue it in. Cut out and glue in the top and bottom trim pieces.

Next cut out the false drawer front and rabbet the back (detail B-B). Divide the board into three parts and cut a ¼″-deep groove on each line. Cut the chamfers on a radial-arm or table saw with the blade tilted to a 45-degree angle. Sand and glue in place.

Cut out the back. To cut the V grooves, tilt the table-saw blade to 45 degrees and set it ¹⁄₁₆″ above the table. Make a trial cut in scrap wood. Set the rip fence to the desired width and rip the grooves. Don't let the thin plywood slip under the fence. Glue the back in place.

Rabbet the ends of the door-frame pieces and cut the rabbets for the glass. Make the center rails ⅜″ thick to allow room behind them for the glass. Glue them in place, flush with the front of the frames. Rout each door front with a ¼″ cove cutter.

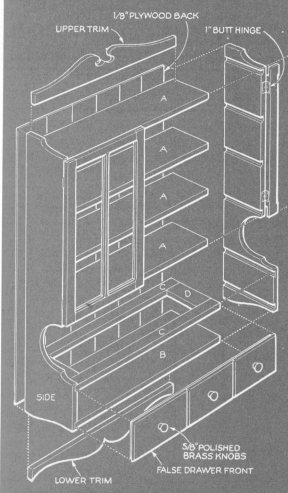

12

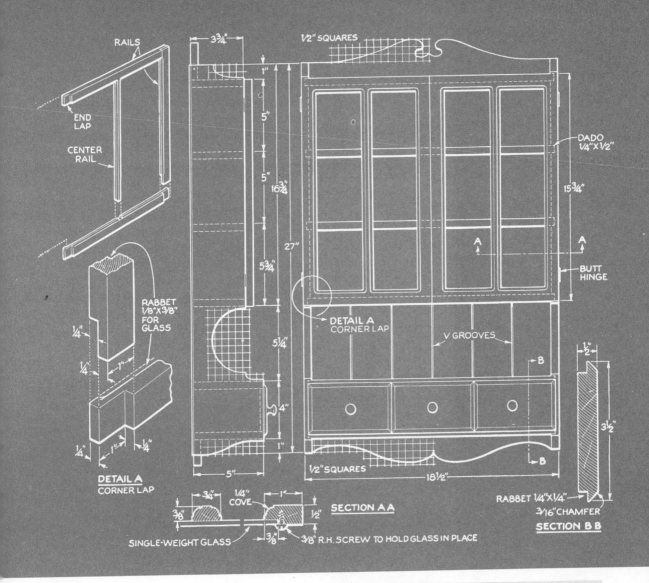

DETAIL A
CORNER LAP

RAILS

END LAP

CENTER RAIL

RABBET 1/8" x 3/8" FOR GLASS

1/2" SQUARES

DADO 1/4" x 1/2"

DETAIL A
CORNER LAP

V GROOVES

BUTT HINGE

SINGLE-WEIGHT GLASS

1/4" COVE

3/8" R.H. SCREW TO HOLD GLASS IN PLACE

SECTION A A

RABBET 1/4" x 1/4"

3/16" CHAMFER

SECTION B B

Locate the hinges 1″ from the ends of the doors. Recess them flush with a sharp chisel. Drill holes for the knobs on the doors and drawer front. Sand the whole project with fine paper, stain if you wish, and finish with semi-gloss varnish.

Use 3/8″ roundhead screws to hold the door glass in place as in detail A-A. You don't need a liner in the planter if you put the plants in small flowerpots.

MATERIALS LIST

2 pc. 1/2" x 5" x 27"	sides
4 pc. 1/2" x 3 3/4" x 18"	shelves (A)
1 pc. 1/2" x 5" x 18"	shelf (B)
2 pc. 1/2" x 1" x 18"	mask sides (C)
2 pc. 1/2" x 1 3/4" x 3"	mask ends (D)
1 pc. 1/2" x 2 1/2" x 17 1/2"	top trim
1 pc. 1/2" x 1 3/4" x 17 1/2"	bottom trim
4 pc. 1/2" x 1" x 15 3/4"	side-door rails
4 pc. 1/2" x 1" x 9 1/4"	end-door rails
2 pc. 3/8" x 1" x 14 1/4"	center door rails
1 pc. 1/8" x 18 1/2" x 27"	back (plywood)
1 pc. 1/2" x 4" x 18"	false drawer front
2 pc. 7 3/4" x 14 1/4"	single-weight glass

SEVEN-IN-ONE GAME TABLE

BY RICHARD C. SICKLER

When television palls, these long winter nights, few things are more fun than playing a game or two with your wife or (after the homework) with the kids. But searching for the desired game through drawers and closets often kills the impulse.

That's why I gathered all our favorite board games—checkers, backgammon, Scrabble, Monopoly, Parcheesi—and designed a playing table around them. The table nests the boards under its marble-like Corian top—which, in itself, makes a fine playing surface for card games, or just for serving refreshments. Two drawers keep all the playing pieces at hand.

You'll probably choose a wood that matches your present furniture—maple, walnut, oak, or pine. If not, do as I did—use Philippine mahogany, filled and stained a rich brown to accent the grain. And trim it with delicate brass highlights, such as square rod tapped into routed grooves with a rubber mallet.

Study the construction drawings. You'll note that the table isn't difficult to build, though the power tools and jigs shown in the photos will speed the work considerably.

How it's built. The understructure is fairly simple. Openings for the two drawers are cut in opposite aprons with a saber saw. Two slats across the center support the gameboard nest and serve as guides for the drawers. (Ten cleats of varying dimensions are screwed to the inner faces of the slats for these purposes.) A square of 3/8″ plywood makes a floor for the gameboard nest, and is hinged to one of the slats. At the opposite side, a rawhide thong is anchored to the underside of the plywood. Enough wood is removed (from cleat, floor, and slat) to create a channel that lets the thong move freely up through the stack of gameboards.

Screws through corner blocks secure the top to the understructure. The finish on a game table should resist water and alcohol spills, plus the foods and juices that usually accompany family fun. I first used a dark mahogany penetrating-stain filler. After it had dried for 48 hours I applied a penetrating resin varnish. With this type of varnish, you brush it on, let it stand for about an hour, then wipe the excess off the surface. Three or four coats are best. The result: a satiny, hard, rubbed finish that brings out the grain of the wood and will wear and wear. One of the best

brands is Tungseal Danish penetrating varnish. You'll find it at most good paint and hardware stores.

Sources of supply. To obtain the other materials:

• Corian is, of course, DuPont's methacrylate panel, with subtle veining in your choice of gray, green, or beige. It comes in 1/4″ and 3/4″ slabs. You may be lucky enough to find a building-supply dealer who will sell you a piece of 1/4″ scrap from which you can cut the 18″ square you'll need. If not, you'll find many project uses for the rest of a full sheet.

If you have trouble finding Corian, write Building Products Div., DuPont & Co., Wilmington, Dela. 19898.

• Brass leg sockets (No. R-12, with 1″-square openings) can be ordered from Period Furniture Hardware Co., 123 Charles St., Boston 02114.

• For the trim, you'll need 24 ft. of 1/8″-square brass rod cut into three-ft. lengths—plus four 1/2″-dia. brass knobs. If you can't buy this locally, write Simon's Hardware Inc., 421 Third Ave., New York 10016.

This handsome marble-top card table . . . has hinged center panel you raise with a thong . . . and prop with a dowel while you choose which gameboard you want for playing.

• The games you may already have. If you want additional boards to complete a set of six, you'll find them at variety or department stores. Parker Bros. and Selchow & Righter offer the best selections of old favorites and modern classics.

Mounting the gameboards. Boards for Monopoly, Parcheesi, and some other games are larger than the 18″-square nest provided here. The actual playing area of all popular games is within these dimensions, however, and you can easily trim down the borders. Use a fine-tooth plywood blade on your table saw. Mount two of these trimmed-down boards back-to-back, taking care to place center folds at right angles. Tape edges with an appropriate color of cloth mending tape for smooth, strong edges.

When the board size is *smaller* than the 18″ nest (like the checkerboard in the photo), glue it to a stiff backing that's been cut to the nest size, and frame it with mitered strips as shown. For backing, I used ⅛″-thick three-ply poplar. Framing strips should be as thick

Mortise four legs before you taper them. While this can be done with hand tools, mortising attachment on your drill press does the job with much greater speed and uniformity.

Cut tapers on both inside edges of each leg, using a tapering jig and a router—or table saw. Plans for such a jig can be found in most instruction books for these tools.

Accurate tenons require a simple tenoning jig that rides on the rip fence of your table saw. Again, you'll find plans for this kind of jig in nearly all books on this tool.

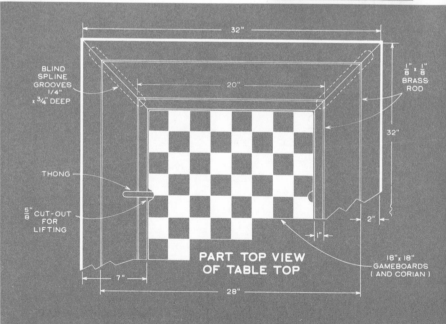

PART TOP VIEW OF TABLE TOP

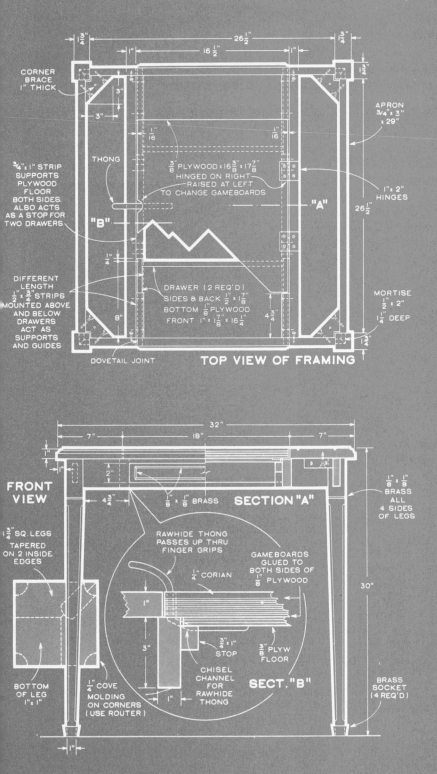

TOP VIEW OF FRAMING

CORNER BRACE 1" THICK

26½" ¾"

1" 16½" 1" ¾"

3"

3"

APRON ¾" x 3" x 29"

¾" x 1" STRIP SUPPORTS PLYWOOD FLOOR BOTH SIDES. ALSO ACTS AS A STOP FOR TWO DRAWERS

THONG

⅜" PLYWOOD x 16⅜" x 17⅞" HINGED ON RIGHT— RAISED AT LEFT TO CHANGE GAMEBOARDS

1⁄16

1⁄16

"B"

"A"

1" x 2" HINGES

26½"

¼"

DIFFERENT LENGTH ½" x ¾" STRIPS MOUNTED ABOVE AND BELOW DRAWERS ACT AS SUPPORTS AND GUIDES

8"

DRAWER (2 REQ'D) SIDES & BACK ½" x 1⅞" BOTTOM ⅛" PLYWOOD FRONT 1" x 1⅞" x 16½"

4¾"

MORTISE ½" x 2" 1¼" DEEP

1½"

DOVETAIL JOINT

FRONT VIEW

32"

7" 18" 7"

2"

1"

⅛" x ⅛" BRASS

4¾"

SECTION "A"

1⅛" x 1⅛" BRASS ALL 4 SIDES OF LEGS

1⅜" SQ. LEGS TAPERED ON 2 INSIDE EDGES

RAWHIDE THONG PASSES UP THRU FINGER GRIPS

¼" CORIAN

1"

GAMEBOARDS GLUED TO BOTH SIDES OF ⅛" PLYWOOD

30"

3"

3"

STOP

¾" x 1"

⅜" PLYW FLOOR

CHISEL CHANNEL FOR RAWHIDE THONG

1"

SECT. "B"

BOTTOM OF LEG 1" x 1"

¼" COVE MOLDING ON CORNERS (USE ROUTER)

BRASS SOCKET (4 REQ'D)

1"

17

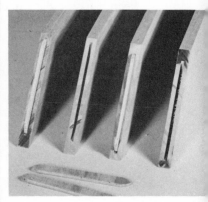

Another simple jig makes mitering easier. The corner angles for the table top are critical, so a jig that rides in the saw-table grooves (and permits no creep) is the kind needed here.

Cut spline grooves into the mitered edges of the top boards, using a dado cutter. Grooves above are ¼" wide and ¾" deep to take 1⅜"-by-7½" splines that are made of ¼" plywood.

Plow channels for ⅛"-square brass, using a veining bit in your router, after assembly of top. Grind 45-degree miters on ends of each strip, force in place with mallet.

as the gameboard. Usually, the same 1/8"
plywood works fine.

Though white glue will do both of these
mounting jobs, you may prefer the instant
adhesion of contact cement. For durability,
brush a coat or two of clear varnish or lacquer
over the face of each game. Let dry thoroughly
before stacking in the table recess. Note that
there's a finger hole at two sides of each board
for easy removal. Always stack the boards so
that these align.

You may wish to partition both drawers to
keep markers, dice, decks of cards, and other
playing paraphernalia neatly compartmen-
talized — especially since the table will be frequently moved. Strips of the 1/8" plywood
slotted for egg-crate assembly, will do the
job.

Size of standard gameboards varies from 15" to 20".
Tabletop nest is 18" sq., so mount smaller boards on
1/8" plywood and frame with mitered veneer strips.

Drawers on opposite sides of table store all accessories for games nested in top. Fronts are dovetailed
and trimmed with brass to match top. Add two brass
knobs.

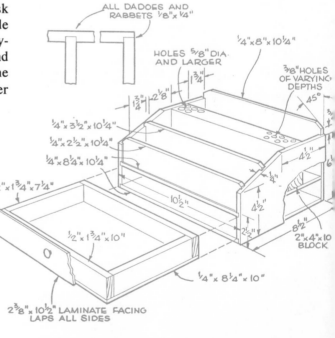

DESK CADDY

All those items that tumble around in desk
drawers are stored neatly in this unit made
from scraps of walnut paneling, or other plywood. It also organizes your stationery and
separates correspondence from bills. The
drawer holds stamps, paper clips, rubber
bands and other small household items.

TELESCOPING WOOD RINGS TURN INTO LAMP

BY ROSARIO CAPOTOSTO

Unusual stripe-accented styling makes this hanging lamp a sure eye-pleaser. Unusual construction techniques make it a fascinating exercise of your shop skills. Turning the relatively thin return-curve walls would be practically impossible by conventional lathe procedures. But by starting with a preformed hollow turning block you eliminate the need for inside turning. This simplifies the job, yet makes it more interesting.

You make the hollow block by "bulging out" a pair of flat boards. Here's how it's done: A series of concentric rings are cut with the jigsaw table set a few degrees off horizontal. This produces rings with angled sidewalls. Pull the center circle upward and each subsequent ring will telescope until the angled sides make binding contact. The result is a bowl-like unit of stepped, interlocking wooden rings.

Thickness of saw kerf and angle of cut determine the amount of telescoping you'll get. Use a thick blade at too slight an angle and the spaces between rings will be too wide to cause binding. The rings will simply slip through one another. The reverse situation — an extra-thin blade and a sharp table angle —

gives you very slight projection of the rings. Ideally, the angled cuts should allow about half the thickness of the stock to project. So make a few test cuts to determine the best tilt for your blade and stock thickness. Somewhere around three degrees should be a good starting point.

Note in the cross sections that half the block is made from rings of equal width; the other half from rings of varying width. Where the steps are equal you'll find the basic profile is a straight line. A curved profile results from varying ring width.

If you follow the dimensions shown, the end result should be a turning pretty close in size and shape to the one illustrated. But the concept is flexible—you can alter the basic form of the turning block by varying the width of the rings and the angle of cut.

Materials for turning. You'll need three pieces of ⅝″ wood, each a foot square. Two are used for expanding, the third for a wide center-stiffening ring. I used a special 11-ply birch plywood to get the thin-striped pattern. This highly specialized wood is used in the steel-rule diemaking industry, but you can get it by mail order. Steel Rule Die Mfg. (53 Toledo St., Farmingdale, N.Y. 11735) will sell you what you need. Ask for three 12″ by 12″ 11-ply panels of ⅝″ birch plywood. Of course you can use oak or pine plywood, or crack-free solid lumber, but watch out for fir plywood. It's prone to splintering on the lathe unless your tools and techniques are very sharp.

Construction tips. After you draw the cutting circles on the boards, bore a small blade-entry hole centered on each circle. Stagger holes alternately side to side about ½″, and pencil in a heavy radius to help you reorient the rings after cutting.

The glue-in is easy. Start with the smallest piece. Brush glue on its sidewall, and coat the inside of the next-largest ring. Force them together with your fingers. No clamps are needed, but be sure to orient rings as they were before the cut. That penciled radius line makes this easy.

You'll need to add a waste block to each end of the turning to mount it in the lathe. To make these, bore a perfectly straight pilot hole through a pair of hardwood circles. Slip a nail through each hole and glue the blocks

2. Cuts can be made freehand—with care. Make test cuts on scrap first. Draw a heavy radius line through disk before cutting so you can realign rings later.

1. Lay out rings using compass made from stick with holes bored at specific distances from pivot nail. Use sections shown in sketch as guides in laying out compasses.

3. Telescoping principle of angled cuts is demonstrated here . . . pull up on the center disk and rings follow. Cut properly, rings should project ½ stock thickness.

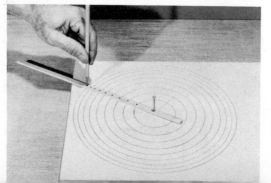

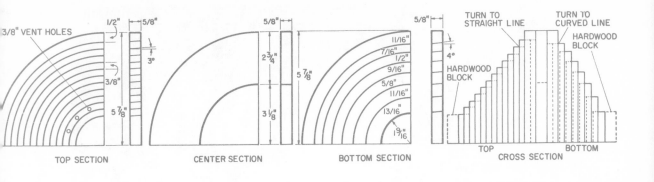

TOP SECTION

3/8" VENT HOLES

1/2" 5/8"

3°

3/8"

5 7/8"

CENTER SECTION

5/8"

2 3/4"

5 7/8"

3 1/8"

BOTTOM SECTION

5/8"

11/16"
7/16"
1/2"
9/16"
5/8"
11/16"
13/16"
19/16"

CROSS SECTION

5/8"

4°

TURN TO STRAIGHT LINE   TURN TO CURVED LINE

HARDWOOD BLOCK

HARDWOOD BLOCK

TOP   BOTTOM

4. Glue-up is easy, requires no clamps. Brush adhesive on both surfaces of rings and press into stack, one at a time. Refer to penciled radius line to orient the rings properly.

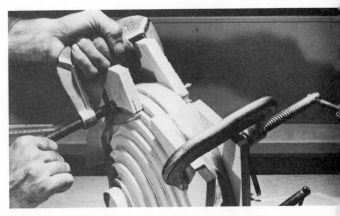

6. Corner cutoffs make good gluing blocks. Use wax paper between blocks and work to prevent sticking. Note end-waste block added here. Mount these as described in the text.

5. Wide middle ring stiffens turning block, helps to prevent distortion on lathe. When assembling two block halves, be sure they have a common axis through the compass nail holes.

7. Skew trims the turning to final stage after the gouge takes off the steps. Refer to drawing and work by eye—no calipers are needed—but remove no more stock than absolutely necessary.

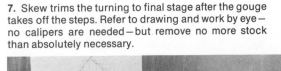

21

8. Cut groove for dropping out bottom, but go no deeper than ⅛". Extra pair of hands can catch the work if it breaks loose. Finally, cut bottom out on groove with a saber saw.

in place with the nails in register with the original compass-point centers on the turning. Accuracy is important to avoid a wobbling turning block.

The turning operation. This goes rather quickly. Use a sharp gouge to shave off the steps and follow up with a skew to trim off any bumps. You won't need a pattern template; the contour will be self-forming as you level off the steps. Stop cutting as soon as the steps disappear.

Before you make the partial parting cut for the lamp opening, sand the turning. This way, you'll be ready to finish if you cut too far on the partial cut. Everything sanded smooth? Go ahead and make the parting cut, but only go in about ⅛". Round the edge of the groove with a diamond point and complete the sanding to this point.

With the turning still in the lathe, brush on a coat of sanding sealer. When dry, fine-sand. Follow with several coats of brushing lacquer, and polish to a soft lustre.

When the finish is hard, remove the turning from the lathe. Using the parting-cut groove as a guide, drop out the bottom with a saber saw. A bit of hand sanding will smooth the cut, and no finish is necessary here.

Now bore a half-dozen holes around the upper section of the cone to provide venting for the lamp.

Hardware? It's available at electrical supply houses or a good hardware store. You'll need a plain socket, one piece of ⅛" threaded nipple, a loop, decorative chain, wire, and a ceiling canopy with a chain-loop fitting. Assemble the unit, and insert a 75-watt mushroom bulb to complete an interesting—and illuminating—project.

ALL-IN-ONE "TURNITURE"

BY LESTER WALKER

Single-unit furniture that "turns into" whatever is needed at the moment is the wave of the future. It makes special sense in a one-room summer cabin or apartment. Why should a bed, used only during sleeping hours, take up precious living space all day long? Make it earn its keep by converting it to other functions—let it become a double couch, let it sprout desks and tables.

Two sheets of ½" plywood, plus a standard double box spring and mattress, can create all the furniture you'll need for your new summer place. And it can have more up-to-the-minute styling than a whole set of conventional furniture pieces.

Placed near the center of a standard room (so that it's free to expand at both ends), Turniture gives an open, casual sense of spaciousness. It is truly a Living Machine, because each part is designed to perform as many functions as possible. The mouse-ear headboard bar not only offers back support for sitting up in bed; it lifts off and bridges headboard and footboard to form a double couch. These end units, in turn, each fold out into a table for two, or join forces to seat four for dining. All the plywood parts can be stored flat or transported in a station wagon.

Duraply is the ideal sheet material for this project because it is virtually warp-free,

Main unit is double bed, based on standard box spring and mattress. Both headboard and footboard are ingeniously designed to fold out into a table for two. With unit set in center of one-room cabin (or apartment), one table assembly can be used for dining (as shown), and other for hobby activities. When floor space is needed, both fold flat.

Tête-à-tête couch is formed by lifting off top bar of headboard, locking it across center of bed and padding with pillows or bolsters. Bar also serves as bundle-board if bed must sleep two guest children.

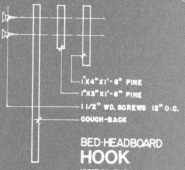

MATERIALS LIST

LUMBER

2 4'X8'X1/2" PLYWOOD SHEETS
2 1"X12"X5'-6" PINE
3 6'-2" 2X4'S
1 1"X4"X1'-8" PINE
1 1"X3"X1'-8" PINE
2 1/2"X1/2"X1' PINE

HARDWARE

4 SETS OF BED HOOKS 6"
2 6' LENGTHS CHROME PIANO HINGE
4 11/2" NO. 8 WOOD SCREWS
6 6"X6" METAL ANGLES W/SCREWS

1"X4"X1'-8" PINE
1"X3"X1'-8" PINE
11/2" WD. SCREWS 12" O.C.
COUCH-BACK

BED·HEADBOARD
HOOK
(SECTION THRU COUCH-BACK)

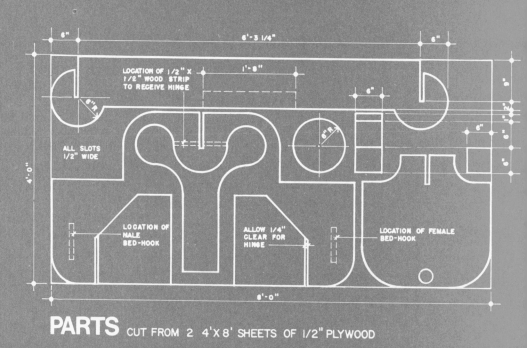

LOCATION OF 1/2" X 1/2" WOOD STRIP TO RECEIVE HINGE

6'-3 1/4"

1'-8"

ALL SLOTS 1/2" WIDE

6" R.

LOCATION OF MALE BED-HOOK

ALLOW 1/4" CLEAR FOR HINGE

LOCATION OF FEMALE BED-HOOK

4'-0"

8'-0"

PARTS CUT FROM 2 4'X 8' SHEETS OF 1/2" PLYWOOD

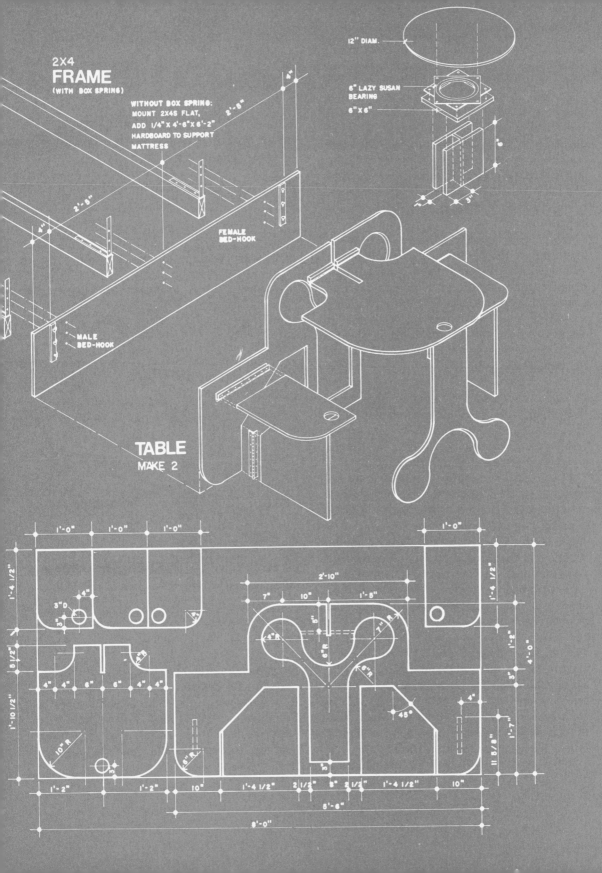

2X4
FRAME
(WITH BOX SPRING)

WITHOUT BOX SPRING:
MOUNT 2X4S FLAT,
ADD 1/4" X 4'-6" X 6'-2"
HARDBOARD TO SUPPORT
MATTRESS

12" DIAM.

6" LAZY SUSAN
BEARING

6" X 6"

FEMALE
BED-HOOK

MALE
BED-HOOK

TABLE
MAKE 2

smooth, and takes paint well. But if you are unfamiliar with this material, a few tips will help you work with it successfully.

Duraply is an exterior plywood with a smooth resin-fiber surface that accepts paint well, with no grain showing through, as often occurs with plywood. (Duraply is only one trademark version of MDO—for medium-density overlaid—plywood; others can be substituted.) This impregnated surface must not be broken or damaged, since patching is difficult.

When laying out the parts on two sheets, as shown in the blueprint, use a soft pencil with a slightly rounded point; a hard, sharp pencil might score the phenolic surface. For similar reasons, sanding of the smooth surface should be avoided. These panels come in single-faced as well as double-faced sheets. For this project you'll need both surfaces treated for painting.

Cutting it out. This is best done with a saber saw fitted with a hollow-ground blade, for straight cuts, and a turning blade for curves. If you use a variable-speed saw, set it high and feed slowly for a smooth cut.

Note from the cutting diagram that cutout pieces must be salvaged for use if you're to get all pieces from two 4-by-8 sheets. This is done by means of cautious cutting, so that a single kerf forms edges on two members. Where the Y-shaped drop leg is concerned, you must start your cut from a hole drilled in an inconspicuous corner. The 3"-diameter finger grips may be made quickly with a circle or compass cutter.

The finish. A bonus in working with this special plywood is that you'll find few voids in the cut edges. Soften sharp corners with medium-grit sandpaper followed with fine grit. Before painting, size all edges with a very thin coat of white glue (just add water) applied with a brush. When set, prime all surfaces.

For durability—and widest color range—I

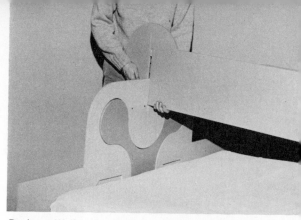

Designer Walker demonstrates ease with which Turniture converts to various functions. Here he has lifted off headboard bar and turned it 90 degrees to slot it down center of mattress for a double couch.

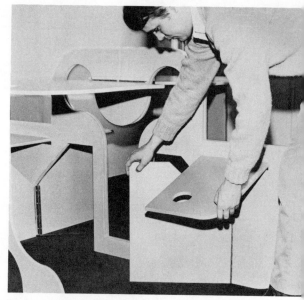

To form dining bench, drop-leaf seat is lifted and support panel swung underneath. Table panel with attached leg has already been folded out of headboard (hooked to identical footboard, here, for double table).

recommend automotive lacquer as the finish.

If you can't find bed hooks locally, order from Constantine and Son, 2050 Eastchester Road, Bronx, NYC 10461. You will need four pairs of the 6" size hooks. The lazy-susan bearings for the turntable may be obtained from the same source.

BUFFET OR DINING TABLE— HERE ARE BOTH IN ONE

BY R. E. SCHULTZ

Here's a table that is as much at home in an apartment dinette as in a banquet-size dining room. During the day it is an attractive buffet —but when the dinner bell sounds, it can be telescoped out to whatever size table you want.

The table shown is built of hardwood to blend with surrounding furniture; but wood,

hardware, and finish can be varied to suit your need. If you use hardwood, some edge-gluing will be necessary because hardwoods are seldom available in widths over 10″. You can have it done at the lumberyard, at nominal cost, if you don't own the equipment to do it.

How to build. Start with edge-gluing. And while the glue is drying you can go to work cutting and shaping the pine framing members for the cabinet. Cut the shelves and back to size, and you're ready for assembly.

Start by joining the shelves and framing; check for square, then attach the back and sides. The shelf support is optional, but it does keep the center shelf from sagging. Attach the stiles and rails to the front and then fasten the top in place. Nails can be used for construction of the frame, but for stronger joinery, screws and dowels were used throughout on this one.

The legs, top, and apron of the movable front assembly should be constructed as

Would you believe this buffet is a table? It is, and the blueprint shows how to build it.

27

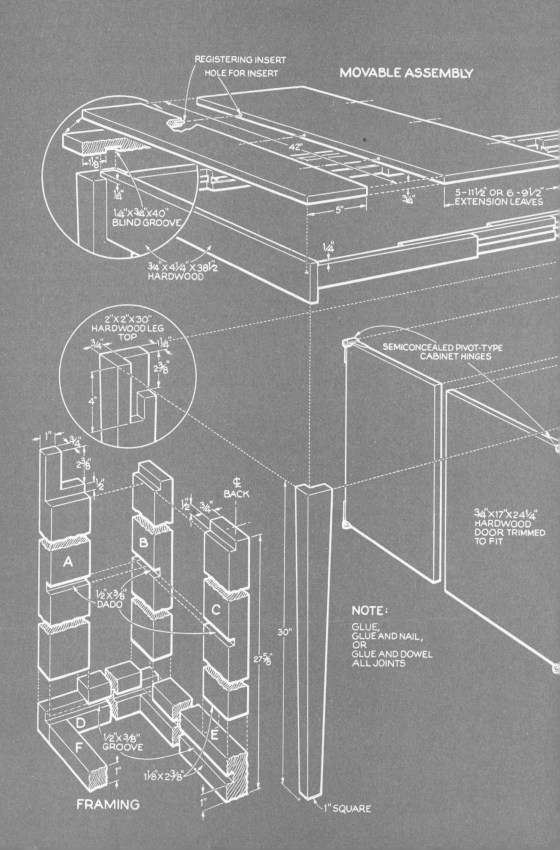

REGISTERING INSERT
HOLE FOR INSERT

MOVABLE ASSEMBLY

42"

1⅛"

¼

¼"x¾"x40"
BLIND GROOVE

5"

¾"

5 - 11½" OR 6 - 9½"
EXTENSION LEAVES

¼"

¾" x 4¼" x 38½
HARDWOOD

2"x 2"x 30"
HARDWOOD LEG
TOP

¾"

1¼"

2⅜"

4"

1"

¾"

2⅜"

½"

SEMICONCEALED PIVOT-TYPE
CABINET HINGES

½"

¾"

₵
BACK

A

B

½"x ⅜"
DADO

C

¾"x17"x24¼"
HARDWOOD
DOOR TRIMMED
TO FIT

30"

27⅝"

NOTE:

GLUE,
GLUE AND NAIL,
OR
GLUE AND DOWEL
ALL JOINTS

D

F

E

½"x ⅜"
GROOVE

1"

1⅛"x 2⅜"

1"

1"SQUARE

FRAMING

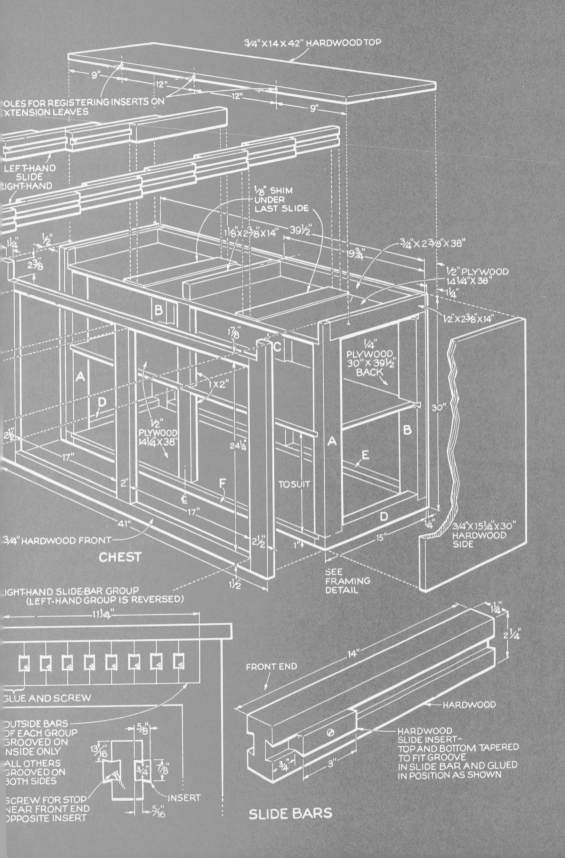

3/4"X14 x 42" HARDWOOD TOP

9"

12"

12"

9"

HOLES FOR REGISTERING INSERTS ON
EXTENSION LEAVES

LEFT-HAND
SLIDE
RIGHT-HAND

1/8" SHIM
UNDER
LAST SLIDE

1 1/8" x 2 3/8"X14"

39 1/2"

19 3/4"

3/4"x 2 3/8"X 38"

1/4

1/2

2 3/8"

1/2" PLYWOOD
14 1/4"X 38"

1 1/4"

1/2"X 2 3/8"X 14"

B

1/4"
PLYWOOD
30"X 39 1/2"
BACK

C

1 7/8"

A

1 X 2"

1/2"
PLYWOOD
14 1/4"X 38"

24 1/4"

30"

A

B

D

E

17"

2"

E

F

TO SUIT

D

2 1/2

1/4"

3/4"X15 1/4"X 30"
HARDWOOD
SIDE

2 1/2

41"

17"

15"

3/4" HARDWOOD FRONT

CHEST

1/2"

1"

SEE
FRAMING
DETAIL

RIGHT-HAND SLIDE-BAR GROUP
(LEFT-HAND GROUP IS REVERSED)

11 1/4"

1/4

2 1/4"

FRONT END

14"

GLUE AND SCREW

HARDWOOD

OUTSIDE BARS
OF EACH GROUP
GROOVED ON
INSIDE ONLY

ALL OTHERS
GROOVED ON
BOTH SIDES

5/8

13/16

3/4

7/8

INSERT

HARDWOOD
SLIDE INSERT-
TOP AND BOTTOM TAPERED
TO FIT GROOVE
IN SLIDE BAR AND GLUED
IN POSITION AS SHOWN

3/4

3"

SCREW FOR STOP
NEAR FRONT END
OPPOSITE INSERT

5/16

SLIDE BARS

MATERIALS LIST
Softwood
  49' pine or fir, 5/4" x 3"
Hardwood
  14' 1" x 3"
  5' 2" x 2"
  4' 1" x 5"
  34' 1" x 10"
  10' 1" x 6"
Plywood
  1 pc. ¼" x 36" x 48"
  1 pc. ½" x 48" x 48"
Misc.
  2 pr. semiconcealed hinges
  1 qt. stain, 1 qt. varnish
  2 drawer pulls, 2 knobs
  screws, glue, dowels

shown in the blueprint. If you have varied any of the cabinet dimensions, this unit must be changed accordingly. Leg design is not critical as long as sufficient space is allowed for attaching the apron and slide bars. Remember, too, to provide enough clearance for the doors to open. Note the blind groove on the underside of the movable top; use a router to make it, and, to prevent the cutter from going off, clamp guides on both sides of the router shoe.

Making the slides. The grooves in the slides are made with a dovetail bit in the router. They're easier to do if you cut them to length before grooving.

The slide inserts must be right on the button, so a little practice with scrap is a good idea. For best results leave the line when cutting them, then sand them down so that they slide freely. Temporarily assemble the slide units to determine exact insert location. When you're satisfied, fasten them with glue and a screw through each. Finally, install the screw stop ¾" from the front edge on each slide as it is added to the assembly. This keeps them from coming apart.

The slide units are attached to the movable front assembly by gluing the first slide of each set to the top, and screwing into the legs. To

Table can be opened to any desired size to accommodate large or small dinner group. Three inserts on each leaf lock into mating holes drilled in the adjoining leaf to keep leaves in place. This table is built of hardwood for durability, but pine can be used.

Slides are made out of hardwood and left unfinished. A little soap rubbed in the grooves reduces friction and helps the assembly to slide more freely.

Left-hand group of slides (see photo) are assembled as shown in drawing. As you determine the exact location of each insert, glue it in place. Add the slide to the assembly and install the screw in the groove, which acts as a stop, and keeps the slide assembly from coming apart. Reverse the inserts to assemble the slides on the right-hand side.

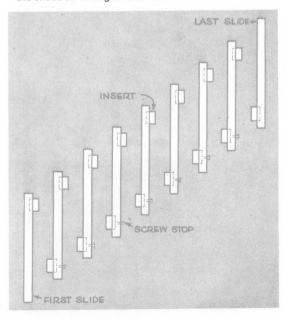

LAST SLIDE

INSERT

SCREW STOP

FIRST SLIDE

attach the slide assembly to the cabinet, place the slides on the top shelf and line up the front with the cabinet to make sure the top pieces are even. Some adjustment may be required; if necessary, the slides can be shortened to eliminate any gap that might be between tops. When aligned, mark location and install the $1/8''$ shim below the last slides. Next, attach the last two slides by screwing through the top shelf into them.

Cut the doors to fit the openings and hang them with semiconcealed hinges. Knobs and drawer pulls are a matter of personal preference and should match room furnishings.

The table leaves. These can be made of hardwood, too, but since they are either stored or covered by a tablecloth, you can save money by using clear pine and staining to match. The leaf inserts can be bought in a hardware store, or you can make your own, using $3/8''$ dowels. Cut them 3" long and glue half the dowel in, then drill $7/16''$ holes in the adjoining leaf to receive them.

After a final sanding with 6/0 garnet paper, the table was finished with oil stain and two coats of varnish, left two weeks, and rubbed with paste wax.

HOW TO ADD A TYPEWRITER TABLE TO A DESK

BY JOHN WOODWARD

A typewriter can be kept out of the way, ready for instant use, with this table that swings into the desk knee space. The table top is attached to a closet pole that turns 180 degrees in desk-mounted supports. A spring-loaded catch, mounted on the desk back panel, holds table and typewriter securely, upside down, in the storage position.

The table can be custom-built to hold any typewriter, but the desk must have at least 24" knee space. It's shown with a portable here, but it works for heavy models, too.

Secure the typewriter to the table with 1¼" #8 bolts in the typewriter supports. Add two pieces of hardwood to prevent the carriage from sliding when the table is swung down. Attach the fixed arm with an L bracket, pivoting arm with a brass screw.

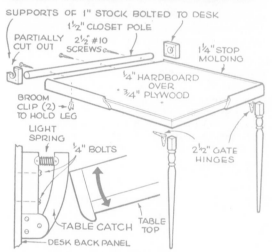

Holder prevents carriage movement when table is down. Recessed head (photo right) fits knob.

Spring-loaded catch (lower left in sketch) is mounted on desk back panel. It supports table when stored.

BOX SHELVES ARE IN STYLE

BY JAMES B. JOHNSTONE

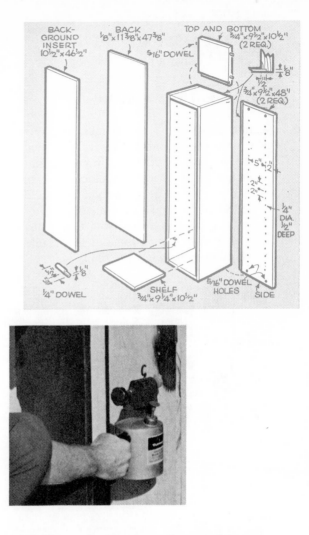

Charring wood, shown at right, should be done outdoors to avoid fire hazards. Above: How the boxes look when finished and mounted.

Art items and knickknacks really stand out in these slim boxes hung in a contemporary grouping. And you can rearrange your display anytime—slip out four support pegs and adjust the inner shelves.

The handsome finish comes from charring the flat-grain fir with a blowtorch. The sides and end pieces have ⅛"-by-½" rabbets to hold the ⅛" tempered-hardboard back.

Drill two rows of ¼" holes ½" deep and 2" apart for the shelf pegs. Assemble the box with resorcinol glue (it holds during charring) and 5/16" dowels at corners.

In a safe spot in your yard, move the blow-torch flame slowly across the wood to produce a yellowish surface flare. Look for a red glow—blow out any flame. Scrape along the grain with a stiff wire brush, and apply paste floor wax or a flat penetrating finish. Char and finish as many shelves as you need.

Mount the hardwood back in the rabbet with glue and ½" brads. Cut a cardboard insert to a loose press fit against the hardboard back, and paint the face or cover it with colored felt. (Besides allowing quick color changes, this slip-out has the added advantage of hiding the wall-mounting screws.) Then hang box frame and install pegs and shelves.

DOUBLE-DUTY CENTERPIECE FOR YOUR HOME

BY ROBERT E. DONEGAN

Interchangeable candlesticks and bowls slip onto the movable arms of this centerpiece to give it a double role in your home. At dinner, it's a flexible candleholder. At a party, it's a dip or hors d'oeuvre server with a difference. Since the arms can swing full circle, the bowls are an easy reach from both sides of the table. And there's room at the middle of the base to stand a bowl of chips.

The sketch gives you the shapes and dimensions you'll need. Note that I turned metal fittings to mate the bowls and candlesticks to the ¼" brass arms, and to mate the arms to the base. If you have no metal lathe, turn the bowl fittings from wood, make the candlesticks entirely from wood, and eliminate fittings on the base.

Candleholder or relish server? Either way, the double-duty centerpiece is a surefire party pleaser. The movable brass arms add flexibility to centerpiece arrangements when the candleholders are in place. Slip on twin bowls filled with relish or dips and the swinging arms put them within easy reach of both sides of the table.

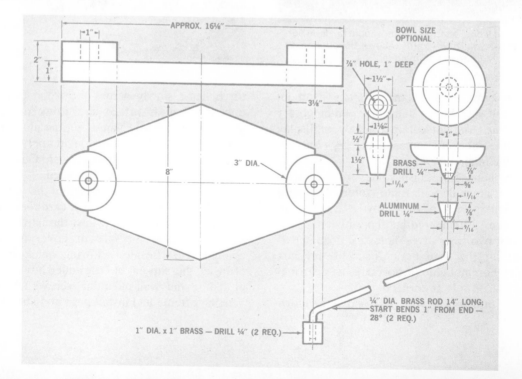

CLASSIC PICTURE FRAME

This frame looks—and even feels—like rich, classic marble. But it's made from a block of ¾″ Corian, cheaper, and easier to work, than real marble. It's ideal for displaying a photo silhouette, or a cherished picture from the past.

Make the outer frame from hardwood, using a shaper or router. Or make it up from picture-frame stock with a ¾″ picture recess.

Making the Corian shine like polished marble after shaping the opening with a router is easy. Wet-sand the opening and face with #400 paper until all scratches and blemishes are gone. Finish by rubbing with DuPont's White Polishing Compound or a similar auto polish.

Inner and outer frame complete? Slip the Corian into the wooden frame and the glass into the recess in the Corian. Now add the picture and tack the back panel in place.

Recess back of Corian to accept nonglare glass. Cut opening, then sand cut smooth before routing to give ripple-free radius.

Mount the picture on a cardboard backing, add a brass ring at top of outer frame for hanging, and assemble frame components.

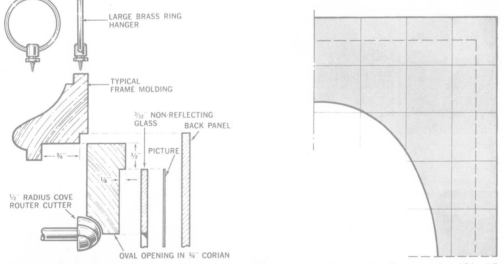

LARGE BRASS RING HANGER

TYPICAL FRAME MOLDING

3/32″ NON-REFLECTING GLASS

BACK PANEL

PICTURE

¾″

½″

⅛″

½″ RADIUS COVE ROUTER CUTTER

OVAL OPENING IN ¾″ CORIAN

Graph-squared layout gives dimensions you need for an elliptical opening. Recess takes 7″-by-9″ glass. Drawing shows how parts fit together. You may have to modify frame stock to accept both Corian and back panel.

ADJUSTABLE SHELF SYSTEM FOR A SHOW-OFF WALL

BY GEORGE S. KANELBA, A.I.A.

Most adjustable wall systems are expensively overengineered. They provide an unlimited flexibility in the arrangement of shelves, but this is rarely needed. Once the average home owner has tailored the arrangement of shelves and cabinets to the needs of his own books and display objects, he rarely needs to alter it.

So I designed a system that permits adjustment without marring any surfaces, but uses economical materials. A series of compartment units is constructed, of varying or identical widths, to fill available wall space. These are locked together with vertical splines, recessed from the front edge to create a neat "shadowline" joint that avoids the need for perfect butting.

I had a 16′-long living-room wall, which I divided into six sections. Starting with 1′8″ as the narrowest desirable compartment, I then added 4″ increments to each succeeding compartment: 1′8″, 2′, 2′4″, 2′8″, 3′, and 3′4″. Allowing for a ½″ gap between all units, I

A lifetime's collecting can be displayed on shelves positioned to match height of books.

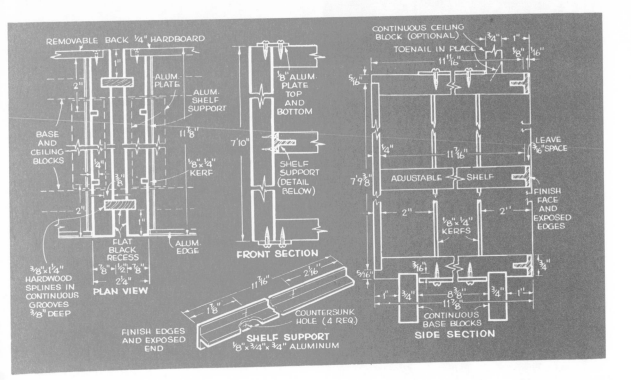

REMOVABLE BACK ¼" HARDBOARD

ALUM. PLATE

ALUM. SHELF SUPPORT

BASE AND CEILING BLOCKS

⅛" x ¼" KERF

FLAT BLACK RECESS

ALUM. EDGE

⅜" x 1¼" HARDWOOD SPLINES IN CONTINUOUS GROOVES ⅜" DEEP

PLAN VIEW

FINISH EDGES AND EXPOSED END

⅛" ALUM. PLATE TOP AND BOTTOM

SHELF SUPPORT (DETAIL BELOW)

FRONT SECTION

COUNTERSUNK HOLE (4 REQ.)

SHELF SUPPORT
⅛" x ¾" x ¾" ALUMINUM

CONTINUOUS CEILING BLOCK (OPTIONAL)
TOENAIL IN PLACE

ADJUSTABLE SHELF

⅛" x ¼" KERFS

LEAVE 3/16" SPACE

FINISH FACE AND EXPOSED EDGES

CONTINUOUS BASE BLOCKS

SIDE SECTION

ended up with a total width of 15′ 2½″, which left space at either end for a filler strip to close the gap at the side walls—always a wise allowance, since walls are never plumb.

I recommend a compartment height of no more than 7′10″, since this allows raising units above the floor on recessed base blocks —even in a room with an 8′ ceiling.

I chose an overall depth of 11⅞″ so I could get four compartment sides from a standard 4′-by-8′ sheet of plywood. This is ample depth for large books and objects, while smaller books can be pushed to the rear of the shelves to make room for small objects in front.

These units can also serve as a room divider, either in a single row, adequately braced to the end wall and ceiling, or in a back-to-back arrangement.

Once you decide on the position of your shelves within a unit, install the aluminum support strips on the inside faces.

Shelf-support strips. These were cut from stock aluminum T. (The front trim strips are the same material, with the face and visible edges polished to a mirror finish.)

Fasten the support strips with screws driven into a pair of kerfs cut the full length of each upright before the units are assembled. These kerfs will conceal screw holes should the shelves later be relocated. (The opposite face of each upright has a groove for the joint spline or filler strip.)

To start, install only one support strip for each shelf (clapping a square against the front edge of the upright to make sure the bracket will be level). Slide one kerfed end of the shelf onto this strip, and place a level near the front edge of the shelf; adjust the shelf's free end until it is level. Then scribe a line on that upright to indicate the position of the second support.

Other components besides shelves— drawers, storage compartments with sliding

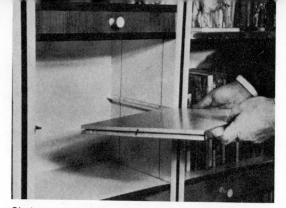

Shelves are kerfed on three edges to accept tongue of aluminum T-strips. Front strip is glued in place for trim. Side strips are screwed to uprights for support of shelf which just slips onto the tongues.

Shallow drawers may be located at random for storage of stationery and other supplies. Glued up from quarter-inch hardboard, with half-inch veneered stock for fronts, they slide between book shelves.

or hinged doors, speaker enclosures—can be installed without support strips. Drive screws from the inside of such units into the kerfs in the uprights.

For special effects, removable color-accent panels can be inserted between shelves as display backgrounds. These panels can be prefinished or painted hardboard, or heavy cardboard covered with fabric or wallpaper.

Because of the variety of color in the objects I wished to display, I finished my unit flat white—including the hardboard backs and the 3/4" plywood shelves.

GROOMING TRAY

Tired of the tangle of bathroom appliance cords? Mount this unit with built-in outlets and tuck electric toothbrushes and razors in their own compartments. Sample dimensions are given for three battery-operated units. The end razor has a self-contained charger, so needs a mating outlet.

All wood used in this tray is 1/4" thick. Adjust your own compartments according to sizes of your appliances. Unit is suspended on flush-mounted hangers.

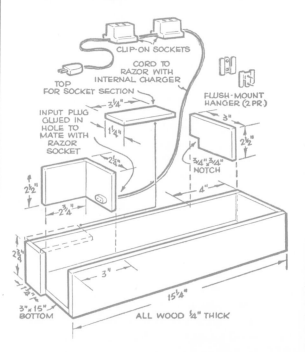

A FINE MARBLE-TOPPED TABLE

BY FRANK GREENWALD

There is a saying in our family that "We can't afford the furniture we like and we don't like the furniture we can afford." So, when the general manager in our household announced she wanted a coffee table, I retired to the drafting board with her specifications.

This marble-topped table is the result. The top should be obtained before you begin.

Mine is a half-inch thick. Most larger cities have firms that cut and grind marble. In many smaller towns a local firm handling the sale and installation of ceramic tile will take an order for a marble top cut to your specifications. Sometimes an antique marble slab can be cut to your pattern by a monument maker. Marble can be supplied with either a polished or honed finish. The honed finish is better for a table top since wet glasses will not leave rings.

Another choice is Corian, a synthetic marble made by DuPont, available from their retail outlets or well-supplied lumber dealers. Or, you might use black Carrara glass 11/32-inch thick, which can be obtained from a glass or mirror company. Phenolic laminate in a marble pattern mounted on 3/8″ or 1/2″ plywood will make a top that looks like marble. A kitchen-cabinet shop can supply it.

Apron. Begin by drawing the skirt pattern on the mahogany stock. Cutting angles can be marked directly on the wood, but check the

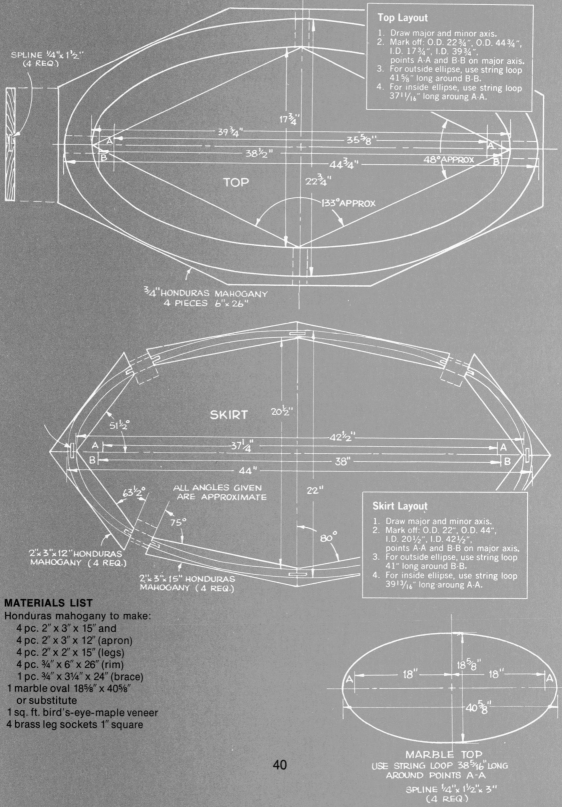

Top Layout
1. Draw major and minor axis.
2. Mark off: O.D. 22¾″, O.D. 44¾″, I.D. 17¾″, I.D. 39¾″, points A-A and B-B on major axis.
3. For outside ellipse, use string loop 41⅝″ long around B-B.
4. For inside ellipse, use string loop 37¹¹/₁₆″ long aroung A-A.

SPLINE ¼″ x 1½″ (4 REQ.)

TOP

39¾″
38½″
35⅝″
44¾″
17¾″
22¾″
48° APPROX
133° APPROX

¾″ HONDURAS MAHOGANY
4 PIECES 6″ x 26″

SKIRT

Skirt Layout
1. Draw major and minor axis.
2. Mark off: O.D. 22″, O.D. 44″, I.D. 20½″, I.D. 42½″, points A-A and B-B on major axis.
3. For outside ellipse, use string loop 41″ long around B-B.
4. For inside ellipse, use string loop 39¹³/₁₆″ long around A-A.

20½″
42½″
37¼″
38″
44″
22″
51½°
63½°
75°
80°

ALL ANGLES GIVEN ARE APPROXIMATE

2″x 3″x 12″ HONDURAS MAHOGANY (4 REQ.)
2″x 3″x 15″ HONDURAS MAHOGANY (4 REQ.)

MATERIALS LIST
Honduras mahogany to make:
   4 pc. 2″ x 3″ x 15″ and
   4 pc. 2″ x 3″ x 12″ (apron)
   4 pc. 2″ x 2″ x 15″ (legs)
   4 pc. ¾″ x 6″ x 26″ (rim)
   1 pc. ¾″ x 3¼″ x 24″ (brace)
1 marble oval 18⅝″ x 40⅝″
   or substitute
1 sq. ft. bird's-eye-maple veneer
4 brass leg sockets 1″ square

18″   18⅝″   18″
40⅝″

MARBLE TOP
USE STRING LOOP 38⁵/₁₆″ LONG
AROUND POINTS A-A
SPLINE ¼″ x 1½″ x 3″
(4 REQ.)

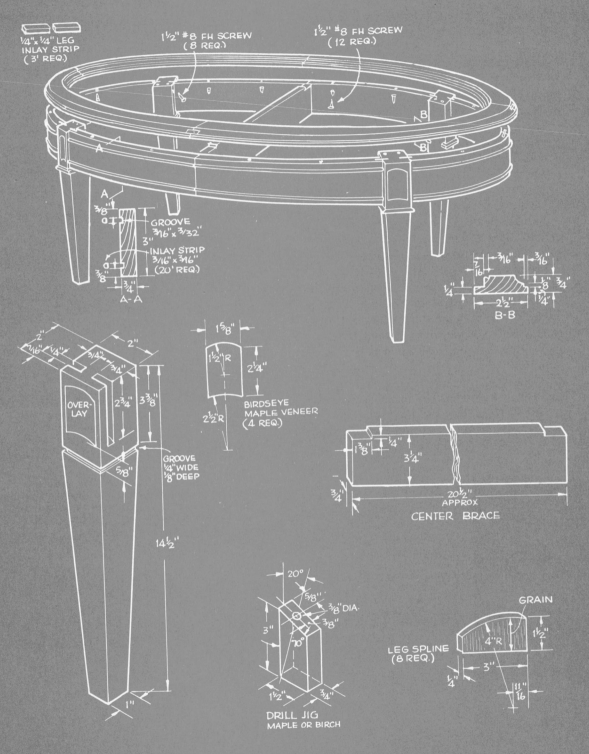

¼"x ¼" LEG
INLAY STRIP
(3' REQ.)

1½" #8 FH SCREW
(8 REQ.)

1½" #8 FH SCREW
(12 REQ.)

3/8"

GROOVE
³/₁₆" x ³/₃₂"

3"

INLAY STRIP
³/₁₆" x ³/₁₆"
(20' REQ.)

3/8"

¾"

A-A

3/16"   3/16"

7/16"

¼"

2½"

1/8"   ¾"

¼"

B-B

2"

3/16"   ¼"   ¾"

¾"

OVER-
LAY

2¾"

3³/₈"

5/8"

GROOVE
¼" WIDE
1/8" DEEP

14½"

1"

1⁵/₈"

1½"R

2¼"

2½"R

BIRDSEYE
MAPLE VENEER
(4 REQ.)

1³/₈"   ¼"

3¼"

¾"

20½"
APPROX

CENTER BRACE

20°

5/8"

3/8" DIA.

3/8"

3"

70°

1½"   ¾"

DRILL JIG
MAPLE OR BIRCH

GRAIN

LEG SPLINE
(8 REQ.)

4"R

1½"

¼"

3"

11"/16

41

cut pieces by actual layout. Since there is ample waste stock, the angles can be altered slightly for an accurate fit.

Using the pattern as a guide, locate a $\frac{1}{4}$"-wide and $\frac{3}{4}$"-deep spline slot in the end of each piece; the slot should be centered after the apron is cut from the rough stock.

The apron stock is first glued together to form two end and two side segments which can be joined by unglued spacers at the leg positions. Next, tape the pattern on top of the segments and transfer the outline of the two ellipses.

A bandsaw does the best job of cutting the ellipses. The inside cut should be made close to the line; leave about $\frac{1}{16}$" outside.

I tried several tools and finally settled on a rasp-type plane to shape and smooth the outside surface. Frequent checks with a square are needed to keep the surface flat. A 3" drum sander will remove any remaining irregularities. Then cut the molding grooves in the apron.

Legs. Start by cutting the four 2"-square legs to $14\frac{1}{2}$". Next, slot the tops to receive the apron splines. My slots were made with a

1. Lay out top and skirt on wrapping paper. To draw ellipse, drive nails at measured points along horizontal axis, loop linen or other nonstretch cord around them. Change dimensions, if necessary, to fit marble top.

2. Cut rough stock for apron at angles given. Check them on pattern. Alignment of leg positions is important, but angles are not critical if stock covers ellipses. Adjust angles, mark them directly on the wood.

3. Fasten cut-offs to outsides of apron members so you can apply clamp pressure. You'll need glue and toenails to take the pull. Check pieces on layout to make sure nails stop within areas to be cut off.

Good detailing adds quality and craftsmanship to the table. Bird's-eye maple veneer tops each leg. Twin beads are inlaid around apron, one on legs.

dado head on a circular saw. It's easiest this way, and it is a simple matter to fit the splines to the curved bottoms of the slot. One word of caution—use a stop block on the saw table. If the cut extends beyond 2¾" it will show below the apron.

Each face of the leg is tapered ½" in 10½". When you use a taper jig on a circular saw, remember that after two adjacent sides are cut the taper setting must be increased to 1" in 10½" for the remaining two sides.

Top rim. Using a full-size pattern, cut and lay out the four pieces of rim stock. Adjust the angles at the joints as well as the splines for tight, dry fit.

After gluing the members, locate the pattern carefully on top, transfer the ellipses, cut out the rim, and mold it to the shape in the drawing. The inner lip dimensions are correct for a ½"-thick top of the size given in the drawing. If other materials are substituted, the ½" dimension may have to be changed. The actual marble top should be used as a template for the recess; allow ¹⁄₁₆" clearance all around.

Before any assembly work is started, sand all pieces thoroughly, first with #1/0 (80) and then with #3/0 (120) aluminum oxide cabinet paper. A reciprocating sander is best for all flat surfaces. If done by hand, use a flat block to obtain good leveling. All corners and edges should be softened (slightly rounded).

Assembly. Start with the four legs and apron pieces and make a trial fit, then disassemble, apply glue to all mating surfaces, and reclamp.

Next, place the rim on the apron and leg assembly and position until the overhang is even. The calculated rim overhang may vary somewhat, but this will not be noticeable after assembly.

After the best position is found, apply glue, clamp and screw up the assembly.

The drawing gives calculated dimensions of the cross brace, but it is wise to check the

4. Use pattern as guide—but allow for any adjustments—to locate ¼"-by-¾" spline slots in ends of apron members. Slots should be centered after removal of excess wood. You can cut them on a table saw.

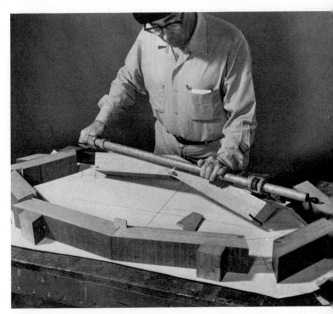

5. Use pipe clamps across each joint to apply even pressure. Glue up end and side segments. Cut 3½"-wide leg spacers from ¼" scrap; insert them in spline slots to space segments 2" at each leg position.

6. Tape apron layout on top of assembled segments and transfer ellipse. Dressmaker's tracing wheel does a good job, or you can use carbon paper. Arrange overlay to center splines between parallel ovals.

7. Ink in transferred lines with a fine fiber pen. All joints are now glued except at leg spacers. Before you disassemble segments, number leg positions to avoid mix-up. Bandsaw and shape the glued pairs.

10. Spline slots are cut in two-by-two stock before legs are tapered. These were made with a dado head, so they curve at bottom. Splines must be shaped to match. Test leg fit before gluing in the splines.

8. Smooth outer faces of skirt, working from crown to end (or glued joint) and checking frequently with a square. When sawing, you should have left 1/16" outside line. The plane whisks off most of this.

9. Finish with a drum sander. Check with your fingers for slight irregularities, bumps and hollows. On inner surfaces you won't have risked much by sawing right to line; they won't need planing or sanding.

11. Web clamp makes quick work of final skirt and leg glue-up. Work on a level surface and use mallet to align members before tightening clamp. Note that legs and skirt are already grooved for inlay.

12. Make drill jig (see drawing detail) to position rim-holding screws. Check jig and stop on scrap. Each leg gets two 1½"-#8 flatheads. Use 12 screws between rim and apron; drill for these after rim is set.

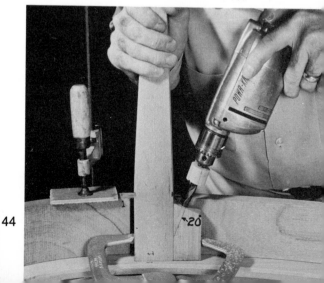

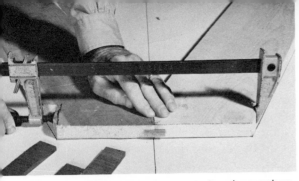

13. Use full-size pattern to arrange top-rim members. Notch waste at corners for clamp seats and adjust joint angles for tight fit before gluing and tracing oval pattern. Splines must fit the slots precisely.

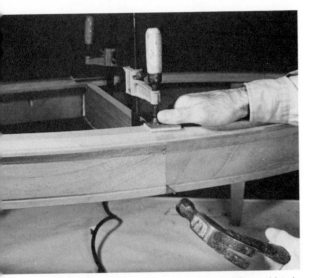

14. Fit and clamp crosswise brace after skirt is grooved, assembled, and lightly sanded and top rim is shaped and rabbeted for top. Sink two holding nails in skirt groove. Brace dimensions are for ½" top.

actual table. Apply glue to the brace, clamp in place, and fasten each side with two eight-penny finishing nails in the apron grooves.

The moldings. I made the rounded-top 3/16″ -by-1³/16″ apron inlay molding with a ¼″ bead cutter (Craftsman 9—2352) on a table saw.

Apply glue sparingly to two or three inches of groove at a time and clamp in the molding as you progress. Apply glue as needed until the molding reaches the next leg where it can be trimmed to length.

The end pieces will be more difficult due to the sharper curve. Notch the molding ¹/32″ deep every ¹/8″ on the back, and use slightly grooved softwood pressure pads under the clamps. Pull the molding into place slowly. If a piece breaks, remove the part already installed and start over.

Installation of the ¼″-by-¼″ bead on the legs is a simple matter. I cut the front section to exact length and left the sides a trifle long. Glue the front in first and then fit the mitered sides. They can be sanded flush at the back after the glue has dried.

To glue the bird's-eye-maple overlays to the leg faces, use softwood pressure pads under the clamps. Apply glue sparingly; little is needed in this joint and all excess will have to be cleaned off.

A final light sanding with 3/0 (120) paper will clean up any rough edges and traces of glue. Use small wood blocks to sand in all

15. Fit and glue the molding in the skirt groove. Do the sides first, starting at a leg. Fit and trim at the next leg. If a piece breaks, remove it, and start over. Notch backs of the end moldings every ⅛″ so they'll take the severe curve at that point.

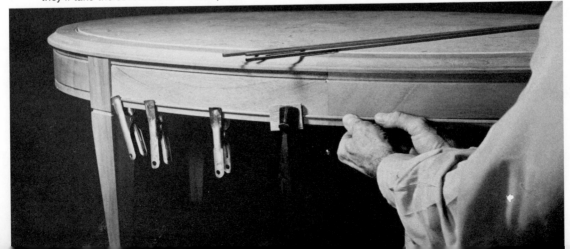

corners, since any glue left on the surface will prevent stain from penetrating. Fit the brass leg sockets to each leg at this time, marking for later assembly.

To keep a natural finish on the bird's-eye-maple, apply a coating of lacquer sanding sealer.

Inspect the whole piece for nicks, dents, or scratches. Small dents and scratches will usually respond to local steaming, done by placing two or three drops of water on the affected area followed by heat from the point of a soldering or a clothing iron. Complete the repair by sanding smooth.

16. Cut three overlong ¼"-by-¼" pieces for each leg bead and fit them by trial so joints are smooth and balanced. Glue front first, then match and glue sides. Sand off excess length of side pieces at rear.

17. Use a ⅝"-wide block to position bird's-eye overlays uniformly above the leg beads. Same block can be used for all four overlays. Leave it in place to keep veneer from slipping as clamp tightens.

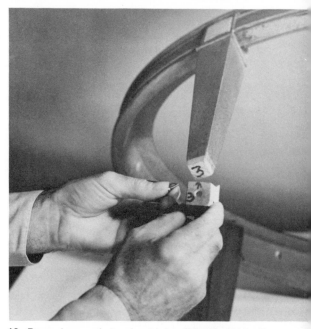

18. Brass leg sockets should be fitted individually to level the table. Mark each socket for the leg it fits (arrow here shows outside). After wood is sanded and finished, attach sockets with ½" screws.

Apply a good finish and you'll have a piece of furniture you'll always be proud of.

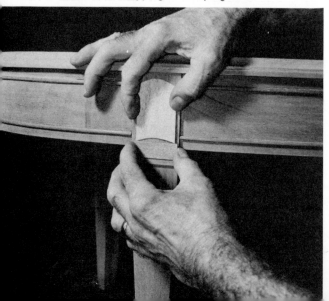

46

PUT THAT CRAWL SPACE TO WORK

BY A. GLOWKA

Crawl space is rarely utilized for storage because it's almost impossible to climb in or out without scraping knees or bumping your head. Result? Valuable space is wasted. By building this double-track version of a monorail, it won't be. Uprights and shelf supports are of one-by-four stock; shelves are $\frac{3}{8}''$ plywood. Three sets of Stanley #2850 sliding-door track, 8' long, provide the transportation. Since crawl space depth here was 13', a shelf unit 12' long was built. For ease of handling, two 6' sections were assembled and joined after both were in place. To line the frame up with the second track, offset the middle upright $1\frac{1}{4}''$ on each unit. For added strength, brace uprights with a 2" strip of plywood at the top. Snap a chalkline under the floor joists (to assure track alignment) and fasten tracks directly to joists. To keep stored items from sliding off, attach a frame to one side and both ends of the shelf. Balance shelf load so that the unit hangs straight.

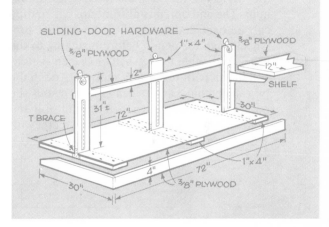

Center upright is offset 1¼" and three legs are tied together with strip of plywood. Note upright shelf standards and brackets.

Adjustable plastic cam on the hanger assembly is removed (shelf weight causes slippage) and hangers are screwed directly to upright.

Rigidity is supplied by T braces on both sides of uprights. Shelf is then scribed around them for a neat fit. Finish with enamel.

BOOKSHELVES

Good-looking bookshelves don't have to be a lot of work to build. The unit shown can be built easily in a weekend because there are no complicated construction details. It's made of ³⁄₄" plywood, aluminum bar and angle (also ³⁄₄"), and tempered hardboard.

Start by building the base. Since the unit will be painted, butt joints can be used throughout. To insure sturdiness, use glue and screws to assemble. For the best fit, cut the hardboard sliding doors to size after the door track is in the cabinet. The legs used are the ready-made variety available at lumberyards and hardware stores.

Use pan-head sheet-metal screws to fasten the uprights—they'll blend well with aluminum. The end uprights at front are cut so they can be bent and screwed to the cabinet top. Check each for plumb before fastening to the base. Add angle to the shelf ends (see sketch) and install both full-length shelves. Attach the two aluminum bars at center and install the bottom shelf and the wooden top rail. Fill and sand all wood, and finish wood and metal with semigloss enamel.

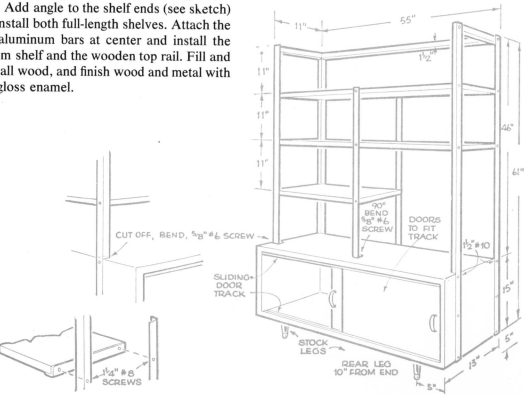

SHALLOW CABINET FOR A HALLWAY

BY THOMAS B. SHEARER

Is there a hall or other narrow area in your home where you can't use a piece of furniture of conventional depth? This shallow cabinet will grace it and give you a lot of useful storage space besides.

The basic parts are cut from one 4'-by-8' panel of ¾" birch plywood. All moldings are stock sizes and should be on hand at a local lumberyard.

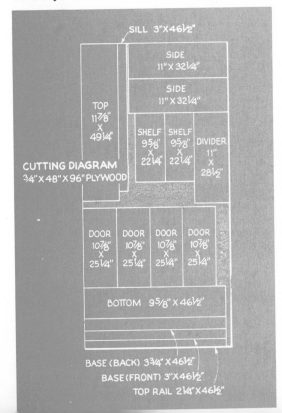

SILL 3"X46½"

SIDE 11"X 32¼"

SIDE 11"X 32¼"

TOP 11⅞" X 49¼"

CUTTING DIAGRAM
¾" X 48" X 96" PLYWOOD

SHELF 9⅝" X 22¼"

SHELF 9⅝" X 22¼"

DIVIDER 11" X 28½"

DOOR 10⅞" X 25¼"

DOOR 10⅞" X 25¼"

DOOR 10⅞" X 25¼"

DOOR 10⅞" X 25¼"

BOTTOM 9⅝" X 46½"

BASE (BACK) 3¾" X 46½"
BASE (FRONT) 3" X 46½"
TOP RAIL 2¼" X 46½"

Drill the two ends and center divider, as shown, for shelf pegs — or use adjustable metal supports. Assemble the bottom first, add the sides, center divider, top rail, and back panel. Check the squareness of the assembly. The back panel can be adjusted to keep the assembly true. Attach eight 1"-by-1" steel angles inside the upper edges of the assembly so the top can be secured from the inside.

Glue together two pieces of ⅜" ornamental molding back to back as shown in the drawing to finish off the edges of the cabinet top. Glue and brad ¼" pine lattice strips to all other plywood edges. Sand them even with the plywood surface.

The doors are ¾" plywood, edged with ¼"-by-1⅜ lattice strips. Moldings are at-

MATERIALS LIST
4'-by-8' panel ¾" birch plywood
4'-by-8' panel 3/16" hardboard
6', ¼"-by-¾" fluted molding
7', 7/16"-by-¾" base shoe
14', ¾" cove
60', ⅜"-by-½" trim molding
7', ½" quarter round
7', ¾"-by-2¼" pine or fir plywood
30', ¼"-by-¾" pine lattice
32', ¼"-by 1⅜" pine lattice
12', ¼"-by-1¼" pine lattice
4 pairs hinges
4 brass pulls

tached as shown. Pivot hinges are used on door tops and bottoms.

Fill all holes with water putty and sand. Apply a primer and two coats of white enamel. Sand between coats. After the final coat, remove gloss by rubbing with pumice stone and water. Antique with cheesecloth dampened with turpentine and artist's burnt-umber oil paint. Tone intensity can be controlled by the amount of oil color and turpentine used. Door-panel molding is finished in gold.

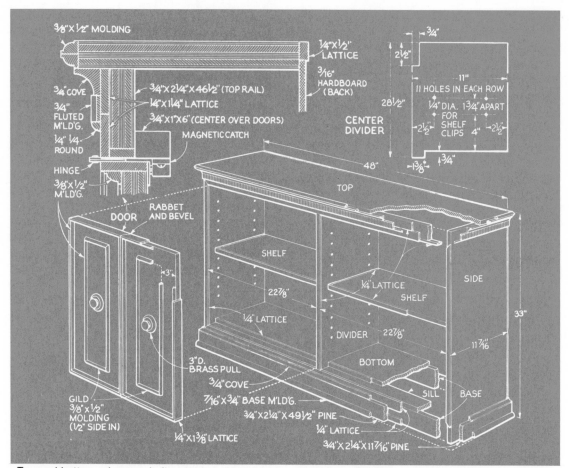

Top and bottom edges are built up using 1″ pine stock and moldings. The plywood top piece is edged with two ⅜″ ornamental moldings glued back to back. Underneath the top edge, front and sides are built up using 1¼″ lattice with ¾″ fluted molding topped by ¾″ cone and finished underneath with ¼″ quarter-round molding. Bottom edges are built up with 1-by-3 pine, plus cone and quarter-round moldings.

SCULPTURED END TABLE

BY MACK PHILIPS

Gracefully sculptured lines give this end table the look and feel of flight. It will give you an interesting exercise of your shop skills. Angled saw cuts, lathe work, dowel-pinned joints, and wood sculpting are all involved. The table's base is weighted for extra stability.

This graceful little table is a conversation piece—not just for its sharp good looks, but because everyone wants to know how you put it together. It almost seems carved out of a solid block. But with today's hardwood prices, a good design must make efficient use of stock, with little waste. This design does—and that professional-look shaping is easy with a few common power tools.

The angled stance of that slender pedestal gives the table a floating feel—you wonder how it stands at all. Well, granted that the table shouldn't hold fragile or expensive glassware, the design is such—with a weighted base—that it's quite stable for normal uses: displaying light objects, even a low lamp, or holding an ashtray.

Mine is a home-shop adaptation of a famous design I could never afford (since it can only be ordered through a decorator). You put it together like a puzzle—the whole thing comes out of a 1½" turning square, an 8" block and a small panel of ¾" hardwood for the top. Once the assembly is sculptured and finished, it's hard for the uninformed to guess how you managed it.

I chose walnut for its contemporary look and easy working. Maple, birch, or cherry would do equally well. Or a splendid version could be made from teak or rosewood. If you wished to avoid gluing up a foot-wide panel for the top, you could substitute plywood in a matching veneer. The sculptured edge, of course, would have to be carefully filled and stained, but the fact that it is always in shadow would help to hide the exposed plies.

All the 1½"-thick stock could be made by gluing up two ¾" boards—with a bonus of more interesting grain patterns after shaping.

Angles are compound. Start by turning the center portion of the pedestal on a lathe. This establishes the diameter and makes it easy to blend in the shaping of the ends. Trim off the ends as shown, and save them. These trim cuts are made at a compound angle to give the pedestal a double tilt.

Turn the center of the pedestal to establish diameter for start of sculpting. Square ends will later be partly rounded by hand.

Trim pedestal ends at compound angle of 12½ degrees. Cut-off pieces have proper angle for use as gussets between foot pairs. Measure angles carefully.

Glue and dowel foot pairs to square ends of pedestal; add gusset blocks. Assemble top end the same, in opposite direction.

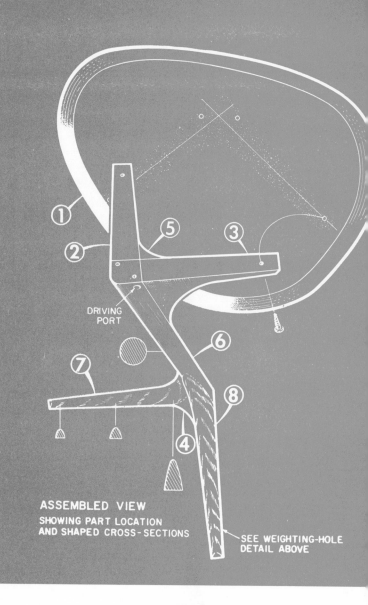

① ② ⑤ ③ ⑥ ⑦ ⑧ ④

DRIVING PORT

ASSEMBLED VIEW
SHOWING PART LOCATION
AND SHAPED CROSS-SECTIONS

SEE WEIGHTING-HOLE
DETAIL ABOVE

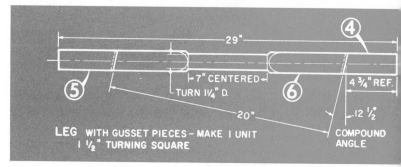

⑤ ④ ⑥

29"

7" CENTERED
TURN 1¼" D.

4 ¾" REF.

20"

12 ½°
COMPOUND ANGLE

LEG WITH GUSSET PIECES – MAKE I UNIT
1 ½" TURNING SQUARE

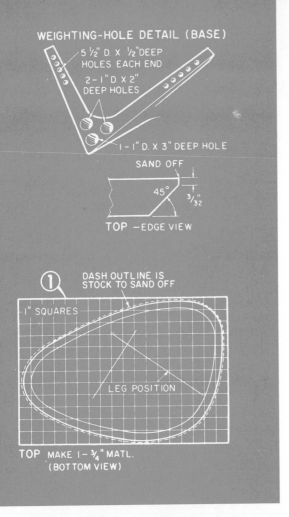

WEIGHTING-HOLE DETAIL (BASE)

5 ½" D. X ½" DEEP HOLES EACH END

2 - 1" D X 2" DEEP HOLES

1 - 1" D. X 3" DEEP HOLE

SAND OFF

45°   3/32"

TOP —EDGE VIEW

① DASH OUTLINE IS STOCK TO SAND OFF

1" SQUARES

LEG POSITION

TOP MAKE 1 - ¾" MATL.
(BOTTOM VIEW)

On your radial-arm or table saw, bevel the edges of the block that you'll cut the feet parts from, then lay out the shapes. A lot of shaping effort can be saved on the assembled leg if you cut away excess stock on a bandsaw. After assembly, check the bases on a flat surface. Correct mismatches by sanding the feet with a belt or drum sander—or by simply rubbing them on a sheet of coarse abrasive tacked to a flat surface.

Drill a series of holes in the bottom assembly, as shown, and pack with lead shot. Weighting improves the stability of the table— especially on a carpeted floor.

Enlarge the graph-squared pattern of the free-form top and trace it on your 12"-by-18" panel. Be sure to mark leg position on the underside.

Sculpting hints. If you own a high speed hand grinder (Dremel and Weller make popular ones) the pedestal can be quickly shaped with burr cutters and rotary files. Cross-sections at various points on the pedestal are shown on opposite page to guide you. I use a good half-round cabinet rasp to follow up after the rotary files. But all the shaping can be done with hand tools. The many types and sizes of Stanley's Surform rasps, for example, would make fast work of it.

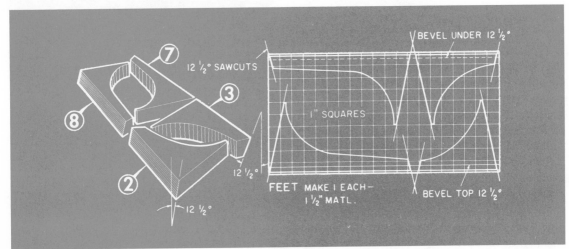

⑦ 12 ½° SAWCUTS

③

⑧

② 12 ½°

12 ½°

BEVEL UNDER 12 ½°

1" SQUARES

FEET MAKE 1 EACH—
1 ½" MATL.

BEVEL TOP 12 ½°

Bandsaw excess stock from feet before assembly if you prefer. Gusset pieces at left have also had preliminary shaping.

Rough-shape the assembly with high-speed burr. Note wood-scrap V blocks clasping center of pedestal in vise for shaping.

Weight base with lead shot in several bore recesses. Cap with epoxy putty or wood plugs to hold shot firmly in place in the recesses.

Rasping cross grain—as you must do on this project—may take a bit more care. Touch up first with a coarse half-round file, finish off with a sharp cabinet scraper.

Finally, sand and blend with 120 grit paper, stroking with the grain as much as possible. Follow with 180-, 240-, and 400-grit sandings, then a rubdown with 4-0 steel wool.

The best finish for this type of contemporary furniture is "Danish" oil. For a satiny sheen, I like Deep Finish Firzite or Watco Danish Oil. Of course, if you want to alter the color of the wood, you can apply a stain—but it may "take" unevenly on sculptured wood.

Where to buy materials. If you can't find the hardwoods locally, you can order them by mail from Constantine & Son, 2050 Eastchester Rd., Bronx, N.Y. 10461, or the Craftsman Wood Service Co., 2727 So. Mary St., Chicago 60608.

Lead shot is available at many hardware stores, and shops selling shotgun-shell reloading supplies.

SLICING PLATFORM

Strips cut from hardwood scraps, assembled with waterproof glue into a 10"-by-15" block and mounted on rubber-tipped legs, will rate cheers from your wife. It's ideal for slicing, chopping, and dicing. The feet prevent sliding or marring, and the hole near one end funnels the cut-up food directly into a bowl, slipped beneath. Slice any 1"-thick hardwood—walnut, oak, maple—into 1" strips and glue and clamp these face-to-face, preferably to present all end grain. After shaping and sanding, apply edible oil or a special salad-bowl finish.

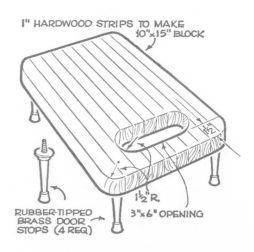

1" HARDWOOD STRIPS TO MAKE 10"x15" BLOCK

1½"R

RUBBER-TIPPED BRASS DOOR STOPS (4 REQ)

3"x6" OPENING

RECLINING CHAIR ADJUSTS FOR COMFORT

BY FRANK TAGGART

Have you ever gone shopping for a contemporary easy chair—one that has the clean lines of Danish furniture but is built to give the solid comfort of old-fashioned chairs? If you have, you undoubtedly discovered what I did. You can find one—but at a price that seems like the national debt.

You can build this one for a fraction of the cost. It's made of walnut, but any knotfree hardwood could be substituted. Unless you want to try your hand at the sewing machine, the project can be a joint effort: You build the chair and your wife makes the cushions.

Construction is simple. If you have never built a modern piece, you're in for a pleasant surprise. All of the angular cutting—except the curved top of the arm—can be done on a bench saw. The arm tops are cut on a bandsaw—or by hand, using a saber saw, or a compass or coping saw.

Keep waste to a minimum by laying out all parts on the stock; mark each piece for identification and cut them all at one time.

You can speed up the job if you shape and sand all parts before assembly. Round the edges, using a 1/4" quarter-round bit in your router. If you don't own a router, a spokeshave and wood rasp can be used.

Assembly. Test the leg and arm units for fit. When you're satisfied, assemble with dowels and glue. The chair itself is completed when these two units are joined with stretchers.

Seat and back come next. These are simple frames with a groove (to accept the cane) cut around the inner edge. Use a 3/16" straight

Danish-inspired chair adjusts to suit the person using it; ottoman gives comfort to legs.

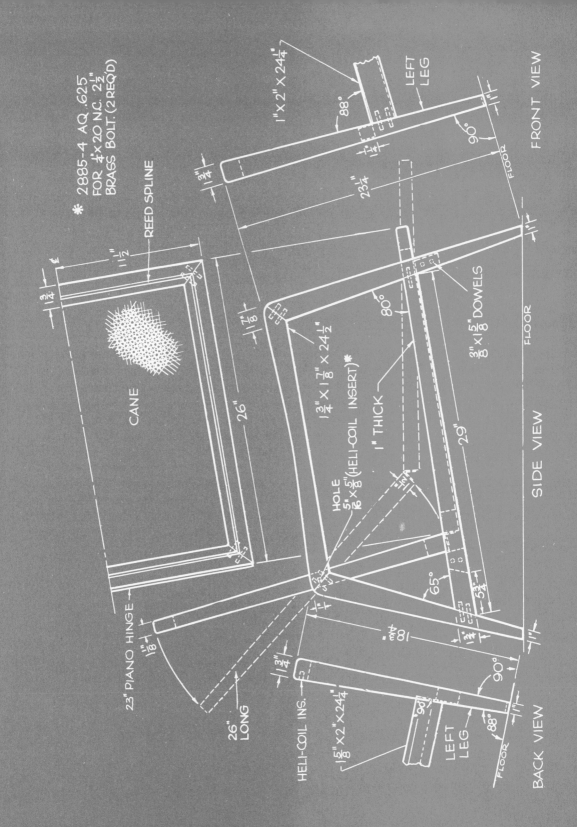

* 2885-4 AQ.625 FOR ¼"×20 N.C. 2½" BRASS BOLT. (2 REQD)

REED SPLINE

CANE

I"×2"×24¼"

LEFT LEG

88°

90°

23¾"

FRONT VIEW

1¾"×1⅞"×24½" (HELI-COIL INSERT)*

80°

⅜"×1⅝" DOWELS

I" THICK

FLOOR

29"

SIDE VIEW

HOLE 5"/16×5/8" (HELI-COIL INSERT)

65°

5¾"

8⅜"

23" PIANO HINGE

1⅛"

26"

1⅞"

I½"

¾"

¾"

26" LONG

HELI-COIL INS.

1¾"

1⅝"×2"×24¼"

LEFT LEG

90°

88°

90°

FLOOR

BACK VIEW

I"

56

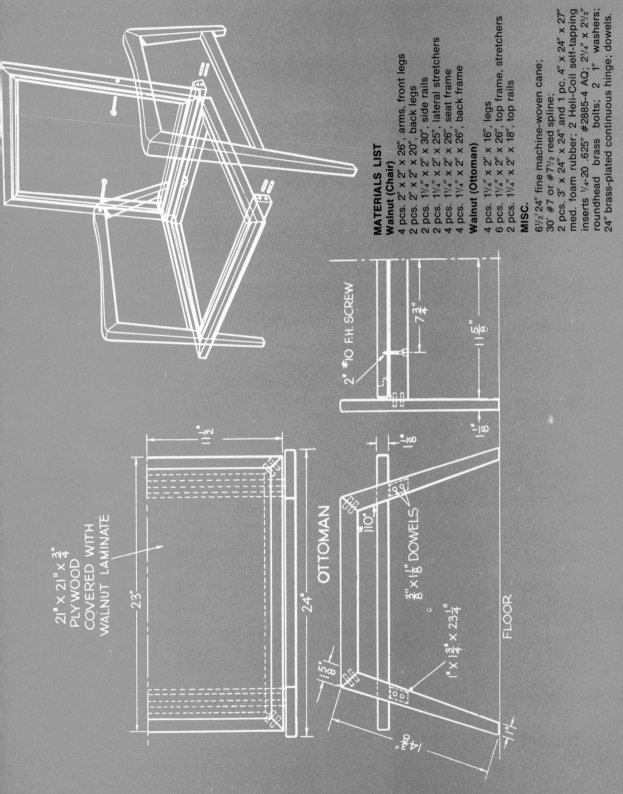

21" x 21" x 3/4"
PLYWOOD
COVERED WITH
WALNUT LAMINATE

23"

11 1/2"

24"

OTTOMAN

2" #10 F.H. SCREW

7 3/4"

11 5/8"

1 1/8"

1 1/8"

110°

3/8" x 1 1/8" DOWELS

1" X 3/4" X 23 1/4"

1 5/8"

FLOOR

1/4"

1 1/4"

MATERIALS LIST
Walnut (Chair)

4 pcs. 2" x 2" x 26", arms, front legs
2 pcs. 2" x 2" x 20", back legs
2 pcs. 1 1/4" x 2" x 30", side rails
2 pcs. 1 1/4" x 2" x 25", lateral stretchers
4 pcs. 1 1/4" x 2" x 26", seat frame
4 pcs. 1 1/4" x 2" x 26", back frame

Walnut (Ottoman)

4 pcs. 1 1/4" x 2" x 16", legs
6 pcs. 1 1/4" x 2" x 26", top frame, stretchers
2 pcs. 1 1/4" x 2" x 18", top rails

MISC.

6 1/2' 24" fine machine-woven cane;
30' #7 or #7 1/2 reed spline;
2 pcs. 3" x 24" x 24" and 1 pc. 4" x 24" x 27"
med. foam rubber; 2 Heli-Coil self-tapping
inserts 1/4-20 .625" #2885-4 AQ; 2 1/4" x 2 1/2"
roundhead brass bolts; 2 1" washers;
24" brass-plated continuous hinge; dowels.

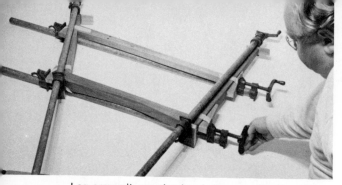

Leg-arm units are glued and clamped after pieces have been shaped and sanded. Frame is checked to assure that it dries with legs, arm, and stretcher in the same plane. Taped-on wedges protect walnut.

Chair unit is complete when lateral stretchers are glued and doweled to the leg-arm units. Work on a level surface, and check frame for square. The next step is to drill the holes for the Heli-Coil inserts.

Foam cushions are cut slightly oversize, fabric actual size. Resulting compression assures smooth slip-covers. Chair back and seat, joined with piano hinge, are attached to chair as in sketch shown.

cutter in the router, set to a depth of $5/16''$, to make them—or cut them on the bench saw. After grooving, all pieces can be mitered to length and the two frames assembled.

Caning. An ancient art, caning has been in use for centuries, as paneling as well as seating material. It's tricky, but also fun to do. Machine-woven cane and reed spline are available from woodworker supply houses such as Albert Constantine, 2050 Eastchester Rd., New York, N.Y. 10461.

Soak the cane in warm (not boiling) water for about 15 minutes. While it's soaking, make the hardwood caning wedge as shown in the sketch.

Lay the wet cane over the frame and, with the narrow tip of the wedge, force the webbing into the first groove. Brush waterproof glue in over the cane and, starting at the corner, tap in the spline with the heavy edge of the wedge. On the opposite side of the frame pull the cane to remove any slack and repeat the procedure. Finish the third and fourth sides in the same manner.

Reclining action. The two Heli-Coil inserts make this possible. They're the pivot point for all movement. The coil bears against the brass bolt, allowing you to tilt the chair while seated. Professional woodworking shops boast a special mandrel for driving the inserts. Since you use only two inserts, the cost makes buying the tool impractical.

Drive them in this way: File $1/16''$ off the tip of a $1/4''$-by-$2\frac{1}{2}''$ bolt on three-quarters of its surface—leaving a point. Screw a nut on, and then the insert until the bolt's point engages the hook on the insert's end. After drilling the hole, use a screwdriver to drive the bolt and a wrench to keep the nut snug against the insert. When it's seated, withdraw the bolt. Done any other way, there's a good chance you'll break the insert. You can order the inserts. from Heli-Coil Corp., Shelter Rock Lane, Danbury, Conn.

The ottoman is also made of walnut with a caned top. If you think you'll call on it to double as a coffee table, ½″ plywood covered with walnut plastic laminate would be a better choice for the top. Construction and assembly are the same as for the chair.

To finish, apply boiled linseed oil with double-0 steel wool. Wait 30 minutes and wipe the excess off. Repeat the procedure the next day. To bring out the walnut grain, wait until the second coat has dried completely and rub with Butcher's wax. Let the wax set for 20 minutes and buff to a sheen. Don't oil the cane; leave it in its natural state.

Heli-Coils in leg-arm units permit reclining action. After locating pivot point, a ⁵⁄₁₆″ hole is drilled ¾″ deep and coil is installed with special mandrel (photo). Text tells how to do it without mandrel.

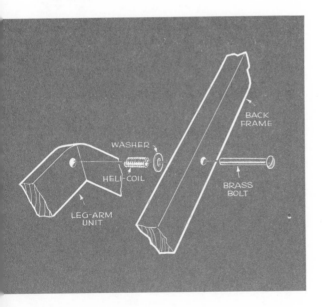

Caning, in three easy steps

Miter the reed spline at the corners and test for fit before starting caning operation. The caning wedge (see sketch) is made of hardwood and used for setting the cane and spline. Sand the butt edge slightly concave to fit the spline; round all edges to prevent wedge cutting the cane.

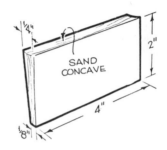

SAND CONCAVE

Stretch wet cane over the frame and force into groove using the narrow tip of the homemade wedge and a hammer. Make certain that the cane design stays parallel to the frame during each step.

Seat the reed spline (after brushing glue in the groove), using wedge's concave butt edge. As each panel is finished, wipe off excess glue and water. Trim cane above the spline with a sharp utility knife.

KEEP THE DIRECTORY NEAR YOUR KITCHEN PHONE

BY GARY GERBER

The whole point of having a classified directory, the ads say, is to "let your fingers do the walking." Yet few of us have found a handy way to keep the directory near the phone—especially in the kitchen. So *we* do the walking to a distant drawer or closet to retrieve it.

Instead, take your pick of these two easy-to-assemble directory holders created by industrial designer Gary Gerber. The stool with the hinged seat offers a bonus: a place to perch while you phone. If you lack power tools, omit dadoes and rabbets and butt-join pieces with glue and screws. If you want the natural finish shown, first apply veneer tape to all plywood edges.

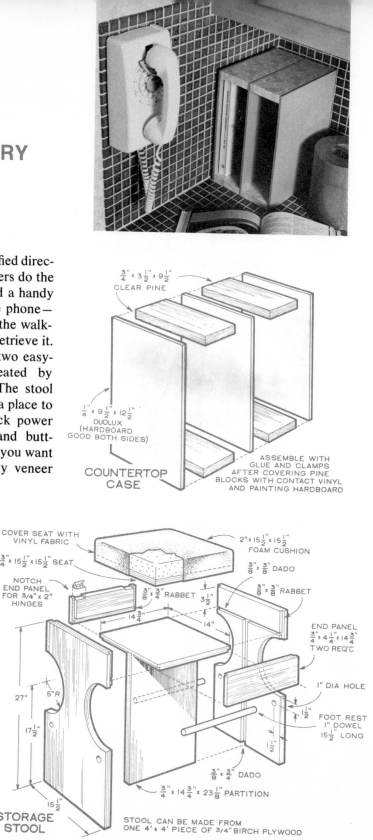

$\frac{3}{4}" \times 3\frac{1}{2}" \times 9\frac{1}{2}"$
CLEAR PINE

$\frac{1}{4}" \times 9\frac{1}{2}" \times 12\frac{1}{2}"$
DUOLUX
(HARDBOARD
GOOD BOTH SIDES)

COUNTERTOP CASE

ASSEMBLE WITH GLUE AND CLAMPS AFTER COVERING PINE BLOCKS WITH CONTACT VINYL AND PAINTING HARDBOARD

COVER SEAT WITH VINYL FABRIC

$2" \times 15\frac{1}{2}" \times 15\frac{1}{2}"$ FOAM CUSHION

$\frac{3}{4}" \times 15\frac{1}{2}" \times 15\frac{1}{2}"$ SEAT

$\frac{3}{8}" \times \frac{3}{8}"$ DADO

NOTCH END PANEL FOR 3/4" x 2" HINGES

$\frac{3}{8}" \times \frac{3}{4}"$ RABBET

$3\frac{1}{2}"$

$\frac{3}{8}" \times \frac{3}{8}"$ RABBET

$14\frac{3}{4}"$

$14"$

END PANEL $\frac{3}{4}" \times 4\frac{1}{4}" \times 14\frac{3}{4}"$ TWO REQ'D

1" DIA. HOLE

$1\frac{1}{2}"$

FOOT REST 1" DOWEL $15\frac{1}{2}"$ LONG

$27"$

$5"$R

$17\frac{1}{2}"$

$1\frac{1}{2}"$

$1\frac{1}{2}"$

$\frac{3}{8}" \times \frac{3}{4}"$ DADO

$\frac{3}{4}" \times 14\frac{3}{4}" \times 23\frac{1}{8}"$ PARTITION

$15\frac{1}{2}"$

STORAGE STOOL

STOOL CAN BE MADE FROM ONE 4' x 4' PIECE OF 3/4" BIRCH PLYWOOD

ONE-SHEET PARTY KNOCKDOWNS

DESIGNED BY LESTER WALKER /
Architect

BY ROSARIO CAPOTOSOTO /
Photos by the author

These two projects will brighten any party. And they'll store flat in a closet until they're needed for guests. Each one is easily and economically cut from a single sheet of plywood, but knowing a few tricks helps. The designer called for MDO (medium-density-overlay) plywood, which is surfaced on both sides with resin-impregnated fibers for smooth, check-free painting. It's double the price of plain fir plywood, which, of course, you can use instead.

For your saber saw, choose a wood blade with set teeth; a no-set blade tends to drift. With the circle jig at far left, you'll make perfect curve cuts. For straight cuts, a portable circular saw is best. For internal cuts you'll need a ripping guide—a 1-by-2 nailed along a straight-edged 1-by-4. This highwalled guide lets you "plunge-cut" by resting the toe of the saw base on the work with the blade above the surface (you'll have to tape up the guard temporarily). Start the saw and slowly drop the blade into the plywood, as shown in the photo, until the base seats solidly, then push the saw forward.

The best way to cut square-cornered notches is with a saber saw and the simple jig shown: The dimensions of the notch should position the blade on each layout line when the saw

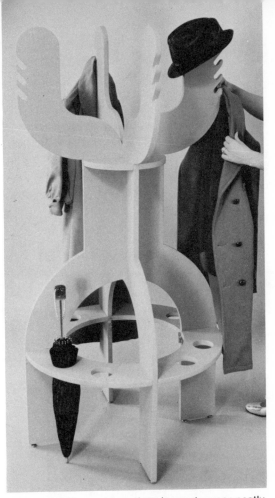

Coat rack solves problem of storing party wraps neatly. Notches at top take coat loops or hooks of wire coat hangers. Hats stack on top. Rainy? Lower ring holds eight umbrellas.

Sturdy table provides serving space for refreshments, doubles as game table. Handy, too, as a work top for projects. It stores flat in three seconds.

base is snug against each side of the notch. Since MDO plywood measures a bit over ¾ thick and you want to allow a hair for paint on each side, lay out all notches slightly oversize. When you've made the two side cuts, repeat passes will remove the waste between. Then slide the saw sideways against the bottom of the jig's notch to smooth the end of the slot. Always clamp the jig in position, of course.

To start a saber-saw cut, drill a blade hole centered on the line. In the case of the coat-rack disk and ring, drill at a slot position and you'll avoid an unwanted edge nick. The table top is cut directly from the panel edge, so no starter holes are required. Follow the sequence for curve cuts on the rack pattern, to preserve pivot points, then section the panel with straight cuts. For the table, you separate the nested leg sections by using both saws.

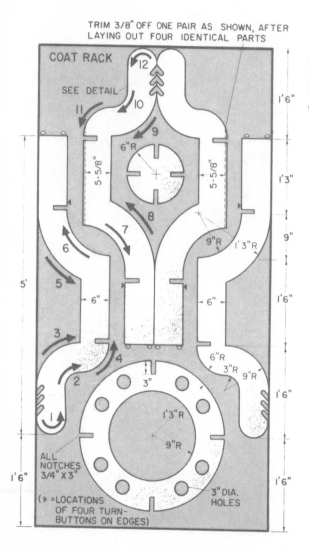

TRIM 3/8" OFF ONE PAIR AS SHOWN, AFTER LAYING OUT FOUR IDENTICAL PARTS

COAT RACK

SEE DETAIL

6"R

5-5/8"   5-5/8"

9"R   1'3"R

6"   6"

6"R
3"R 9"R

3"

1'3"R

9"R

ALL NOTCHES 3/4" X 3"

3" DIA. HOLES

(▸ =LOCATIONS OF FOUR TURN-BUTTONS ON EDGES)

1'6"

1'3"

9"

1'6"

1'6"

1'6"

5'

1'6"

Designed for minimum waste, members are nested edge-to-edge on 4-by-8 sheet of ¾" MDO plywood. Best cutting sequence is shown for coat rack. For step-by-step party-table construction, see photos.

5-1/8"

DRILL 3/4" HOLE

1"

2"

2"

TURNBUTTON DETAIL

DRILL FOR SCREW 1/2" FROM EDGE OF SLOT

COAT-HOOK DETAIL

Lay out and cut coat rack as shown in photos on these pages. After marking off straight lines, fill in radii, using a stick tacked through pivot point at given distance from the hole for pencil.

62

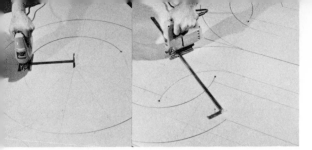

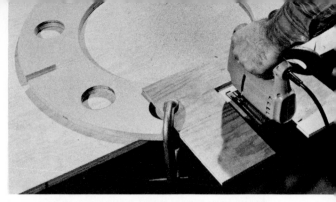

Cut umbrella ring with circle jig (left). Cut outside first to preserve pivot point for inner cut. Ring is laid out with pivot stick, then divided into 30-degree parts. Drill starting holes for saber saw in waste when possible (right). Some curve cuts can be started in previously cut straight center kerfs. Run blade up to straight layout lines on inside corners, as here.

To cut identical slots in disk, ring, and uprights, make jig from scrap with notch to guide base of saber saw and stop blade at proper depth. After making the two side cuts, repeat passes will clear slots.

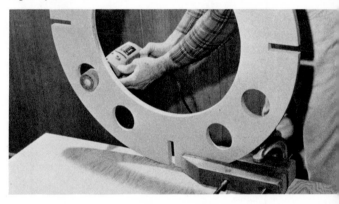

Make all straight cuts with a circular saw held snug against a clamped-on guide—after radius cuts are made. Some straight lines must be plunge-cut, so lightweight 4½" Trim Saw comes in handy.

Drum sander in portable drill makes quick work of smoothing all hole edges. Just take care to keep axis square with work. MDO plywood faces need no sanding for paint.

Circle-cutting bit does neatest job of cutting umbrella holes, but note that the cutter spins too fast to be seen; keep hands away. Use a backup scrap and clamp work securely to drill press.

To assemble coat rack, push four uprights into mating notches of disk and ring. Four turnbuttons, screwed to inner edges of uprights (see sketch on opposite page), lock them to the ring.

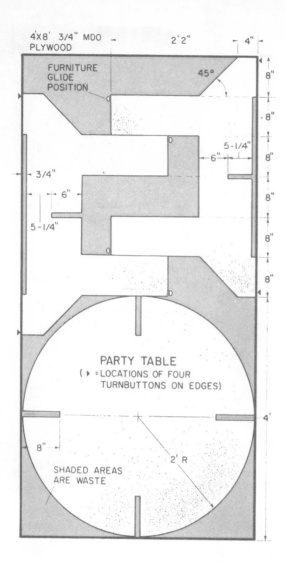

4'x8' 3/4" MDO PLYWOOD

FURNITURE GLIDE POSITION

45°

2'2"

4"

8"

8"

5-1/4"

6"

8"

3/4"

6"

8"

5-1/4"

8"

8"

PARTY TABLE
(▶ =LOCATIONS OF FOUR
TURNBUTTONS ON EDGES)

4'

8"

2' R

SHADED AREAS
ARE WASTE

To complete ends of internal cuts insert saber saw into the kerf, since circular blade leaves underside of cut short of mark.

To separate nested sections, seven cuts are required. Z-shaped waste area at the center is then removed without plunge-cutting.

Clamped-on guide is used again to make angled cuts. As before, run circular saw up to line. Complete cut with saber saw.

Internal slit cuts require series of plunge cuts against clamped-on high-wall guide. Just pivot spinning blade into the plywood.

Cutting four-foot disk for the table top is simple with home-made jig (see drawing below) to align teeth of saber-saw blade with nailed pivot point.

Optional second jig has V cut to take base of router with straight cutter to smooth edge. This can be done by sanding, instead.

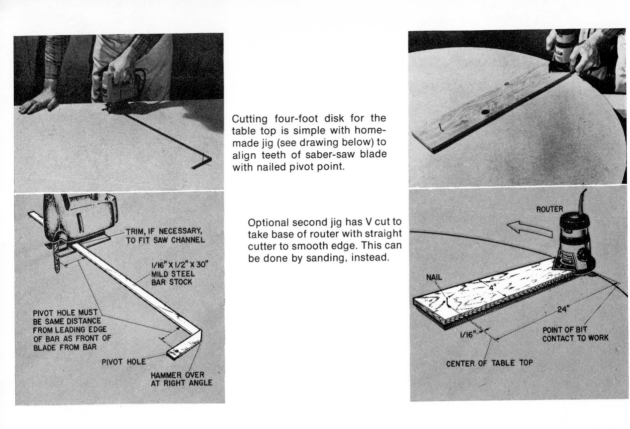

TRIM, IF NECESSARY, TO FIT SAW CHANNEL

1/16" X 1/2" X 30" MILD STEEL BAR STOCK

PIVOT HOLE MUST BE SAME DISTANCE FROM LEADING EDGE OF BAR AS FRONT OF BLADE FROM BAR

PIVOT HOLE

HAMMER OVER AT RIGHT ANGLE

ROUTER

NAIL

4"

24"

1/16"

POINT OF BIT CONTACT TO WORK

CENTER OF TABLE TOP

Trial assembly checks mating slots—made slightly oversize to allow for the paint layer. Test-fit the top on leg assembly.

Drive turnbutton screws 1" from edge of each leg after drilling pilot holes. Omit these if table is not to be lifted for moving.

PLYWOOD ROCKER-TABLE FOR 4-IN-1 PATIO FUN

BY LESTER WALKER / *Architect*

The passing of the front porch left a void in neighborly relaxation that has been filled by the backyard patio. I designed this four-man rocker as a replacement for the old porch swing, but realized it would have to earn its space with other outdoor functions. So it converts to a picnic table/playhouse or a service bar by merely being flipped onto its back or side.

The unit is structurally engineered to avoid any necessity for framing. The plywood panels, bolted to two-by-two cleats, brace one another to form a stable structure no matter how the unit is positioned. If you want a

ROCKER

PICNIC TABLE

PLAYHOUSE

BAR

cleaner corner on the cleats, you can substitute poplar for the standard pine lumber called for in the plans. Glue all cleats in place before drilling for and driving flathead screws from the opposite face. All heads are countersunk to set flush and are merely painted over in the model shown. But, since all cleats are permanently attached, you can sink the heads deeper and putty over them if you prefer.

One of the advantages of MDO plywood (if your lumber dealer doesn't stock it, have him order three sheets of exterior grade for you) is that it needs no surface sealing or undercoat. Before you apply the exterior enamel, be certain to sand all cut edges carefully, then give them a couple of extra coats of the enamel to guard against splintering. If you plan heavy use of the rocker on a rough surface, you may want to protect the curved edge from wear by nailing on aluminum strap or sections of split garden hose.

Since assembly takes only 20 minutes, you may want to knock down the unit and cart it along to a summer cottage. The parts fit easily into a station wagon, or could be carried on the top of a sedan.

Designer Lester Walker has come up with this delightful piece that serves all the patio functions shown. It's easily made from MDO (medium-density overlay) plywood, assembled with two-by-two cleats and 30 wingnut/bolt/washer sets. It knocks down for flat winter storage or transport in a station wagon. Close ends of crawl-through tunnel and it becomes a roofed playpen for a toddler.

Finger-snug all the wingnuts for easy disassembly. Along with the 3"-long bolts and the 1⅜"-diameter washers, wingnuts should be of the galvanized variety to resist weather exposure.

67

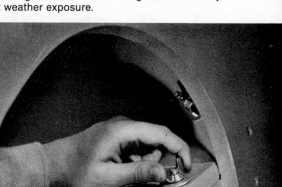

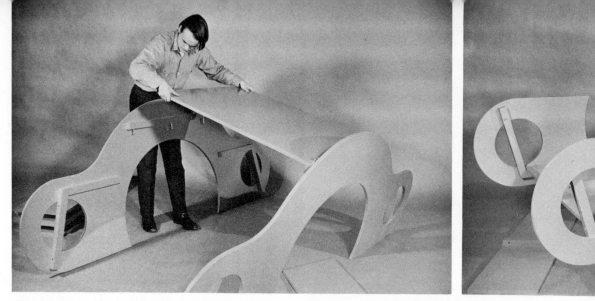

One-man assembly starts (in table position) by bridg-
ing rocker panels with tabletop. Anchor one end (left)
before positioning other. Flip unit over to rocker position (center); bolt in both seat bottoms: drop in seat

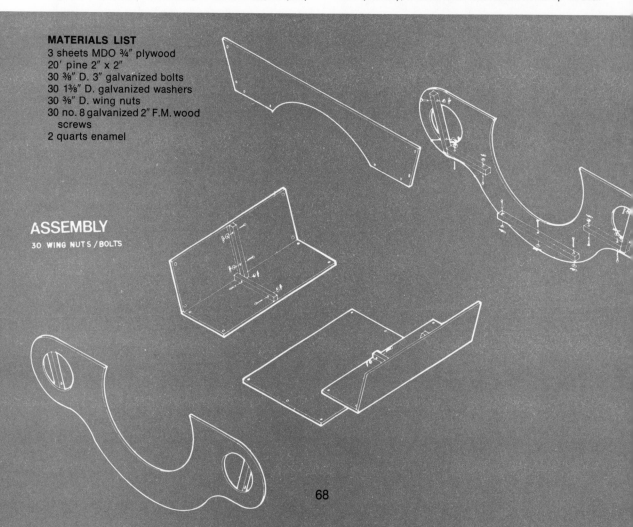

MATERIALS LIST

3 sheets MDO ¾" plywood
20' pine 2" x 2"
30 ⅜" D. 3" galvanized bolts
30 1⅜" D. galvanized washers
30 ⅜" D. wing nuts
30 no. 8 galvanized 2" F.M. wood
   screws
2 quarts enamel

ASSEMBLY

30 WING NUTS / BOLTS

68

backs against cleats set 15 degrees from vertical. Slide tension bar (right) between two-by-two cleats at center of seat panels. A ¾" space is provided between these cleat pairs to allow perfect fit for tension bar.

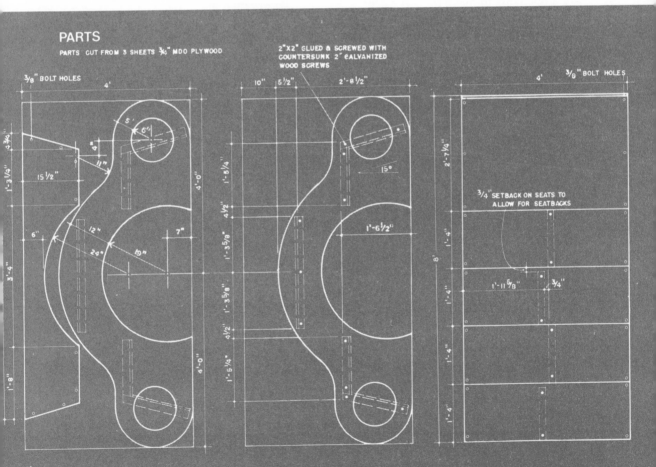

PARTS

PARTS CUT FROM 3 SHEETS ¾" MDO PLYWOOD

2"X2" GLUED & SCREWED WITH COUNTERSUNK 2" GALVANIZED WOOD SCREWS

⅜" BOLT HOLES

¾" SETBACK ON SEATS TO ALLOW FOR SEATBACKS

A SLATE-TOPPED BUFFET

BY DONALD RUTHERFORD

Don't let the slate top or the Mediterranean good looks of this buffet scare you off—it's easier to build than you think. The sketch shows all you need to know to start, but here are a few hints to make the job easier:

First cut the base to size. Add the frame members and backstop. If your wall is wavy, scribe and bandsaw the backstop for a good fit. Groove the picture-frame molding as shown and fasten it in place with glue and finishing nails. Set nails and fill holes with spackle.

Lay the slate as shown here. While the mastic sets for a couple of days, apply three coats of black enamel to skirt and backstop. Sand lightly between coats.

Mount the buffet on the wall. Then apply the grout. After it has set for a few minutes, go back over it with a damp sponge, cleaning the slate and smoothing the joints at the same time. Keep sponging until the slate is as clean as you can get it. Cover with wet cloths for two days to allow for a crack-free cure.

Finally, wash the counter with detergent, let dry, and apply two coats of slate dressing. Allow the dressing to dry and your buffet is ready to take on its first dinner party.

Unfinished picture-frame molding makes the attractive skirt. Lumberyards and frame shops carry it in a variety of cuts and sizes. Molding shown here is 3½″ wide. Fasten with glue and finishing nails.

MATERIALS LIST

Base—½″ plywood, 19″ × 85½″
Frame—clear fir or pine, 2″ × 2″
  (1½″ × 1½″ actual), 2 pcs. 85″ long, 5 pcs. 15¾″ long
Backstop—clear pine, 1″ × 4″, 85″ long
Filler—pine, 1″ × 2″, 3 pcs. 18¾″ long
Skirt—unfinished picture-frame molding, 3½″ wide, 12′ long
Brackets—wrought iron, approx. 12″ × 18″, 3 reqd. (available at lumberyards)
Mastic—1 quart
Grout—20 lbs. (use equal parts Portland cement and fine sand, plus 2 lbs. powdered lampblack)
Hardware—4d and 6d finishing nails, six ¼″ × 1″ lag bolts, six ¼″ × 2½″ lag bolts, 48 1¼″ #8 FH screws
Finish—white glue, putty, spackle, black satin-finish enamel, slate dressing
Slate—10-sq.-ft. floor-tile kit (made by Buckingham-Virginia Slate Corp., 1103 E. Main St., Richmond, Va.

Slate sets in place on a bed of mastic applied with notched spreader. Scraps of ½″ plywood between blocks maintain uniform intervals for the grout to be applied later between slate blocks.

Work mayonnaise-thick grout into joints with a trowel or rubber spatula. Let set a few minutes, clean up, smooth with damp sponge. Cover with wet cloths for two days so it will dry slowly and crack-free.

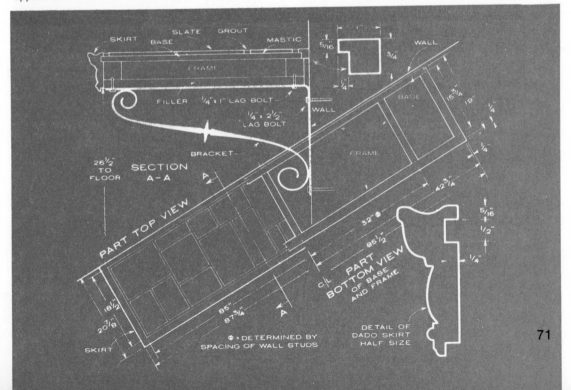

71

COFFEE MUG HOUSE

The coffee-mug craze has left many homes with mugs that have too much appeal to be hidden away. One clever way to display them —and keep them handy for use—is a wall-hung mug house styled to match the architecture of your home. The photo shows a rack built of walnut and scrap counter-top laminate, to match a split-level house. From the basic dimensions shown here, the other sketches can be adapted.

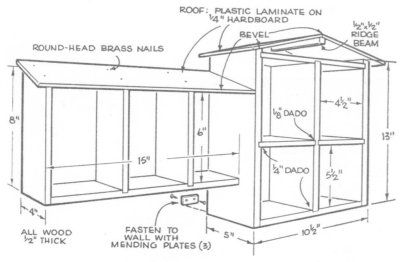

ROOF: PLASTIC LAMINATE ON ¼" HARDBOARD

BEVEL

½"×½" RIDGE BEAM

ROUND-HEAD BRASS NAILS

8"

6"

15"

4"

⅛" DADO

4½"

¼" DADO

5½"

13"

10½"

5"

ALL WOOD ½" THICK

FASTEN TO WALL WITH MENDING PLATES (3)

SPLIT-LEVEL STYLING

TWO-STORY

RANCH

GARAGE

MODERN

WESTERN-STYLE TRESTLE DESK AND BENCH

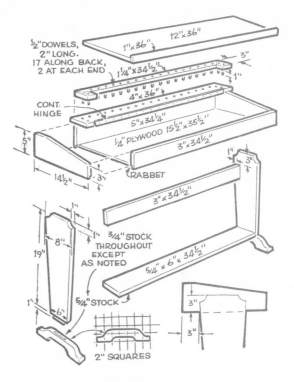

Simplified joinery makes this desk with a western flavor an easy one to build. The desk top gives a large work area and just below it is a generous-size storage bin. Though it's designed to withstand rough kid treatment, it goes together surprisingly fast.

Dowels (½″) are used throughout to assemble the pieces. Note that those at the top pass through the rail and top board into the back. To assemble, drive them in from above, then saw and sandpaper them flush.

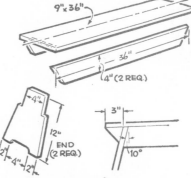

Though equally rugged, the bench is even easier to build. Cut the pieces as shown and assemble with the splayed legs set in 3″ from each end at a 10-degree angle. Finish with stain and varnish.

AIR FORCE ACADEMY DESK

Dormitory rooms at the Air Force Academy at Colorado Springs are designed for fast cleanup and maintenance, leaving the cadets with more time for out-of-classroom study. Although the furniture is equally easy to maintain, it's extremely good-looking.

Just how important *is* environment to good study habits and grades? Lt. Gen. Thomas Moorman, the Academy's Superintendent, feels that "a good study atmosphere is conducive to good grades." So when a new dorm was in the planning stage, all aspects of human behavior were taken into account to assure that the new quarters would "make it possible for members of the cadet wing to maintain a high degree of academic excellence," as the General put it.

To achieve the desired atmosphere, the architects and engineers leaned heavily on experience gained in the original dormitory. Since space was at a premium when the academy first opened, three cadets were billeted to a room. This proved unsatisfactory. One of the two beds was a double bunk, and it was impossible to provide independent study areas.

Study environment. Former Dean of Faculty Brig. Gen. McDermott explained it this way: For most students, the environment for study is affected by three variables — interruptions

from visitors and noise, the number of students assigned to a room, and the appearance and layout of the room. The first condition can be controlled by rules and regulations, the other two by planning the study space.

An important part of such planning is the choice of furniture. In the case of the new dormitory, nothing was left to chance. Each piece was custom-designed for cadets, and constructed to government specifications.

The Academy supplied the specifications and plans for the dormitory desk so that it could be made for use in the home.

Built of walnut and aluminum (as are matching chest and bed), the desk is rugged enough for years of service. Judging by its sleek good looks, you would expect it to be tough to build. It's not. It is simply an aluminum frame with end panels and a box-like drawer case.

To make it possible to build the desk of materials that are readily available, we've made a few changes. But, as can be seen in the photos, the appearance is barely altered. Overall dimensions are the same. The changes:

• The original specs called for 1¼″ aluminum angle, channel, and square tubing. All three are available only through wholesale supply houses at premium prices. Instead, Reynolds do-it-yourself 1″ square tubing has been substituted and used throughout the frame.

• The drawer pulls on the original are custom-made ones, so they were changed, too. A search turned up Knape and Vogt's flush pulls. Installed, they give the same contemporary or military-chest appearance as those on the Academy desk.

• The invisible welded joints called for in the specs require special equipment and would up the cash outlay slightly. Our wood-plug method holds strongly and uses shop scrap.

Building the desk. Start by cutting the aluminum tubing to length and plugging the ends, as shown. To insure neat joints, squirt a bead of aluminum paste (or use aluminum epoxy)

Desk as it appears in room of cadet at Air Force Academy. Before they get to fly a plane, cadets spend long hours piloting a desk.

MATERIALS LIST

Reynolds Do-It-Yourself Aluminum
Frame—6 6′ pcs. 1″-square tubing (#4860)
Drawer strips—1 6′ pc. ½″ angle (#2406)

Tempered Hardboard
Drawer bottoms, dividers—1 pc. ¼″ x 4′ x 4′

Particleboard
Top—1 pc. ¾″ x 3′ x 5′

Lumber
Upper drawer—1 pc. pine ½″ x 4″ x 6′
Lower drawer—1 pc. pine ½″ x 8″ x 6′
Drawer edging, slide front—walnut, 1″ x 1″ x 10′
Filler cleats, plugs, straddle strips—scrap

Plywood (Walnut)
End panels, drawer fronts, case—¾″ x 4′ x 8′

Plastic Laminate
Top—1 sheet, 3′ x 5′ Pionite Alpine White Encore

Hardware
14 oval-head screws 2¼″-8; 12 F.H. screws 2¼″-8; 32 sheet-metal screws ⅝″-8; 10 R.H. screws ¾″ 8; F.H. screws 1¼″-8; and 1½″-8; 4 Domes of Silence 1″ diam.: 2½″ bullet catches; 2 Knape & Vogt #819 flush pulls; 3 pr. Alta glides, 14 1″ corner braces

Miscellaneous
Aluminum cement or epoxy; 4d finishing nails; 1 qt. contact cement; glue; stain, lacquer; wood plastic or putty stick

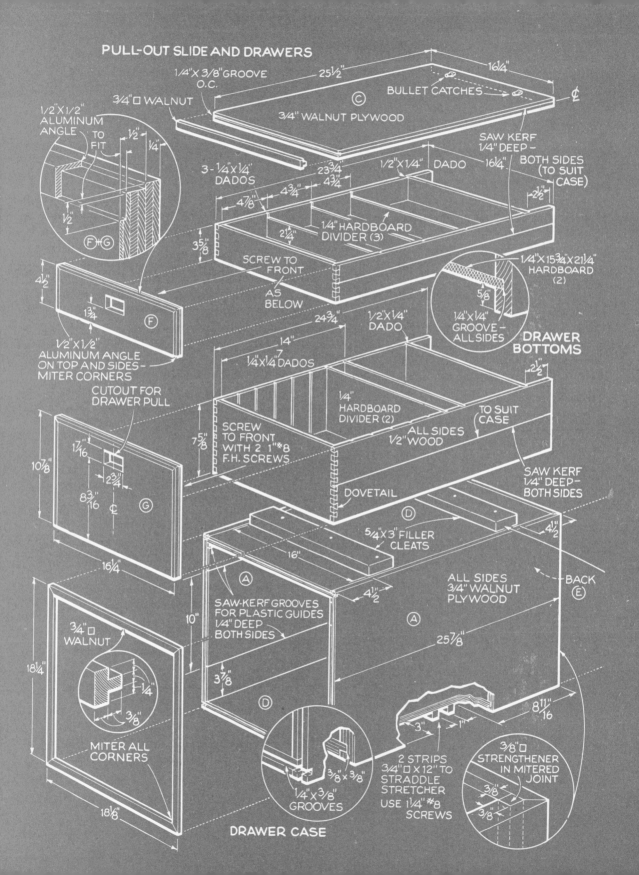

PULL-OUT SLIDE AND DRAWERS

1/4" X 3/8" GROOVE O.C.

3/4" □ WALNUT

25½"

16¼"

BULLET CATCHES

¢

3/4" WALNUT PLYWOOD

C

1/2" X 1/2" ALUMINUM ANGLE

TO FIT

1/2"

1/4"

1/2"

SAW KERF 1/4" DEEP – BOTH SIDES (TO SUIT CASE)

16¼"

3- 1/4" X 1/4" DADOS

23¾"

1/2" X 1/4" DADO

16¼"

2½"

F↔G

4¾"

4¾"

4⅞"

3⅝"

2¼"

1/4" HARDBOARD DIVIDER (3)

SCREW TO FRONT AS BELOW

1/4" X 15¾ X 21¼" HARDBOARD (2)

5/8"

DRAWER BOTTOMS

4½"

1¾"

F

1/2" X 1/2" ALUMINUM ANGLE ON TOP AND SIDES– MITER CORNERS

1/4" X 1/4" GROOVE– ALL SIDES

CUTOUT FOR DRAWER PULL

24¾"

14"

1/4" X 1/4" DADOS

1/2" X 1/4" DADO

2½"

1⅛₁₆"

2¾"

10⅞"

8³⁄₁₆"

¢

G

SCREW TO FRONT WITH 2 1" #8 F.H. SCREWS

7⅝"

1/4" HARDBOARD DIVIDER (2)

TO SUIT CASE

ALL SIDES 1/2" WOOD

SAW KERF 1/4" DEEP– BOTH SIDES

16¼"

DOVETAIL

D

4½"

5/4" X 3" FILLER CLEATS

16"

A

4½"

ALL SIDES 3/4" WALNUT PLYWOOD

BACK

E

18¼"

3/4" □ WALNUT

10"

SAW-KERF GROOVES FOR PLASTIC GUIDES 1/4" DEEP BOTH SIDES

A

25⅞"

3⅞"

MITER ALL CORNERS

D

1/4" X 3/8" GROOVES

3/8" X 3/8"

3"

1"

2 STRIPS 3/4" □ X 12" TO STRADDLE STRETCHER USE 1/4" #8 SCREWS

8¹¹⁄₁₆"

3/8" □ STRENGTHENER IN MITERED JOINT

3/8"

3/8"

18⅛"

DRAWER CASE

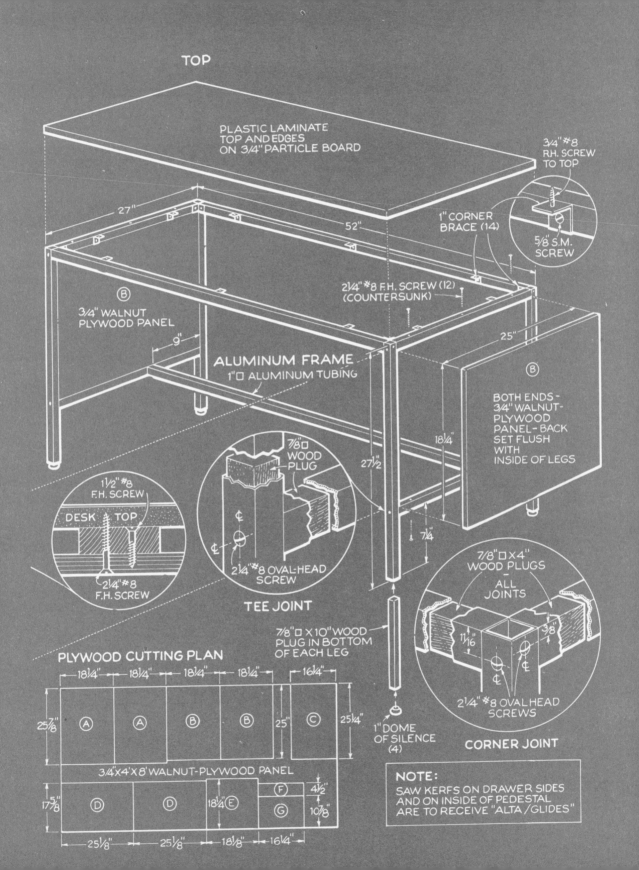

TOP

PLASTIC LAMINATE
TOP AND EDGES
ON 3/4" PARTICLE BOARD

3/4" #8
R.H. SCREW
TO TOP

1" CORNER
BRACE (14)

5/8 S.M.
SCREW

27"

52"

2 1/4" #8 F.H. SCREW (12)
(COUNTERSUNK)

3/4" WALNUT
PLYWOOD PANEL

9"

25"

B

BOTH ENDS -
3/4" WALNUT-
PLYWOOD
PANEL - BACK
SET FLUSH
WITH
INSIDE OF LEGS

ALUMINUM FRAME
1" □ ALUMINUM TUBING

18 1/4"

7/8 □
WOOD
PLUG

27 1/2"

1 1/2" #8
F.H. SCREW

DESK   TOP

2 1/4" #8
F.H. SCREW

2 1/4" #8 OVAL-HEAD
SCREW

TEE JOINT

7/4"

7/8" □ X 10" WOOD
PLUG IN BOTTOM
OF EACH LEG

7/8" □ X 4"
WOOD PLUGS
- ALL
JOINTS

1 1/16"

3/8"

2 1/4" #8 OVAL HEAD
SCREWS

CORNER JOINT

PLYWOOD CUTTING PLAN

18 1/4"   18 1/4"   18 1/4"   18 1/4"   16 1/4"

25 7/8"   Ⓐ   Ⓐ   Ⓑ   Ⓑ   Ⓒ   25   25 1/4"

3/4" X 4' X 8' WALNUT-PLYWOOD PANEL

1" DOME
OF SILENCE
(4)

5"
17 7/8"   Ⓓ   Ⓓ   18 1/4" Ⓔ   Ⓕ   4 1/2"
                                      Ⓖ   10 1/8"

25 1/8"   25 1/8"   18 1/8"   16 1/4"

NOTE:
SAW KERFS ON DRAWER SIDES
AND ON INSIDE OF PEDESTAL
ARE TO RECEIVE "ALTA/GLIDES"

To frame drawer fronts with recessed angle, first rabbet all four edges, then plough the face.

Temporarily assembled drawer is checked for slide-fit. If tight, front and back can be trimmed. Tacked-on braces keep drawer square during this step.

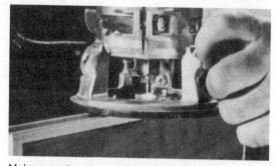

Make repeat pass on edges, with router shoe riding high edge to restore diminished width of rabbets.

View from the back shows Alta drawer glide being tapped into saw kerf. Glide is set in ¾" from forward edge to allow clearance for drawer front.

Mitered angle sets flush with both face and edge. Cut test-edge first on scrap to judge right depth.

on the wood plug before joining. Frame assembly goes easiest if you put the two end sections together first, then join them with the rails and lateral stretcher.

Walnut end panels go in next. Since they just butt the frame, and no gap-hiding moldings are used, cut them carefully. To insure perfect joints, I cut two pieces of plywood slightly oversize and used each frame as a marking template. Panels are held with flathead screws through top and bottom rails only.

Do the top next, starting with the edge strips. Apply the strips at the ends first, then the front and back. Cut the laminate for the top with an ⅛" overhang on all four sides. After it's bonded, trim the excess with a straight carbide cutter in the router, or with a sharp iron in your block plane. Finish the top by beveling all edges slightly with a smooth file. Attach the top to the frame as shown.

Making the drawer case. This rests on the lateral stretcher, and can be butted against either end panel, to suit the user and the location of the desk. To assemble the case, use well-set 4d finishing nails and white glue. Set the nails and fill with wood plastic or a putty stick. *Note:* You must run the slide-holding kerfs in the sides of the case before assembly.

With one bottom cleat attached, place the case on the lateral stretcher. After aligning the unit, clamp it to the leg to prevent movement while you fasten the second cleat. Finally, run the screws up into the top.

Two bullet catches installed in the back edge of the slide-out shelf aid in pulling it out. A slight push on the front springs it forward enough to be gripped with your fingertips.

The drawers are of ½" stock and dadoed to take hardboard dividers. Shape the drawer-front edges and attach the angle before fastening the fronts to the drawers.

The drawers slide on glides made of Delrin installed in the drawer case in sawkerf grooves mated to those in the drawers. You'll need three pairs (available from Alta Industries, 3015 N.W. Industrial, Portland 97210).

Finishing the piece. Use walnut oil stain followed by a sealer such as thinned shellac, and a coat of lacquer. We followed Academy specs and gave all exposed wood a second coat of lacquer. Let the finish cure for two weeks, then use double-0 steel wool, and follow with two coats of paste wax. Buff the surface to a sheen with a stiff, clean brush. To give the aluminum a "grain," rub it with fine steel wool or use a fine-wire wheel chucked in your drill. A coat of lacquer will keep the metal bright.

FIVE EASY STEPS TOWARD A WELDLESS ALUMINUM FRAME

Fine-tooth cutoff blade slices aluminum fast, cuts even better when it's sprayed with silicone. Put on safety goggles—a must—for this operation.

To secure screw plugs, cut them slightly oversize, so they are "shaved" by tubing when driven. Next, apply aluminum cement or epoxy as at right.

After drilling and countersinking aluminum tubing, frame is joined with oval-head screws. Excess aluminum paste squeezes out, fills any voids in joint.

Aluminum cement is cleaned off as soon as screw is turned home. After scraping off bulk, clean away any traces with rag and solvent before paste dries.

SWIVEL-TOP PROJECTION CABINET

BY THOMAS W. COTTON

One reason you don't show your slides as often as you'd like—to yourself or to your friends—is the fuss involved. You don't want to make a production out of dragging the projector from storage, clearing off or setting up a table for it (usually with a stack of books to get the proper height), then hunting through drawers for the slides you want.

With this clever, good-looking cabinet, everything for your show is at hand. Not only does it provide a sturdy projection stand with built-in height adjustment, but when it's not in use, it doubles as a lamp table or smoking stand you'll be proud to have in your living room.

I built my cabinet out of bird's-eye maple, but any inch-thick hardwood (actual thickness: ³/₄″) would do. The compartmented core is made of ¹/₄″ birchveneer plywood. You'll also need some ¹/₂″ ply for the height-adjustment slides and cabinet bottom. Construction is detailed in the blueprint, and is much simpler to *do* than to show. The unit is basically a box, with hinged double doors on the front and a pivoting drop-leaf door on the rear. These give access to two 25-compartment storage bins of egg-crate (halfflap) partitions, set back to back against a center bulkhead. This core is made separately and set in place during assembly of the cabinet.

The raisable top consists of a framed

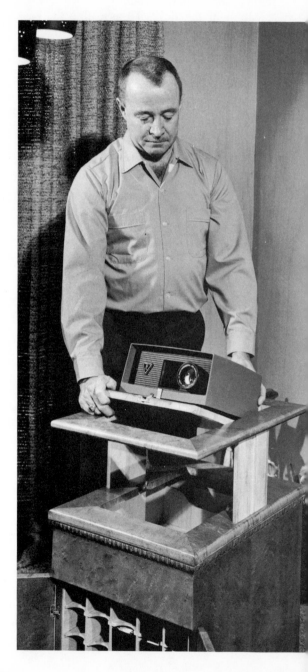

When the lights are on, it's a handsome side table. At show time, the top goes up and flips your projector into position for showing the trays of slides that store behind front and back doors.

swivel panel with the projector clamped to the underside. Extending vertically from the frame are two support slides that flank the compartmented core, riding in grooves routed into the inner faces of the cabinet walls. The slides lock at various heights by means of spring-loaded dowels. When the unit is telescoped, the pivoting center panel rests on the wider frame of the false top beneath. But once the top is raised and a latch slid back, the panel is free to swivel 180 degrees, pivoting the projector right-side up. The latch is then moved into a second socket to lock the panel in this position. There are bins at either end of the projector recess for storing such items as the power cord and remote-control handset.

Before figuring out the materials required, check the blueprint dimensions against those of your projector. If your machine is too large to clear the frame when mounted on the swivel panel, either the top sections or the entire cabinet must be enlarged. The slide-tray compartments are scaled for any tray that will slip into a space 2¾″ wide, 2⅝″ high, and 9¼″ deep. If your trays exceed these dimensions — (or are of "donut" variety) — adjust the egg crate accordingly.

I pivoted the rear door at the top (and pro-

vided a support brace) to create an extension leaf for the convenience of the projectionist. As shown above, it's handy for keeping other trays ready — and for an ashtray or refreshments during the show. Once the show is over, the unit closes up quickly to provide dustfree storage for the projector and slides until the next time. Yet the projector is easily detached for use elsewhere.

Projector hangs upside down on pivoting center panel of liftable top. Egg-crate compartments at front and rear hold 50 40-slide trays — 2,000 slides.

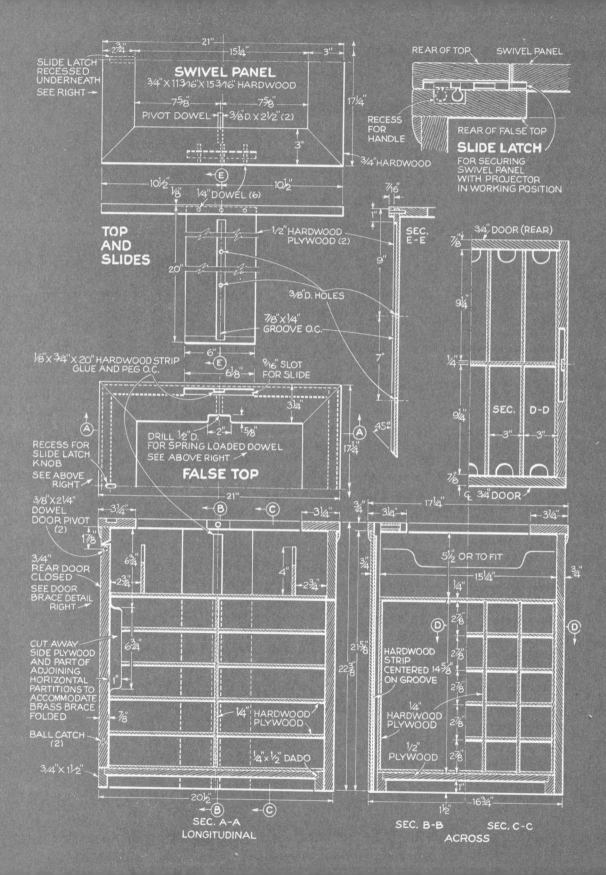

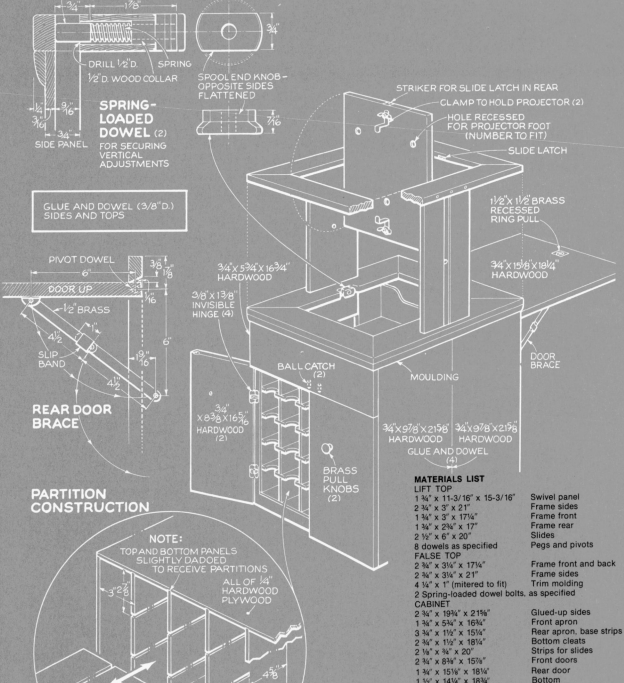

3/8" X 25/8 DOWEL – TURN DOWN TO FIT 3/8" SPRING AND SPOOL

3/4"
1 7/8"

DRILL 1/2"D.   SPRING
1/2" D. WOOD COLLAR

3/4"

SPOOL END KNOB –
OPPOSITE SIDES
FLATTENED

7/16"

**SPRING-
LOADED
DOWEL** (2)
FOR SECURING
VERTICAL
ADJUSTMENTS

1/4"
3/16"
9/16"
3/4"
SIDE PANEL

GLUE AND DOWEL (3/8"D.)
SIDES AND TOPS

PIVOT DOWEL
6"
3/8"
1 7/8"
DOOR UP
1/16"
1/2" BRASS
4 1/2"
1"
SLIP
BAND
4 1/2"
19/16"
6"

**REAR DOOR
BRACE**

**PARTITION
CONSTRUCTION**

STRIKER FOR SLIDE LATCH IN REAR
CLAMP TO HOLD PROJECTOR (2)
HOLE RECESSED
FOR PROJECTOR FOOT
(NUMBER TO FIT)
SLIDE LATCH

1 1/2" x 1 1/2" BRASS
RECESSED
RING PULL

3/4" x 15 1/8" x 18 1/4"
HARDWOOD

3/4" x 5 3/4" x 16 3/4"
HARDWOOD

3/8" x 1 3/8"
INVISIBLE
HINGE (4)

BALL CATCH
(2)

3/4"
X 8 3/8 X 16 5/16"
HARDWOOD
(2)

BRASS
PULL
KNOBS
(2)

DOOR
BRACE

MOULDING

3/4" x 9 7/8" x 21 5/8"
HARDWOOD   3/4" x 9 7/8" x 21 5/8"
HARDWOOD
GLUE AND DOWEL
(4)

NOTE:
TOP AND BOTTOM PANELS
SLIGHTLY DADOED
TO RECEIVE PARTITIONS

ALL OF 1/4"
HARDWOOD
PLYWOOD

3" 2 7/8"

INTERLOCK

4 5/8"

4 5/8"

4 5/8"

4 5/8"
1/2"

MATERIALS LIST
LIFT TOP

1 3/4" x 11-3/16" x 15-3/16"	Swivel panel
2 3/4" x 3" x 21"	Frame sides
1 3/4" x 3" x 17 1/4"	Frame front
1 3/4" x 2 3/4" x 17"	Frame rear
2 1/2" x 6" x 20"	Slides
8 dowels as specified	Pegs and pivots

FALSE TOP

2 3/4" x 3 1/4" x 17 1/4"	Frame front and back
2 3/4" x 3 1/4" x 21"	Frame sides
4 1/4" x 1" (mitered to fit)	Trim molding
2 Spring-loaded dowel bolts, as specified	

CABINET

2 3/4" x 19 3/4" x 21 5/8"	Glued-up sides
1 3/4" x 5 3/4" x 16 3/4"	Front apron
3 3/4" x 1 1/2" x 15 1/4"	Rear apron, base strips
2 3/4" x 1 1/2" x 18 1/4"	Bottom cleats
2 1/8" x 3/4" x 20"	Strips for slides
2 3/4" x 8 3/8" x 15 7/8"	Front doors
1 3/4" x 15 1/8" x 18 1/4"	Rear door
1 1/2" x 14 1/4" x 18 3/4"	Bottom

SLIDE-TRAY CORE

2 1/4" x 15 1/4" x 19"	Top and bottom
2 1/4" x 4 1/8" x 19"	Sides
1 1/4" x 14 1/4" x 14 3/4"	Center bulkhead
8 1/4" x 9 1/4" x 14 1/4"	Vertical partitions
8 1/4" x 9 1/4" x 14 3/4"	Horizontal partitions
2 1/4" x 4" x 15 1/4"	Upper partitions

BRASS
Door knobs and ring, slide latch, brace, projector
clamps (with wingnuts), invisible hinges (4), ball
catches (4), 2 1/4" ball casters with mounting plates (4)

83

SPANISH-STYLE TILE TABLE

BY R. J. DE CRISTOFORO

There's always demand for heavy Spanish-style furniture like this coffee table. An interior decorator keeps an eye on everything that comes out of my shop. When she made a good offer for the table, I figured others might like to know about it, too.

It's a pretty straightforward project. The tiles, a full ½" thick, are made for floors. All wood parts of the original are pine. You can substitute a hardwood if you prefer, but I think the pine and a walnut finish give the right feeling for this sort of project. Besides, pine is easy to work.

The tile base is a used solid-core door. To get the heavy look in the legs and stretcher, I wanted a full 2" stock. So I checked lumberyards to uncover a 14' length of 2-by-12 pine in the rough. I have a planer to work with, but there isn't so much smoothing involved that you can't do it with a belt sander.

Have the tiles on hand—enough to cover about 13 or 14 sq. ft.—before you start. Since these are an important feature of the table, spend some time looking for and selecting them. Avoid conventional tiles; you don't want to end up with something that looks like part of a kitchen counter set on legs. Spanish styles are good; so are handmade Mexican

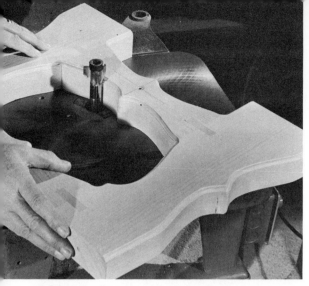

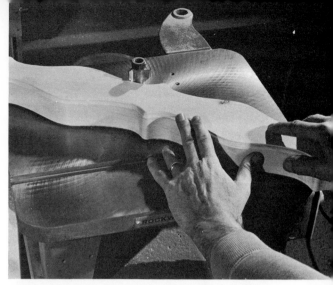

1 Edge shaping should be done after the leg assemblies are put together and sanded well. The author used the bead section of bead-and-cove cutter for this. You may prefer some different shape at edge.

2 Shape edge of stretcher in the same way as the legs. Since material is the same thickness, no change is needed in cutter setting. Be sure to work with a shaper guard, removed here to photograph work.

varieties. Generally, tile made for floors is better for this kind of project than those designed for counter use.

Lay the tiles out. Use pieces of ¼″ or ⅜″ plywood as spacers so you can determine the overall size of *your* table. It's not likely you'll hit the exact size shown in the drawings; on the other hand, since tile modules don't vary too much, you shouldn't be far off. An inch or two in width and length—one way or the other —won't be critical. This procedure will determine the size of the base on which you place the tiles. Have the tile dealer cut the tiles as necessary—or do it yourself with an abrasive wheel on a grinder.

Cut pieces for the leg assemblies to overall size and form the notches for the splines. Don't be tempted to make the splines a tight fit; a *slip* fit is better since it provides room for glue to bond everything together.

Make all *inside* pattern cuts on the leg pieces, but do not shape the outside edges of the vertical pieces. Finish this up *after* you have glued and clamped the pieces together.

Pattern cuts can be made on a bandsaw or a jigsaw, or even with a saber saw; but be sure, after cutting, to smooth all edges on a drum sander. This is very important for the shaping cuts that come later.

Now make the stretcher. Cut it to overall size, and lay out the straight lines shown in the drawing. This will diagram a wide, shallow chevron. On these lines, lay out the pattern using the same template employed on the legs. At this point, you can do the shaping on the stretcher and the leg assemblies. If you lack a shaper or a portable router or necessary drillpress accessories, you can do the shaping by simply rounding off with a file and sandpaper.

Drill the lag-screw hole in the legs and assemble temporarily to the stretcher. Place the assembled pedestal on the underside of the tile base and mark lag-screw points. Drill and counterbore for all lag screws. Make the assembly by applying glue to all mating surfaces before driving the screws.

I made the frame for the top from ¾″ pine,

3 Lag screw is driven through the leg assembly into end of stretcher. Be sure to make a trial assembly before you do the final one—a good rule to follow in all sorts of home-shop construction.

4 Use three lag screws through top into each leg, one down through each vertical piece and one between. After trial assembly, remove screws, counterbore for the heads, apply glue before final assembly.

shaped on the outside top and bottom edges with the same cutter used on the legs and stretcher. You can substitute a fancy molding. The width of the frame pieces should equal the thickness of the tile base, plus the thickness of the tile, plus about $1/16''$ allowance for the mastic. After the top frame is glued and nailed in place, you can lay the tile.

Use a regular tile mastic. Apply according to the directions on the container. I found it best to place the perimeter tiles first and then those between, using the same plywood spacers I

cut when doing the original layout. When you place the tiles, swivel them a bit to get good contact with the mastic. Let the mastic set overnight before doing the grouting.

Use a grout that is grayish in tone and has sand in it—not the velvety material used on kitchen tile. Add water slowly and mix thoroughly until you have a very plastic mixture. It should "pour" like a very thick salad dressing. Work it over the tiles with a small trowel or piece of wood, but be sure to fill all the joints completely.

After it has set a whole, wipe off the excess with a piece of old, rough towel. Check to be sure all joints are full. Repeat the wiping process with a damp cloth until the joints are smooth and the tiles are clean. Allow to set until the grout is dry. Then you can finish with a regular tile-and-grout sealer.

5 Use an escutcheon to conceal the head of the leg-to-stretcher lag screw. You can buy a Mexican- or Spanish-style nail from a hardware store, or modify a drawer pull by sawing off post and drilling holes.

6 Plywood spacers help place the tiles as you want them. Note the grout joint between the perimeter tiles and the frame. Be sure to use the plywood spacers to determine table-top size and to set tiles.

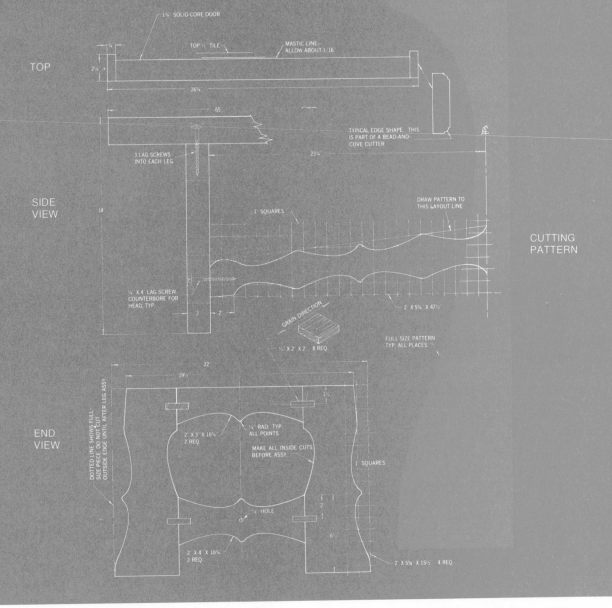

Finishing the wood. Use a dark, filler-type walnut stain, applying it generously by brush and then wiping after about 30 minutes. After drying, rub it with steel wool, wipe clean and apply two or three coats of satin-finish Vara-thane. Let each application dry thoroughly and smooth down with a fine steel wool before doing the next coat. Rub the last coat with steel wool, wipe clean, and then finish with a couple of applications of hard paste wax. The tile top will also take the wax application.

One hint before you go to buy the tile: Luck and persistent checking over of what's available can save you money. Keep an eye out for good seconds, or tag-ends at sale prices. Also, broken tiles can be used at table edges.

CORIAN-TOPPED SERVER IN THE CLASSIC STYLE

BY PHIL MC CAFFERTY

Fold-down top, made of Corian slab ¾" thick, looks like costly old-world marble.

Marble is often associated with fine furniture of the past. Nowadays home shops can turn out furniture of equal quality using Corian—a modern material that looks like marble but is much easier to work.

Styled with the elegant flavor of the Mediterranean countries, this classic server features rich dark wood, heavy moldings and carvings, and a fold-down Corian top that looks for all the world like fine old-world marble. Hidden under the base are global casters for easy moving. Inside there is room to store party and serving things; and if you wish, a "marble" wine-storage rack.

Materials needed. Idaho pine "widewood" was used for the server case. This is narrow strips pre-glued, planed, and sanded, supplied by many lumberyards in wide widths. About 12 linear feet of widewood 24" wide is needed for the base, doors, and shelf. Trim is a combination of standard stock white-pine moldings and embossed hardwood trim. The "carvings" on the doors are stock plastic simulations.

A piece of Du Pont's ¾" Corian 20" by 62" makes the three-piece top and the turned knobs. A wine rack requires a 13"-by 23" piece of ¼" Corian and ¾" hardwood dowels.

Embossed trim around the doors and the bottom and top of the base was Craftsman Wood Co's #E-175, ¹³/₁₆" material. Six four-foot lengths were used. (For catalog, write to Craftsman Wood, 2727 S. Mary St., Chicago, Ill. 60608). Four Panel-Crafts 8"-by8" "Ponce" design plastic carvings were trimmed to 6" by 6" to use on the doors. These are typical of simulated carvings you can buy at building-supply stores.

Five pairs of H-shape full-surface hinges with a wrought look, 3½" long, were used for the doors and hinging top leaves. Two pairs of 8" drop-leaf supports hold the leaves in the open position. A set of 3" plate-type casters is mounted under the recessed bottom of the base.

Butt-joint corners. These simplify assembly of the base. The front is cut from one piece of widewood, as shown. This glued-up material has a slight tendency to warp. The base was designed to minimize this problem. Everything except the doors is held in alignment by the bottom piece, shelf, and top mounting strips. The cleats on the back of the doors help hold them flat and provide handy holes for storing dinnerware and utensils.

Cut out all the base parts, making sure the front is cut from one piece as shown. Bevel the center edges of the door pieces slightly.

"Weather" and distress the base before applying the trim and molding. After the trim is applied, weather that, too, and work it for a distressed effect. "Weathering" can be done with a wire wheel. Distressing is a matter of taste. Some things you can do: dropping a heavy chain on the wood, drilling small "worm" holes, rounding edges with a rasp and fine sandpaper to stimulate wear, scorching with a torch.

Working with Corian. Blank out the three-piece top and two pieces for the knobs. A fairly fine-toothed blade used in a radial or table saw will provide an edge that requires only light sanding. Center the top piece over the base and mark the hold-down screw locations. Drill and tap for 1/4" machine screws, being careful not to drill the holes through the top. If an error is made, the holes can be hidden pretty well by plugging with a mixture of epoxy glue and powdered Corian shavings.

Rout or shape the edges of the top. This can be an ogee and drop-leaf shape, or cove and quarter round. Using 3/8" cove and 3/8" rounding cutters makes a neat job.

Mount the drop-leaf hinges with 3/16" machine screws and assemble the top to the base. The drop-leaf supports can then be installed.

Rough-sand the top with 150- or 200-grit paper and finish with 400 grit. Polish to a high marble-like luster with Du Pont automotive White Polishing Compound.

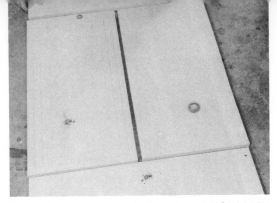

Front of server was made from board 24" wide by cutting and reassembling, as here.

Pre-drill holes in top mounting strip for later fastening of the slab of 3/4" Corian.

Give wood weathered look by brushing away the soft parts with a fine wire brush.

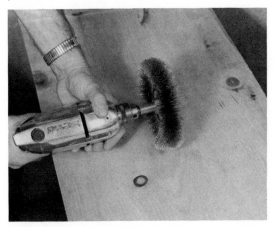

Install casters on the pre-stained bottom as close to corners as swiveling allows.

Lathe-turn knobs after routing edge. Drill and tap back to bolt work to faceplate.

Epoxy-glue polished knobs to finished doors, centering between plastic moldings.

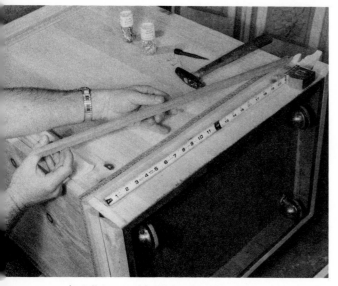

Install top and bottom trim with glue and brads. Cut and trial-fit all the pieces first.

Finish the back so server can be used anywhere. Brush stain coats but do not wipe.

Tarnished pewter look was given hinges by wire-brushing off original black paint.

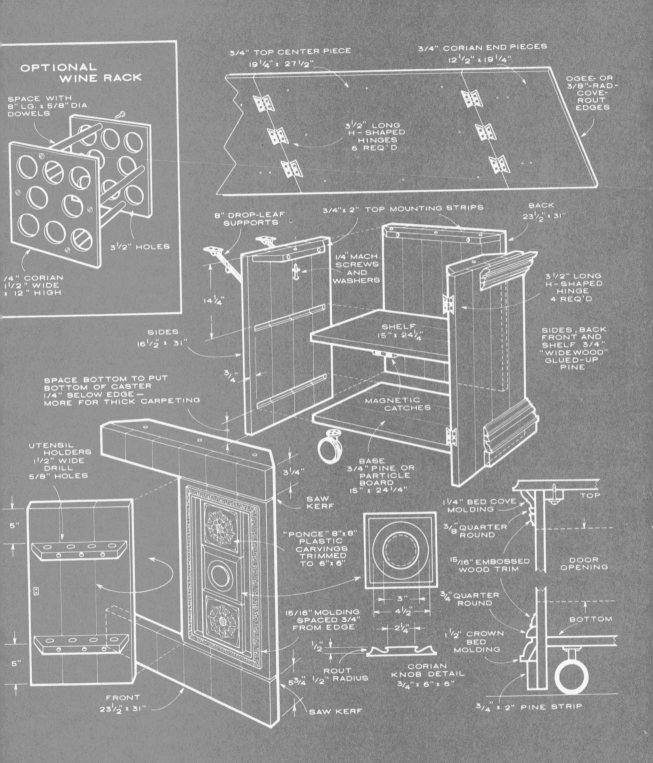

OPTIONAL WINE RACK

SPACE WITH 8" LG. x 5/8" DIA DOWELS

1/4" CORIAN 1 1/2" WIDE x 12" HIGH

3 1/2" HOLES

3/4" TOP CENTER PIECE 19 1/4" x 27 1/2"

3/4" CORIAN END PIECES 12 1/2" x 19 1/4"

OGEE- OR 3/8"-RAD-COVE-ROUT EDGES

3 1/2" LONG H-SHAPED HINGES 6 REQ'D

8" DROP-LEAF SUPPORTS

3/4" x 2" TOP MOUNTING STRIPS

BACK 23 1/2" x 31"

1/4" MACH. SCREWS AND WASHERS

3 1/2" LONG H-SHAPED HINGE 4 REQ'D

14 1/4"

SIDES 16 1/2" x 31"

SHELF 15" x 24 1/4"

SIDES, BACK FRONT AND SHELF 3/4" "WIDEWOOD" GLUED-UP PINE

3/4"

SPACE BOTTOM TO PUT BOTTOM OF CASTER 1/4" BELOW EDGE— MORE FOR THICK CARPETING

MAGNETIC CATCHES

3/4"

SAW KERF

BASE 3/4" PINE OR PARTICLE BOARD 15" x 24 1/4"

UTENSIL HOLDERS 1 1/2" WIDE DRILL 5/8" HOLES

5"

"PONCE" 8" x 8" PLASTIC CARVINGS TRIMMED TO 6" x 6"

3"

4 1/2"

2 1/4"

1 1/4" BED COVE MOLDING

TOP

3/8" QUARTER ROUND

15/16" EMBOSSED WOOD TRIM

DOOR OPENING

3/4" QUARTER ROUND

1 1/2" CROWN BED MOLDING

BOTTOM

5"

15/16" MOLDING SPACED 3/4" FROM EDGE

1/2"

ROUT 1/2" RADIUS

5 3/4"

CORIAN KNOB DETAIL 3/4" x 6" x 6"

3/4" x 2" PINE STRIP

FRONT 23 1/2" x 31"

SAW KERF

91

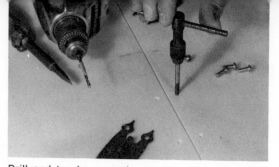

Drill and tap leaves and server top for three hinges on each side, but avoid drilling through.

Cut holes for wine rack with adjustable cutter. Sand off sharp edges of holes.

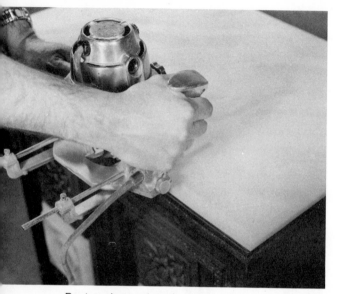

Rout or shape edge of top. Routing center piece after it's attached to server is best.

Finishing the base. This can be done before or after installing the top. Lightly sand the distressed, wire-brushed wood, trim, and moldings. Brush on one coat of regular oil stain made by mixing two parts ebony-tone stain with one part dark walnut-tone stain. Brush out but do not wipe. When dry, sand lightly and brush on two coats of a commercial "maple," "Salem maple" or "Antique maple" colored stain/finish material such as Dayco Blond-it Wood Finish. Brush out but do not wipe. Sand lightly after first and second coats. Apply two coats of a semiflat clear finish such

as McCloskeys Heirloom Eggshell Finish, sanding lightly between coats. This gives practically the same tone to the plastic "carvings," embossed hardwood molding, softwood trim, and pine.

Corian facts. You have your choice of three color veins. (Each sheet has its own unique vein pattern.) We used Regal Gray. It's also available in Dawn Beige and Olive Mist. If your lumber dealer won't order it for you, write Building Products Div., Du Pont, Wilmington, Del. 19898.

BALCONY SHELVES FOR APARTMENT DWELLERS

BY L. O. REXRODE

If you live in a high-rise apartment, as I do, you probably spend a good deal of time out on the balcony during the warm months. There's never enough room for end tables or snack carts, so finding a spot for drinks, ashtrays, and the like can be a problem. I solved this problem by building take-apart shelves that can be stored flat when they're not in use.

The shelves in the photo were made of redwood, but cedar or pine would do just as nicely. To achieve a rustic effect, the tenons are peg-shaped and protrude ½" beyond the sides. For the best-looking job, select the lumber carefully. Pick a straight piece with an attractive grain, free of knots.

Building is simple. Outline the parts and make the cuts with a saber saw. Hint: After cutting the first side, use it as a pattern for the second. Use the same procedure for cutting the extensions. The notch on the extensions must be custom-cut to fit your balcony wall. Use the wall thickness, plus ⅛", to determine this cut.

Drill the ¾" holes in the sides and, to avoid splintering when the bit breaks through, use a backup board. Cut the shelf as shown, and round the tenons to fit the holes. The extensions are attached with screws. Countersink the heads so they will be out of sight. When joining sides and extensions, apply a dab of glue to prevent twisting.

After sanding, finish by applying a coat of clear furniture oil—such as Danish oil. Follow this with a light coat of liquid wax to protect the shelves from stains and spills. Hang them up, and bring out the guests.

Hanging shelves take the place of tables or carts without taking up valuable floor space. They're designed so that they can be taken apart for storage.

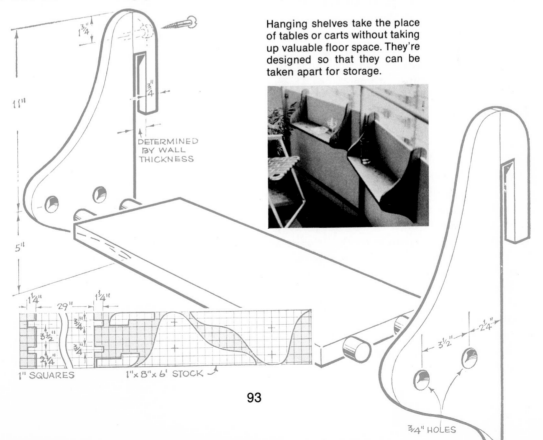

HOW TO REPRODUCE A PEMBROKE TABLE

How many times have you wandered through an Early American restoration, or museum, admiring antique furniture? And how many times have you gotten the urge to make an authentic duplicate for your own home? It can be frustrating, unless you have the time and the authorization to take measurements on the spot. Even then, each goof means a trip back to check—or settling for a guess, which means sacrificing authenticity. Now you can build those copies without traveling any farther than to the lumberyard.

Like most folks, E. Carlyle Lynch enjoys antique furniture. Unlike most, he took the time to copy a number of fine pieces—faithfully and carefully. The result is his book, *Furniture Antiques Found in Virginia* (Bonanza Books Div. of Crown Publishers, 419 Park Ave. So., NYC 10016). The book is a good one; it's chock-full of handsome furniture. From it we've chosen this table.

The name probably refers to the Earl of Pembroke, who may have been the first to order such a table, back in the 18th century. The special characteristics of a Pembroke are the short drop leaves and swing-out supports.

In building our reproduction, we've simplified construction to make the project easier. The table is walnut (with a little pine for drawer and interior construction). Details are given in the blueprint.

The veneer borders and drawer pull are from Albert Constantine and Son (2050 East-

This elegant American version of an 18th-century classic Pembroke table will fit nicely in any home.

chester Rd., Bronx, N.Y. 10461). Borders come in one-yard lengths, so you'll need two No. 82 and one No. 77.

Cutting the stock. Begin by edge-gluing the top and drop leaves. If the 2″ walnut for legs is not available—or if it will save a few dollars—laminate ¾″-by-1½″ stock. On each leg, make the first pass on the bench saw, rotate the leg 90 degrees, and make the second pass. The legs are tapered on the two inside planes only and the top 5″ is left square. Make the jig, as shown, and test for accuracy with scrap.

Next cut the three aprons to overall length. Cut the fixed apron (9¾″) off each side apron, then tackle the swing-out supports. On these parts you are working with two angles. The

Cut finger-grip bevel on drop-leaf support with rip fence set so bottom outside edge remains full 5″ width. Bevel cuts are 52½ degrees; apron cut, 60.

Better-looking rule joint results when hinge knuckles are gained (see hinge detail on blueprint). Mark around hinge and use small gouge to cut groove.

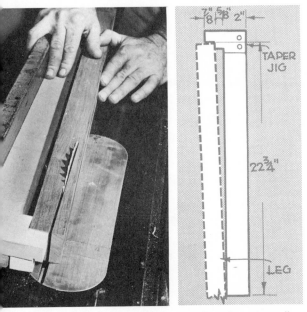

Taper legs quickly and accurately by using a taper jig. Sketch shows how to build one. Make sure leg is fully seated and held firmly to cut the taper.

angle on the apron is 60 degrees; the bevel cut on the two edges of the support is 52½. Cut the finger-grip bevel as shown, and mortise for the support hinges.

Glue and clamp the two front rails to a pair of legs, and the back apron to its legs. Attach the four ⅞″-by-5″ filler strips to each leg. When dry, fasten the sub-aprons in place and clamp the table, checking squareness. Spread glue on the sub-aprons, clamp on the walnut ones, and secure with 1½″-#8 flathead screws.

Make the drawer before you attach the top. It's easier this way to check for fit and to locate slides and stops.

The inlay. If you have a router, use it (with clamped guides) to make grooves for the inlay. If you don't own one, some old-fashioned mallet and chisel work will make the piece all the more authentic. Either way, plough the grooves to a depth that will leave the veneer slightly above the walnut surface. After the veneer is set, sand it flush with the walnut and shellac it so it won't absorb stain.

Now shape the top. Sears shaper cutters No. 9-3291 and 9-3290 used on a spindle-shaper make the rule joint as shown. A drill press will do the job too. For the best-looking rule joint—with leaves down—gain the hinge knuckles into the top's underside. To complete assembly, flip the top, position the table on it, and fasten with ⅝″ screws and ¾″ corner braces. At the front, use 1¼″-#8 screws through the top rail.

The table shown was finished with oil stain and walnut filler, followed by two coats of Minwax antique oil finish.

95

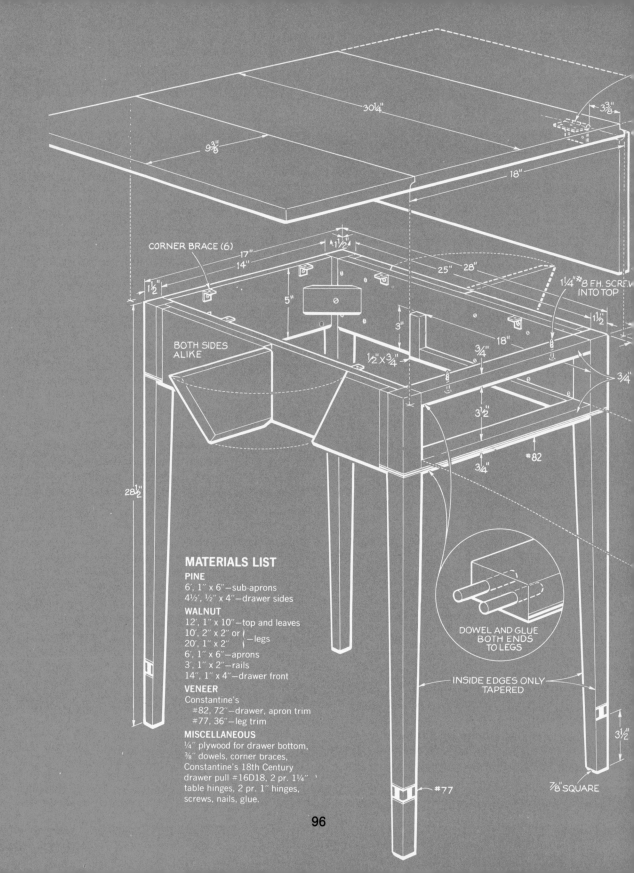

30¼"

9⅜"

3⅜"

18"

CORNER BRACE (6)

1½"

17"
14"

25" 28"

1¼"#8 FH. SCREW
INTO TOP

1½"

1½"

5"

BOTH SIDES
ALIKE

½" x ¾"

3"

18"

¾"

¾"

3½"

#82

¾"

3¾"

28½"

MATERIALS LIST

PINE
6', 1" x 6"—sub-aprons
4½', ½" x 4"—drawer sides

WALNUT
12', 1" x 10"—top and leaves
10', 2" x 2" or \
20', 1" x 2" / —legs
6', 1" x 6"—aprons
3', 1" x 2"—rails
14", 1" x 4"—drawer front

VENEER
Constantine's
  #82, 72"—drawer, apron trim
  #77, 36"—leg trim

MISCELLANEOUS
¼" plywood for drawer bottom,
⅜" dowels, corner braces,
Constantine's 18th Century
drawer pull #16D18, 2 pr. 1¼"
table hinges, 2 pr. 1" hinges,
screws, nails, glue.

DOWEL AND GLUE
BOTH ENDS
TO LEGS

INSIDE EDGES ONLY
TAPERED

3½"

#77

⅞" SQUARE

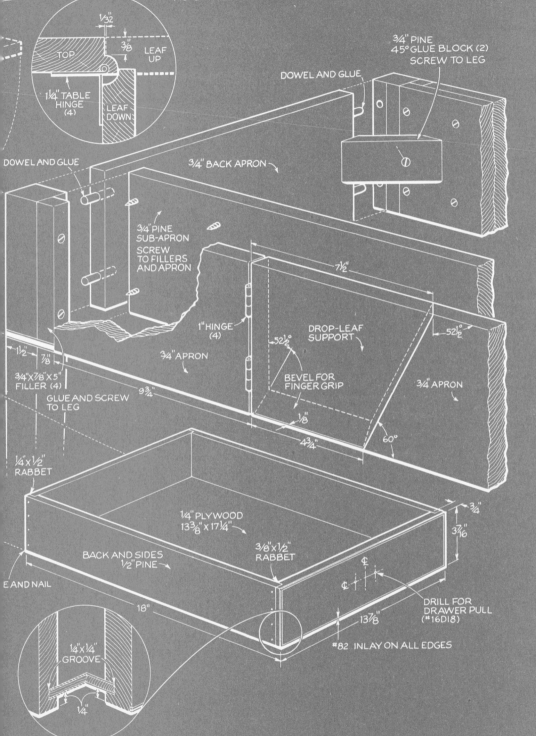

NOTE:- ALL WOOD IS WALNUT UNLESS OTHERWISE INDICATED

TOP

LEAF UP

1/32

3/8

1/4" TABLE HINGE (4)

LEAF DOWN

3/4" PINE 45° GLUE BLOCK (2) SCREW TO LEG

DOWEL AND GLUE

DOWEL AND GLUE

3/4" BACK APRON

3/4" PINE SUB-APRON SCREW TO FILLERS AND APRON

7 1/2"

1" HINGE (4)

DROP-LEAF SUPPORT

52 1/2°

52 1/2°

3/4" APRON

3/4" APRON

1 1/2"

7/8"

3/4" x 7/8" x 5" FILLER (4)

GLUE AND SCREW TO LEG

9 3/4"

BEVEL FOR FINGER GRIP

1/8"

4 3/4"

60°

1/4" x 1/2" RABBET

1/4" PLYWOOD 13 3/8" x 17 1/4"

3/4"

3 7/16"

BACK AND SIDES 1/2" PINE

3/8" x 1/2" RABBET

E AND NAIL

18"

DRILL FOR DRAWER PULL (#16D18)

13 7/8"

#82 INLAY ON ALL EDGES

1/4" x 1/4" GROOVE

1/4"

97

tom. Fold ends down and around the end of the foam and tack in place with a few stitches.

Now build the cushion frame around the foam. Position the crossbars in the frame $1/2''$ from the top, fasten with screws and 1" L brackets. Cut and assemble the leg-handles. Position so that handles rest on the foam. Fasten assemblies in place with screws from inside the frame, a pair at each point.

LOW-COST HIGH-STYLE OTTOMAN

BY W. J. HAWKINS

Looking for a weekend furniture project that will keep you busy but not broke? This contemporary ottoman requires no special tools or skills.

Round banister stock serves for legs and handles; strips of 1" pine make up the cushion tray. Crossbars support the cushion, giving it a flexible feel. Dimensions of the tray depend on the size of your foam cushion, so cut and cover the foam first. I used a 30"-by-15" blank.

Pull the material tightly around the foam and sew a seam down the center of the bot-

Simple lines and simple construction make the ottoman an excellent weekend project.

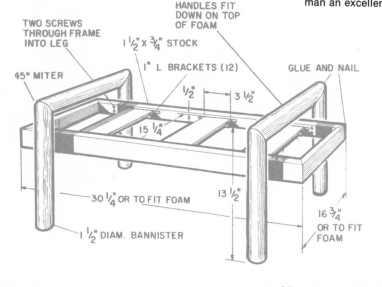

TWO SCREWS THROUGH FRAME INTO LEG

HANDLES FIT DOWN ON TOP OF FOAM

$1\frac{1}{2}'' \times \frac{3}{4}''$ STOCK

1" L BRACKETS (12)

GLUE AND NAIL

45° MITER

$\frac{1}{2}''$ $3\frac{1}{2}''$

15 $\frac{1}{4}''$

30 $\frac{1}{4}''$ OR TO FIT FOAM

13 $\frac{1}{2}''$

$1\frac{1}{2}''$ DIAM. BANNISTER

16 $\frac{3}{4}''$ OR TO FIT FOAM

SHAKER SETTEE

BY DAVID WARREN

The only place the early Shakers liked embellishment was in their religion. Their name comes from an ecstatic dance performed as part of their worship. In contrast, their everyday community life was based on the no-nonsense principles of celibacy and self-sufficiency.

These attitudes are reflected in the furniture they produced for their settlements—especially those along the New York-Massachusetts border, several of which are now museums. The original of this bench is on display in one of them, though its name comes from Canterbury, N. H., where it was found.

It's typical of Shaker design—strictly utilitarian, without frills or unnecessary parts. Of all period furniture, Shaker pieces make the most direct appeal to modern tastes. This bench will be at home in any room style.

You'll note it lacks lateral stretchers to strengthen legs or back. It is reasonable, therefore, to question the bench's sturdiness. But I built two for use in the family recreation room and our six shaking youngsters haven't been able to loosen a joint. The reason: quality-designed, deep-set hardwood joints.

Where to start. Edge-glue and dowel the seat boards to the required width. When the glue has dried, you can start the scooping operation. An electric power plane or router are laborsavers here, but a scrub or jack plane will do the job, too—it just takes a little more

Bench is right at home whether indoors or out. Use waterproof glue and exterior varnish on a bench that will be exposed to weather.

99

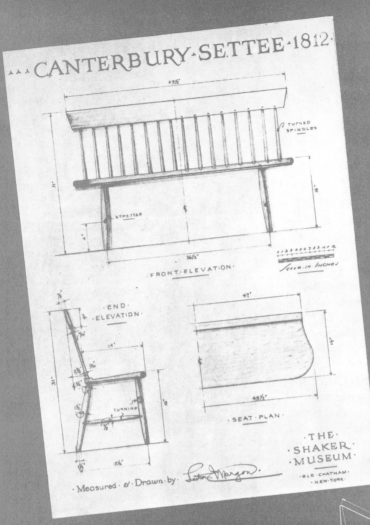

CANTERBURY·SETTEE·1812

FRONT·ELEVATION·

SCALE·IN·INCHES

END ELEVATION·

SEAT·PLAN·

TURNED SPINDLES

STRETCER

TURNING

·Measured· & ·Drawn·by· Lester Margon

THE SHAKER MUSEUM

·OLD·CHATHAM· ·NEW·YORK·

The blueprint for this settee is based on the drawing at left, taken from Lester Margon's book, *Masterpieces of American Furniture* (copyright 1965 Architectural Book Publishing 10 E. 40th St., New York, N.Y. 10016). Margon made the drawing after measuring the Canterbury settee on exhibit at the Shaker Museum, Old Chatham, N.Y. The name refers to the still-active Shaker community—Canterbury, N. H.—where the bench was made around 1812.

MATERIALS LIST
CHERRY WOOD
2 pcs. 2″ x 8″ x 51″, seat
4 pcs. 2″ x 2″ x 18″, legs
2 pcs. 1″ x 1″ x 18″, stretchers
16 pcs. 1″ x 1″ x 14″, spindles
1 pc. 1″ x 1″ x 51″, backboard
MISC.
4 chair glides, glue, shellac

16 SPINDLES - APPROXIMATELY 2¹⁵/₁₆ APART IN 44″

49½

47″

47″

49½

1½″

1½

14″

BACK

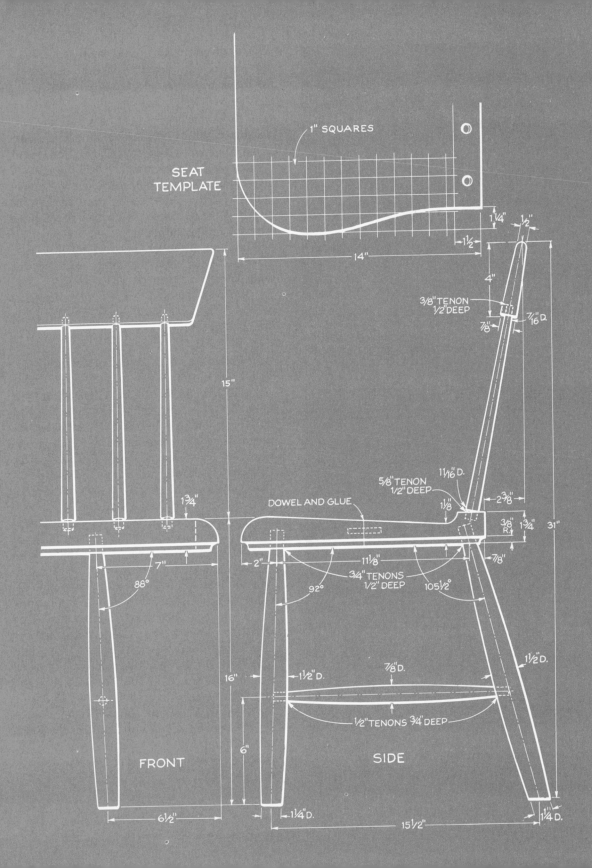

SEAT
TEMPLATE

1" SQUARES

14"

1¼" ½"

1½"

4"

⅜"TENON
½"DEEP

7/16"D.

7/8"

15"

1¾"

11/16"D.

5/8"TENON
½"DEEP

2⅜"

1⅛"

31"

DOWEL AND GLUE

⅜"
R.

1¾"

7"

88°

2"

11⅛"

¾"TENONS
½"DEEP

105½"

7/8"

92°

1½"D.

7/8"D.

16"

1½"D.

½"TENONS ¾"DEEP

FRONT

SIDE

6"

6½"

1¼"D.

15½"

1¼"D.

side until you have turned the legs. Then, if the tenons are overcut, you can compensate with a smaller drill bit to assure a snug fit.

The lathework. The best way to turn the spindles and legs is by taking dimensions from a full-scale end-view drawing. Size the tenons by setting the calipers to the drill bit you will use for the mating holes. Make the straight portion of the leg tenon $3/8''$ shorter than the depth of the seat hole; this leaves room in the hole for setting the leg flare.

Drill the stretcher holes in the legs last. Caution: Once two legs and a stretcher are joined and driven into the seat, they are locked in. Removal without breaking the stretcher would be difficult. To be safe, test for fit before final assembly.

Easiest way to turn legs (above) and spindles is by taking measurements from a full-scale end-view drawing. Each leg takes a half-hour to turn—spindles 20 minutes. Shellac padded on (below) builds to a smooth sheen quickly. Lubricate the pad with linseed oil and avoid getting shellac on the tenons.

Assembling the back. Taper and sand the backboard and cut the waste off both ends. To lay out the spindle holes set your dividers at about $2^5/16''$ and tick off 16 points on the bottom edge. Adjust the dividers until the distance from the first point to the 16th is precisely $44''$. Next make a mark $1^1/2''$ in from the first end. Walk off the remaining 15 points— the 16th should be exactly $1^1/2''$ from the other end.

Line the backboard up with the seat and transfer the marks with a try square. Drill the spindle holes and set the angle of the back on the bevel square. From here on you have to move at a steady clip. Glue and assemble the entire back, weighting it as shown in the photo.

I finished my bench by padding shellac on while the pieces were spinning. It's a fast way of building a high, lustrous polish. Use a lint-free cloth for the pad and keep it lubricated with a few drops of linseed oil. But keep shellac off the tenons; it seals the wood, reducing the strength of the glue joints. If you're building the bench for patio use, protect the wood with several coats of exterior varnish. Chair glides ($7/8''$) on the legs compensate for any slight wobble.

energy and patience. After scooping, make a cardboard template for marking the curved seat ends. Cut with a saber saw and finish shaping with a spokeshave. Carve the cove detail in the lower edge with a router and cove cutter, or use a $3/4''$ No. 6 gouge.

Don't drill the leg holes in the seat under-

Temporary stretchers, 35″ long (above), are wedged between legs to hold the leg cant while the glue dries. Back is held at uniform angle (right) by weighting. As each wrench is added, check with bevel square.

EARLY-AMERICAN DOLL CRIB

Four square feet of ¼″ plywood, 15 feet of ⅜″ dowel, and some shop scrap—if put together in the shape of a crib—is sure to please the littlest lady of the house. Start the project by turning four posts from 1⅛″ stock. Next, cut the end panels and glue and assemble a pair of posts to each panel. After drilling and ripping two pair of rails, cut the dowels to length and assemble the sides. Finally, apply glue generously and assemble all parts using clamps. The crib shown was stained, then given two coats of orange shellac. A nursery decal at each end completes the job.

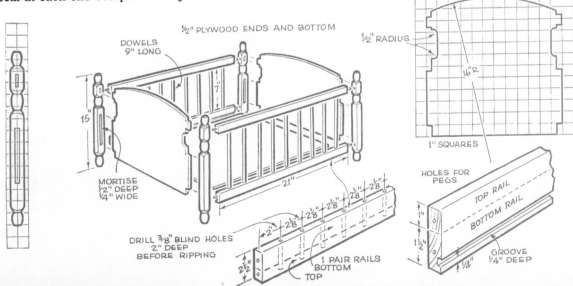

½″ PLYWOOD ENDS AND BOTTOM

DOWELS 9″ LONG

½″ RADIUS

16″R

7

15

1″ SQUARES

MORTISE ½″ DEEP ¼″ WIDE

HOLES FOR PEGS

21″

DRILL ⅜″ BLIND HOLES 2″ DEEP BEFORE RIPPING

2″ 2⅛″ 2⅛″ 2⅛″ 2⅛″ 2⅛″ 2⅛″ ¼″

1 PAIR RAILS BOTTOM TOP

2½″

TOP RAIL

BOTTOM RAIL

GROOVE ¼″ DEEP

¼″

1″

1½″

LOCKUP GUN CABINET

This cabinet displays a collection of guns, yet keeps them away from children. A locking bar guards the rifles and shotguns and, although the model shown displayed two pistols for the photo, shells and pistols are normally stored in a locked compartment. The cabinet is finished inside and out with matching Masonite walnut paneling and perforated board, making it practically maintenance-free.

The framework is built of one-by-two pine. Since it is covered with ¼″ paneling you can use corrugated nails and butt joints. Panels were bonded to the frame with Royalcote panel adhesive. Particle board was used for the top, bottom, shelf, and gunstock rack.

How you build it. Start by building the framework for the two sides, front, and back. Next, bond the paneling to the inner surface of both sides. Attach the top and the bottom to the laminated sides, and stand the unit upright.

Shape the gunstock rack from the particle board and the barrel rack from pine. Use ½″ stock for the locking bar and attach it to the rack with a small hinge at one end. Cut a slot at the other end so that the locking bar will slip over a staple that receives a small padlock. Install these parts, and the shelf, by screwing 2″-No. 6 wood screws through the frames. Don't drive the screws home until all three pieces are set in the cabinet. After the interior pieces are in, attach the front frame and bond the perforated board in place at bottom. To do

To minimize cutting and fitting, the framework is paneled inside before the shelf and the gun racks go in. Tighten the screws after you have all three pieces in place. Locking bar is hinged on gunstock rack.

the back, bond the perforated board to the frame first, then attach the assembled back to the unit.

Paneling the case. Panel the top of the cabinet first, then the sides. By doing it in this order, you will hide the edge. Use a few brads to hold the panels in place while the adhesive is drying. The last step in paneling the cabinet is to apply the trim strips to the exposed edges on the front of the frame.

The compartment door is made of $5/8''$ par-

ticle board and attached to the cabinet with a $25''$ continuous hinge, along with a hasp for a small padlock. The knob on the door is optional and if one is used it is centered on the door, $1''$ from the bottom edge. Panel the door edges first, then panel both sides (again to hide the edge). Stain all unfinished stock, with walnut stain, to match the prefinished material. To prevent the pine from showing through the perforated board, the front and back frames should be stained prior to bonding. Allow 24 hours' drying time before paneling.

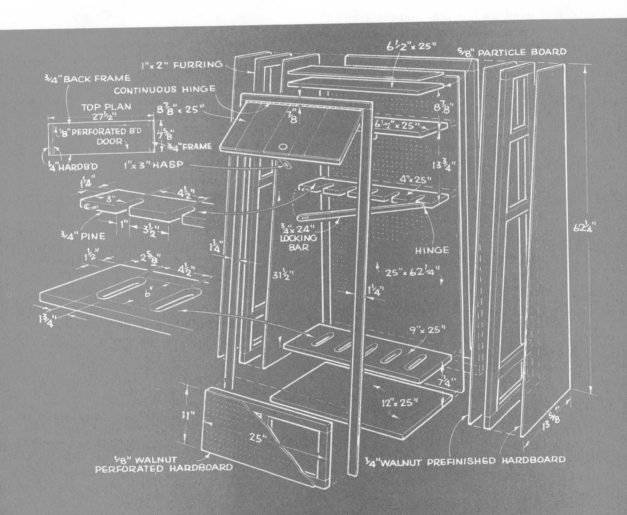

105

CHILD'S WARDROBE: A "Housekeeper" You Can Build

BY RO CAPOTOSTO

Just about the only way you can keep kids from messing up the house is to make it easier for them to be neat than sloppy. This wardrobe near your home's service entrance gives the kids a place to stow their books, baseball gloves, and jackets the minute they walk in the door. The slant-in design provides a place to sit while they remove muddy boots and

Always ready at the door, the wardrobe handles the kids' belongings as soon as they step inside, before they can clutter up the house.

shoes, and the drawers provide cover-up storage for the dirty footwear.

The wardrobe is easy to build from ¾" plywood. This double unit serves two children, but you can vary the number of stalls to suit your family needs.

The easiest way to make the angled cut in the vertical members is with a portable power saw. Clamp a guide board to the work to make the cuts smooth and straight. For a neat, strong unit, set the shelves into dadoes cut in the verticals.

When you cover the edges of the plywood with pine facing strips, you'll also hide the dadoes. Two or three coats of enamel provide a protective finish and add color.

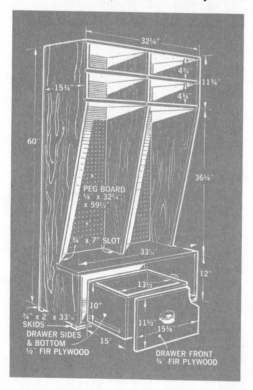

Blind dadoes, cut into the verticals using a saw or router, contain the shelves and seat solidly, so you can use glue and nails for quick, easy assembly.

Strips of clear ¾" pine are used to face the exposed edges of the plywood. They cover dadoes and take finish better than raw plywood edges.

COFFEE TABLE THAT SOLVES A PROBLEM

BY CARLTON G. BUCHER

Table is just the right height for use in front of a sofa. The planter in the center occupies only a small part of that space. Remainder of the shelf behind it is handy for storing current magazines.

Keeping an encyclopedia set where you and the children can use it freely is only one function of this coffee table. It has two spillproof surfaces for serving beverages, and between them a top big enough to hold serving trays, ashtrays, and board games. The big open space in the center below could take other books, magazines, records, radio or record player—even planters.

Encyclopedia volumes—or other books—are stored spines up under the glass at each end. Titles are convenient to read, and selection is easy.

Start construction by cutting the parts as shown in the cutting pattern in the blueprint. The sides (C and D) are the only pieces that require any further detail. Notch them as shown for the table top; then groove them for

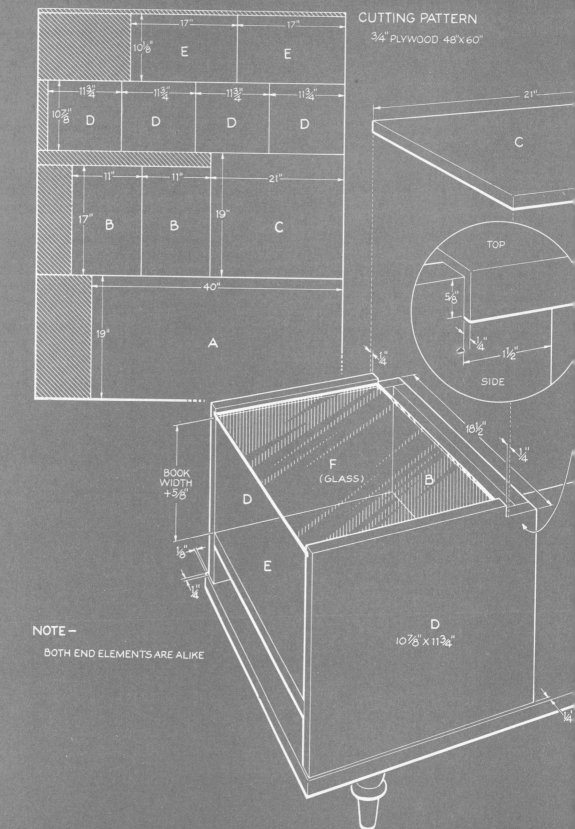

CUTTING PATTERN
3/4" PLYWOOD 48"x60"

17" 17"
10 1/8" E E

11 3/4" 11 3/4" 11 3/4" 11 3/4"
10 7/8" D D D D

11" 11" 21"
17" B B 19" C

40"

19" A

21"
C

TOP

5/8"
1/4" 1 1/2"

SIDE

1/4"

BOOK WIDTH +5/8"

F (GLASS)

18 1/2"
1/4"

D B

1/8"
1/4" E

D
10 7/8" x 11 3/4"

1/4"

NOTE –

BOTH END ELEMENTS ARE ALIKE

108

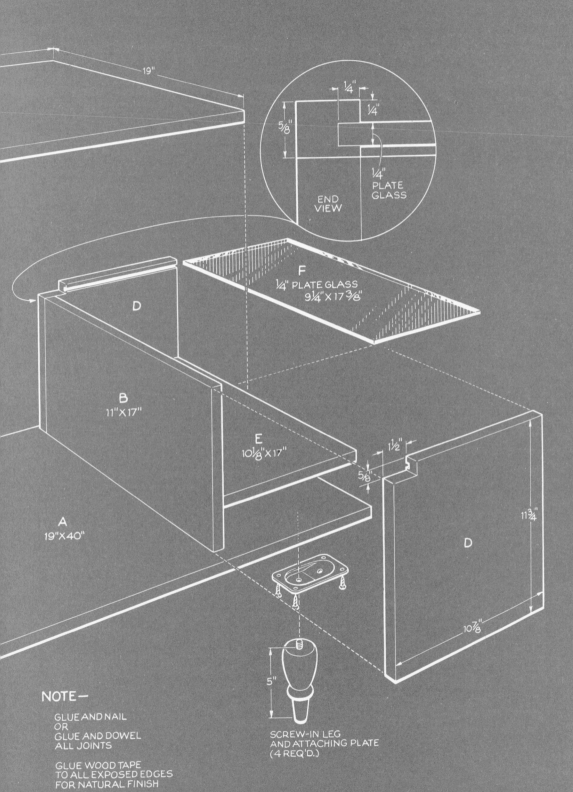

19"

END VIEW

¼"
¼"
⅝"
¼"
PLATE GLASS

F
¼" PLATE GLASS
9¼" X 17⅜"

D

B
11" X 17"

E
10⅛" X 17"

1½"
⅝"
11¾"
10⅞"

D

A
19" X 40"

NOTE—

GLUE AND NAIL
OR
GLUE AND DOWEL
ALL JOINTS

GLUE WOOD TAPE
TO ALL EXPOSED EDGES
FOR NATURAL FINISH

5"

SCREW-IN LEG
AND ATTACHING PLATE
(4 REQ'D.)

109

the plate-glass panels. The rest of the job is assembly.

Check the size of your encyclopedia before assembling the end units. Note that the distance of bookshelf shown the glass is book width plus 5/8". With this determined, assemble both end units and attach them to the bottom with screws from beneath. Finally, attach the top.

Order the plate glass cut to size for an easy fit in the grooves. The 5" factory-made legs go on last.

If you're going to use an enameled or antique finish, you can save money by making the table of fir plywood. And you can assemble it with glue and well-set nails. If the table is to be stained or left natural, birch or walnut cabinet-grade ply is recommended. Use dowels to assemble, and wood-tape the ply edges for a professional-looking job.

The table shown was designed so that each bookshelf holds 10 volumes of a popular set. Measure your set before cutting the stock, and change the shelf width and height if necessary.

KITCHEN-TOWEL HOLDER

Those new bordered paper towels are just the thing for this Early American towel holder-cabinet made from 1/2"-cherry.

First lay out and cut the sides. Dado the grooves for the dividers, and then cut the dividers and glue them in place. Next cut the back and front trim pieces and glue them in position.

Saw out the front and back sections of the drawer, rabbet the back, and dado a 1/8" groove to receive the sides. Divide the front into three equal parts and dado 1/4"-deep

grooves along each line. Tilt the blade on a radial-arm saw to 45 degrees to cut the chamfers. Cut the remainder of the drawer parts, dado the sides, and assemble with glue and brads.

Cut the hinged lid for the chest top and the spacer strip to which the hinges will attach. Glue this strip in place. Bevel and round the lid and set it aside.

To form the spindle, drill a 17/64" hole at each end of a 1"dowel and insert and glue 1/4" dowels in these holes so that they protrude 1".

Sand the entire project with fine sandpaper and stain with antique cherry, following up with a semigloss varnish. Finally attach the lid with the hinges and mount the brass knobs.

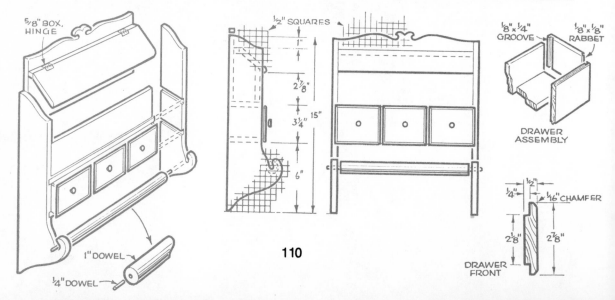

MOBILE PLANTER FOR HEAVY HOUSEPLANTS

Four casters hidden beneath this redwood planter let you roll even the heaviest houseplant to a sunny window during the day and back to a better display area in the evening. And if you spill while watering, clean-up is easy: Just roll the plant out of the way and mop up.

To start construction, cut out the four 3/4″ redwood sides, miter the ends, and make a 3/4″ groove in each side to hold the bottom of the planter. Locate the groove so the top edge of a large clay saucer placed in the planter is flush with the top of the planter. Another groove, this one 5/8″, holds the corner gussets to which the casters are screwed. Locate this groove so the casters hold the planter 1/8″ off the floor (or perhaps 1/4″ or more if the planter is to be used mostly on a carpet).

Now cut the gussets from 5/8″ plywood and the bottom from 3/4″ plywood. The bottom is a square with corners cut off to clear the casters. Assemble the sides, gluing the bottom into the 3/4″ groove. Glue the gussets into the top groove. Then cut the separators to size and glue and screw them between the gussets and bottom. Screw the casters to the gussets and finish the job with varnish.

Put the saucer in the planter and fill all around with crushed rock. Now it's ready for the potted plant. Dimensions, which are for a 13″ saucer, can be changed to suit your needs.

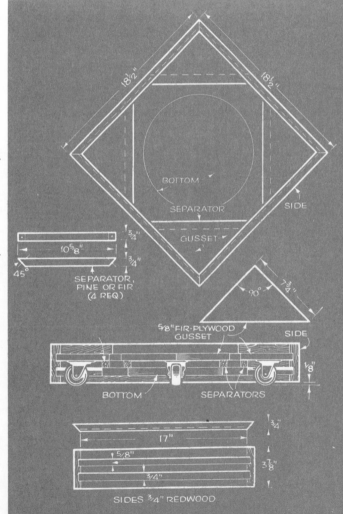

111

OUTDOOR—INDOOR FURNITURE

BY RICHARD C. SICKLER

When we began to settle into the "second" home we'd just built, we needed a lot of furniture in a hurry—on a tight budget. Since we'd be doing considerable summer entertaining, we had to furnish the porch with comfortable matching pieces that would stand up to exposure. But when the weather chased us inside, we needed furniture that would serve equally well in the den.

Just try to find such versatile pieces in the stores! Porch or patio furniture can seldom be used anywhere else. So I built my own, starting with a basic design for a big, relaxing armchair that would fit into any setting, from rustic modern to Early American.

With this done, I doubled its width for a pair of settees that have single armrests on oppo-

112

site ends. If your wife likes to rearrange furniture, these units will delight her. She can group them with a table to turn a corner or butt them together for an 8' couch.

Using the same tapered and chamfered leg design, I added a king-size ottoman that converts the armchair into a chaise lounge, and a 5' cocktail table.

The dual purpose of the furniture ties right in with the current rage for outdoor-indoor carpeting. To dramatize this for the photographs, I moved both furniture and carpet from the porch to the den. The carpet is Mohawk's new Boundless, ·made of Herculon olefin fiber. Like the furniture, it's unfazed by weather exposure.

Why Philippine mahogany? You may be surprised by my choice of wood. Philippine mahogany isn't as familiar—or respected—as it should be. It's inexpensive and easy to work, takes a paste filler readily, accepts stain well, and can be varnished and buffed to an attractive satin finish. And it holds up well.

The seat and back cushions are interchangeable between chairs and settees. The padding is 4" urethane foam; fabric is a 100-percent-cotton print intended for draperies and slipcovers. It's been treated with a water and oil repellent that wards off stains. The covers have zippers along one side for easy removal.

Settee version of chair has one armrest omitted and front leg shortened. Seat and back panels are attached as for chair (see sketch), except that number of screws along bottom stretcher should be increased.

I sized this set to furnish a 10'-by-20' area on our screened porch, so the basic chair has generous dimensions, with a 22"-by-23" seat. You can make it (and the matching pieces) smaller to fit the space you have.

The accompanying rough-cut list for the chair will guide you in buying your lumber. Multiply it by the number of chairs you plan to make. It's easy to compile a similar list for the other three pieces from the dimensions on the blueprint.

Gauging the work. Making furniture by the set has certain advantages. With a bit of planning you can keep waste to a minimum. And since the same basic construction techniques are used throughout, you can set up a virtual production line to cut all units at once, then prepare all mortise-and-tenon joints, carefully marking pieces for later assembly.

Though these joints aren't difficult to make by hand (with a backsaw, chisel, and file), they go a lot faster with the special jointer

ROUGH-CUT LUMBER—ONE CHAIR		
Legs		
Front	2	1½" x 1½" x 23"
Rear	2	1½" x 1½" x 20"
Stretchers		
Side	2	5/4" x 2" x 27"
Front, back	4	5/4" x 2" x 25"
Arms	2	5/4" x 2½" x 28"
Back		
Sides	2	¾" x 2½" x 20"
Rails	2	¾" x 3" x 23"
Slats	5	½" x 1½" x 17"
Seat		
Front	1	¾" x 3½" x 24"
Back	1	¾" x 2½" x 24"
Sides	2	¾" x 2½" x 23"
Plus corner braces, plywood		

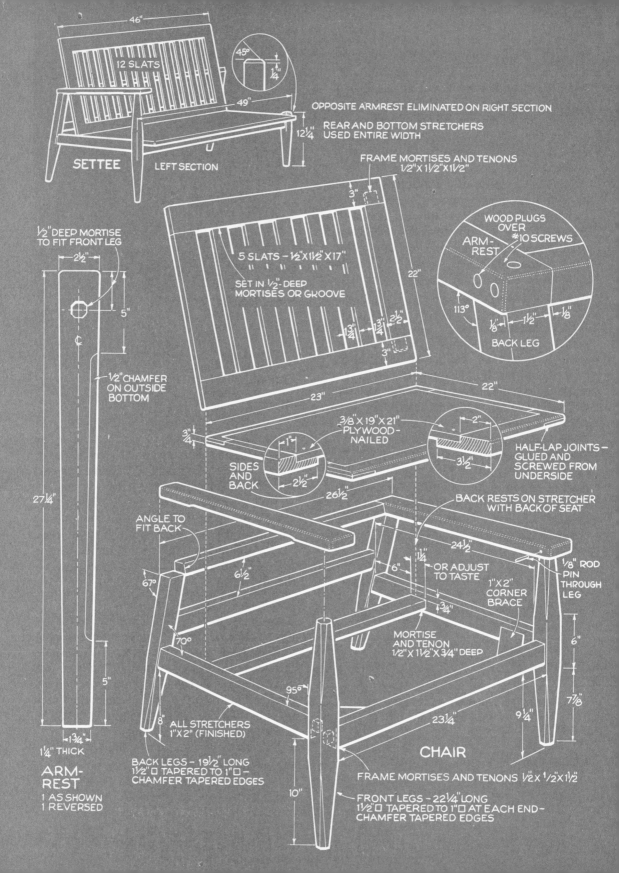

SETTEE LEFT SECTION

46"

12 SLATS

49"

12¼"

45°

¼"

OPPOSITE ARMREST ELIMINATED ON RIGHT SECTION

REAR AND BOTTOM STRETCHERS USED ENTIRE WIDTH

FRAME MORTISES AND TENONS ½"X 1½"X 1½"

3"

5 SLATS – ½"X 1½" X 17"

SET IN ½"- DEEP MORTISES OR GROOVE

22"

1¾"   3¾"   2½"

3"

WOOD PLUGS OVER
*10 SCREWS

ARM-REST

113°

⅛"   1½"   ⅛"

BACK LEG

23"

22"

3"
¾"

3/8" X 19" X 21"
PLYWOOD-
NAILED

1"

2½"

SIDES
AND
BACK

2"

3½"

HALF-LAP JOINTS-
GLUED AND
SCREWED FROM
UNDERSIDE

BACK RESTS ON STRETCHER
WITH BACK OF SEAT

26½"

24½"

½" DEEP MORTISE
TO FIT FRONT LEG

2½"

5"

½"CHAMFER
ON OUTSIDE
BOTTOM

27¼"

5"

1¾"

1¼" THICK

**ARM-
REST**

1 AS SHOWN
1 REVERSED

ANGLE TO
FIT BACK

67°

6½"

70°

95°

8"

ALL STRETCHERS
1"X 2" (FINISHED)

BACK LEGS – 19½" LONG
1½"□ TAPERED TO 1"□ –
CHAMFER TAPERED EDGES

1¼"

6"

OR ADJUST
TO TASTE

¾"

1"X 2"
CORNER
BRACE

MORTISE
AND TENON
½"X 1½"X ¾" DEEP

⅛" ROD
PIN
THROUGH
LEG

6"

7⅞"

9¼"

23¼"

CHAIR

10"

FRAME MORTISES AND TENONS ½"x ½"x1½"

FRONT LEGS – 22¼" LONG
1½"□ TAPERED TO 1"□ AT EACH END–
CHAMFER TAPERED EDGES

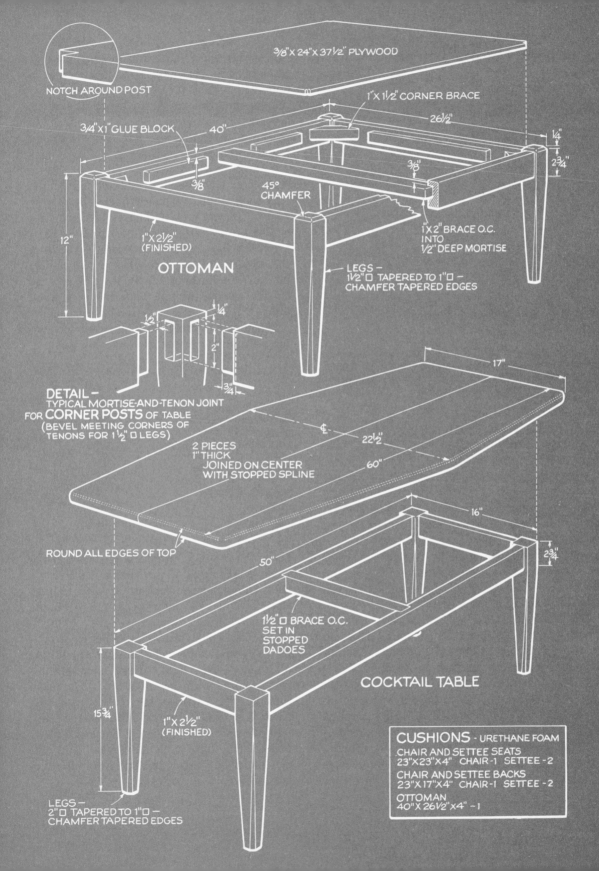

3/8" X 24" X 37 1/2" PLYWOOD

NOTCH AROUND POST

1" X 1 1/2" CORNER BRACE

3/4" X 1" GLUE BLOCK

40"

26 1/2"

1/4"

2 3/4"

3/8"

3/8"

45° CHAMFER

1" X 2" BRACE O.C. INTO 1/2" DEEP MORTISE

12"

1" X 2 1/2" (FINISHED)

OTTOMAN

LEGS – 1 1/2" ☐ TAPERED TO 1" ☐ – CHAMFER TAPERED EDGES

1/4"

1/2"

2"

3/4"

DETAIL –
TYPICAL MORTISE-AND-TENON JOINT
FOR CORNER POSTS OF TABLE
(BEVEL MEETING CORNERS OF
TENONS FOR 1 1/2" ☐ LEGS)

17"

2 PIECES
1" THICK
JOINED ON CENTER
WITH STOPPED SPLINE

22 1/2"

60"

16"

2 3/4"

ROUND ALL EDGES OF TOP

50"

1 1/2" ☐ BRACE O.C.
SET IN
STOPPED
DADOES

COCKTAIL TABLE

15 3/4"

1" X 2 1/2"
(FINISHED)

CUSHIONS - URETHANE FOAM
CHAIR AND SETTEE SEATS
23" X 23" X 4" CHAIR - 1 SETTEE - 2
CHAIR AND SETTEE BACKS
23" X 17" X 4" CHAIR - 1 SETTEE - 2
OTTOMAN
40" X 26 1/2" X 4" - 1

LEGS –
2" ☐ TAPERED TO 1" ☐ –
CHAMFER TAPERED EDGES

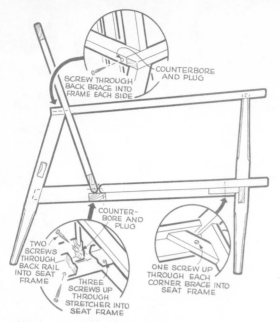

Attach seat and back with flathead screws as shown in cross section with underside and rear details. Choose lengths that won't pierce front surface. Where visible, cap heads with wood plugs.

jig available for most drill presses. If your press lacks a tilting table, you'll have to make a bed to hold units at the proper angle for mortise-drilling. Angles are given on the plans.

Preplanning is the key to fast, efficient work. You can use the drill-press jig to cut the slat mortises for the chair back, or you can simplify this operation by cutting ½"-by-½" slots along the inside edges of the top and bottom rails, filling in the spaces between slats with glued-in ½"-by-½"-by-1¾" blocks. Either way, assembly is a bit tricky, since the slats must be dropped into position at the time the frames are assembled and glued. It's not necessary to glue the slats in place.

The tapering of the legs can be done with a hand plane, on a bench saw, or with a portable router. The latter calls for a ¾" straight bit and a special jig, described in the instruction manual that comes with most routers. The end of the leg that is to be reduced is shimmed up into contact with the bit by means of a wedge while the router rides atop a unit resembling a big miter box. Chamfering is done with a hand plane, after tapering.

I cut the armrests on my bench saw, using a standard tapering jig, then cut the underside chamfers (for an easier fingergrip) with my portable router.

Assembly. For the most durable assembly, lock each tenon into its leg mortise by driving a metal pin through it. This is especially desirable at the joint where the top of the front leg enters the armrest. Always drill first, from the inside surface, through the tenon. The pin can be a finishing nail. Set it well below the surface and fill the hole with matching wood putty.

When constructing the chair or settee, complete the frame first, then make the seat and

Sturdy construction is evident in underside view of chair unit. All frame members are assembled with glued mortise-and-tenon joints, including stretcher at base of back. Corner braces add muscle.

back panels to fit. Some adjustment in the angle of the back is possible by setting the back frame farther forward on the support stretcher, or by altering location of the stretcher.

All pieces should be sanded before assembly. Apply a rich brown mahogany penetrating oil stain. Follow with a paste filler that has been colored with the stain. Since this furniture will be exposed to weather, sunlight, alcohol, and other deteriorating agents, finish with a quality bar varnish. I brushed on four coats, smoothing with steel wool and fine sandpaper between each. The resulting satin-gloss finish needs no waxing.

SHELVES THAT MOVE WITH YOU

BY R. W. WEED

Built-in shelving enhances the utility of a home, but why leave it behind if you move? This simple design solves the problem. A hidden wedge in the top press-fits the unit between floor and ceiling.

Measuring approximately half the desired shelf width, the wedge slides from a retracted position to one that is parallel with and about 1″ above the sides of the ceiling box. Sliding the wedge holds the shelves tightly in place.

Construct each component as shown and apply the selected stain or finish while they are dismantled.

When you're ready for final construction, install the self-supporting strips with the hardware supplied and mount the ceiling and base boxes to the sides with 1½″ wood screws.

Tip the unit into place, tapping the wedge against the ceiling with the thin edge of a carpenter's square until a firm pull will not move the unit. As a final touch, add crown molding over the ceiling gap.

By adding more units you can cover an entire wall.

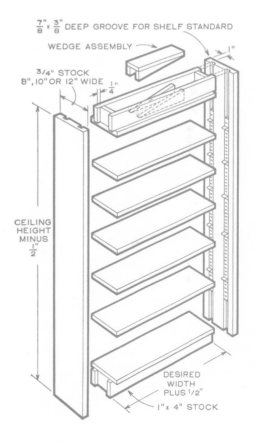

117

FLIP-TOP TABLE: TWO GAMES IN ONE

BY JOHN CAPOTOSOTO

Bumper pool or knock hockey—which is your piece of the action? You can take your choice with the flip of a table top.

This unique table sports a regulation-size bumper-pool table on one side and a satisfactory hockey table on the other. When you want a change of pace, simply flip the top over and a new game appears.

Sturdily built, the table features a simple but positive locking device that assures solid-as-a-rock rigidity—so important to a game of pool. The flip-top mechanism is so simple even a child can operate it.

The table is built of pine, both ¾" and 1⅛" stock. The bed is of U.S. Plywood's Novoply, an excellent material because of its smooth surface and, more important, its warp resistance. The bed size is 32" by 48", which is one third the size of a standard 4'-by-8' sheet.

Build apron first. Use 1-by-8 common pine, which actually measures ¾" by 7½". If you choose your lumber carefully, you can eliminate most knots. Rip the boards 7¼" wide, make the ball-return cutouts and bushing holes, then assemble with glue and nails. Use galvanized finishing nails for tightness if you can.

Before nailing, size the end grain of the end pieces with white glue thinned with water. Brush on and allow to air-dry about five min-

A slow, deliberate game of bumper pool turns to a fast game of knock hockey at a flip of the table. Bumper-pool table is full-size, sturdy, and easy to level, even on a rippled floor, thanks to special adjustable jacks in the table legs.

utes. Apply more glue full strength, then join the sections. For accuracy, temporarily nail a couple of diagonals to the frame as the glue sets.

Making the legs. Use ⁵/₄ stock (⁵/₄ stock measures 1¹/₈″). Again, choose the lumber carefully to avoid knots. The table shown was made of common lumber, yet no knots show. Location of the stretcher is important. Improperly positioned, it may interfere with tilting the table. Best way to handle this is to make a kraft-paper pattern of the leg including the cutout for the stretcher (the 1¹/₈″-by-5¹/₂ rectangle).

Trace the cutout onto the board: then, when assembling, you can use the traced cutout to align the stretcher on the legs. To keep the legs from moving during assembly, drive a couple of nails into them. Then you can drill the pilots accurately at your convenience.

To drill the holes for the leveling jacks into the bottom of the legs, use a ¹/₂″ drill, and be sure to drill square and straight, and perpendicular to the floor—not at the angle at which the leg is mounted.

To simplify assembling the legs to the apron, clamp a 1¹/₄″-wide cleat across the top of the apron to serve as a gauge for the leg tops. Drill pilots and screw them inside through the apron into the legs, using glue and 1¹/₄″ screws.

Sub-apron. This is a frame similar to the apron but made with clearance so it will swing freely

on its pivot. Clearance of ³/₈″ is allowed at the ends, ¹/₃₂″ at the sides. Cut and install the bed support to the inside of the sub-apron, using a 2¹/₂″ gauge block to position the support. Tack the support in place with brads, then screw permanently after drilling pilots and applying glue. You can toenail the two cross members, or you may prefer to nail from outside the support. If so, nail the long side pieces to the cross members, then install the assembly as a unit. Add the ball-box ends and sides.

Cushions. The cushion supports are mitered at 45 degrees, and you will note they measure ¹/₈″ less in length and width than the inner dimensions of the sub-apron. Clearance for the cloth is needed at the ends.

After cutting the cushions to size, apply rubber cement to the upper face of the support as well as the rear of the cushions. Allow the cement to set, then press the rubber cushion firmly into place. Let the ends of the rubber overhang. The cross section of the cushion rubber is not symmetrical, so be sure to posi-

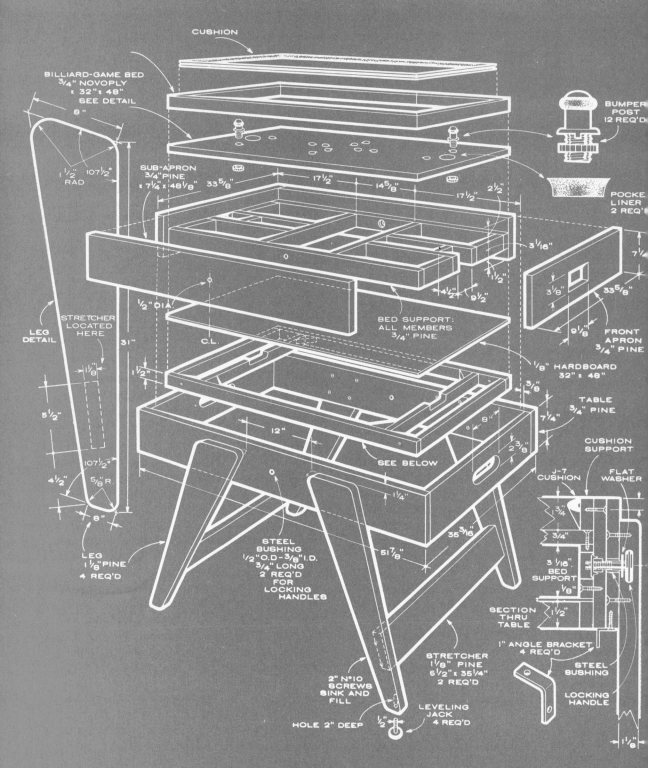

CUSHION

BILLIARD-GAME BED
3/4" NOVOPLY
x 32" x 48"
SEE DETAIL

8"

1 1/2"
RAD

107 1/2°

BUMPER
POST
12 REQ'D

POCKET
LINER
2 REQ'D

SUB-APRON
3/4" PINE
x 7 1/4" x 48 1/8"

33 5/8"

17 1/2"

14 5/8"

17 1/2"

2 1/2"

3 1/16"

7"

1 1/2"

1/2" DIA

C.L.

31"

LEG
DETAIL

STRETCHER
LOCATED
HERE

1 1/8"

1/2"

BED SUPPORT:
ALL MEMBERS
3/4" PINE

4 1/2"

9 1/2"

33 5/8"

9 1/8"

FRONT
APRON
3/4" PINE

1/8" HARDBOARD
32" x 48"

5 1/2"

107 1/2°

5/8" R

4 1/2"

6"

3/8

3/8

12"

TABLE
3/4" PINE

7 1/4"

8"

CUSHION
SUPPORT

J-7
CUSHION

FLAT
WASHER

3/4

3/4

LEG
1 1/8" PINE
4 REQ'D

STEEL
BUSHING
1/2" O.D - 3/8" I.D.
3/4" LONG
2 REQ'D
FOR
LOCKING
HANDLES

SEE BELOW

1 1/4"

2 3/8"

3/16"
BED
SUPPORT

1/8"

1/2"

SECTION
THRU
TABLE

35 3/16"

51 7/8"

1" ANGLE BRACKET
4 REQ'D

STEEL
BUSHING

LOCKING
HANDLE

STRETCHER
1 1/8" PINE
5 1/2" x 35 1/4"
2 REQ'D

2" N°10
SCREWS
SINK AND
FILL

HOLE 2" DEEP

LEVELING
JACK
4 REQ'D

1/2"

1 1/8"

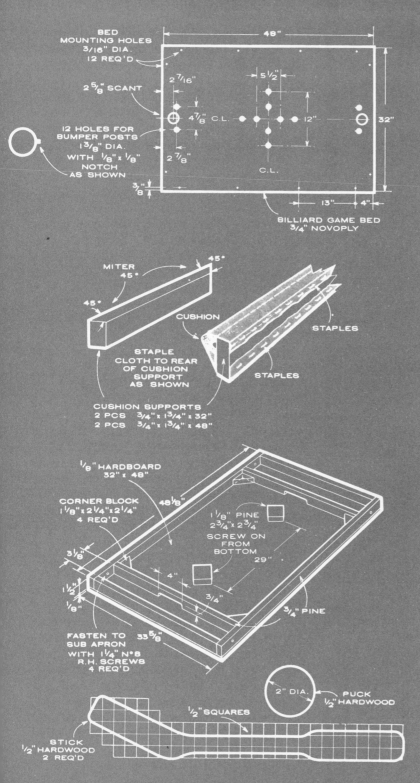

BED MOUNTING HOLES 3/16" DIA. 12 REQ'D

48"

2 7/16"

5 1/2"

2 5/8" SCANT

4 7/8" C.L.

12"

32"

12 HOLES FOR BUMPER POSTS 1 3/8" DIA. WITH 1/8" x 1/8" NOTCH AS SHOWN

2 7/8"

C.L.

3/8"

C.L.

13" 4"

BILLIARD GAME BED 3/4" NOVOPLY

MITER 45°

45°

45°

CUSHION

STAPLES

STAPLE CLOTH TO REAR OF CUSHION SUPPORT AS SHOWN

STAPLES

CUSHION SUPPORTS
2 PCS 3/4" x 1 3/4" x 32"
2 PCS 3/4" x 1 3/4" x 48"

1/8" HARDBOARD 32" x 48"

CORNER BLOCK 1 1/8" x 2 1/4" x 2 1/4" 4 REQ'D

48 1/8"

1 1/8" PINE 2 3/4" x 2 3/4"

SCREW ON FROM BOTTOM

29"

3 1/8"

4"

1 1/2"

3/4"

1/8"

3/4" PINE

FASTEN TO SUB APRON WITH 1 1/4" N° 8 R.H. SCREWS 4 REQ'D

33 5/8"

2" DIA.

PUCK 1/2" HARDWOOD

1/2" SQUARES

STICK 1/2" HARDWOOD 2 REQ'D

121

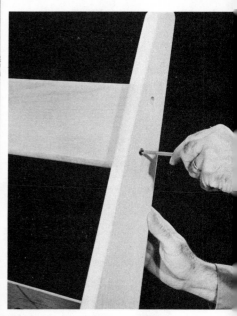

Heavy-duty T nuts support a good portion of the table's weight. Drill their mounting holes through sub-apron and drive in place.

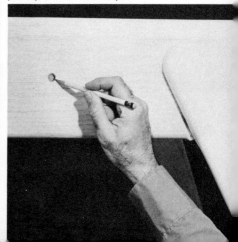

Rigidity required for a good game of pool is added to legs by stretch-ers. Glue and screw them in place —don't use nails here.

A bushing lines the hole in apron through which the locking bolt passes. Bolt also serves as the pivot point for table top.

Sub-apron goes together with glue, screws, and nails. Use the screws to fasten the four main frame pieces and the two cross braces. You can get by with nails at other joints.

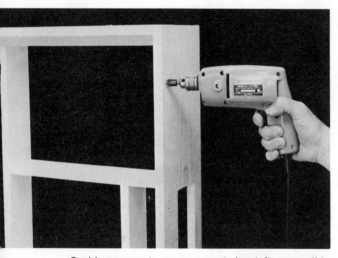

Cushion-support screws must be left accessible (above). Use flatheads, and countersink them just below the surface. Drill bumperpost holes with a spade bit (below). Use saber saw to cut larger holes.

tion it properly. When correctly installed, the nose of the cushion should be 1-1/32″ from the bottom of the support. If *incorrectly* installed, it will measure $1^3/_8$″.

Trim the overhanging rubber with a very sharp knife or razor. Dip the blade into water to cut the rubber cleanly. Continue the angle of the miter when trimming the rubber.

Cover the cushions with the same material purchased for the bed. Cut four strips 5″ by 60″, leaving the rest for the bed. Wrap the cloth around the cushion so the edges are at the rear. Staple above every inch or so, pulling the cloth taut as you staple. Start at the center and work toward the ends. Cover the miters by cementing. Apply rubber (or contact) cement to both wood and cloth. Allow to dry (it should not be tacky), then pull the cloth over the ends and gather it so excess is at the middle of the miter. Trim with a razor and press loose ends firmly in place.

Making your bed. Lay out and cut the holes for the posts and liners as shown. The post holes can be made with a spade bit and portable drill. The larger holes are best cut with a saber saw. Before making the cutout for the pocket liner, cut a trial piece for fit. The liner should fit snugly with cloth in place.

The saber saw is also used to make the $1/_8$″ notches in the post holes. The notches prevent posts from turning when tightening nuts from below.

Cover the bed with the remaining cloth. Dust off the board carefully first. Staple the cloth to the edges, working from the center. Do the long sides first, then ends.

Cross-slit the cloth for the hole cutouts, stopping just a trifle before the edge of the hole. The free ends of the slitted cloth around the pocket liner cutout should be stapled to the underside of the table. No stapling is required at other holes.

Mount the bed to the support with $1^1/_2$″ No. 8 FH screws. Next, install the cushions, driving screws from the upper edge of the sub-apron. Sink the heads slightly.

The hockey board. Drill the holes for the deflectors and mount with the ¾" RH screws. The board simply lies on the bed support, held in place by the frame, which is screwed to the subframe as indicated.

To eliminate painting the hardboard, we used prefinished Marlite. This material has a very hard, smooth surface ideally suited to the game. If unpainted hardboard is used, paint with a quality gloss enamel.

The pivot hardware is installed using a flat washer between the apron and hand wheel. Install the four angle brackets with FH screws so the bracket can swing out of the way without binding when you flip the table top, then swing back into position to hold the bed level. Tighten the screws all the way, then back off ½ turn.

The specialty items such as cushion rubber, bumpers, balls, cloth, and the pivot bushing are available from The Armor Company, Box 290, Deer Park, N.Y. 11729. Write for a free price list.

Cement cushion rubber to support with the end overhanging slightly. Then trim to proper length and miter with a sharp knife.

Cushion cloth is stapled to backs of supports except at ends, where it is trimmed with a razor blade and cemented in place.

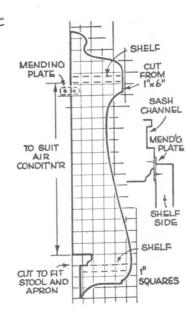

AIR-CONDITIONER SHELF

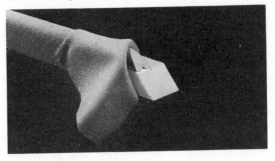

Nothing intrudes so much on a cozy room—especially a room with a period decor such as Early American—as an air conditioner thrusting through the window. It's particularly true if you leave it in place all year round—during winter months it's a functionless eyesore. Assuming it's a front-blower unit, you can camouflage it nicely—and get handy display space—with a shelf built around it. Make the shelf of pine to fit the window, and finish it to match the trim.

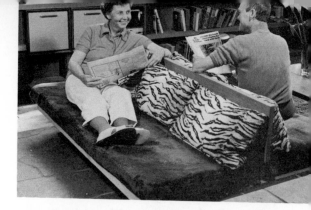

TWO-FACED COUCH
IS A REAL SLEEPER

BY DARRELL HUFF

Built-ins you build beat furniture you buy. You can make them fit your situation and needs exactly. You can make their style match your room. Take this double couch: It's decorative. It divides a room. It seats half a dozen. It sleeps two, separated or together. And its deep upholstery over foam and goose down push it into a luxury bracket you would not enjoy paying for.

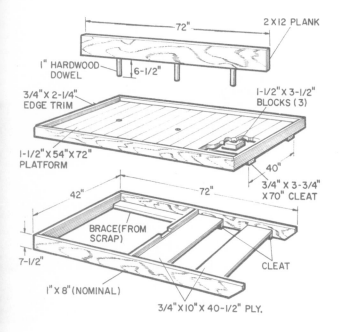

72"
2 X 12 PLANK
1" HARDWOOD DOWEL
6-1/2"
3/4" X 2-1/4" EDGE TRIM
1-1/2" X 3-1/2" BLOCKS (3)
1-1/2" X 54" X 72" PLATFORM
40"
3/4" X 3-3/4" X 70" CLEAT
42"
72"
BRACE (FROM SCRAP)
7-1/2"
CLEAT
1" X 8" (NOMINAL)
3/4" X 10" X 40-1/2" PLY.

To build it, make a supporting box about 7½" high. If this is open at one end, it will give you a place to stow such hard-to-store items as a card table.

Make the platform 54" by 72" to fit atop the box. We chose that size because readily available foam-plastic pads fit it, and it gives double-bed width. Don't hesitate to change the length if you have more room or happen to find longer cushions easier to buy.

The platform is 2-by-6 tongue-and-groove pine, held together by cleats that fit within the supporting box. The divider plank—ours is oak—has dowels to support it rigidly, yet permit removal when the couch becomes a bed. Edge trim is both for appearance and to hold the mattresses in place. Since it is highly visible, it should be chosen and finished to match the plank. The box is almost hidden, so any softwood will do.

The 27"-by-72" seat cushions (from surplus stores, mail-order houses) are foam plastic for durability and comfort over the base. Our 4"-thick ones are great for sitting, acceptable for sleeping. If you'll use the couch regularly as a bed you may prefer 6" thickness.

No fancy sewing is called for. Seat covers are simple sacks, like pillow slips, machine sewed on three sides and then hand-sewn at one end with the foam pad inside. If you find the pad hard to slip inside, dust it with talcum.

Six ordinary bed pillows make backrests. Cut the covers slightly undersize so they'll stuff plumply. Three sides of the covers are sewn; the fourth has Velcro strips for easy removal for bed-pillow use.

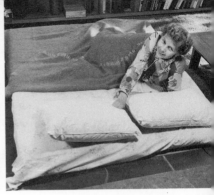

Slip off pillow covers, and couch quickly makes up into a pair of beds for guest sleeping or regular use in a child's room.

Divider back is held firmly upright by three dowels that slip between padded seat cushions into support platform. The hardwood dowels fit into holes supported by 1½" by 3½" wood blocks.

With divider removed you have a double bed. Greater length might be obtained by shopping around to find 75" foam pads.

A MAKE-UP STAND

BY ROBERT WORTHAM

Built into this handsome make-up stand are two wife-pleasing features: soft, even lighting, and a two-sided mirror that gives both a normal and a magnified view. To make the stand, start with a 12" square of ¾" plywood. In the center, cut an 8¼" hole for the mirror. Around the edges, drill six ⅝" holes for the pin-type lamp sockets. The wire stand of the mirror—bought at the dime store—is stapled to the back of the square. Frame the square with 2" cove molding.

Antique the frame and cover the plywood and inside edge of the cutout with textured wallpaper, contact paper, or burlap. Install the lamp sockets and wiring in parallel with a toggle or twist-type switch below the mirror.

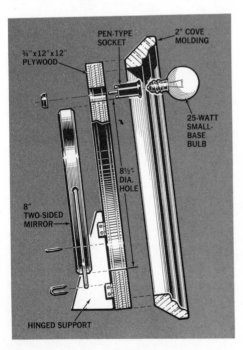

PEN-TYPE SOCKET

2" COVE MOLDING

¾"x12"x12" PLYWOOD

25-WATT SMALL-BASE BULB

8½" DIA. HOLE

8" TWO-SIDED MIRROR

HINGED SUPPORT

125

THE FURNITURE THAT SERVES YOU FOUR WAYS

DESIGNED BY LES WALKER

**BUILT AND DESCRIBED
BY R. J. DE CRISTOFORO**

PHOTOS BY WILLIAM EYMANN

Modern sculpture results when you stack the stools as pictured above. They can also be used as footstools, end tables, seats.

You can limit this woodworking adventure to one easy chair and one stool, and have a multipurpose unit for a single person (great for a youngster's room). Or you can go all out and build four of each and have a houseful of furniture even if you live in a single room.

Construction is quite interesting and presents the opportunity to check out the bend-by-kerfing method that you may have heard about but never actually tried. Tools needed are minimal; a table saw and a saber saw will do the job. A portable router can be a big help and, if you go for four units, I suggest that you rent one for a half day or so if you don't own one.

Materials you'll need. The plans call for solid lumber on all parts except the seat and back on the chairs. A good grade of ¾" plywood is better here because it lends itself to the bending technique. Since these parts should be coated with a high-gloss enamel, it's best to avoid fir and similar grain-prominent woods, or those with tough-to-fill pores. This pretty much limits your choice (in terms of readily available stuff) to a maple or birch or a pine-faced plywood.

For the sides of the chairs and for the stools, I elected to work with Georgia-Pacific's "Wide Panel" edge-glued pine. This material is available in ¾" stock with widths running to 30" and lengths to 16'. It's great because you have ready-made, wide-panel, solid material and that sure beats having to build width from narrow boards.

Building tips. Makes a ¼" hardboard template that duplicates the profile of the chair sides. Clamp this to the stock and follow it with a router for the cutting. This yields edges that require little smoothing.

The pine is soft. If you own or rent a heavy-duty router and equip it with a sharp ¼" bit, you can cut through in one pass. If your equipment can't handle the one-pass thing, go through halfway the first time and repeat,

You have a desk of convenient height when you tip up the chair so its back becomes the top. Stool is just right for the desk.

Chair has curved seat and back formed by kerfing birch plywood. Because of the curves, seat is comfortable even without padding.

Dining table for two or four results when you shove the main furniture units together as you see below and on opposite page. Separated, units could completely furnish an apartment.

127

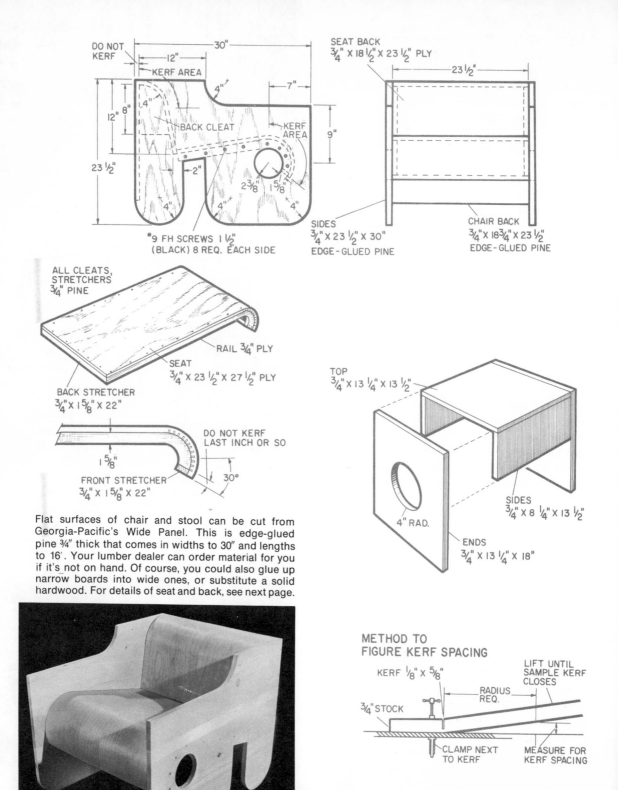

DO NOT KERF

KERF AREA

30"

12"

4"↗

7"

BACK CLEAT

KERF AREA

4"

12" 8"

4"

12"

23 ½"

2"

2 ³⁄₈" 1 ⁵⁄₈"

4"

4"↗

4"

4"

#9 FH SCREWS 1 ½"
(BLACK) 8 REQ. EACH SIDE

SEAT BACK
¾" X 18 ½" X 23 ½" PLY

23 ½"

9"

SIDES
¾" X 23 ½" X 30"
EDGE - GLUED PINE

CHAIR BACK
¾" X 18¾" X 23 ½"
EDGE - GLUED PINE

ALL CLEATS,
STRETCHERS
¾" PINE

RAIL ¾" PLY

SEAT
¾" X 23 ½" X 27 ½" PLY

BACK STRETCHER
¾" X 1 ⁵⁄₈" X 22"

DO NOT KERF
LAST INCH OR SO

1 ⁵⁄₈"

FRONT STRETCHER
¾" X 1 ⁵⁄₈" X 22"

30°

TOP
¾" X 13 ¼" X 13 ½"

SIDES
¾" X 8 ¼" X 13 ½"

4" RAD.

ENDS
¾" X 13 ¼" X 18"

Flat surfaces of chair and stool can be cut from
Georgia-Pacific's Wide Panel. This is edge-glued
pine ¾" thick that comes in widths to 30" and lengths
to 16'. Your lumber dealer can order material for you
if it's not on hand. Of course, you could also glue up
narrow boards into wide ones, or substitute a solid
hardwood. For details of seat and back, see next page.

METHOD TO
FIGURE KERF SPACING

KERF ⅛" X ⁵⁄₈"

LIFT UNTIL
SAMPLE KERF
CLOSES

RADIUS
REQ.

¾" STOCK

CLAMP NEXT
TO KERF

MEASURE FOR
KERF SPACING

128

You can also handle the job with a saber saw or even with a jigsaw. The size of the panels would make the job difficult on a home-shop bandsaw. If you do the job by sawing, tack-nail together two panels and cut and mark them as mates for individual chairs.

Next step is to draw a layout on one of the sides to show positions of the rails, cleats, back, and seat. From this you can make a cardboard template for the back cleat and the seat rail to use in marking stock. Here, your choice of cutting methods is very broad; almost any tool will do, but be sure to be accurate, for these parts have much to do with forming the curves on back and seat.

Bending technique. This is no more than a series of parallel cuts to remove stock so you can arc the wood. The test method shown in the drawing will come close to telling you how far apart the kerfs should be spaced. Ideally, after this test you should be able to make the bend and close the kerf gaps. Results can differ, depending on the wood used and even differences in woods of the same species. So regard the test itself as a guide. The kerfs may be deepened and brought closer together if this gives an easier, smoother bend.

Unless you are a purist I see no harm in arbitrarily cutting the kerfs a little more than $5/8''$ deep and spacing them about $1/4''$ apart. This should do, no matter what wood you use.

The final part for the chair is the back. This is straight cutting, following the drawing.

Assembling the parts. Start by gluing and nailing the back cleats to the inside faces of the chair sides. Position these so there's a $3/4''$ setback at the top and the back edge. Next, use glue and finishing nails to assemble chair-back to sides. The top edge of the back must be flush with the top edge of the cleat.

The assembly so far gives you firm support for forming the seat back. Start this by ap-

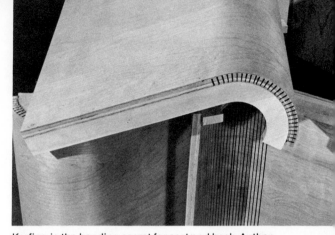

Kerfing is the bending secret for seat and back. Author spaced kerfs $1/4''$ and cut them $5/8''$ deep. This allowed wood to conform to shape of side rails. If they bother you, conceal kerfs on underside with application of self-adhesive sheet veneer.

plying glue to all mating edges and nailing through the rear edge of the seat back into the top edge of the chair back. Then fold the seat back to conform to the shape of the cleat. Use a couple of nails beyond the kerfed area to keep the part in place. If you own bar clamps, it won't hurt to snug the sides together until the glue has dried thoroughly.

Make a subassembly of the rails and two stretchers for the seat. Apply glue to mating areas and attach the seat by first nailing across the back edge and then working toward the kerfed area. At this point, use light clamp pressure to conform the seat to the rails and end up by nailing through the front edge of the seat into the front stretcher. Leave the clamps on until the glue dries.

Coat the rails with glue and put the seat in place between the chair sides. Alignment won't be difficult since the bottom edge of the rails should line up with the edges of the cut-outs in the sides. It will be difficult to accomplish this without smearing glue where you don't want it but, after applying clamps to hold the seat in place, use a damp cloth to wipe off the excess.

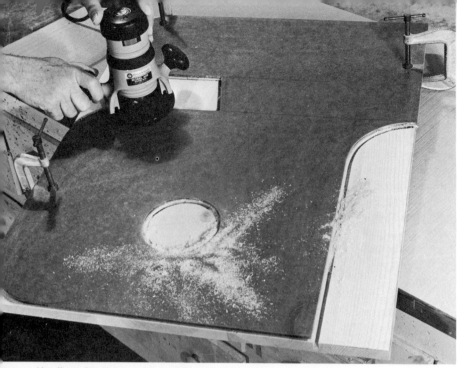

Begin assembly by attaching cleats to inside surface of sides, then add the chair back. The back is inset between the sides. In photo, also note the ¾" setback from top edge of sides.

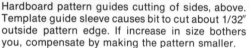

Hardboard pattern guides cutting of sides, above. Template guide sleeve causes bit to cut about 1/32" outside pattern edge. If increase in size bothers you, compensate by making the pattern smaller.

Attach curved seat back by applying glue to all mating edges, then nailing across top edge. Curve back downwards to conform to cleat and snug sides together with bar clamp. Drive nails to secure the back.

Now locate and drive home the eight #9-1½" F.H. wood screws on each side. I had no problem driving these flush without a countersinking job. This may not be the case if your wood is harder than pine. In any event nothing was done to hide the screws.

Making stools. This is straightforward cutting and assembly, using glue and finishing nails throughout. The circular cutouts can be cut with a template and a router or you can pad two pieces at a time and cut with a saber saw or on a jig saw.

The best assembly procedure is to nail top to sides and then nail the ends. Be careful with dimensions. If you fudge in any way it may be difficult to stack the stools.

Finishing. Do a good sanding job on all parts before assembly. After assembly, go over everything with a pad sander and pay special attention to edges. Don't leave glue spots on parts to be finished clear.

Remove sanding dust, then brush a full coat of sealer over everything. After about ½ hour, remove excess sealer with a lint-free cloth. Pad-sand again, dust, and do the enamel job on ends of stools, chair seat, and front and rear of the chair back.

After the enamel is fully dry, brush a full coat of clear, urethane varnish over all other parts. Wait out the drying time, then do a light smoothing job with fine steel wool, even on the enamel. Finish up with two applications of hard paste wax rubbed to a polish.

GLASS-TOPPED COFFEE TABLE

BY RONALD BENREY

It's an instant coffee table—make the base from plywood, add a plate-glass top. The simple "wine-rack" design and the use of walnut veneer add to the look of elegance.

There's nothing simpler than a glass-topped coffee table—it's just a slab of plate glass resting on a sturdy base. That's why I was dumbfounded by the high prices these tables fetch.

We really wanted a glass-topped table, though. They look great, and just as important, they *stay* looking great. The glass top ignores food spills, drink splashes, and cigarette embers that will mar most wood tables.

The solution? Build a table myself. I designed the base in a "wine rack" style, using plain ¾" plywood.

As the plans indicate, only four edges must be bevel cut; all the others are simple 90-degree angles. When the base is assembled, veneer (I used walnut) brings the plywood up to the same level of elegance as the glass top provides.

The glass itself must be plate glass—the structurally strong stuff used in storefront windows. Minimum safe thickness is ½" (it actually measures about ⁷⁄₁₆"), but for more money, you can go up to ¾". And you have a choice of three shades: clear, smoky gray, or bronze.

You can get plate glass through your local glass shop, probably on special order. For looks and safety's sake have the edges finished. The simplest finish—the one I chose—is to have the corners ground smooth, and then cork-polished. This gives you a smooth translucent edge. You might ask for a "bulb" edge—a half-rounded edge that has a rich look. Price will vary from place to place.

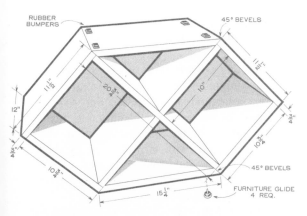

RUBBER BUMPERS

45° BEVELS

45° BEVELS

FURNITURE GLIDE 4 REQ.

HOW TO BUILD
A TABLE
THE CHINESE WAY

BY DAVID WARREN

Despite its sleek modern look, the table shown here conceals an ancient secret— fantastic joints that have characterized the best Chinese furniture-making for centuries. Built of Thailand teak and East Indian rosewood, this "all-Eastern" table stands 22″ high and measures 15″ by 26″. And that challenging joinery is more than a stunt. You've probably admired tri-mitered corners on expensive modern furniture—but they're weak at best. Try them with oily, glue-resistant teak and rosewood, and their inadequate gluing surfaces just won't hold. The joints detailed below are not merely intricate and beautiful— they're strong.

The Chinese have long treasured rosewood (or Huali) for its striking color and grain and its scent of musk rose. So they evolved a unique system of joinery to lock this exotic hardwood together—without glue. True Chinese joinery avoided nails and screws, too —even dowel pegs were used sparingly. But only a high-tensile-strength wood such as Huali permits such refined joinery.

This project typifies Chinese frame-and-panel construction. It was inspired by the first two of 34 drawings illustrating Chinese joinery in Dr. Gustav Ecke's book, *Chinese Domestic Furniture,* published by Chas. E. Tuttle.

Author modified a commercial design, altering dimensions and woods (rosewood frame, teak top) and reinstating authentic Chinese joints. For brass stretchers, he created special lock joint.

Here's how the parts mesh. First, the center panel is clamped to the stiles by sliding dovetails. Then the rails are secured to the stiles with wedged tenons. Next, the aprons are dadoed into the frame and tenoned into the double-mitered legs. Finally, the legs are tenoned into the top frame, tying all together —dry!

With today's power tools, it's comparatively easy to duplicate these cleverly engineered Chinese joints. However, since our western heritage does make oriental joinery unfamiliar, here are three hints: Supplement your fine, incised markings with white chalk to show miter directions and waste portions clearly. (Tailor's chalk works fine.) Second, compare those markings with our illustrations before you cut. Third, since actual measurements

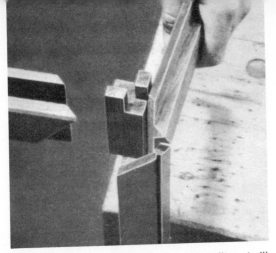

Tricky joint locks double-mitered aprons to "turreted" top of each leg. Assembly (sketched below and dimensioned on next page) is carefully adapted from actual joint in Chinese cabinetry.

aren't as important as having corresponding widths, thicknesses, rabbets, grooves, etc., of uniform size, test your machine adjustments on scraps. Then, assure uniformity by mass-producing all corresponding cuts at that adjustment. You'll be most satisfied in the long run if you take these precautions.

I ordered my wood from Craftsman's Wood Service (catalog from 2729 So. Mary St., Chicago 60608).

Top frame. Start by laying out and ripping the rails and stiles. Cut the stiles slightly longer than 26″ so their tenons will extend through the rails, then sand flush after assembly.

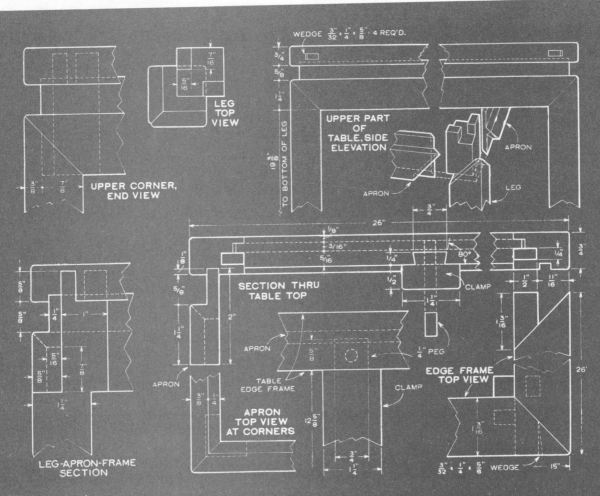

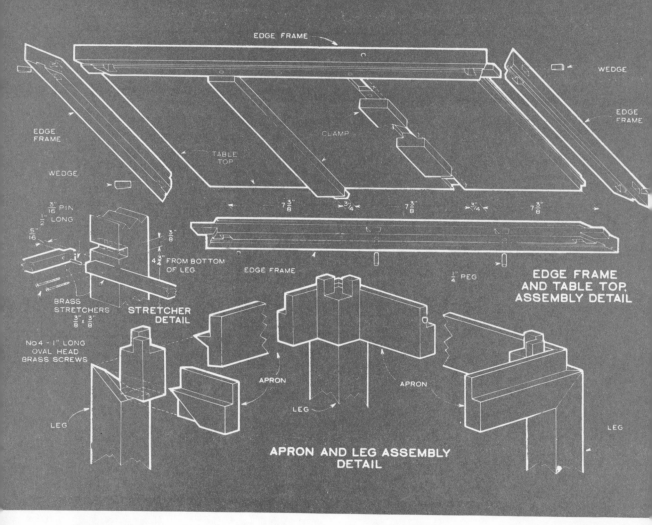

Clamp rails and stiles together and sand the edges so they're all equal width. Saw plow cuts on the inside edges and on the undersides. Then miter the ends, and bore mortises in each rail.

Lay out miters on the stiles next. Use a dado cutter to make the tenons by removing waste from top and botton surfaces. Then cut the $1/4''$-thick triangular tenon down to $1/2''$ width, using a jig or dovetail saw. Complete the frame by tapering mortises and tenons so the wedges fit. Now, bore clamp mortises in the stiles.

Aprons. Rip out apron stock, reduce to $5/8''$ thick, and plane the four pieces to equal width.

Rabbet the sides so each apron fits snugly into its groove in the top. With dado head set for $5/16''$, form the triangular tenons. Miter both ends of each apron with a disk sander.

Legs. Plane four sides of the leg stock enough to reveal its color and grain. Rip waste from the lighter or imperfect sides so the stock is slightly oversize. Then sand or scrape to $1^5/8''$ square. Next, select and label the position of each leg. Try to make the top with straight grain, outer sides darker, and the grain in each pair—viewed from side or end—to curve inward, like parentheses.

Saw $1/8''$ off the top to square that end. (Cut the bottom of leg to finish length after you

Gang sanding is quickest way to smooth four legs uniformly. Rip each to about 1 11/16", clamp them together as shown, and sand one set of sides at a time until 1⅝" square is achieved.

Leg turrets can be cut with hand tools, but jig or band saw works faster to square inside edges of tenons. Use sharp chisel to remove waste, creating flat shoulder for top to rest upon.

Accurate mortises will fit leg tenons snugly to draw rails and stiles together. You can pare mitered ends with chisel to butt tightly. The secret is frequent trial fitting and adjustment.

Dovetail groove for clamp was cut with bench saw tilted 10 degrees; after outline cuts were made (in opposite directions), waste was removed with additional passes, cleaned with hand router.

have fashioned the top.) Mark the mitered haunches with a fine dovetail saw or knife; then miter the haunch with your dado cutter adjusted to cut ⅝" deep.

Rosewood is so hard that when it's struck with mallet and chisel, it shatters into flying particles. So, eye protection is desirable when chopping mortises. Use hold-down push sticks to move rosewood through your jointer and table saw.

Use plain white paper to draw an original and three carbon copies of the top view of the leg, showing both tenons. Cut these 1" squares and paste one on the end of each leg. Stand legs in their relative positions and make sure plans are located correctly. Then saw both ½" long chisel. Bore the 5/16" triangular mortise next. Reduce legs to 1¼" square by cutting the shoulders and removing ⅜" waste from the two sides opposite the mortises. (I used a planer blade, finishing with a portable jig saw.) Cut dadoes and bore mortises for the brass stretchers next. Cut the incised molding in the outer corner of each leg, sand, and saw off to proper length.

Assemble the frame and clamp together while you mark the mortises in the rail and stile for the leg tenons. Cut these mortises accurately so the leg tenons draw the frame together. Use a chisel to pare the mitered ends so the frame, apron, and leg miters butt tightly.

135

Top panel. While the frame is assembled, verify measurements for the teak panel, including its tongues. Cut the panel to overall size; cut a tongue on four sides. Then rout dovetail clamp grooves across the bottom. Saw mating dovetail clamps from scrap hardwood. Assemble and bore the peg holes.

Brass stretchers. These are a modern garnish. You can use solid brass as I did, or reduce your costs by using square brass tubing.

Cut brass to finish length. Form tenons at the ends of two short rods with hack saw and file. Drill holes for ³/₁₆″ round pins. Use No. 32. bit to drill body holes through longer rod for No. 4 screws. Countersink, and use a No. 44 bit to bore ⁵/₈″-deep pilot holes in rosewood. Screw stretchers in place.

Disassemble table. Round all edges to a ³/₁₆″ radius, and sand thoroughly. Brighten brass with liquid brass polish. Reassemble. (If you wish, apply a dab of epoxy glue to each leg joint — sparingly, so it doesn't ooze. Epoxy is an adhesive that bites into these woods.) Drive pegs through stile into clamp. Drive wedges into their mortises, sand flush. Tap furniture glides into legs. Use razor-sharp wood carver's parting tool or ¼″ chisel to form heart-shaped carving at upper end of each leg. Carve so chisel does not dig into grain.

Finish. I simulated the classic Chinese finish by rubbing in clear polish — no stain, no filler. Use a 4/0 steel wool pad (nothing coarser) to rub a generous coat of linseed oil into the teak. Then use a 4/0 pad to rub a mixture of equal parts shellac and linseed oil into both woods. Rub in additional coats with the grain as previous coats dry. Continue polishing until there is a rich, satin finish. As you polish, the 4/0 pads will become rose color. Avoid transferring this coloring to the teak. For final touch, use wax — it helps prevent checking as wood ages. It's easy to keep your T'iao Chi looking mod by repolishing marred areas.

136

SPACE-SAVING SPICE RACK

BY PATRICK ABBEDUTO

Rack fits neatly into the wasted space beneath your kitchen cabinets and stores a full selection of spices within easy reach.

After an unsuccessful shopping trip in search of a spice rack, my wife decided we'd have to design and build our own. The Early American style available just didn't fit our modern kitchen — in terms of space or style. The rack I came up with fits snugly in wasted space under our cabinets. Its perforated-hardboard front provides hanging storage for pots and kitchen utensils.

Buy a matched set of spices first, then size the rack to fit the set. Be sure to allow space for the hooks to engage the rack in front of the bottles. The unit shown is designed to fit a corner, but is easily adapted to one-wall service.

The rack goes together quickly with brads and glue. Drill pilot holes through the hardboard. If you don't, the brads will bend and the board will chip.

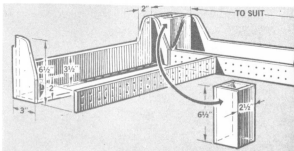

STORAGE CABINETS MADE EASY

BY R. S. HEDIN

Storage cabinets are handy to have, but tricky to make—especially the drawer slides.

When I needed a small cabinet to store negatives, I used a design that simplifies slide construction. The drawer bottoms are made of $\frac{1}{8}''$ hardboard $\frac{1}{2}''$ wider than the drawers.

This gives the bottom $\frac{1}{4}''$ tongues along the sides that fit into $\frac{1}{4}''$-by-$\frac{1}{4}''$ grooves cut in the sides of the cabinet.

The drawing shows construction details. Choose dimensions to suit your needs. This design is for a small cabinet, just a little over a foot in height, but you can expand to a much larger size by beefing up the drawers. Switch to $\frac{1}{4}''$ hardboard for the bottoms, and $\frac{5}{8}''$ plywood for front, back, and sides.

When the cabinet is complete, hand-sand the sharp corners off the drawer slides. Then rub them lightly with paraffin.

Small cabinet is open at rear; larger size will need a back to reinforce frame.

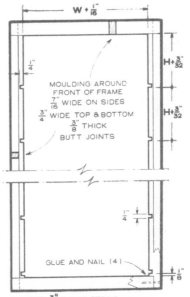

FRAME $\frac{3}{4}''$ THICK STOCK
"L" INCHES DEEP

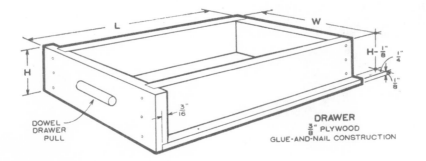

DRAWER
$\frac{3}{8}''$ PLYWOOD
GLUE-AND-NAIL CONSTRUCTION

137

YOUR CHOICE: TWO PHONE BENCHES FOR YOUR HOME

BY AL LEES and WILLARD ALLPHIN

Either of these seats for phoning can be the focal point of your entry hall, or will dress up a corner of the living room. Both provide handy shelves for telephone directories beneath a table for jotting messages. In addition, the modern floating design collects the week's newspapers for bulk disposal, and has two shallow drawers, set at right angles, that keep track of appointment books, keys for house and car — or store cartons of cigarettes.

Each design calls for less than a full 4-by-8 sheet of ¾-inch cabinet plywood (walnut veneer was chosen for these models). To avoid waste, partial sheets can often be purchased from cabinetmakers or self-service lumber outlets. For the modern bench you'll need a sheet at least three feet long in order to achieve the wrap-around grain effect of the mitered tabletop and sides. This project is especially designed so that good-one-side plywood can be used; you don't need a quality veneer on the back face since the interiors of the compartments are enamelled black.

Making the modern unit. The pedestal of this bench (also painted black) was made the same height as the existing baseboard, for appearance. It consists of mitered 2-by-3s set on edge and recessed ¾" from the front and ends of the seat box.

The ⅜" birch dowel pegs serve both deco-

Floating design by Al Lees needs no legs under table section, which is cantilevered from seat and screwed to wall cleat under directory shelf. Wire to phone jack is coiled around cuphooks in bottom of cleat (see photo, below). Open seat box serves as newspaper caddy.

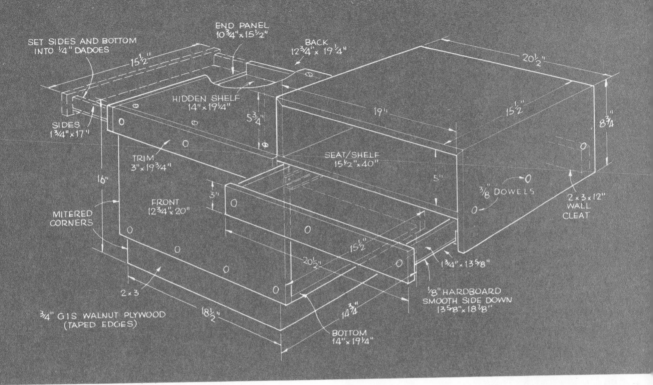

SET SIDES AND BOTTOM
INTO ¼" DADOES

END PANEL
10¾"×15½"

BACK
12¾"× 19¼"

15½"

HIDDEN SHELF
14"×19¼"

5¾"

20½"

19"

15½"

8¾"

SIDES
1¾"×17"

SEAT/SHELF
15½"×40"

TRIM
3"×19¾"

16"

3"

FRONT
12¾"×20"

5"

⅜" DOWELS

2×3×12"
WALL
CLEAT

MITERED
CORNERS

20½"

15½"

1¾"×13⅝"

2×3

¾" G1S WALNUT PLYWOOD
(TAPED EDGES)

18½"

14¾"

⅛" HARDBOARD
SMOOTH SIDE DOWN
13⅝"×18⅛"

BOTTOM
14"×19¼"

rative and practical functions, securing some joints without additional fasteners. These should be 1¾" long, driven in place with glue.

The front drawer slides on two iron angles, the end one on a hidden shelf beneath the seat panel. The three mitered table members are joined to this full-length panel that serves as both seat top and directory shelf. (This panel need not be cabinet ply since all its surfaces and edges will be enameled black.) The short end of the table can be glued into a ¼"-deep dado cut across this panel, or merely butted against it and fastened with glue and screws

Bench-table by Allphin replaced a phone table with separate stool which was clumsy to pull out while answering phone. Legs were tapered from 2-by-2 turning squares mail-ordered from Constantine. Sides and rails (¾" ply) are mortised into legs; so are front edges of ½" shelves which are glued and then nailed into the table sides.

from below. This assembly is screwed to the seat box and wall cleat as the final step.

Cushion to suit. The 16"-by-19" reversible cushion was custom-made (vinyl over four-inch foam rubber) by an upholsterer. You can buy a ready-made cushion and tailor the construction to its dimensions.

For the traditional bench-table, tenons on the sides and rails are not full width. The 8" sides have pairs of 2"-wide tenons at each end. The 3" rails have 2½" tenons except where indicated on the drawing (see detail). Smaller tenons, here, prevent weakening the cross rail.

Mortises were made by drilling a row of ⅜" holes and chiseling out between. Tenons were cut on a table saw with the blade set ⁹/₁₆" from the fence. Tabletop and seat are anchored by means of corner blocks, glued and screwed underneath. Fasten the top before gluing in the shelves so you'll have access to these corner blocks.

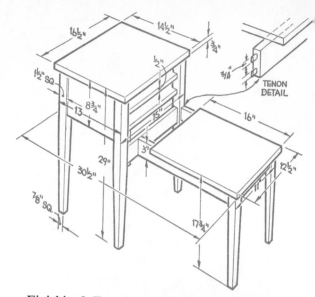

Finishing? For the traditional design, you can use two coats of Satinlac followed by furniture wax. For the modern unit, apply Watco Danish Oil to all veneer surfaces.

A LOG HAMPER

BY JOHN RIEDEL

Oak stair tread—it looks rugged and it is rugged—is a perfect material for hearthside log hamper. It even has one edge finished round, just the way you want it for this project. The hamper I made, dimensions shown, holds four or five average logs and some kindling. The feet are fir two-by-six, the bottom is a scrap of one-by-six pine. Everything goes together quickly, with glue and countersunk flathead brass woodscrews. After sanding, I stained the wood to match my furniture, and brushed on some low-gloss varnish.

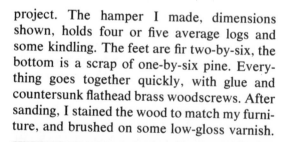

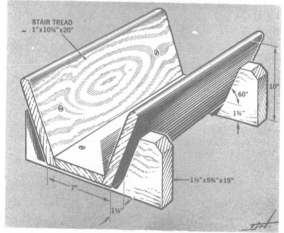

Integral lights on headboard and over work table plug into outlet that's visible under the bed. So do electric tools, clock, or typewriter.

HOW TO BUILD
THE MICRODORM

BY KEN ISAACS

A psychiatrist who is a research specialist in child adjustment tells me that my newest Living Structure does great things for a child. It satisfies, he says, the "territorial imperative." In plain language, this means that the structure makes the child feel more secure and independent by giving him a place he can call his own.

Newest living structure is first Isaacs has designed specifically for the young. A small house within a room, it includes drawer storage and a full-length bed topside (see photos), plus a private study with seat, table, and bookshelves.

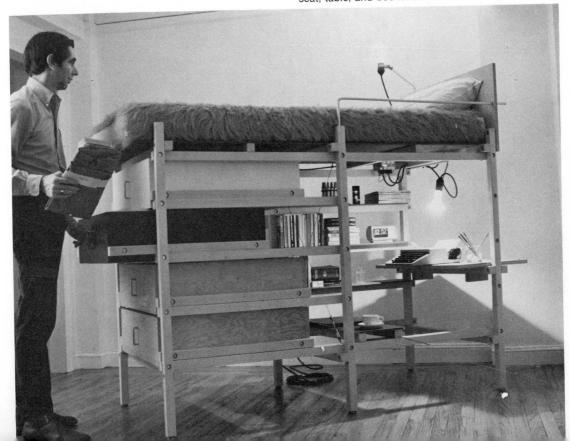

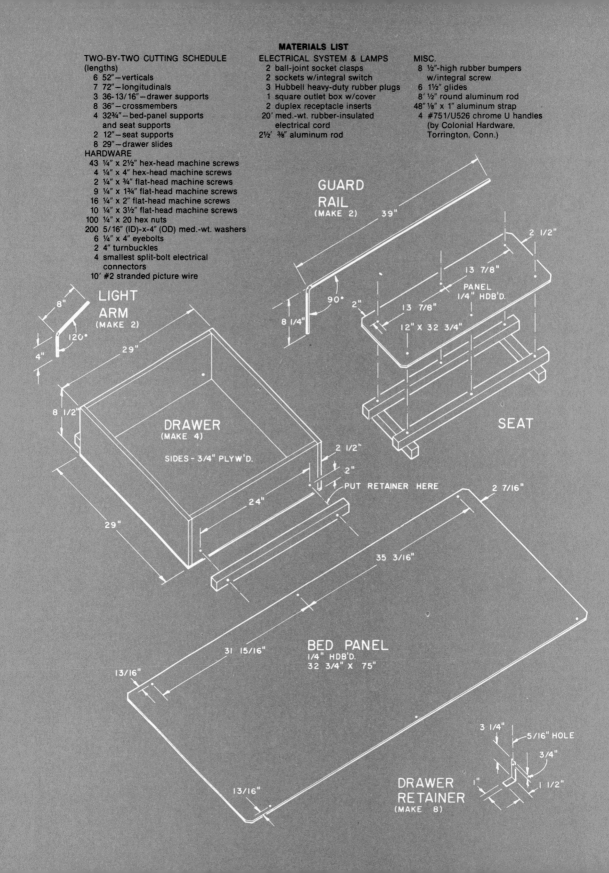

TWO-BY-TWO CUTTING SCHEDULE
(lengths)
- 6 52"—verticals
- 7 72"—longitudinals
- 3 36-13/16"—drawer supports
- 8 36"—crossmembers
- 4 32¾"—bed-panel supports and seat supports
- 2 12"—seat supports
- 8 29"—drawer slides

HARDWARE
- 43 ¼" x 2½" hex-head machine screws
- 4 ¼" x 4" hex-head machine screws
- 2 ¼" x ¾" flat-head machine screws
- 9 ¼" x 1¾" flat-head machine screws
- 16 ¼" x 2" flat-head machine screws
- 10 ¼" x 3½" flat-head machine screws
- 100 ¼" x 20 hex nuts
- 200 5/16" (ID)-x-4" (OD) med.-wt. washers
- 6 ¼" x 4" eyebolts
- 2 4" turnbuckles
- 4 smallest split-bolt electrical connectors
- 10' #2 stranded picture wire

MATERIALS LIST

ELECTRICAL SYSTEM & LAMPS
- 2 ball-joint socket clasps
- 2 sockets w/integral switch
- 3 Hubbell heavy-duty rubber plugs
- 1 square outlet box w/cover
- 2 duplex receptacle inserts
- 20' med.-wt. rubber-insulated electrical cord
- 2½' ⅜" aluminum rod

MISC.
- 8 ½"-high rubber bumpers w/integral screw
- 6 1½" glides
- 8' ½" round aluminum rod
- 48" ⅛" x 1" aluminum strap
- 4 #751/U526 chrome U handles (by Colonial Hardware, Torrington, Conn.)

GUARD RAIL (MAKE 2)

39"

2 1/2"

13 7/8"

PANEL 1/4" HDB'D.

13 7/8"

12" X 32 3/4"

90°

2"

8 1/4"

LIGHT ARM (MAKE 2)

8"

120°

4"

29"

8 1/2"

DRAWER (MAKE 4)

SIDES - 3/4" PLYW'D.

SEAT

2 1/2"

2"

PUT RETAINER HERE

2 7/16"

24"

29"

35 3/16"

31 15/16"

BED PANEL
1/4" HDB'D.
32 3/4" X 75"

13/16"

13/16"

DRAWER RETAINER (MAKE 8)

3 1/4"

5/16" HOLE

3/4"

1"

1 1/2"

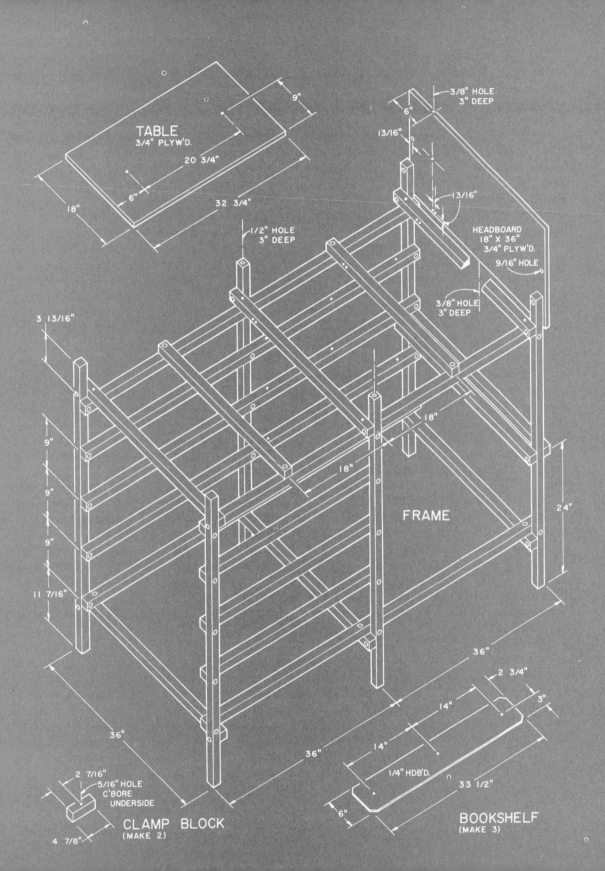

TABLE
3/4" PLYW'D.

9"

20 3/4"

6"

32 3/4"

18"

3/8" HOLE
3" DEEP

6"

13/16"

13/16"

HEADBOARD
18" X 36"
3/4" PLYW'D.

9/16" HOLE

3/8" HOLE
3" DEEP

1/2" HOLE
3" DEEP

3 13/16"

9"

9"

9"

11 7/16"

18"

18"

24"

FRAME

36"

36"

36"

2 7/16"

5/16" HOLE
C'BORE
UNDERSIDE

CLAMP BLOCK
(MAKE 2)

4 7/8"

2 3/4"

3"

14"

14"

1/4" HDB'D.

33 1/2"

6"

BOOKSHELF
(MAKE 3)

The Microdorm integrates a bed, study-work-eating area (with seating), bookshelves, lighting, and more than 16 cubic feet of drawer space for clothing and tools (approximately the storage capacity of two ordinary chests of drawers). All these functions are organized within a geometric Matrix framework of my design that takes up the same floor space (three by six feet) as an army cot. This multiplicity of uses is available *all* the time without the necessity of making adjustments or moving any elements.

The Microdorm is an expression of the Matrix Idea in design. Traditional design is concerned with fragmented solutions to one aspect of a problem; the Matric Idea attacks the whole problem at once and aims at providing the hardware for a new way of life.

The Microdorm was conceived as a Living Structure that could grow up with a child. He can begin using it at five or six. It should mean a lot to the child to have his own *private* piece of architecture rather than a hodgepodge of traditional furniture, most of which was designed for adult use. We all will appreciate what a Living Structure can mean to a youngster by recalling the excitement we had at age eight or so in playing in a large corrugated box.

I think we learn to live best when our physical environment supports order and alertness, encouraging us toward study, understanding, and constructive action. If our surroundings are chaotic and based on superficial notions about life values, our approach to life may end by being haphazard and cynical. If there are no shelves for books, few will read. If there is no privacy, few will think.

The Microdorm was also designed with consideration for the day-to-day problems of cleaning and maintenance. From the housekeeping point of view, it makes cleaner room spaces possible because it is open and easy to clean. Heating and cooling are better because the grid allows free air circulation.

The structure requires so little floor space that it will work in an extremely small bed-room and still leave extra square footage for activities. A slightly larger room will accommodate two children with a central space remaining for car tracks, games, and other uses in common. The emotional pressures that may be generated in children by forced sharing—a feature of traditional furniture designs—will be relieved by the fact that now each has his own structure. There is none of the old-fashioned overlapping use of tables, chairs, and shelves—a source of conflict.

The Microdorm fulfills the living equation so comprehensively that it will work just as well for the high-school student as the eight-year-old. Actually, as study and work requirements increase with maturity, the basic features acquire increasing importance. It is usable throughout a youngster's school years.

Building the Microdorm. Select the driest, straightest Douglas fir (or white fir) two-by-twos in the lumberyard. Following the cutting schedule, mark lengths on top and two sides of the two-by-two with a square. Saw slightly beyond these lines, then use them as a guide for rasping the ends as smooth and square as you can.

Study the drawing before beginning hole layout. Holes are made with a $5/16''$ drill. The counterbores are $5/8''$ deep and can be made with a $7/8''$ spade bit. All holes are on the longitudinal centerline of the two-by-two.

Assemble the two longitudinal (side) frames first. Then add the 3' crossmembers and the two table supports. Secure the two extra crossmember bed-panel supports last—18'' on either side of the center posts.

Cutting and drilling the panels. Cut the bed and seat panels from $1/4''$ hardboard. The three bookshelves can be cut from scraps of hardboard. Cut $3/4''$ off each corner at a 45-degree angle to prevent snagging. Lay out holes and drill with a $1/4''$ bit and countersink for flathead machine screws. The headboard and table are cut from $3/4''$ plywood.

Note that the guard-rail holes in the head-board are drilled $9/16''$ diameter (oversize) to ease fitting problems. The two $3/8''$ holes for the light arms (in headboard edge, top and bottom) are a little ticklish, so take time and sight well. The headboard is secured to the frame with two $2\frac{1}{2}''$ and two $4''$ hex-head machine screws. Put four washers on each.

Assembling the drawers. Cut the drawer sides from $3/4''$ fir plywood. Drawer bottoms can be $1/4''$ hardboard. If you plan to store equipment or heavy items in addition to clothing, better use $3/8''$ plywood. There is plenty of clearance for the added thickness. It is easier to sand, drill, and countersink holes in the sides before assembly. Use a stapling gun in the plywood edges to hold the pieces together before nailing and gluing. This makes nailing easier and the fit will be more precise. Be sure of good glue coverage, with a $1''$ brad every $4''$ to keep the bottom from pulling loose.

Last step is to bolt two-by-two slides to the drawer, using $2''$ flathead machine screws with heads countersunk *inside* the drawer. The drawer retainers are bent in a vise from aluminum strip, drilled with a $1/4''$ bit, and sandwiched between drawer and slide on the rear bolt. Use two washers on the front bolt to

Wire crossbracing in middle frame makes unit fully rigid. Drawer support rungs serve as a ladder to reach bed for casual study, sleep.

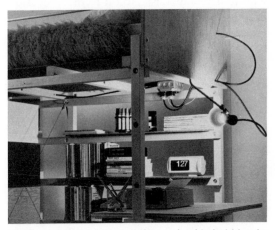

Hardboard shelves next to the work table hold books and equipment. Table clamps to crossmembers with two-by-two blocks, $4\frac{7}{8}''$ long.

Study area is a total work center with equipment close at hand. Light pivots on arm with adjustable ball joint at socket clamp; cords thread through holes in head-board. A loose cushion can be used on seat, which can be adjusted by sliding it back and forth on the lowest side members.

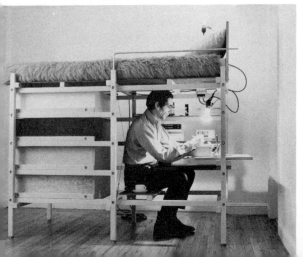

equalize the thickness. The bottom, or horizontal, leg of the retainer bears against the underside of the drawer support, and prevents the drawer from tipping when it is pulled out past its balance point. As a further safety measure (to prevent the drawer from being pulled all the way out and falling), screw a $1/2''$-high rubber bumper on the bottom side of each of the eight drawer-support members near the drawer-face end.

The guard rails are bent of $1/2''$ aluminum

rod, using a vise and a scrap of water pipe slipped over one end as a lever. Bend the two light arms of ³⁄₈″ aluminum rod at the same time. File the cut ends flat and clean before inserting in holes or attaching socket clamps.

Tension cables. Two tension cables (with turnbuckles) anchored at the centers of the longitudinal frame members (see photo) counteract stresses caused by using the drawer supports as a ladder to reach the bed. To install, replace the appropriate 2½″ bolts with eyebolts. Open the bottom eyebolts to take turnbuckle eyes. Secure all cable end-loops with electrical connectors.

The electric outlet is a standard steel box with four receptacles. Bolt it to the underside of the bed panel with ¾″ flathead machine screws. It services the table lamp and the reading lamp on the headboard. In addition it offers two extra plug-ins for typewriter, soldering gun, etc. The supply cord is threaded

through a ³⁄₈″ hole in the middle crossmember and another in the short transverse bed-panel support. It is guided to the floor by two eyebolts inserted in place of two of the frame bolts in the vertical member at the end of the bookshelves. The lamp sockets will take 50- or 75-watt reflector flood bulbs, which need no shades and give high-intensity light.

Finishing up. To eliminate splinters, round the long corners of all two-by-twos with a plane and rasp. Sand all surfaces smooth with fine aluminum-oxide paper. Apply three coats of a deep-penetrating clear resin sealer (Firzite), sanding between coats. Finish with fine steel wool, paste wax, and rub with a soft cloth.

Sand all hardboard panels and edges smooth. Then roller-coat with a flat paint. The drawers can also be roller-coated, but leave the two-by-two slides natural. Wax to decrease friction.

DUAL-PURPOSE HAMPER

BY BOB GILMORE

Perforated sides on this wheeled hamper ventilate soiled laundry stored in it. Come washday, an inserted muslin bag transports wet wash and clothespins. The bag is grommeted to fit over dowels projecting from the frame top, and hooks cut from coat hangers.

The hamper is made from ⅛″ perforated hardboard, one-by-two pine or spruce, and 1″ oak dowels, assembled with glue and small nails. Cut the bottom from ¾″ plywood, cutting saw kerfs at front and rear edges for the hardboard panels. Aim for a tight fit at the rear, a loose fit at front. Also saw-kerf the dowels that top the front and back panels. My hamper has hard-rubber wheels on axles of cold-rolled rod but casters could be used, as in the drawing.

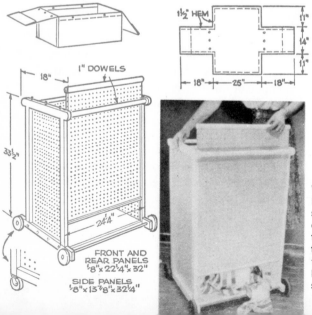

Work-saver extraordinary, this hamper collects and stores soiled clothes in airy fashion during the week, wheels them to the laundry on washday, and then carts them after washing to the clothesline. Front panel lifts in grooves for emptying soiled clothing (photo left).

NO-TOOL KNOCKDOWN PUZZLE BOOKCASE

BY RICH OLIVER

Nobody enjoys moving day. But it's a lot easier to take if your furniture knocks down for transport. That was the idea in the back of my mind when I began designing a bookcase that would fit into my nomadic lifestyle.

The final result turned out better than I had imagined. It has modern good looks, assembles and knocks down like a Chinese puzzle—without tools of any kind. Like a Chinese puzzle, it's made entirely of wood. And unlike most commercial knockdown units it's sturdy, inexpensive, and holds a lot of books.

I made it from ordinary fir two-by-fours, 1-by-12 pine, and some ³⁄₈″ dowels. As dimensioned in the sketch, the case stands 5′ high by 5′ wide. But by changing the lengths of the horizontals and uprights you can easily custom-fit the units to your needs without having to change the dado design.

Construction is simple. But you may need a little guidance on the trick of putting the puzzle together: First assemble two A and two B pieces to form a rectangle on your floor. Add a pair of uprights at one end and slip a couple of dowels into their holes to stabilize things. Move to the other end of the rectangle and do the same thing. Now slip the bottom shelf into place. This will prevent the bottom ends of the uprights from slipping out of place while you move operations to the top of the unit and continue with the assembly.

Insert the supporting dowels for the top shelf and set the shelf in place. Slip both B pieces into their dadoes, then drop the A pieces into position. This accomplished, everything is locked together. Place the remaining dowels and shelves, and your case is ready for books.

All framing joints are simple, sturdy halflaps. Make trial cuts in scrap wood to assure tight flush fit. Dowels should fit smoothly but snugly in their holes.

A: FOUR – 19″ LONG, TWO DADOES
B: FOUR – 60″ LONG, FOUR DADOES
C: FOUR – 60″ LONG, TWO DADOES
D: TWELVE DOWELS, ³⁄₈″ X 18″
ALL FRAMING 2 X 4 FIR

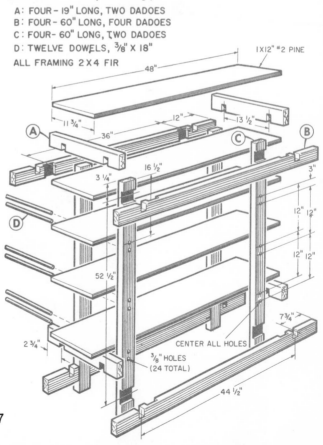

147

GUEST ROOM IN A TEN-INCH SPACE

BY AL LEES / *PS Home Workshop Editor*
Design by KEN ISAACS
Constructed by ROSARIO CAPOTOSTO

The guest room is a forgotten luxury in today's homes. Who of us can set aside that kind of space for infrequent use in the squeeze of family life? So what do you do with over-nighters—especially the unexpected or emergency types who don't give enough advance warning to let you ship the kids off to the neighbors?

You put them up on the living room couch. But even if you have one that folds out into a bed, it makes a shambles of the room as your guests search awkwardly for places to stow their belongings—and feel like ward patients next morning, when the family walks through.

Handsome wall panel gives no hint that full equipment for sleeping two overnight guests is stored behind. The unit doesn't interfere in any way with the normal use of the living room or den.

Pivot the panel out at one end (other end is hinged to shallow shelf unit behind) and you have access to a pair of folding cots, linen, towels. Note that outer corner rolls easily on large caster.

With beds set up, storage compartments serve as a double wardrobe. Hinged panel becomes a privacy wall, masking guests from major traffic lanes of host family.

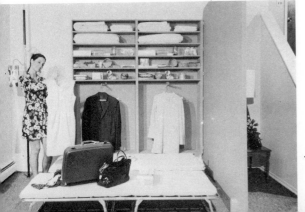

All this is solved with our 10-inch-deep guest room. It takes no usable floor space. You need only one free wall to hang a seven-foot-square panel on, as in the photo above. It floats in front of the wall, like minimal sculpture. We made ours of prefinished plywood and left it plain. You may prefer to dress up the front surface with a cluster of framed prints. Or you could mount a window-shade projection screen near the top, to pull down for showing your slides or movies. Or cover most of the panel with a giant map.

The decorative potential is limited only by your ingenuity and the existing room setting. Designer Isaacs points out that the unit might be a "living wall," with one or two cutouts matched up to shelving compartments, behind, tailored to your prize pieces of sculpture or trophies. Or, if you wish to make sections of the shelf space easily accessible for storing often-used items, just pierce the panel with random doors in bright, contrasting colors, so you can reach items without pivoting the full panel.

Ease of construction was a prime consideration in designing the storage unit and privacy screen for overnight guests, shown here.

You don't even need stationary power tools. If you don't own a portable circular saw for cutting the large panels, you can easily rent one. For smooth edges, a hollow-ground plywood blade is recommended.

The storage cabinets are made up as two identical units and simply mounted side by side. Cut all parts from $5/8''$ fir plywood and sand the faces before assembly. You'll need a dozen spacer blocks about $1\frac{1}{2}''$ wide and exactly $5\frac{3}{4}''$ long to simplify shelf alignment, as shown.

Temporarily nail the five inner shelves to one of the back panels with $1\frac{1}{2}''$ finishing nails only partly driven in. Pull this assembly apart, apply glue and reassemble, driving the nails home. Then drill countersunk holes for $1\frac{1}{2}''$ No. 8 flathead screws. Add the top and bottom pieces (note they're $5/8''$ wider to lap the

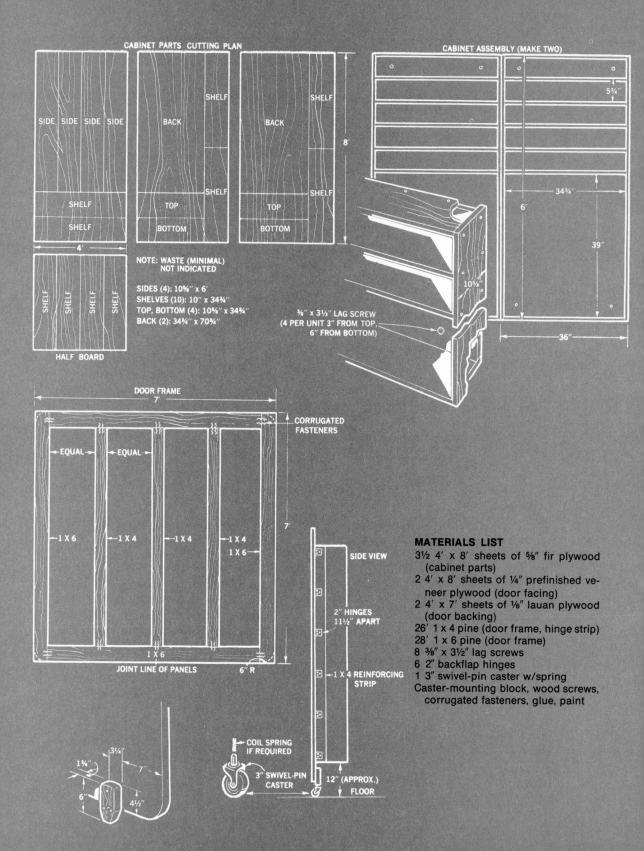

CABINET PARTS CUTTING PLAN

SIDE SIDE SIDE SIDE

SHELF

BACK

SHELF

SHELF

TOP

BOTTOM

8'

SHELF

BACK

SHELF

SHELF

TOP

BOTTOM

SHELF

SHELF

4'

SHELF SHELF SHELF SHELF

HALF BOARD

NOTE: WASTE (MINIMAL)
NOT INDICATED

SIDES (4): 10⅝" x 6'
SHELVES (10): 10" x 34¾"
TOP, BOTTOM (4): 10⅝" x 34¾"
BACK (2): 34¾" x 70¾"

⅜" x 3½" LAG SCREW
(4 PER UNIT 3" FROM TOP,
6" FROM BOTTOM)

CABINET ASSEMBLY (MAKE TWO)

5¾"

34¾"

6'

39"

10⅝"

36"

DOOR FRAME
7'

CORRUGATED
FASTENERS

EQUAL   EQUAL

1 X 6   1 X 4   1 X 4   1 X 4
                               1 X 6

7'

1 X 6

JOINT LINE OF PANELS   6" R

SIDE VIEW

2" HINGES
11½" APART

1 X 4 REINFORCING
STRIP

1¾"
3¼"
7"
6"
4½"

COIL SPRING
IF REQUIRED

3" SWIVEL-PIN
CASTER

12" (APPROX.)
FLOOR

MATERIALS LIST

3½ 4' x 8' sheets of ⅝" fir plywood
  (cabinet parts)
2 4' x 8' sheets of ¼" prefinished veneer plywood (door facing)
2 4' x 7' sheets of ⅛" lauan plywood
  (door backing)
26' 1 x 4 pine (door frame, hinge strip)
28' 1 x 6 pine (door frame)
8 ⅜" x 3½" lag screws
6 2" backflap hinges
1 3" swivel-pin caster w/spring
Caster-mounting block, wood screws,
  corrugated fasteners, glue, paint

edge of the back panel) and then nail, glue, and screw on the sides.

The cabinet assemblies are heavy, so must be anchored to at least two wall studs per cabinet. Prop them up against the wall, roughly centered between floor and ceiling (assuming your ceiling is a standard eight-foot height). Mount with lag screws.

Decide which side the door panel should hinge from to provide the best privacy, and beef up that side panel with a hinge strip, as shown on the plans.

The panel door is a big seven-foot square. Don't assemble it in your shop until you've checked doors and turns on the path to the appointed wall. If you have doubts about clear passage, cut the pieces in your shop, assemble them "at the site."

If you wish to duplicate our Japanese teak facing, check your lumber yard. They may not stock it, but they'll order it for you. I economized on the door's back panels, using 4-by-7 sheets of ungrooved lauan plywood. You can often pick these up at low cost in $3/32''$ thicknesses.

Prepare an ample supply of scrap wood strips to serve as clamping blocks.

After brushing glue on both the frame and the panel back, where it will make contact, position the panel and keep it from slipping when clamped by anchoring it with a couple of thin brads.

Hanging the door isn't difficult. Just prop it against the mounted cabinets, make certain it is level, and mark the six hinge locations on the back of the door. The hinges called for in the Materials List below have 2"-square leaves. They spread the "purchase" over a wider band than the ordinary butt hinge.

Caster bears the weight. Although these hinges will anchor the door, its width requires a swivel caster on the outer end to take the strain off the hinge line and cabinet. A 3"-diameter wheel about 1" wide will roll easily

1 Portable circular saw makes quick work of cutting large panels into components shown in sketch on next page. Guide is tacked down.

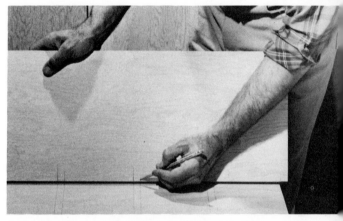

2 Transfer shelf locations from back panel to sides. Lines show where to apply glue. To position shelves, tack on blocks cut to match space between, gapping them with scraps of shelf stock. Don't drive nails in — blocks are removed before glue sets.

3 Apply white glue to face of panel and to edge of shelves; spread so excess won't ooze much when shelves are set in blocks.

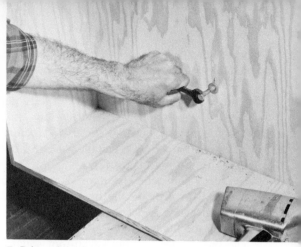

4 Holes for screws are easy if you check drill housing against square to keep it vertical. Full-length sides complete unit.

7 Drive eight lag screws up tight, washers under heads. It's easier to paint units after mounting.

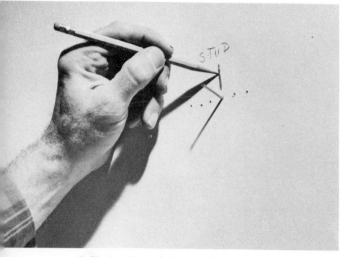

8 If floor is not even, drill socket hole deep enough to take compressed spring. This keeps caster in contact with floor at all locations.

5 Find wall studs by probing with thin nail or drill. Locate and mark center of one; others should be 16" from it—but check.

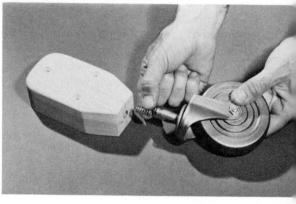

6 Prop both cabinets against the wall at mounting height, clamp at center. Drill pilot holes for lag screws through back and into studs—one at each corner.

9 Assemble frame flat with scrap blocks under joints to even out bumpy floor. Make sure frame is square.

10 Secure assembly with pair of ⅝″ corrugated fasteners across each joint so you can flip it and drive second pair across each joint. No gluing is needed, if joints are snug.

Gang panels for face and back, and trim all to size at once, with straight board as guide. Leave panels slightly oversize.

Apply back panels with glue, brushing it on for quick, even spread. Secure with several brads and flip over.

13 Apply facing panels in same way, secure with a few brads. Have lots of clamps handy to clamp sandwich while glue sets. Note that pressure is applied along center seam by bowing a long board across stacked boards (below), centered on seam.

14 Final trimming is done with circular saw, after glue sets, to bring oversize panels flush with frame. For straight cut, tack on guide.

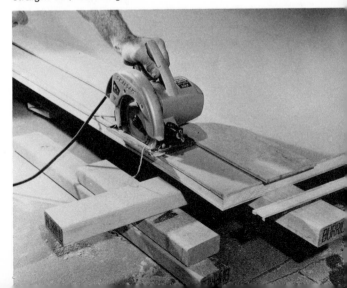

15 Cut corner radius with saber saw, using medium-tooth hollow-ground blade. Sand edges, stain to match veneer.

16 Attach hinges by clamping straight strip on back to assure pins will align. Then prop door against cabinet to attach.

over any type of floor. If your floor is not level, bore the hole for the caster pin deep enough to take a compression spring, as shown in the sketch. This will keep the caster in contact with the floor at all locations. The snap-in collar usually supplied with this type caster isn't used here, so the pin can move freely up and down. But bore the socket for a snug fit to prevent side play.

Paint the fir-ply cabinet units. To tame the wild grain, apply a coat of Firzite first. If you plan to paint the lauan back, fill the open grain with a paste wood filler. I dressed up the caster by spraying it bronze.

Attach garment brackets to the rear walls of the cabinets, to take clothes hangers. I used one called Spacemarker 101 that is sold at houseware stores. The notched arm pivots back flat when not in use.

You're ready for company as soon as you stock the shelves with essentials for overnighting: sheets, blankets, pillows and cases, face and bath towels—and the folding cots. These come in varying sizes and prices. Standing height, folded, averages about 38″, with widths from 25″ to 30″. The average front-to-back dimension, with mattress, is about 6″.

Shopping tips: Select your plywood panels personally; ask for A/B grade fir for the cabinets. As for the pine, get straight kiln-dried lumber.

Don't need a guest room? Consider the alternatives. The unit could as well serve as a sewing center or hobby shop. With a couple of drop-leaf tables in the cot compartments, you'd have generous workspace.

154

A TILT-TOP TABLE

BY DAVID WARREN

With space at a premium in most Colonial homes, the local cabinetmaker was frequently called upon to build a piece of furniture that performed more than one function. This table is typical of such pieces. In addition to its basic role, it was often used—with the top tilted—beside the hearth; the top reflected warmth to where it was wanted.

Though many tilt-top tables were larger (some served for dining), the size of this one makes it ideally suited for use as an occasional, or end, table. With top tilted, it takes little space when stored against a wall and it's easy to move around to serve as a snack table wherever needed.

Since the top is in full view when vertical, I made mine of bird's-eye maple. Its distinctive figured grain is decorative and adds an authentic look to the piece. All other wood members are of white maple. Both are available from woodworking-supply houses such as Craftsman Wood Service Co., 2727 S.

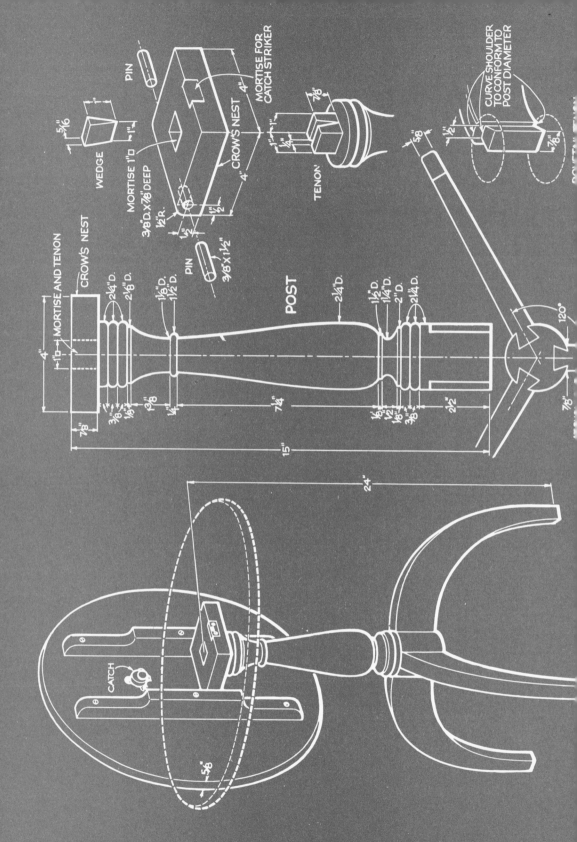

PIN

WEDGE

$\frac{5}{16}"$

$1"$

MORTISE 1"☐

MORTISE 1"☐ DEEP

$\frac{3}{8}"$D. X $\frac{7}{8}"$ DEEP

$\frac{1}{2}"$R.

$\frac{1}{2}"$

$\frac{1}{2}"$

CROW'S NEST

$4"$

MORTISE FOR CATCH STRIKER

$4"$

PIN

$\frac{3}{8}" X 1\frac{1}{2}"$

$\frac{7}{8}"$

TENON

$\frac{1}{4}"$

MORTISE AND TENON

CROW'S NEST

$4"$

$\frac{7}{8}"$

POST

$2\frac{1}{4}"$D.

$2\frac{1}{8}"$D.

$1\frac{1}{8}"$D.

$1\frac{1}{2}"$D.

$\frac{3}{8}"$

$\frac{1}{8}"$

$3\frac{1}{8}"$

$\frac{1}{4}"$

$7\frac{1}{4}"$

$2\frac{1}{4}"$D.

$1\frac{1}{2}"$D.

$1\frac{1}{4}"$D.

$2"$D.

$2\frac{1}{4}"$D.

$\frac{1}{16}"$

$\frac{1}{2}"$

$\frac{1}{8}"$

$\frac{3}{8}"$

$2\frac{1}{2}"$

$15"$

$\frac{5}{8}"$

$\frac{1}{2}"$

$\frac{7}{8}"$

CURVE SHOULDER TO CONFORM TO POST DIAMETER

$120°$

$\frac{7}{8}"$

CATCH

$24"$

$\frac{5}{8}"$

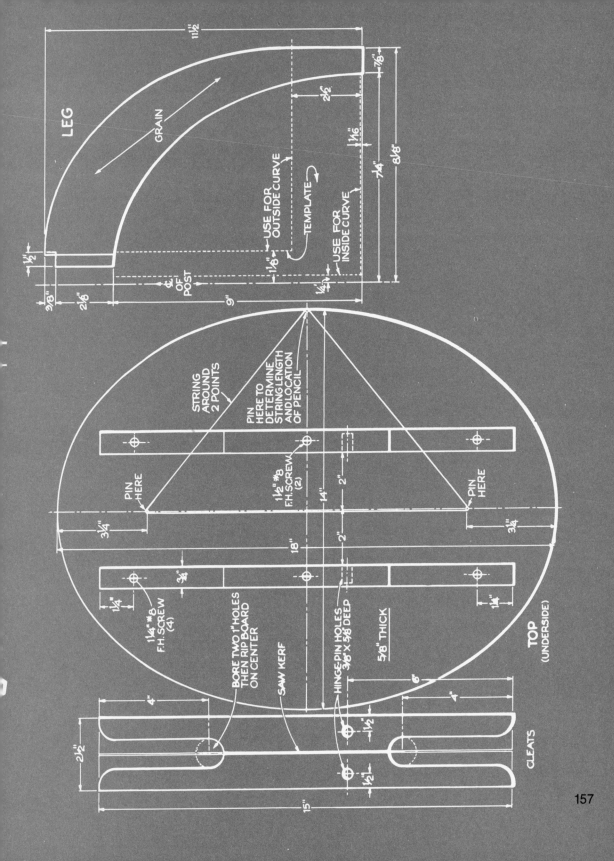

LEG

GRAIN

1½

1⅛"

2⅛"

USE FOR OUTSIDE CURVE

TEMPLATE

USE FOR INSIDE CURVE

¢ OF POST

1⅛"

¼"

2½"

7⅛"

1 1/16"

7¼"

8⅛"

9"

STRING AROUND 2 POINTS

PIN HERE TO DETERMINE STRING LENGTH AND LOCATION OF PENCIL

PIN HERE

PIN HERE

1½"*8 F.H. SCREW (2)

14"

2"

2"

3¼"

3¼"

18"

¾"

1¼"*8 F.H. SCREW (4)

¼"

14"

BORE TWO 1" HOLES THEN RIP BOARD ON CENTER

SAW KERF

HINGE-PIN HOLES 3/8" x 5/8" DEEP

5/8" THICK

TOP (UNDERSIDE)

6"

4"

4"

2½"

1½"

½"

½"

15"

CLEATS

157

Boards for top are tongue-and-grooved, glued, and clamped. For best appearance, grain runs with cleats.

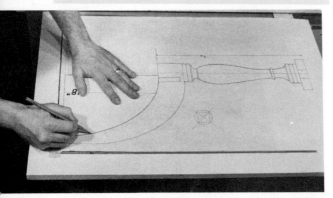

Quarter section of cardboard template for top serves as guide for marking legs. To make top template (above), draw 14" and 18" intersecting lines at right angles. Drive a 2d nail 3¼" in from each end of the longer line and at one end of the 14" line. Tie string tightly around all three nails; remove the nail on the 14" line. To draw accurate ellipse, hold pencil vertical, keep string taut as pencil moves.

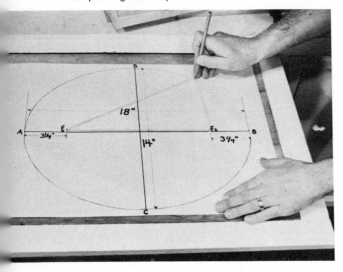

After cutting to shape, sand top down to ⅝" thickness. Then edge is rounded with spokeshave.

Square, wedged tenon provides good gluing surface, should be cut using mortise in crow's nest as guide.

Mary St., Chicago 60608, and Albert Constantine, 2053 Eastchester Rd., Bronx, New York, N.Y. 10461.

Laying out the table. The top is an ellipse, not an oval, with 14″-semicircle ends. Using the string-and-pencil method shown, lay it out on a piece of cardboard. To insure symmetry, score the template in quarter sections and fold it to check the edge in both length and width. If necessary, trim it with sharp scissors or a utility knife until the edges match perfectly.

After cutting tongues and grooves, glue and clamp the boards for the top. When dry, transfer the outline, using the template, and cut the top. To reduce top thickness to $5/8″$, scrape or sand $1/16″$ off each side. I found that a hand plane had a tendency to chip out some of the "eyes" of the maple. A belt sander with a medium-grit belt is better. (If any eye voids do result, they can be filled with tinted wood putty after staining.) Round the edge using a $1/4″$ quarter-round cutter in your router. If you lack power, it can be rounded with a spokeshave.

In the long run, you'll save time by preparing a full-size drawing of the post and one leg. Transfer three leg outlines onto $7/8″$ stock and cut out the legs. Use a disk sander to finish the outside curve, a drum sander on the leg's inner curve. Shape the top edge of the legs, mark and cut the dovetails with a fine saw. Using a gouge, work the shoulder of the dovetail concave, so it will fit the curved post snugly.

Turning the post. Take all dimensions for the post from your drawing. Note: The top pin is turned $1\frac{1}{2}″$ in diameter to allow for the 1″-square tenon. Since maple seems to be particularly susceptible to cross-grain scratches, sand the post carefully with 6/0 (220 grit) paper. Burnishing the piece with a scrap of leather while it spins in lathe polishes surface and reveals these scratches; it may also cut down amount of stain the wood absorbs.

Catch on table top's underside snaps into striker on crow's nest when top is lowered to horizontal.

Dovetail sockets are cut with drill and small chisel. Leg dovetail serves as pattern for marking.

Dust particles are knocked off prior to waxing by smoothing varnish with pumice stone and water.

After removing the post from the lathe, locate the three dovetail sockets. Using the leg dovetails you've cut as a pattern, mark and cut the sockets. Bore the waste stock in the sockets with a 3/8″ drill and finish cleaning with a sharp chisel.

The crow's nest. Cut the 4″-by-4″ block from 7/8″ stock. Bore a 1″ hole in the center and cut the mortise square. Drill the 3/8″ pin holes for

the dowels and round the edge. Now, using the mortise, mark the round tenon on the post and cut it square. Slot the tenon and cut the wedge so that it fits snugly.

Finally, cut the cleats and drill all holes. Since bird's-eye is an especially tough hardwood, drill the right-size body and pilot holes. (Rubbing a little soap or wax on the threads makes turning in the screws easier.)

Assembly. Make a trial assembly without glue to check the table for plumb and level. With the table on a level surface, check the post with a framing square and the top (in the horizontal position) with a level.

The brass tilt-table catch can be fitted and installed at this time. The one used here is number 48 from Horton Brasses, Box 95, Brooks Hill Rd., Cromwell, Conn. 06416.

Do the gluing in two steps. First, glue the dowels in their mating holes in the crow's nest. Secure one cleat to the top, position the crow's nest, and fasten the second cleat. (Note: Dowels are not glued to the cleats). The legs can be glued to the post at this time. Later, glue the crow's nest to the post, fit the mortise-and-tenon, apply glue, and drive the wedge in. When dry, cut the wedge flush with the tenon.

The table shown was stained with Minwax Ipswich Pine, then rubbed with linseed oil. Since it was to be used occasionally to serve snacks, final finish was a coat of polyurethane varnish for durability. If you follow the same procedure, allow the oil (which is used generously) to dry for at least 72 hours before applying the varnish. After two or three weeks of curing, rub the surface to a soft luster with Butcher's wax.

SMART FISH BOWL UNDER THE TABLE

BY JACKSON HAND

A chairside table with a plastic top that's really spillproof . . . An aquarium that can never leak . . . A lamp designed to spotlight the aquarium and provide the soft illumination every room needs . . .

Here's a colorful and intriguing lamp table that's all of these. And it's easy to make, despite its unique design. Interesting, too, because the materials you use aren't the same old workshop humdrum:

• A 20″ hemisphere bowl made of clear-acrylic plastic, ideal for a fish tank because its parabolic shape reflects and seems to multiply the number of specimens swimming about. And another 12″ plastic bowl for the lampshade. (Both available by mail from the Edmund Scientific Co., Barrington, N.J. 08007.)

• A 24″ disk of clear ¾″ Plexiglas, now sold by the sheet at hardware, lumber, and other specialty outlets.

• Leather strapping that forms the crisscross sling supporting the hemispheric tank snugly and securely.

• A length of ⅜″ flexible chromium-plated plumber's tubing. Under the gleaming chrome, it's brass or copper—easy to bend into the graceful arc that conceals the lamp cord and supports the lamp.

• Rugged, strong-grained oak stair tread—more than an inch thick—to give the transparent table a solid look.

Lamp table is alive with fish in sleek aquarium hung in leather sling on oak supports—all illuminated by a lamp on gleaming chrome stem. You buy plastic bowls for aquarium and lampshade, build simple half-lapped frame as shown in sketch, next page. Perforated funnel in gravel gives filtration and aeration.

The drawings show dimensions and assembly of the oak base, with details of drilling and routing operations that provide runs for the lamp cord and the small plastic tube that feeds the aerator. It all goes together quickly and easily if you do it this way:

1) Cut out the basic pieces: two of them 3½″ by 22½″; four of them 3½″ by 15″. Leave the taper cuts until last so you work as long as possible with easy-to-handle, on-the-square pieces.

2) Cut the half-laps at the centers of the two crosspieces. With the two interlapped, drill a ⅜″ hole through both members. This will accept the 3″ length of threaded tube that acts as a bolt to hold the parts together, and as a tube through which the air hose goes.

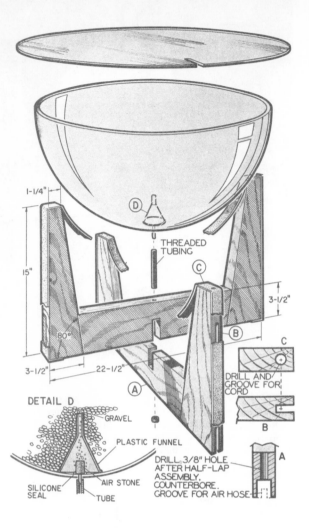

1-1/4"

15"

D

THREADED
TUBING

C

3-1/2"

80°

B

C

3-1/2"

22-1/2"

A

DRILL AND
GROOVE FOR
CORD

B

DETAIL D

GRAVEL

PLASTIC FUNNEL

SILICONE
SEAL

AIR STONE

TUBE

DRILL 3/8" HOLE
AFTER HALF-LAP
ASSEMBLY.
COUNTERBORE.
GROOVE FOR AIR HOSE.

A

in from the outside (or routed) edge of the upright. It should meet the top of the groove, forming a continuous passageway from top to bottom. This hole is a socket for the lamp stem.

Half-lapping the uprights. Cut these half-laps first—a simple on-the-square operation. Set your saw to cut exactly halfway through the stock. Make the shoulder cut first—very carefully. Then make a series of cuts close together—even overlapping, until you reach the end. Clean up the cut with a chisel.

Then make the taper rips on the four uprights. The drawing shows the taper as 80 degrees, as close as it will measure on a home-shop miter gauge or protractor.

When you make the angled half-lap cuts on the crosspieces, however, you may be wise to lay the upright over the other piece, holding it perfectly square on the outside, and scribe the angle carefully, *as it actually exists.* Then error will match error, if any, and you'll get a neater joint. Fasten uprights to crosspieces with a plastic resin glue. Pair up the grooved upright (B) with the grooved end of the crosspiece (A).

(Why not put all the taper on the uprights *above* the crosspieces, making the half-laps

Underside of cross-lap base has counterbored hole to pass threaded tube and seat nut on end (flange at right screws on top, locking units together). Groove takes air tube to edge.

Counterbore a ³⁄₄" hole about ³⁄₄" deep in the lower crosspiece, to recess the nut and allow the air hose to make its turn to travel to the outer edge.

3) Rout a groove not over ¹⁄₄" wide and about ¹⁄₂" deep in the bottom edge of the lower crosspiece from the counterbored hole out to the edge to recess the air hose.

4) Run a groove from the bottom of one upright to 4" from the top, while your routing equipment is set up. This groove will carry the light cord.

5) Finally, drill a ³⁄₈" hole 4" deep straight into the end of this upright. It must be ³⁄₈"

square on both members? Go ahead—but it will detract somewhat from the design of the piece.)

When the glue at the four joints has set, put the two halves of the base together, fastening them with the threaded-tube "bolt." You'll find the hardware for this at any electrical shop or well-stocked hardware store.

Put the finish on the framework now so it can dry while you work on the rest of the project. Ideal for oak is a penetrating wood finish such as Deep Finish Firzite, Dura SEal floor finish, or DuPont penetrating wood finish. Give the wood two coats. But keep the finish off the outside edges, where the leather will be glued.

Preparing the lamp. An ordinary electric light socket will fit over the end of the $\frac{3}{8}''$ plumber's tubing used for the lamp stem. Connect lamp cord to socket, then run the cord through the tube. With pressure and a twisting motion, force on the socket, then tighten the setscrew.

Bend the upper 12″ of the tube into a half-circle with 6″ radius. An easy way to do this: Cut out a bending jig with a saber or band saw. (The length of tube determines height of light above the table; a 36″-to-48″ length is about right.)

Drill a $\frac{3}{8}''$ hole through the *exact* center of the 12″ hemispheric reflector. Spray the inside with two coats of white Krylon. Then spray on two coats of any dark color for opaqueness. Finish with another coat of white for reflectiveness. Don't get paint on the outside of the plastic. When the last coat is dry, slip the cord and the bent tube through the hole in the shade, but don't put a plug on the end of the wire—yet.

The leather slings. You need two leather straps about 6′ long for the slings. If you can find a fairly decent leather-working shop, the dealer can cut the straps the exact width you want: as wide as the uprights are thick. Otherwise, buy the closest width possible and trim later.

Glue leather slings to edge of uprights, clamping with strip of wood as here. Note 1″ or so bottom turn-under. Anchor only one end of straps to permit adjustment after trial with bowl.

Straps can be trimmed flush after glue sets—if you can't buy them in width to match thickness of wood. Be sure blade is very sharp, and hold plane at angle to avoid marring finish.

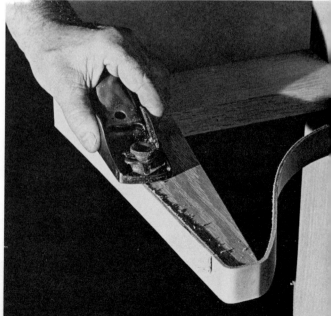

Airstone activates filtering current in water. Shank goes through hole drilled in exact bottom of bowl. Leakproof it with fillet of silicone all around stone.

Slot the back edge of the disk to fit around the light stem (above). Cope it, rasp, and sand smooth.

Plexiglas-disk top can be removed for aquarium maintenance (above). It's locked in position by three little Plexiglas cleats fastened to the underside with a special solvent cement (below) that forms a chemically welded transparent bond. Locate them so they'll be equally spaced around the bowl rim.

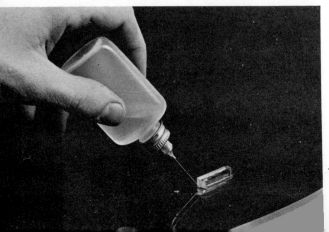

Glue *one* end of each strap to the outer edge of an upright, over the top, and under the bottom, as shown. When the glue has set, draw up the free ends of the straps, put the big plastic bowl in position temporarily, and adjust the slings for proper tension. They should hold the bowl perhaps 2″ up off the frame; they'll stretch a bit with the weight of the water-filled aquarium.

Glue the two free ends, then open up the hole through that special upright by boring through the leather at top and bottom. Punch holes through the slings where they cross — precisely at the bottom — for the air tube.

Making the tabletop. Cut the Plexiglas into its circular shape and make the slot for the light stem before you peel off the paper. For a smooth edge to gain the bright rim of lighting that Plexiglas can produce, treat it like wood: Use a rasp to remove saw marks, then work the edge with progressively finer sandpaper. Finish with No. 400 grit waterproof paper.

From bowl to aquarium. All you need for a healthy marine environment in the bowl is an air compressor, some flexible tubing, an "airstone," and enough gravel to fill a two-pound coffee can, available at pet shops or tropical fish stores. Also get a 3″ plastic funnel. All these go together at the bottom of the tank.

Drill a hole to accept the shank of the airstone. Seal the stone in place by running silicone caulk around it. Lay the tube to exit via the groove routed in the crosspiece. Now punch or drill several holes in the funnel, place it over the airstone, and pour in the gravel.

The water in the bowl goes down through the gravel, into the funnel, then up again, forced by the action of the bubbles rising in the inverted funnel. The bubbles pass through the stem with a piston-like action. This circulation of water takes advantage of the gravel's filtering effect. Meanwhile, the continuing flow of bubbles keeps the water heavily oxygenated. (The pump runs continuously.)

Installing the lamp. Slip the lamp socket and lampshade over the flexible tube, feed the lamp cord down its hole in the upright and out at bottom. The last 4″ of the tube slips into that hole you drilled in the top of the upright. Put a plug on the end of the wire and light up.

Now—after all this—you say you're no Aquarius and fish turn you off? Okay. Think what a great addition to the room you'd have if you left out all the aquatic paraphernalia and planted the clear-plastic bowl as a terrarium.

ADJUSTABLE BOOK RACK FOR DESK

BY SERGEY KOREN

Keeping books neatly organized on your desk may seem like a trivial problem. If you own the obvious answers, a book rack or bookends, you know their downfalls. Book racks are rigid, and unless they're completely filled, you suffer the consequences. Bookends are too flexible, and sometimes end up toppling to the floor.

This adjustable book rack, however, takes the good points from both. Glued and nailed together, the sides make the container rigid enough for the largest of books. And the movable end-support allows you to adjust the rack to fit the number of books you wish. A wingnut tightened against the front holds the movable end solidly in place.

You might stain pine to match your furniture. You could also make the book rack of solid walnut and use a natural finish.

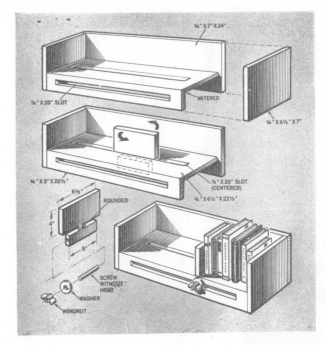

165

MODERN VANITY FOR A SPARE CORNER

It's a rare home that can't use another bathroom. Here's one quick way out: Install *part* of a bathroom. You can set this modern washbasin into an easily built cabinet in just about any available corner—in the corner of a bedroom, for instance.

Being corner-mounted, the storage cabinet that hides the plumbing is economical of materials. You only have to build one side, a door, and the counter top.

Lavatory and dressing table take little space from a bedroom. Buy framed mirrors or design your own frames; choose wall lamps to suit your own taste.

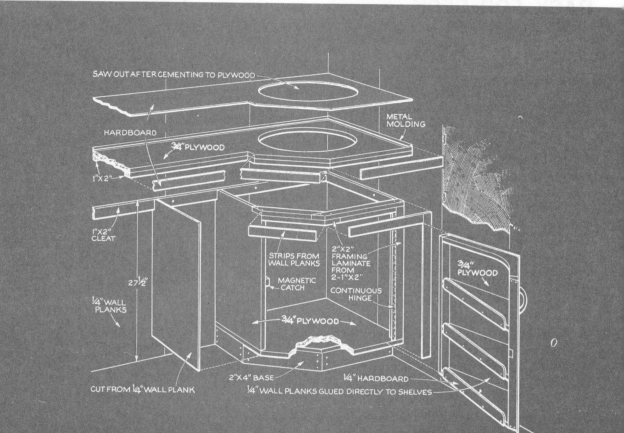

SAW OUT AFTER CEMENTING TO PLYWOOD

METAL MOLDING

HARDBOARD

¾" PLYWOOD

1"X2"

1"X2" CLEAT

27½"

¼" WALL PLANKS

STRIPS FROM WALL PLANKS

MAGNETIC CATCH

2"X2" FRAMING LAMINATE FROM 2-1"X2"

CONTINUOUS HINGE

¾" PLYWOOD

¾" PLYWOOD

CUT FROM ¼" WALL PLANK

2"X4" BASE

¼" HARDBOARD

¼" WALL PLANKS GLUED DIRECTLY TO SHELVES

A two-by-four 6' long, a 4'-by-8' sheet of ¾" waterproof fir plywood, and about 36' of one-by-two pine are basic materials. The original cabinet was covered with the same ¼" Marlite wall planks used on the walls. A sheet of ⅛" Marlite in a black and gold pattern topped off the dressing-table counter to give the luxurious look of marble.

Use waterproof glue to assemble the parts. The shelves are the supporting members for the door, so make sure they all have the same angle. Otherwise they'll twist the door out of shape. Use strips of planking to make the lips on the front of the shelves, and to cover the cabinet base.

Paint the inside of the cabinet, the front edge of the cabinet floor, and the shelves to match the outside.

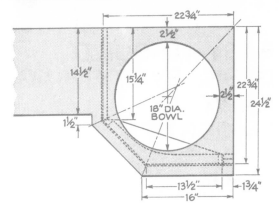

NO-CLUTTER SHOE RACK

BY W. P. BROTHERS

I ended shoe-cluttered closet floors in our house with a simple rack that I made in about an hour. I used four ¾" dowels 4' long and three pieces of ¾" plywood cut and drilled as shown in the drawing. To line up the holes, I clamped the pieces together for drilling. The dowels were glued in place. I put furniture glides on the bottom edges of the plywood so the rack would slide easier.

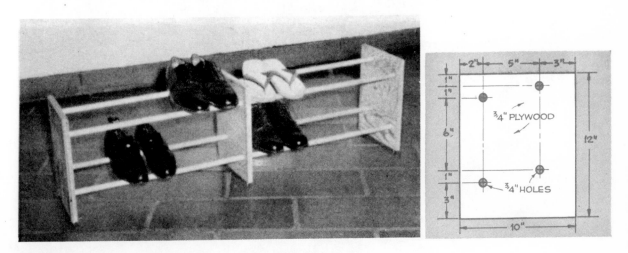

EASY-TO-BUILD DESK: EVERYTHING AT YOUR FINGERTIPS

BY JIM ABBOTT

A good desk is hard to find. Locate one and it's hard to pay for. After a lot of searching and pricing, I decided to build my own. It's conventional in appearance, but conceals features that keep things at your fingertips in minimum space.

There's a pullout for a typewriter. Below

that, nestled into the side of a large drawer, is a shallow drawer for index cards. Other drawers are sized to take file folders.

This desk is not a project to be tackled only by master craftsmen. I deliberately designed this piece of furniture with the average home-shop worker in mind. There are no fancy cuts or tricky joints, no expensive woods to match. The basic material is stock plywood, and total material costs ran me less than $50.

Round up your materials. The list can serve as a guide, but you may want to use different woods and finishes. Note that I've confined the width to 48″. This will enable you to make all the parts from standard 4-by-8 plywood sheets and, at the same time, create a water-fall effect without piecing.

An attractively grained plywood such as birch or walnut can be used for the top, front, and sides. Less expensive fir may then be used for the other pieces if you want to keep the price down.

Desk has typewriter pullout, file folder drawers, and side-of-drawer index-card storage (directly below typewriter) to put everything you need within easy reach.

Cut out all the parts first. Follow the dimensions carefully. Especially critical is the top. Unless these rabbets are accurately cut the edges will not be a good match. In fact, if you can remove all but $1/16''$ of the top veneer in making these rabbets, all the better. But, be careful! That thin veneer is susceptible to splintering, both during and after the cutting. For this reason, I've allowed for a full $1/8''$ in the drawing. If you do decide on a $1/16''$ lip, be sure to correct the other sizes.

The basic plywood cuts may be made with a portable power saw on a cutting table, but once the sheets have been reduced to manageable size, switch to a table saw to ensure the utmost in accuracy.

The assembly. Begin from the bottom up, starting with the pedestal bases and fastening the bottom boards to these. Attach the side pieces next (drawer runners previously placed), using white glue at all joints and clinching with finishing nails, driven from the bottom up to avoid marring the sides.

Complete the "boxes" by attaching the drawer-runner fronts and backs, then the two longer cleats that will bring the pedestals into position for the top and center drawer parts.

Test-fit the top and do any necessary sanding before applying glue to the top edges of the base. Secure the top with $1¼''$-#8 screws driven upward through the cleats as shown. Next, apply the faceboard, using glue and clamps to ensure a neat, tight fit along the front edge.

Since the front parts of the base will be concealed by drawer fronts, it is not really necessary to cover the edges of the wood. Just fill in the flaws and holes with putty, sand smooth, and finish with the desired stain. However, you may want to glue veneer tape to these edges. The stuff comes in a variety of woods, in eight-foot rolls, and is easily applied with glue.

Drawer construction. This is largely a matter of preference. I used a simple, box-like as-

sembly. Build the boxes as shown, then attach the drawer fronts with glue and brads. Remember that the "box" slides more easily when weight rests on the two side pieces rather than on the entire bottom, hence the grooved slots for the drawer bottoms.

The drawer just below the typewriter pull-out on most desks is generally a lost cause unless you want to move the machine and push in the support whenever access is desired. To circumvent this problem I decided to put the openings in the side of a drawer, in this case sized for $3''$-by-$5''$ index cards. It would be just as easy to install drawers or shelves for paper and envelopes, or storage space for a small portable.

The pullout. Assembly is not difficult. Fasten parts (C) to the inside of the left pedestal with $1¼''$-#8 flatheads, positioning them $1/2''$ back from the front edges. Insert parts (B) and fasten board (D) to the bottoms, making sure that the assembly will slide easily, but not loosely. Finally insert pre-assembled box (A) until it clears the front edge of (D). Fasten a stop cleat to this edge and attach the drawer front.

To vary the length of the slide, simply increase or reduce the width of (D). However, a width of less than $4''$ is not recommended since the typewriter's weight might be too much for it.

The back panel and brace. Install the back brace running the full length of desk. The back, $1/4''$ plywood, may cover the entire back or just the two pedestals and center-drawer

MATERIALS LIST
¾ x 4 x 8 birch plywood: 1 panel
½ x 4 x 8 fir plywood: 1 panel
¼ x 4 x 8 fir plywood: 1 panel
¾ x 2 x 5 fir plywood: 1 piece
1 x 6 clear pine: 24 feet
Drawer pulls: 7
1¼ #6 flathead screws: 12
1¼ #8 flathead screws: 50
Various brads, finishing nails, white glue, wood putty, oil stain, sandpaper, and urethane varnish

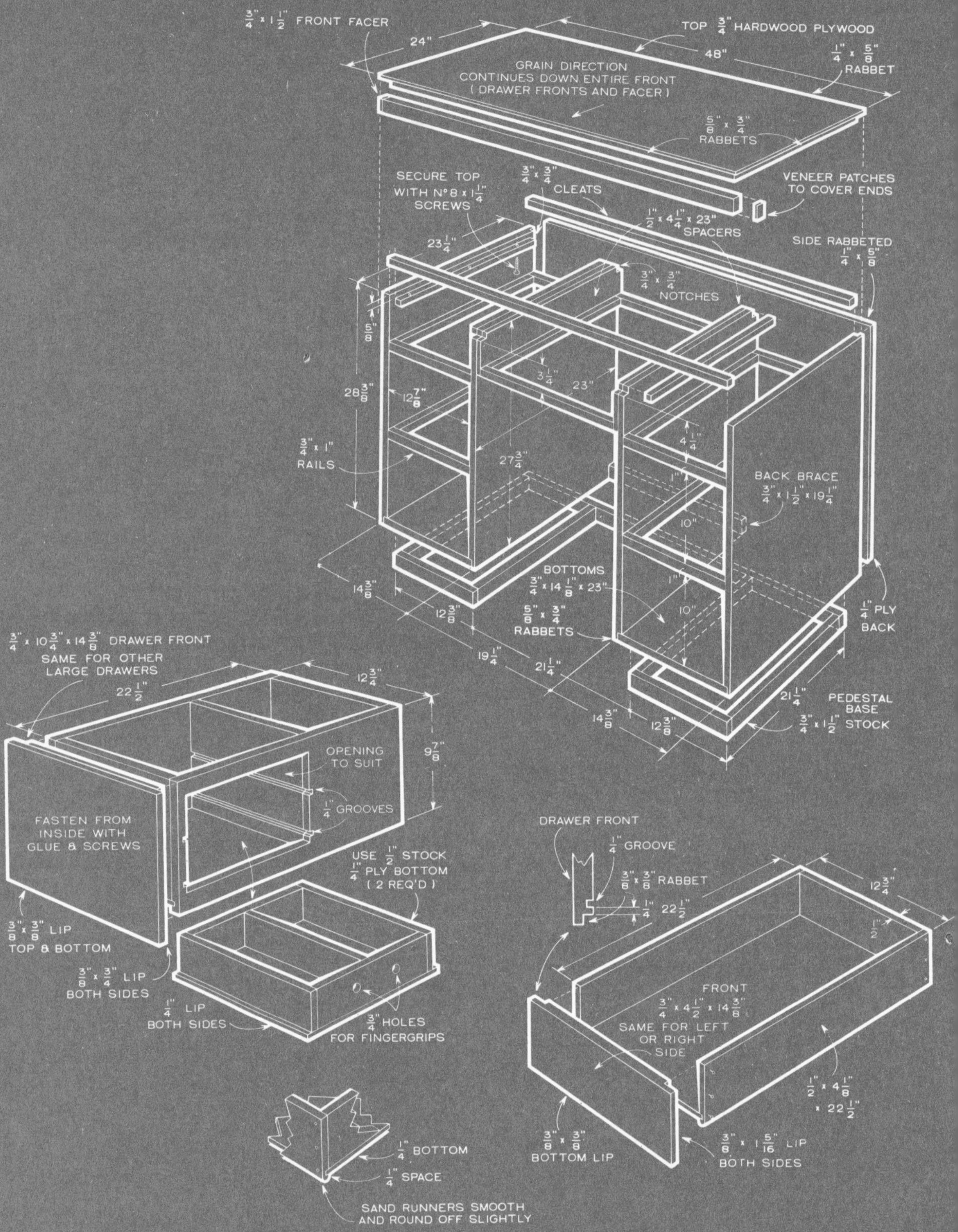

3/4" x 1 1/2" FRONT FACER
TOP 3/4" HARDWOOD PLYWOOD
24"
48"
GRAIN DIRECTION CONTINUES DOWN ENTIRE FRONT (DRAWER FRONTS AND FACER)
1/4" x 5/8" RABBET
5/8" x 3/4" RABBETS
SECURE TOP WITH N°8 x 1 1/4" SCREWS
3/4" x 3/4" CLEATS
VENEER PATCHES TO COVER ENDS
1/2" x 4 1/4" x 23" SPACERS
SIDE RABBETED 1/4" x 5/8"
23 1/4"
3/4" x 3/4" NOTCHES
5/8"
28 3/8"
12 7/8"
3 1/4"
23"
3/4" x 1" RAILS
27 3/4"
4 1/4"
BACK BRACE 3/4" x 1 1/2" x 19 1/4"
1"
10"
BOTTOMS 3/4" x 14 1/8" x 23"
14 3/8"
12 3/8"
5/8" x 3/4" RABBETS
1/4" PLY BACK
19 1/4"
21 1/4"
21 1/4"
PEDESTAL BASE 3/4" x 1 1/2" STOCK
14 3/8"
12 3/8"
3/4" x 10 3/4" x 14 3/8" DRAWER FRONT SAME FOR OTHER LARGE DRAWERS
22 1/2"
12 3/4"
9 7/8"
OPENING TO SUIT
1/4" GROOVES
FASTEN FROM INSIDE WITH GLUE & SCREWS
USE 1/2" STOCK 1/4" PLY BOTTOM (2 REQ'D)
3/8" x 3/8" LIP TOP & BOTTOM
3/8" x 3/4" LIP BOTH SIDES
1/4" LIP BOTH SIDES
3/4" HOLES FOR FINGERGRIPS
DRAWER FRONT
1/4" GROOVE
3/8" x 3/8" RABBET
1/4"
22 1/2"
12 3/4"
1/2"
FRONT 3/4" x 4 1/2" x 14 3/8" SAME FOR LEFT OR RIGHT SIDE
1/2" x 4 1/8" x 22 1/2"
3/8" x 3/8" BOTTOM LIP
3/8" x 1 5/16" LIP BOTH SIDES
1/4" BOTTOM
1/4" SPACE
SAND RUNNERS SMOOTH AND ROUND OFF SLIGHTLY

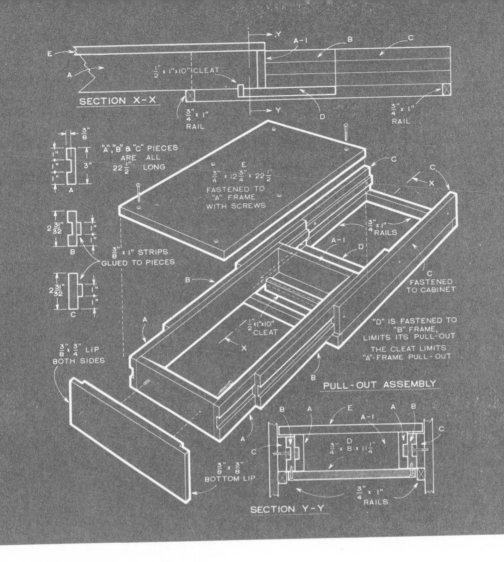

SECTION X-X

E
A
Y
A-1
B
C
½" x 1" x 10" CLEAT
¾" x 1" RAIL
¾" x 1" RAIL
Y
D

⅜"
1"
1"
1"
3"
A

2 31/32"
1"
B

2 31/32"
1"
C

"A", "B" & "C" PIECES ARE ALL 22½" LONG

⅜" x 1" STRIPS GLUED TO PIECES

⅜" x ¾" LIP BOTH SIDES

⅜" x ¾" BOTTOM LIP

E
¾" x 12¾" x 22½"
FASTENED TO "A" FRAME WITH SCREWS

C
C
X
A-1
D
¾" x 1" RAILS

C FASTENED TO CABINET

B

½" x 1" x 10" CLEAT
X

A

B

A

"D" IS FASTENED TO "B" FRAME, LIMITS ITS PULL-OUT
THE CLEAT LIMITS "A"-FRAME PULL-OUT

PULL-OUT ASSEMBLY

B   A   E   A   B
A-1
D   ¾" x 8 x 11¼"
C
Y
¾" x 1" RAILS

SECTION Y-Y

To build desk, make two box-like pedestals, joining them with cleats. Top goes on with screws driven up through the cleats.

Drawer below typewriter pullout is inaccessible when pullout is in use, so author installed card storage in side of drawer.

area. In either case, a back is recommended since it provides added structural strength.

If the back of your desk will be visible, the same type of plywood as used in the top is suggested. When fastening this plywood, start at the top and attach with glue and brads, then square up the assembly and fasten similarly along the sides and bottom. Countersink and wood-putty the holes.

The final step is the finishing—one of the most important, but tedious, steps in cabinetry. Begin by filling all holes and flaws with a good grade of wood putty. Sand smooth, but don't overdo it, keeping in mind that the hardwood veneer on most plywoods is quite thin.

Remove all dust from the surfaces before you apply the desired stain. I generally use a good oil-base stain, wiped on with a cloth. Once the stain has set, follow up with several coats of urethane varnish, sanding lightly between coats with a number-320 paper. Knock the gloss off the final coat with fine steel wool, and finish up with paste wax for a deep, low-luster glow.

A DROP-LEAF TABLE WITH A NEW TWIST

BY J. F. BOGASH

A drop-leaf dining table is always practical because of the space it saves while serving as a small table between meals.

You'll have to be careful to locate and mount the 6″ or 7″ ball-bearing swivel and rotation stops exactly as indicated, but otherwise the table is easy to make. It's best to use veneer hardwood for the leaves, but you can glue up solid wood if you wish.

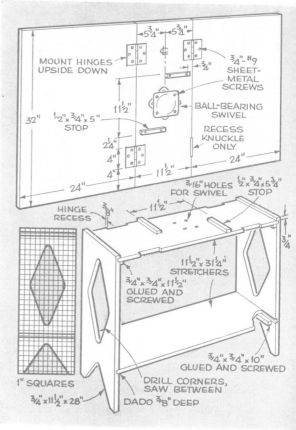

The whole top turns on a ballbearing swivel, and the two hinged leaves drop to make a compact table between meals. Stops allow top to turn correct amount.

172

KNOCKDOWN DESK IS A KNOCKOUT

DESIGNED BY LESTER WALKER
BUILT BY ROSARIO CAPOTOSTO

Snug it into a corner as a telephone table, correspondence desk, or record-keeping center. Or build one for the student in the family and let him take it along to college. Since it's slot-assembled (no glue or fasteners), it can easily be knocked down for moving or temporary storage. Yet a dozen turnbuttons keep it sturdy while it's in use. Best of all: It's cleverly designed for layout on a single sheet of plywood, as shown in the plan above right —with virtually no waste. And the only trick in its construction is cutting those interior slots in the two sides.

There are 14 such slots to be cut with square-cornered precision. The job might give a professional cabinetmaker pause, yet with the jig shown here—plus a saber saw with the blade mounted backwards—the slots are a cinch.

How would you go about it? A router is out, because it would leave rounded corners. How about boring two square holes at each end with a mortising bit, then carefully cutting out the waste in between? Just one problem: We want to use MDO (medium-density-overlay) plywood, because the treated surface resists splintering and takes paint well—but ½″ MDO is actually *over* ½″ in thickness. You can't adjust a mortising bit to cut oversize.

So the answer is a jig with a cutout to guide the base of a saber saw. You get the square

You cut it from a sheet of half-inch plywood. Tab-and-slot assembly lets you take it apart.

ends on the slots by moving the front of the base back and forth against the end of the jig's cutout. And since we're cutting enclosed slots, you might assume it's a simple matter of sawing out the waste in one direction from the entry hole, then turning the saw around and continuing on toward the other end. But no, it's not all that simple.

The problem: The base of a saber saw isn't centered in respect to the line of cut. At best, it's centered over one edge of the blade. And the blade has thickness. So when the base is turned 180 degrees to cut in the opposite direction, the jig is useless because the cut will be offset.

173

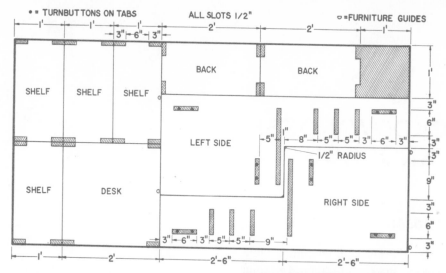

Solution? First make all required cuts in the normal saw direction. Then take out the blade and insert it backward, so the teeth point to the rear. Now just push the saw in the opposite direction to clean out the rest of each slot.

Make the jig in two parts. First cut an open-ended rectangle in a piece of hardboard (to match the dimensions of your saw); then butt up with a back piece. Just tape the two together. Four corner nails hold the jig securely in place on the work. It's easy to fill the nail holes before you paint the finished pieces. If you use a plywood blade, you shouldn't have to do much edge-sanding before assembly.

Turnbuttons are practical means of locking key parts together—and they add a decorative touch. Standard sizes are 1½" and 1¾"; if you find hub section a bit too wide to pass through notches, grind a flat on each side before screwing them onto the ends of the bottom-shelf and two back panels. Their locations can be seen in photos and on layout plan at top of page.

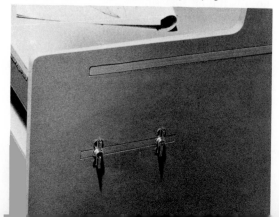

Cutting the slots is tricky

1 When laying out the pieces, consider the thickness of the saw kerf as waste. You can't get full 1' multiples out of a 4'-wide plywood panel, of course.

2 Drill an entry hole or saber-saw blade near one end of each slot. Use bit of a diameter just a little smaller than that of slot width.

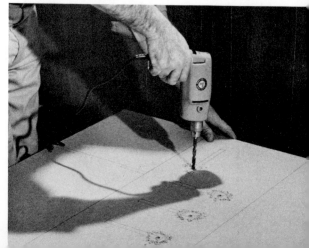

3 Align hardboard jig with slot layout. For top accuracy with speed, use a strip of cardboard for spacing template as shown.

4 Nail jig firmly to the plywood. Note masking-tape shim along one edge, added to obtain final accuracy when jig was cut.

5 Make initial cuts in conventional forward direction from entry hole along both layout lines. Make additional cuts in waste between, then square end.

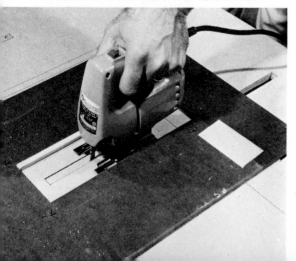

6 Slot is nearly complete when all forward cuts are made. You can work all slots this far before turning blade, or complete each separately.

7 Reverse blade to complete unfinished end of slots. On most saws, the blade is easy to switch, so it could be done for each slot.

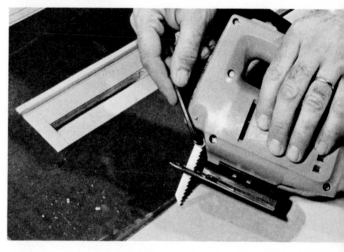

8 Push saw backward, repeating outline and waste-removal cuts. Square end of cut by moving base back and forth until all wood is removed.

Separate the side members with one cut, keeping tight radius around corners.

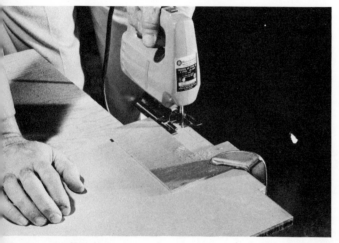

Notching out shelf ends to make tabs is best done with an L-shape jig like this.

All these pieces are cut from a single plywood sheet. If done with care, trial fit (before finishing) should go smoothly. Screw turnbuttons on last.

SLAW-BOARD TABLE

BY JACK PAYNE

An old cabbage shredder inspired this coffee table. In its original use the slaw board usually had no legs; a cabbage was placed in the sliding frame and passed back and forth over the knives, shredding it into slaw. A barrel under the knives would catch the vegetable shreds. We eliminated the barrel and added turned legs that are in the period style — and the result is a handsome table.

The board is made from a solid piece of $5/4''$ pine. After cutting in the leg notches, round off the end to suit your eye. The opening for the knives is made at a 30-degree angle across the board to the dimensions shown. Add the $1/4''$ strip to the edge of the cutout for the ends of the blades to rest on. A piece of oak, set in as a crosspiece, holds up the back of the front knife. The knives are not fastened, but held in place by the rails.

Lay out and cut the rectangular holes for the pegs; when making the two side rails, be sure that the peg holes line up with the holes in the board. The box is made of $5/4''$ pine and dovetailed at each corner. If you prefer, corners can be rabbeted. The guides are $3/4''$ and added to the box. Solid oak is used for the

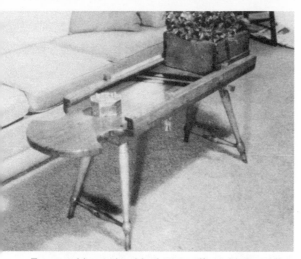

Turn a cabbage shredder into a coffee table by adding turned legs. The charm of an Early American device, plus its useful function as a table, add up to a pleasing project that will be a prime conversation piece.

pegs and lockpins; these are fitted individually to each hole. Position and attach the legs as shown—if you use ready-turned legs, you can substitute heavy dowel for the turned spindle. Make the knives of steel. Since you're probably not going to shred cabbage in the living room, for safety's sake, keep them dull.

Choice of finishing technique is up to you. The table shown was treated with a clear finish that brought out the beauty of the oak. Remember, there's no bottom on the box. Make a receptacle out of copper that will fit snugly inside the frame and you have an attractive showcase for plantings—or for storing ice cubes for a short time. Make sure that the joints are well soldered; test for watertightness before you drop the liner into the box. Or, you might locate a waterproof plastic container that will fit nicely inside the box.

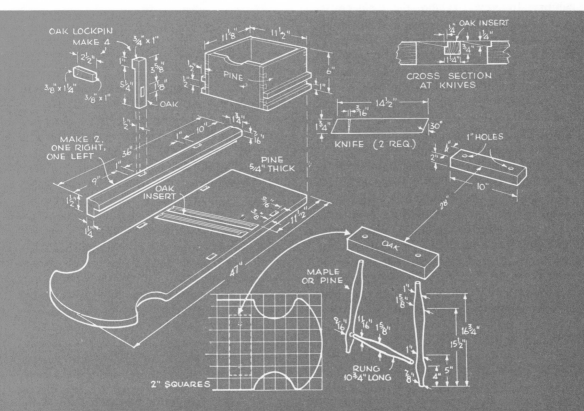

SAILMAKER'S BENCH

This double-duty bench will serve as a coffee table or seat. Stick to the job and you can build and finish one of these in a weekend.

This version of a sailmaker's bench is a variation of those in wide use during the 18th century. In New England, the local craftsmen stitched sails while seated comfortably on benches such as this. The construction details are simpler than you would expect in a bench of this type. For example, note the mortise-and-tenon detail in the photograph. As you read on you will discover that pictures can indeed lie; a clever woodworker can employ tricks and skills that simplify the task, yet do not sacrifice authenticity.

Start the project by cutting the lumber to rough dimension (cut slightly oversize) for the seat, legs, and rails. Seat and rails are $5/4''$ pine; all other wood is $3/4''$ pine. Plane edges that are to be joined to insure that they are square. Glue, dowel, and clamp the pieces that will be the seat and legs. Corrugated nails can be substituted for the dowels. However, on the legs where they will show, set them deep with a nail set so that on the finished product they will give the illusion of being distress marks. While these parts are drying you can go to work cutting and shaping the rails. The two grooves are made in the seat as shown to receive the rails. The cleats are cut from one-by-

three stock, grooved and attached to the legs. Mark the bench seat for the four false mortises. Drill starting holes and complete the cutout with a saber or keyhole saw.

Professional craftsmen sand the parts before assembly. By using this method you will avoid swirls that tend to occur in corners as a result of post-assembly sanding. It will also shorten the time it takes to do the job. After sanding, you're ready to put the bench together.

The rails are fastened with 6d common nails; remaining joinery is accomplished with screws as indicated. Use glue on all joints. When attaching the rails with the 6d nails, set the heads deep and roughen the holes slightly. Glue and insert the false tenons. For the wedges, use any shop scrap. A different species of wood—walnut, for example—offers an interesting contrast. In the bench shown, cedar shingles were at hand and proved to be a good choice.

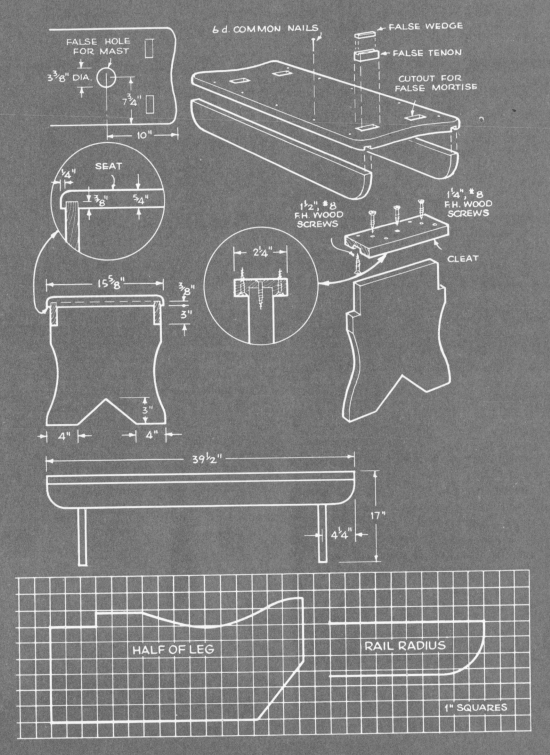

FALSE HOLE FOR MAST

$3\frac{3}{8}$" DIA.

$7\frac{3}{4}$"

10"

6 d. COMMON NAILS

FALSE WEDGE

FALSE TENON

CUTOUT FOR FALSE MORTISE

SEAT

$\frac{1}{4}$"

$\frac{3}{8}$"

$\frac{3}{4}$"

$1\frac{1}{2}$", #8 F.H. WOOD SCREWS

$1\frac{1}{4}$", #8 F.H. WOOD SCREWS

CLEAT

$15\frac{5}{8}$"

$\frac{3}{8}$"

3"

$2\frac{1}{4}$"

3"

4"

4"

$39\frac{1}{2}$"

17"

$4\frac{1}{4}$"

HALF OF LEG

RAIL RADIUS

1" SQUARES

179

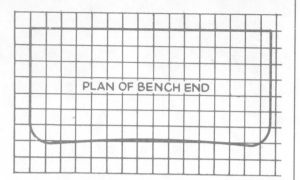

PLAN OF BENCH END

Mortise and tenon? No, just a clever carpenter's trick. The drawing (on page 179) shows you how to achieve this effect—quickly and simply.

The authentic sailmaker's bench had a hole on the surface that accommodated a mast to which the sails were attached. Eliminate this detail if you intend to use the piece as a sitdown bench. However, if it is to be used as a coffee table the hole will make an excellent receptacle for a planter. If your wife has a favorite vase or jug, the hole can be custom-cut to receive it. The bench in the photo was finished by applying knotty-pine oil stain, followed by two coats of semigloss varnish. After a week of drying it can be waxed and buffed to give the bench the appearance of being hand-rubbed.

BUFFET WITH WOVEN PANELS

BY JERROLD R. BEALL

The buffet was a standard fixture in dining rooms 30 years ago. Today's popular "dinette sets" for smaller dining areas usually include only a hutch-type cabinet with the table and chairs. And that creates a problem in most homes. There never seems to be enough room for storing linens, cutlery, and other dining accessories. Building this chest not only solves that storage problem, but adds a new technique to your woodworking skills as well.

The chest itself is simply constructed—the sides and doors are actually four identical frames. You can use a molding head and cutters on your table saw to make the lattice. If your shop lacks these accessories, this project alone could justify buying a set. Or you can have the dadoes cut at your lumberyard for a slight charge.

Building the cabinet. If you can't get wide enough stock for the top, base, and shelves, edge-glue narrow stock to the required width. Note that the top and base are exactly the same size. If you eliminate the shaped edges, cut both pieces 1" shorter in length and 1/2" less in width than the dimensions on the blueprint. After shaping and sanding, set the pieces aside.

Cut the stiles and rails for all four frames. Before assembling them, rip the grooves on

Cut the lattice stock to 10″ by 28′. Using a try square, measure and mark off 10 increments spaced 2¼″ apart along the edge of the board. Install the molding cutter (see sketch) in the head and mount it on the saw to cut to a depth of ⁵⁄₁₆″. Dado the 10 cuts across the board using the miter gauge and a work holddown. Flop the workpiece and make another 10 passes, each cut exactly opposite its mate on the first side.

Next, mount a hollow-ground planer blade on the bench saw and set the rip fence ¹⁄₁₆″ from the blade. Rip off 32 strips—enough to do the four panels.

To find the exact length of the 16 vertical strips, fit one into the bottom groove on a panel and trim the other end until it can be snugly inserted into the top groove. When

Top and base are shaped with molding cutters. Numbers shown are for Sears cutters.

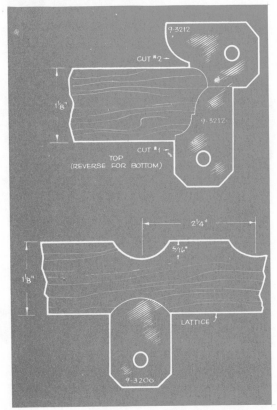

the inside edges to accept the lattice. Since the grooves must be ¹⁄₁₆″ wide, use a planer blade (with no set on the teeth) to cut them. The frames shown were butt-joined with dowels, but mortise-and-tenon, half-lap, or mitered joinery could be used. The shaped inside edge is made with a bead cutter (see sketch) in the router after the frames have been assembled.

The lattice. Select an absolutely flat piece of ⁵⁄₄″ stock (actual size 1⅛″) for the lattice. Even a slight warp will show up in the finished work. Twisted stock will cause the dadoes to vary in depth, making a neat weaving job just about impossible.

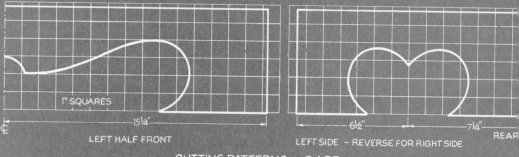

1" SQUARES

15¼"

LEFT HALF FRONT

6½"

7¼"

LEFT SIDE - REVERSE FOR RIGHT SIDE

REAR

CUTTING PATTERNS - BASE

MATERIALS LIST

PINE (clear or knotty)

1 pc. 1" x 16" x 6' (top, base)
1 pc. 1" x 14" x 5' (shelves)
1 pc. 1" x 6" x 5' (legs)
3 pcs. 1" x 3" x 8' (stiles, rails)
1 pc. 1" x 4" x 2' (shelf knee supports)

CLEAR PINE

1 pc. 1¼" x 12" x 30" (lattice strips)

PLYWOOD

1 pc. ¼" x 22" x 28" (back)

HARDWARE

2 prs. V658-4A hinges ⎫
2 knobs V274-4A ⎬ National Lock
2 backplates V6331-4A ⎭
2 magnetic catches

MISC.

Glue, ⅜" dowels, sandpaper, ¾" #8
f.h. screws, antiquing kit

NOTE –
BLIND DOWEL AND GLUE ALL JOINTS

14"

14"

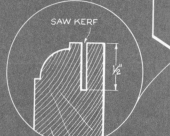

SAW KERF

½"

3/4" x 2½"

DOORS

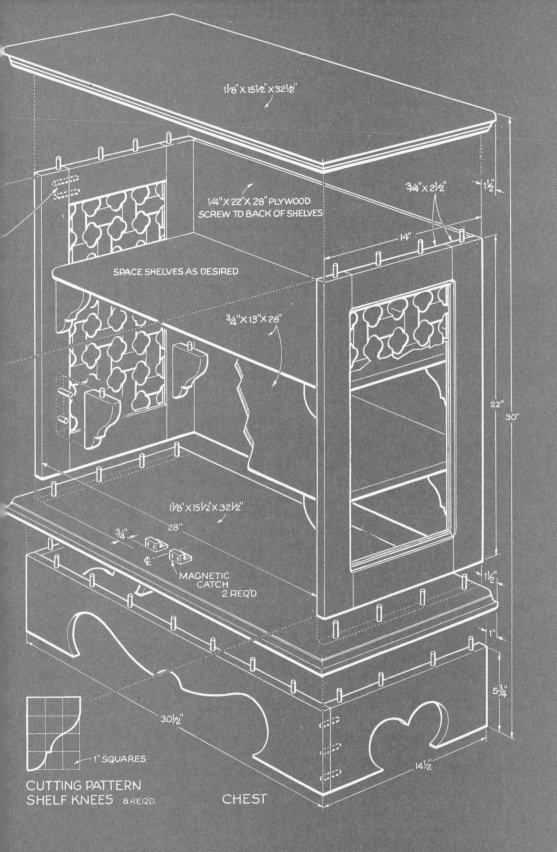

1⅛" X 15½" X 32½"

1½"

¾" X 2½"

¼" X 22" X 28" PLYWOOD
SCREW TO BACK OF SHELVES

14"

SPACE SHELVES AS DESIRED

¾" X 13" X 28"

22"

30"

1⅛" X 15½" X 32½"

28"

¾"

₵

MAGNETIC
CATCH
2 REQ'D.

1½"

1"

5¾"

30½"

14½"

1" SQUARES

CUTTING PATTERN
SHELF KNEES 8 REQ'D.

CHEST

Dadoes are cut on both sides of 5/4" stock, using a miter gauge and work hold-down.

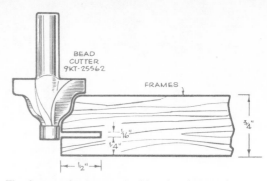

The frame edges are cut with a bead cutter in router after frame assembly.

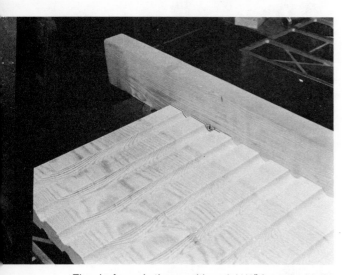

The rip fence is then positioned 1/16" from the blade (above) and 32 strips are ripped. First nine strips off the production line (below) illustrate why clear, knot-free stock must be used to make the lattice.

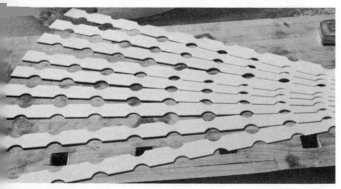

you're satisfied with the fit, trim 15 more strips to the same length. Horizontally, you will need 32 strips. Using the same method for sizing, you'll get two strips from each of the remaining 16 strips.

The weaving operation is simple. A standard over-and-under basket weave is used and each strip is aligned as it is placed. Glue is unnecessary; friction of the strips against each other holds them firmly in place.

Assembling the buffet. The coped legs are attached to the base first, the end panels and top added, and the shelves installed on their fancy knee supports. Finally, the 1/4" plywood back is glued and screwed to the shelves. Blind dowel joinery was used throughout (except for the back). But if you are going to paint your buffet, well-set nails could be used for all assembly and the holes filled and sanded.

Finishing. Since accent color was wanted in the room in which the buffet shown would stand, it was finished with an antiquing kit. If your plans call for a natural finish to match existing dining-room furniture, stain and finish the lattice strips before the weaving operation. It's easier to do in reverse order and goes a lot faster. If color accent is desired with a stained cabinet, tack material, such as burlap, inside the lattice.

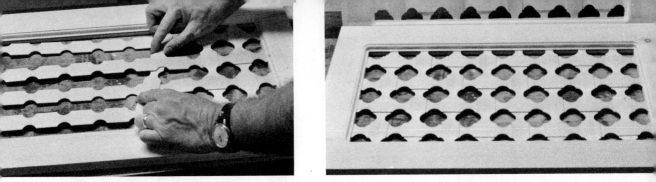

Simple over-and-under basket weave is used to form geometric shapes with a Mediterranean theme. Strips are forced into saw kerf; tension holds them there. Each panel uses four full strips vertically, eight half-strips horizontally. If buffet is to be left natural, stain and finish strips before weaving.

LUGGAGE RACK FOLDS COMPACTLY FOR STORAGE

BY RALPH TREVES

A folding luggage rack is a perfect gift, and it's easy to make, too. You can get an attractive natural finish on almost any wood with a straight grain, but hardwood such as maple is best.

You'll need 16' of $1^5/_{16}$"-by-$1^5/_{16}$" wood. If you buy milled hardwood, the $1^1/_4$" thickness will be fine. You also need three yards of plastic or canvas webbing.

All joints are held by $^1/_2$" dowels. First, drill $^1/_2$" holes through the four legs exactly at midpoint for the pivots. Use no glue on the pivot dowels that join the two leg assemblies —just a small finishing nail to lock in the dowel on one side while the other leg turns freely on the dowel. A metal washer with a $^1/_2$" hole separates the legs.

Round off the top corners of the two rails with a plane or spokeshave. Tack the webbing from underneath, taking care that when the rack is open all webbing is evenly stretched.

$1^5/_{16}$" SQ. x 22" (2 REQ)
2" x $21^1/_2$" PLASTIC TAPE
TACK UNDER RAILS
ABOUT 14"
$^1/_2$" x $2^3/_4$" DOWEL, IN $^1/_2$" HOLE, NOT GLUED
$10^1/_2$"
$1^5/_{16}$" SQ. x 19"
$3^1/_2$"
$1^5/_{16}$" SQ. x 16"
$1^5/_{16}$" SQ. x 21" LEGS
WASHER BETWEEN LEGS

A ROOMFUL OF 2x2s

BY KEN ISAACS

With a handsaw, a wrench, and a portable drill, plus a few ordinary two-by-twos, you can quickly furnish a handsome den-library or television room. Sturdier, less-expensive, or easier-to-make furniture would be hard to conceive.

All three units shown below evolved from my Matrix Idea as applied to what I call Living Structures — open-space-frame designs that relate the functions of furniture to the

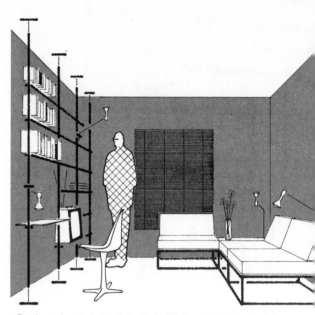

Designer's sketch of typical 10'-by-12' room shows how three designs (plus a desk chair) can combine to create airy modern study and television den. At right, three seating modules are grouped with table. Guest bed is formed by removing bolsters and sliding cushion of single module onto corner table.

Seating module has rugged masculine look, with comfort assured by loose foam cushion and bolster. Attached reading light eliminates floor lamp.

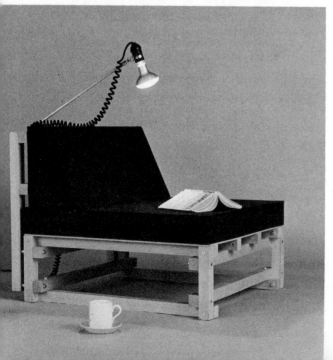

Coffee table is same unit minus back, with ¾" plywood top replacing thinner seat platform. Plastic-laminate surface is best. Clamp-on lamp is optional.

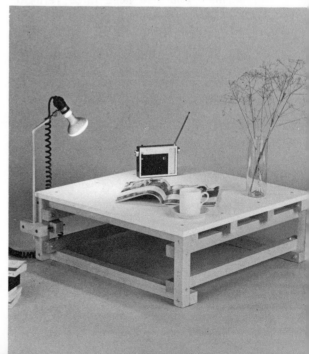

total environment, or matrix. Here, the room itself is the matrix, and the individual pieces are integrated toward a single solution of the room's multiple needs.

The sketch shows only a sample grouping, however. The pieces can be used individually elsewhere. The seating module, upholstered in vinyl, would be ideal for an outdoor deck or patio. It can be built as a double unit, or two single units can be butted for the same effect, with greater flexibility for future arrangements.

The corner grouping. If you plan to follow the arrangement shown you may want the top of the matching table the same height as the seat platforms; if so, cut the table legs only 9½" long to compensate for the extra-thick top.

The storage grid. This unit offers unlimited variations on the arrangement shown. For average books, no actual shelving is needed; the paired two-by-two rails with their center gap will support them. The clamp-on desk and the platforms (for a portable TV, hi-fi components, large books, or art objects) can be positioned to suit you. Since the unit doesn't depend on wall support, it can be used as a room divider, too. It's not fastened to the floor or ceiling, so it can easily be moved to a new location as your space needs change.

After deciding which units you want to build, consult the cutting schedules to determine the running feet of two-by-two you'll need. At the lumberyard, select the straightest and driest Douglas fir (or white fir) on the rack.

To lay out cutting lengths (for hand-sawing), mark cut lines on top and two sides of the two-by-two, using a square. Leave these lines intact and cut slightly beyond them; they'll serve as a guide to finishing the ends square with a rasp. It's best to rotate the piece as you work.

Assembling base frames. For the seating module or table, lay the two-by-twos on the floor in final position and mark holes for drilling. All holes are drilled on longitudinal centerlines. Use a brace and bit or an electric drill for the 5⁄16" holes through which the corner joints are bolted. Fasten with ¼"-by-3½" flathead machine screws, countersunk just flush.

Cut the 32"-square seat panel from ¼" hardboard; the same size tabletop from 3⁄4" plywood. Lay out mounting holes carefully and drill them with a ¼" bit, countersinking for the flathead machine screws that bolt the panel to the frame. Note that each of these passes through a pair of crossed support rails.

Each seating module requires a 32"-square, 4"-thick cushion of foam rubber or plastic. A firm, high-density foam is best. Have your foam supplier cut the bolster to shape. Cover both cushions with the simplest kind of box covers, zippered along one edge for easy removal.

Let there be light. To bend the 3⁄8"-diameter aluminum rod for the lamp's support arm,

Storage grid is anchored securely between floor and ceiling by two-by-two feet at end of threaded rods. Height-adjustment nuts wedge upright units tightly.

STORAGE GRID

HARDWARE

⅜"-dia. aluminum rod
Ball-joint socket clasp
Socket with heavy cord, plug
(Table light: bolts for clamp)

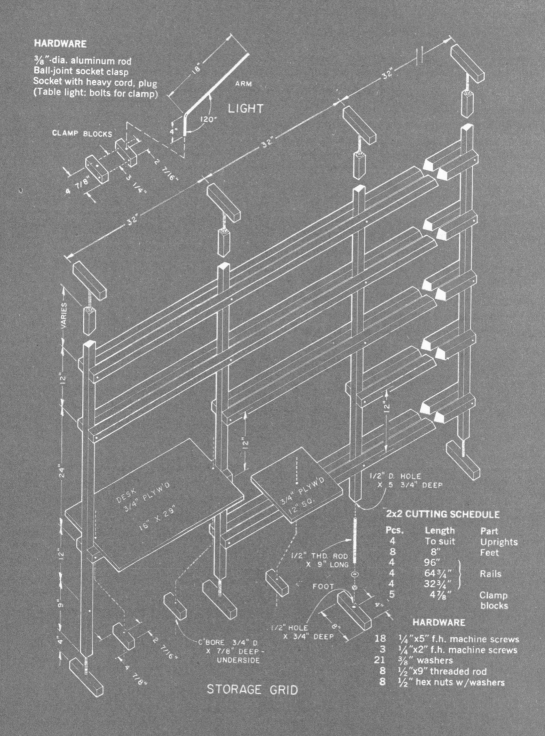

LIGHT

CLAMP BLOCKS

2x2 CUTTING SCHEDULE

Pcs.	Length	Part
4	To suit	Uprights
8	8"	Feet
4	96"	
4	64¾"	Rails
4	32¾"	
5	4⅞"	Clamp blocks

HARDWARE

18	¼"x5" f.h. machine screws
3	¼"x2" f.h. machine screws
21	⅜" washers
8	½"x9" threaded rod
8	½" hex nuts w/washers

STORAGE GRID

SEATING MODULE & TABLE BASE

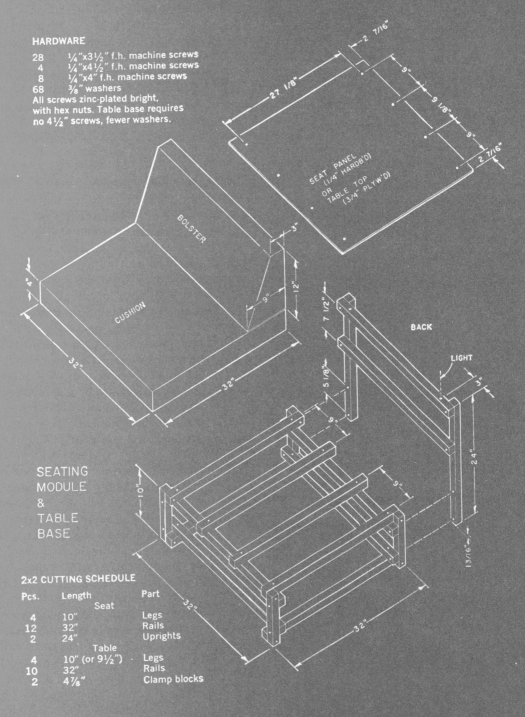

HARDWARE

28	¼"x3½" f.h. machine screws
4	¼"x4½" f.h. machine screws
8	¼"x4" f.h. machine screws
68	⅜" washers

All screws zinc-plated bright,
with hex nuts. Table base requires
no 4½" screws, fewer washers.

SEAT PANEL
(1/4" HARDB'D)
OR
TABLE TOP
(3/4" PLYW'D)

2 7/16"
27 1/8"
9"
9 1/8"
9"
2 7/16"

BOLSTER

CUSHION

4"
32"
32"
3"
9"
12"

BACK

LIGHT

7 1/2"
5 1/8"
9"
9"
2 4"
3"
13/16"

SEATING
MODULE
&
TABLE
BASE

32"
32"
10"

2x2 CUTTING SCHEDULE

Pcs.	Length	Part
		Seat
4	10"	Legs
12	32"	Rails
2	24"	Uprights
		Table
4	10" (or 9½")	Legs
10	32"	Rails
2	4⅞"	Clamp blocks

Back brace bolts through typical three-member joint with four 4½" machine screws. Gang of 16 washers acts as bushing between back and frame. Countersink screw heads; use washer under each nut.

Integrated light for all three units is similarly made. Note photographic ball-joint clamp that grips socket for reflector flood at end of aluminum-rod support arm. Black spiral cord adds design interest.

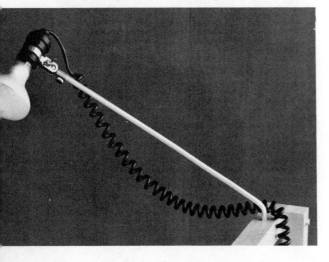

Top back rail of seating module is drilled through near both ends to provide snug fit for removable light—which pivots and swivels for still more reading adjustment, or can be aimed up at the ceiling.

clamp one end in a vise and slip a piece of water pipe over the other, for leverage. File cut ends flat and clean, and attach the ball-joint socket clamp. Insert the other end of the arm in a snug hole in the top rail of the seating module—or in a clamp block, in the case of the table or storage grid.

Use two ¼"-by-5" flathead machine screws, countersinking the heads, to draw each clamp tight against the upright. The sockets will take 30- or 75-watt reflector-flood bulbs, which need no shade and give a high-intensity light.

The storage-grid poles. The vertical compression units of the uprights are like screw-type auto jacks. As each upright is positioned and plumbed between floor and ceiling, the nuts are turned to wedge the units firmly. It's a good idea to cement a friction pad (of inner-tube rubber or felt) on the face of the foot block that butts floor or ceiling.

You can bore straight, deep sockets for the threaded rod by clamping each pole to your workbench and then sighting along the bit and two-by-two while drilling.

To determine the length of these uprights, measure your ceiling height and subtract 11". Have all uprights in place before you cut the horizontal rails to length. Drill these members, then use them as a guide for drilling the uprights, after positioning them with a level. You can make adjustments, after assembly, by turning the nuts on the lower threaded rods to bring members level, then turning the upper nuts for final wedging action.

Round all long corners slightly with a plane and rasp and smooth all surfaces with fine aluminum oxide paper. For a natural finish, apply three coats of a clear penetrating-resin sealer, sanding between coats. Buff with steel wool, apply paste wax, and rub with a cloth.

The best surface for the tabletop, desk, and platforms is plastic laminate. If you don't want to drill through this, bolt the plywood in place first, countersinking the heads. Cap the heads with water putty, sand flush, and apply the laminate right over them.

190

AN I TABLE AND A SET OF CUBE CHAIRS

BY KEN ISAACS

The table in this project takes its name from resemblance to cross section of the letter "I". The cube chairs stack as shown at the right, taking a minimum of floor space. Interiors of the cubes can be used for storage of magazines or other items.

In developing my Matrix idea, I explored in great depth and detail traditional forms of furniture. As a result, I designed a number of pieces based on past ideas of furniture. These were distinguished by their small scale, and extreme directness and simplicity of construction. The "I" table presented here is one of these designs. It offers the user advantages in an era of shrinking space in housing.

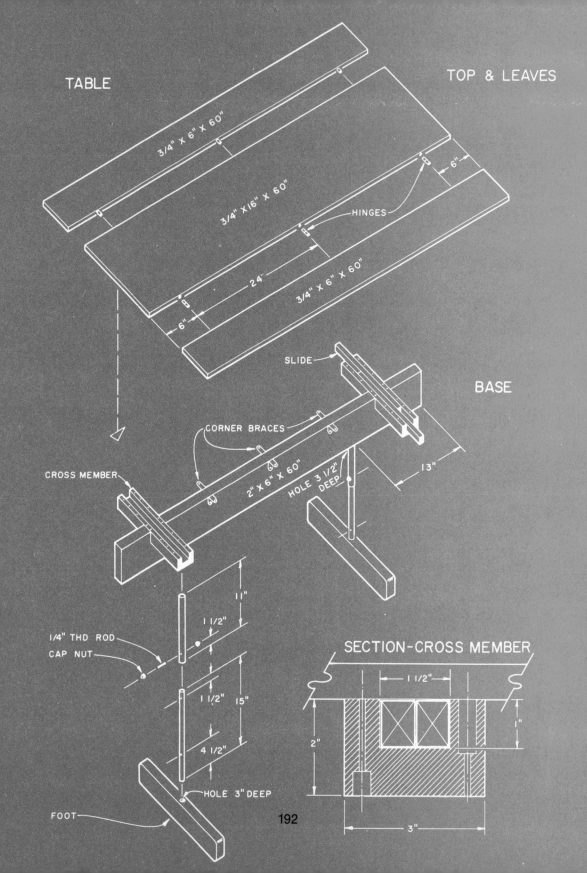

TABLE

TOP & LEAVES

3/4" X 6" X 60"

3/4" X16" X 60"

6"

HINGES

24"

6"

3/4" X 6" X 60"

SLIDE

BASE

CORNER BRACES

CROSS MEMBER

2" X 6" X 60"

HOLE 3 1/2" DEEP

13"

11"

1 1/2"

1/4" THD ROD

CAP NUT

1 1/2"

15"

4 1/2"

SECTION-CROSS MEMBER

1 1/2"

2"

3"

HOLE 3" DEEP

FOOT

192

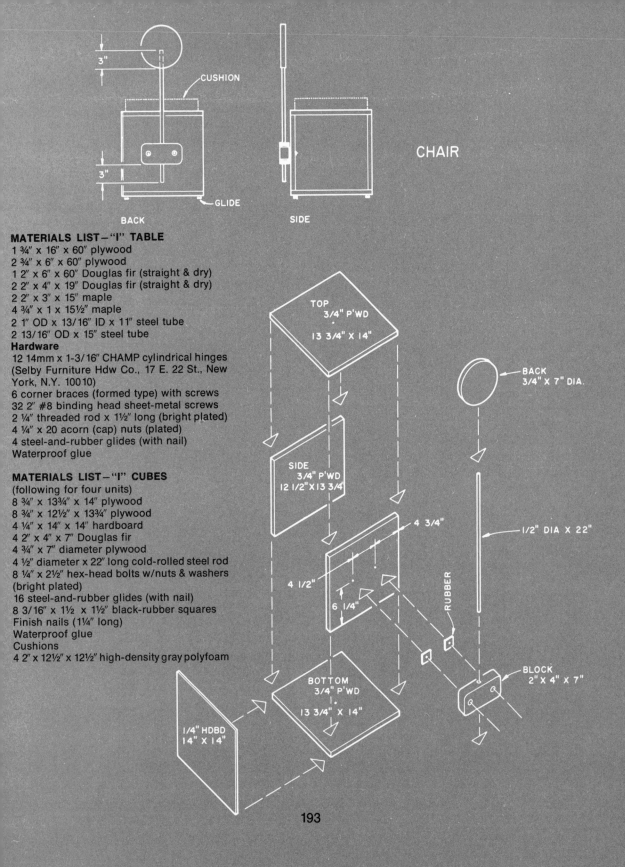

3"

CUSHION

3"

GLIDE

BACK

SIDE

CHAIR

MATERIALS LIST—"I" TABLE

1 ¾" x 16" x 60" plywood
2 ¾" x 6" x 60" plywood
1 2" x 6" x 60" Douglas fir (straight & dry)
2 2" x 4" x 19" Douglas fir (straight & dry)
2 2" x 3" x 15" maple
4 ¾" x 1 x 15½" maple
2 1" OD x 13/16" ID x 11" steel tube
2 13/16" OD x 15" steel tube

Hardware
12 14mm x 1-3/16" CHAMP cylindrical hinges
(Selby Furniture Hdw Co., 17 E. 22 St., New
York, N.Y. 10010)
6 corner braces (formed type) with screws
32 2" #8 binding head sheet-metal screws
2 ¼" threaded rod x 1½" long (bright plated)
4 ¼" x 20 acorn (cap) nuts (plated)
4 steel-and-rubber glides (with nail)
Waterproof glue

MATERIALS LIST—"I" CUBES

(following for four units)
8 ¾" x 13¾" x 14" plywood
8 ¾" x 12½" x 13¾" plywood
4 ¼" x 14" x 14" hardboard
4 2" x 4" x 7" Douglas fir
4 ¾" x 7" diameter plywood
4 ½" diameter x 22" long cold-rolled steel rod
8 ¼" x 2½" hex-head bolts w/nuts & washers
(bright plated)
16 steel-and-rubber glides (with nail)
8 3/16" x 1½ x 1½" black-rubber squares
Finish nails (1¼" long)
Waterproof glue
Cushions
4 2" x 12½" x 12½" high-density gray polyfoam

TOP
3/4" P'WD
13 3/4" X 14"

SIDE
3/4" P'WD
12 1/2"X13 3/4

BACK
3/4" X 7" DIA.

4 3/4"

4 1/2"

6 1/4"

RUBBER

1/2" DIA X 22"

BLOCK
2" X 4" X 7"

1/4" HDBD
14" X 14"

BOTTOM
3/4" P'WD
13 3/4" X 14"

193

With the leaves down, the table is only 16 inches wide and occupies little space against the wall of a small apartment. With the leaves up, six can eat with elegance. Moreover, telescoping legs allow it to be used at coffee-table height if desired.

The "I" cube was designed as the Matrix chair for both working and eating. The unit is neat and small scale. It offers good storage space for books, magazines, etc. Up to four cubes may be stacked, forming a storage column and taking up little floor space. At the same time, the cubes remain ready to serve as chairs on short notice. The back is resilient and moves in a springy arc when one leans against it, due to the rubber square in the mounting.

Building the table. Pick a straight, dry Douglas fir two-by-six and trim it to 60″ in length. If possible, run the top edge through a jointer to insure the top going down at a precise 90-degree angle. Cut two notches for the cross members carefully.

Use maple (or equal-performing wood) for cross members and slides. Dado the groove carefully and then size the slides for the closest possible fit without binding. Remember that the leaf action depends on the accuracy of these pieces. After fitting the cross members to the notch in the two-by-six, counterbore four holes in each (as shown in large section on plan) 1⅛″ deep. Use good waterproof glue and 2″ screws to secure.

Shop for tubing for the legs, using the given diameters as a guide. Get pieces with a good close fit. Size and drill ¼″ stop holes. Legs should be bright chrome-plated because paint will not hold up. An automotive plater can probably do this for you along with the ½″ rod for the cube backs.

Cut two pieces of Douglas fir two-by-four to a length of 19″ for the feet. Put a ¾″ radius on the corners as shown in the photographs. Drill a hole to fit the lower leg section of your tubing. A friction fit should work. If you have trouble, you might epoxy this joint.

Drill two holes in the bottom of the two-by-six to fit your upper leg-section tubing. Put off final assembly until finishing is done because force fits are involved for several of the pieces.

Top and leaves are cut from ¾″ plywood (some of the Japanese lumber-core-birch im-

Special cylindrical hinges which you can order by mail from a source in the parts list do neat job on table leaves, but author also suggests you may prefer simpler job of installing back hinges.

Chair back is attached like this. Making the tubing a press fit in the block may be sufficient, but for greater security you may prefer to put a pin through tubing above block. Mount block on rubber pads.

ports are excellent). You will probably want to use plastic laminate on upper surface and edges. Just be sure you apply the proper backing sheet to balance the panel and eliminate warping. The cylindrical hinges are very attractive, but do involve the extra expense of purchasing a drill to install them. Back-flap hinges may be used instead. The top is secured to the cross members by 12 screws through each of the cross members. Holes for these are counterbored exactly ½″. Exercise care to avoid spoiling your top. If the backing sheet will accept glue, use it here. The corner braces supply additional strength when screwed to the top and the two-by-six.

Building the Cubes. Here's your chance to get in the mass-production business. Size all the plywood pieces accurately to insure fine glue joints. You might even want to set up a little quickie jig to help your assembly. Glue and nail the four plywood sides together as shown, taking care with squareness. Cut the fifth hardboard side ¹⁄₁₆″ over 14″ to allow for sanding. Make the two-by-four blocks from Douglas fir with a ⅞″ diameter counterbore ½″ deep. The bolt holes are ⁵⁄₆″ for the ¼″ bolts.

Drill a ½″ hole vertically for the chrome-plated rod. You can pin these from the back with nails if you like. The 7″-diameter back should be left free to turn, for comfort.

I used polyfoam without covering for the prototypes and recommend it in the dark gray color. The texture of this cushioning material is great and, in my opinion, it makes a fine appearance, but you can cover it if you must.

A spanking white tabletop goes great with the feet and two-by-six in natural fir finished with Firzite and wax. Cubes should be done in bright, saturated colors with rolled enamel. All these combinations are fine with the bright chrome plating of the table legs and back rods. Drill a ⁵⁄₁₆″ hole in the exact center of the cube top and bottom for a safety bolt and wing-nut if absolute security is important when chairs are stacked.

A STURDY TYPEWRITER STAND

BY J. W. CLEMENT

This plywood stand for a portable typewriter can be put together in an afternoon or evening. It's lighter than a typewriter table, yet quite sturdy. Sit at the stand with knees astraddle the center upright and you'll have plenty of leg room. Use ¾″ plywood for the top and base, ½″ plywood for the back and center support. Assemble with finishing nails and glue. Avoid driving nails through the top where they will show by gluing a strip of scrap plywood on each side of the center support.

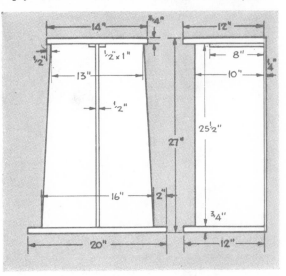

SHAKER CANDLE-STAND . . . AND CANDLESTICK, TOO

BY DAVID WARREN

Shaker-style furniture is unique. Its simplicity of design and clean lines blend with practically any furniture style. The design and construction of these two pieces is typical of those produced 150 years ago—except that you'll build yours a lot faster than the original craftsmen did.

The table is made of cherry, which is not usually available in $\frac{1}{2}''$ or $\frac{5}{8}''$ thickness; so its necessary to plane down $\frac{3}{4}''$ stock. Or you can have it done at the lumberyard mill; the cost is nominal. Since the candlestick will be painted—make it out of less expensive pine.

Making the table. Begin construction with the top. Match the grains and mark the best arrangement. Tongue-and-groove the boards and glue them together. When the top is dry, plane 1/8" off each surface. Next, draw the circle on the underside and mark the center. Cut the top, and round the edge with a router and 1/4" quarter-round bit. Use a Forstner bit to bore the 1" hole for the post.

Turn the post on a lathe to the dimensions shown; maintain a close tolerance in the diameter of the 5/16" stub that fits into the top. Size the calipers to the Forstner bit to make sure of an accurate cut for the 1" hole.

Next lay out the 5" disk on a piece of 5/8" stock. The 1 5/8" hole is bored with an expansion bit; practice on scrap first and test-fit to the post. When the bit is set correctly, bore the hole and cut out the disk.

Cut the legs (also 5/8" stock) and round the edges. The most important construction detail here is the dovetail where the legs slide into the post. If the fit is loose, the joint will be weak; too tight, and you can split the post. Mark and cut the tenons on the legs. Use a coping saw on each shoulder where the leg joins the post. On the base of the post carefully lay out the three dovetail mortises an equal distance apart. Use the tenons as templates. Cut the mortises with a 1/4" chisel and mallet so each leg fits snugly.

Putting it together. Assemble the table with glue and place it on a level surface. Check the top with a level and the post with a framing square. When you are satisfied that top and post are true, center a 10-pound weight on the top until the glue dries — at least 24 hours.

After a final sanding, finish the table with your preferred method. The table shown was finished with shellac.

The candlestick. This one is made of wood, styled after the metal candlesticks used by the Shakers. It's easily turned from four-by-four stock.

If your lathe is equipped to drill, turn the candlestick with the top toward the headstock so you'll be set up for boring the candle hole later.

Turn the piece as shown and cut the bottom slightly hollow with the parting tool, to about 1". Then cut off the upper end. Bore the 3/4" hole for the candle with the base of the candlesticks held firmly against the tailstock center.

Glue felt to the bottom and paint the candlestick to simulate metal. Apply a coat of aluminum paint and let dry. Then brush on flat black enamel, and when it is tacky wipe lightly with lint-free cloth.

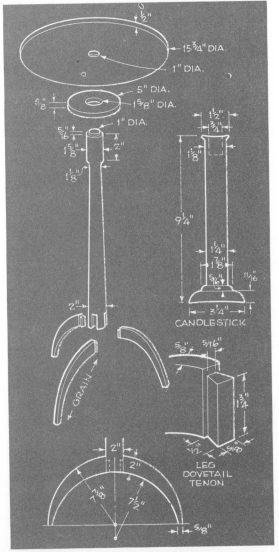

197

DESK . . . HOBBY BENCH . . . AND IT'S ALSO A BAR

BY HOWELL M. BURKE JR.

Have you considered building a home bar but decided against it because you'd use it too infrequently? Well, here's one that can be the life of many a party—and also work throughout the year as a giant desk or hobby bench.

It converts from one function to another fast and easy. When the party's over, you remove a couple of wingnuts and screws, pull the perforated-hardboard panel from the bar front, and lift the unit off the leg extensions that raise it to bar height. Screwed to the opposite side, the hardboard now serves as a

workbench backboard. A strip of the panel extending above the counter top is handy for hanging tools or hobby equipment.

The versatility of the piece comes from putting the major sections together with screws instead of nails. You can take it apart and move it anywhere in the house.

The desk-bench-bar design makes construction economical because it can be built with little waste. The plywood components are cut from 1½ 4'-by-8' panels of ¾" plywood. In addition, you'll need 8' of one-by-twelve pine, for shelving; 8' of one-by-six pine, for the lengthwise backbone of the lower structure; 8' of one-by-two furring strips; a 4'-by-8' piece of perforated hardboard, a 2'-by-10' piece of plastic laminate; contact cement; white glue; three steel right-angle brackets with ³⁄₁₆" holes; and assorted screws and nails.

An electric drill and saber saw will make the job go faster, but it's easy to build with hand tools, too.

Lay out the indicated parts on the two plywood panels and make the necessary cuts. Lightly plane or sand the cut edges reasonably square and smooth.

Begin by gluing and nailing positioning

cleats and the front edge strip to the underside of the plywood top. Space the two sets of short crosswise cleats so that each middle leg will be 30″ from the leg of the corresponding end. Keep the ends of the crosswise cleats flush with the back edge of the plywood panel.

Now assemble the legs to the top, placing each between its proper pair of cleats, and install the one-by-six backbone piece. Screw it to the back edge of each of the two middle legs and its ends to short pieces of one-by-twos placed vertically inside the end legs. Glue and nail in the two end shelves 15″ from the floor, but install cleats to support the center one. This shelf can be removed to provide desk and workbench kneehole space.

Assemble the leg-extension pieces, raise the structure to bar height, and you're ready to assemble the perforated-hardboard panel. This gets its rigidity from a strip of plywood, screwed lengthwise to one edge, and two short pieces at the ends.

The two short plywood pieces rest on the counter top when the unit is set up as a desk and hobby bench. The strips are on the back face of the panel when it's in place on the bar. Attach the panel with wingnuts on bolts through the backbone piece.

When the unit is taken off the extension pieces for use at desk or bench height, remove the wingnuts and screw the panel against the edges of the legs on the opposite side.

Finish the counter top by attaching the plastic laminate. In cutting the piece for the top surface, allow for a slight overhang all around and you can then put a 45-degree bevel on the edges to miter the side panel to the top. A metal-cutting blade in a saber saw is a good tool for slicing through plastic laminate. Cut the edge strips slightly wide so the lower edge can be planed flush after assembly. Attach the laminate with contact cement used according to the maker's instructions.

A good choice for decorating the unit is a light-colored, washable, semigloss paint that will harmonize with the plastic-laminate counter top.

When used as a desk (opposite page) and hobby center, hardboard panel extends above top to hold tools or hobby equipment.

Add leg extensions to sides, place perforated hardboard panel on front, and presto—you have a bar. Inset shows extension details.

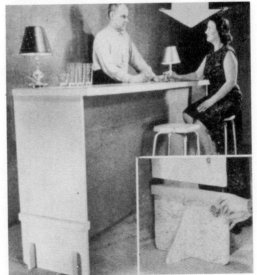

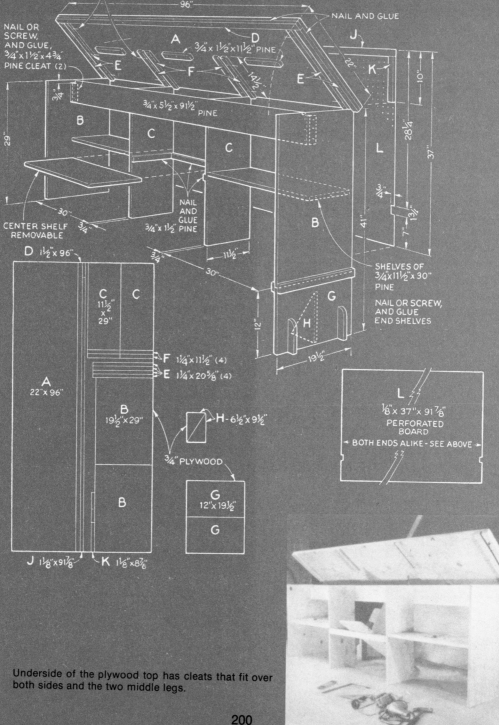

FINISHING NAILS PARTLY DRIVEN THROUGH ALL CLAMPS WHEN TOP IS IN PLACE

96"

NAIL AND GLUE

NAIL OR SCREW, AND GLUE, 3/4" x 1 1/2" x 4 3/4" PINE CLEAT (2)

A D 3/4" x 1 1/2" x 11 1/2" PINE

J

E F E K

3/4" 14 1/2"

3/4" x 5 1/2" x 91 1/2" PINE

22"

10"

29" B C C L

NAIL AND GLUE 3/4" x 1 1/2" PINE

B

3/4"

28 1/4"

37"

CENTER SHELF REMOVABLE 3/4"

3/4"

13 1/2"

7"

13 1/2"

11 1/2"

30"

41"

SHELVES OF 3/4" x 11 1/2" x 30" PINE

D 1 1/2" x 96"

12"

G

H

19 1/2"

NAIL OR SCREW, AND GLUE END SHELVES

C C 11 1/2" x 29"

A 22" x 96"

F 1 1/4" x 11 1/2" (4)
E 1 1/4" x 20 5/8" (4)

B 19 1/2" x 29"

H - 6 1/2" x 9 1/2"

3/4" PLYWOOD

B

G 12" x 19 1/2"

L 1/8" x 37" x 91 7/8" PERFORATED BOARD
◄ BOTH ENDS ALIKE - SEE ABOVE ►

G

J 1 1/8" x 91 7/8"   K 1 1/8" x 8 7/8"

Underside of the plywood top has cleats that fit over both sides and the two middle legs.

200

COFFEE-TABLE MUSIC CENTER

BY H. V. HUSTON

Are your stereo components scattered all over the living room? On shelves, perhaps, or sitting on top of the mantel? After your wife has looked at (and dusted) the set for awhile, you're probably hearing what she thinks about the whole setup. Solution? Build this table/music center and you can both be happy. She'll have a handsome new table, and you the hi-fi.

What will it hold? The table is designed to house a Scott Stereomaster 382 amplifier, a Lafayette 830 tape deck, and a Garrard 40 Mk. II turntable. If you already have your components or buy equipment with different measurements, change the table dimensions accordingly.

The parts for the pentagon music center are cut from one sheet of ¾" birch plywood (see blueprint). The only other lumber needed is pine for the cleats, ¼" stock for the splines and tilting-rack stops, and some molding.

Because the units generate heat, they must be ventilated. Space at the top is provided by the cleats, which are set ⅛" above the side panels. The cleats are 12" long and are centered on the panels, leaving a space at each end for air flow.

On the opposite side, between the amplifier and tape deck, a diagonal cleat is used because of lack of space. In addition to supporting the top, it also strengthens the corner. Three legs, equally spaced, provide ventilation and toe space at the bottom.

To keep down the size of the table, the components are placed very close together. This means that all parts must be cut accurately and the dimensions must be exact.

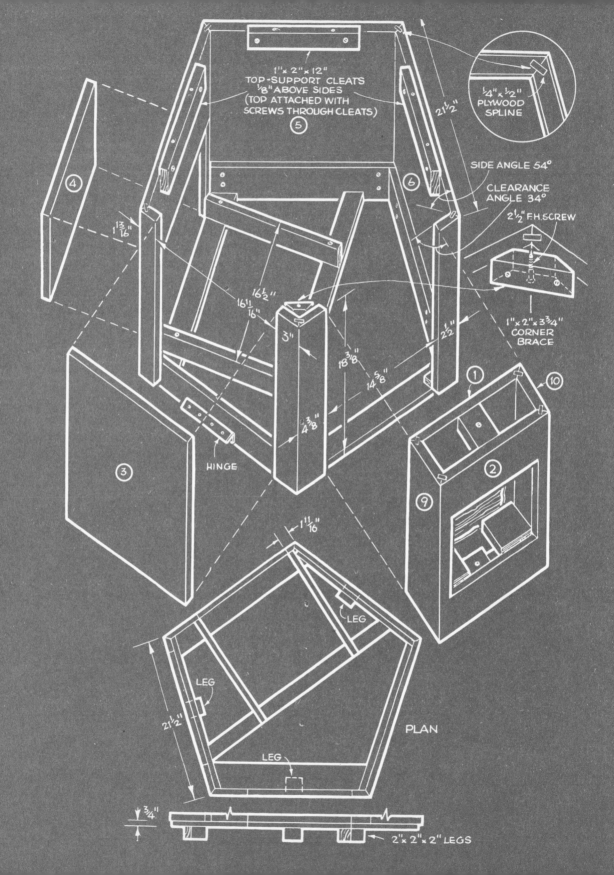

1"× 2"× 12" TOP-SUPPORT CLEATS ⅛" ABOVE SIDES (TOP ATTACHED WITH SCREWS THROUGH CLEATS) ⑤

¼"× ½" PLYWOOD SPLINE

2½"

④

SIDE ANGLE 54°

CLEARANCE ANGLE 34°

2½" F.H.SCREW

⑥

1 13/16"

16½"

16 11/16"

3"

2½"

18 3/8"

14 5/8"

1"× 2"× 3¾" CORNER BRACE

4 3/8"

①

⑩

③

HINGE

②

⑨

1 11/16"

LEG

LEG

21½"

LEG

PLAN

¾"

2"× 2"× 2" LEGS

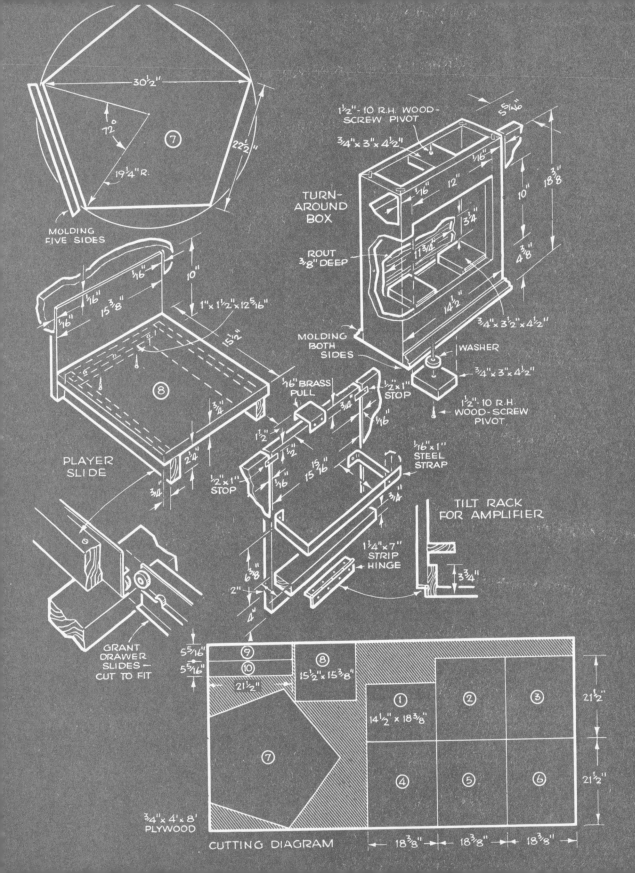

MOLDING
FIVE SIDES

30½"

72°

22½"

19¼" R.

⑦

TURN-AROUND BOX

1½"-10 R.H. WOOD-SCREW PIVOT

¾"x 3"x 4½"

5⁵⁄₁₆"

1/16"

12"

1/16"

3/4"

11¾"

10"

18³⁄₈"

4³⁄₈"

ROUT ⅜" DEEP

14½"

¾"x 3½"x 4½"

WASHER

¾"x 3"x 4½"

1½"-10 R.H. WOOD-SCREW PIVOT

MOLDING BOTH SIDES

10"

1/16"

15³⁄₈"

1/16"

1"x 1½"x 12⁵⁄₁₆"

15½"

¾"

⑧

2¼"

¾"

PLAYER SLIDE

1/16" BRASS PULL

½"x 1" STOP

3/4"

1/16"

1½"

½"

1½"

15⁵⁄₁₆"

½"x 1" STOP

1/16"

1/16"x 1" STEEL STRAP

3/4"

TILT RACK FOR AMPLIFIER

1¼"x 7" STRIP HINGE

3³⁄₄"

GRANT DRAWER SLIDES – CUT TO FIT

6³⁄₈"

2"

4"

5⁵⁄₁₆"

⑨

5⁵⁄₁₆"

⑩

⑧

15½"x 15³⁄₈"

21½"

⑦

①

14½" x 18³⁄₈"

②

③

21½"

④

⑤

⑥

21½"

¾"x 4'x 8' PLYWOOD

CUTTING DIAGRAM

18³⁄₈"   18³⁄₈"   18³⁄₈"

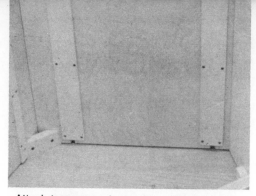

Attach temporary cleats with screws to hold the panels securely when you are gluing them.

MATERIALS LIST

1 panel ¾" x 4' x 8' lumbercore birch plywood (top and sides of pentagon; sides, back, platform, and swivel parts of tape-deck box; turntable platform)

14' 1 x 3 pine (3 top-support cleats, 2 lower cleats, tilt-rack cleat, 3 turntable platform supports)

5' 1 x 4 pine (3 lower cleats)

20' ¾" x ¾" maple or birch (for forming molding trim)

Misc.: scrap ¼" and ½" stock (splines and tilt-rack stop), 6" 2 x 2 (3 legs), flexible wood tape (for covering edges), white glue.

Hardware: 3' 1/16" x 1" steel strap, 1 pr. Grant #335 drawer slides, 1¼" x 7" piano hinge; brass strip (tilt-rack handle), 1 washer, 1 rivet, assorted nails and wood screws

How to build the table. Since it would be difficult to make the panel cutouts after the piece is assembled, cut them out beforehand and use temporary cleats to hold them in place. A rope clamp is used when gluing the sides together; a band clamp is fine, too, but you'll need one with a 9' capacity.

Use care when cutting the angles of the parts. Three are involved. The sides are 54 degrees; clearance angle for the turn-around box is 34 degrees; and the turn-around box miters are 45 degrees. Since the saw arbor will not tilt more than 45 degrees, set the blade at 36 degrees when cutting the side miters; this leaves a 54-degree angle for the cutting.

To cut the miters for the sides, mount a wood strip on the rip fence, and carefully adjust the blade so it just kisses the top edge of the wood being cut. Make some trial cuts on scrap before you cut the panels.

The grooves for the splines are cut with the dado cutters set at the same angle. Adjust the rip fence so that the groove is centered and pass the work through vertically.

After the miters are cut, make the necessary cutouts for the amplifier, tape-deck box, and turntable. For greater accuracy, assemble the temporary cleats as shown in the photos before cutting the panels. After the cuts are made, the sections remain in place until after gluing.

White glue sets fast, so have all the equip-

Rope clamps work fine for gluing the sides together. Corrugated cardboard protects corners.

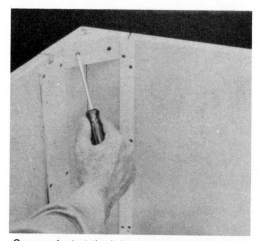

Corner cleat at the joint between amplifier and tape-deck panels braces and strengthens joint.

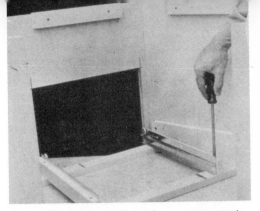

Mount the drawer-slide hardware on supports before installing them to simplify the job.

How cleats and hinge are installed is seen from bottom. Three two-by-two blocks serve as legs.

Table partially assembled shows placement of tape-deck supports that allow access to pivot.

ment ready and within easy reach. If rope is used for clamping, loop one end beforehand. Use corrugated board at the corners to prevent damage to the cabinet from the rope clamp. Use wood blocks for wedges and a turnbuckle to increase the pressure, if necessary. Cut the needed cleats and attach with glue and wood screws.

The works. To make the turn-around box, cut the various sections to size, and miter the corners. Make the cutout for the tape deck. If the Lafayette 830 is used, it is necessary to rout the area (as shown in the blueprint) at the rear of the chassis. *Note:* The rear panel of the chassis is repositioned so the line cord and jacks will not be blocked by the flush side of the turn-around box. When remounting the panel, be careful not to break or short any wires. Actually this tape deck was easy to rework and posed no problems.

Use a washer at the lower pivot of the turn-around box so that it will turn freely. Wires from the tape deck can be passed through the top or bottom of the box. The two supports for the deck are set toward the sides so one hand can be inserted at the center to facilitate mounting the pivot screw. The tape deck simply slides into place and rests on the supports.

Cut the pieces for the record-changer slide and assemble with glue and screws. Cut the cleats for the turntable support and attach the sliding-drawer hardware before attaching cleats. To complete assembly, install the cleats and slides.

Shape and attach the metal for the amplifier tilt rack. Attach the stop tab with a Pop rivet. If you don't have one, a nut and bolt can be substituted. Mount the wood supporting strip and brass pull, and slide the amplifier into place.

For the trim, $3/4''$-by-$3/4''$ maple was shaped with a router. The feet are simply three pieces of two-by-two attached to the bottom of the cleats. The exposed edges of the tilting rack,

turn-around box, and turntable drawer should be covered with flexible wood tape for a finished appearance.

Finish the table to match your furniture. Mine was stained walnut and given three coats of clear lacquer. After waiting a week, I applied paste wax.

Movable tab on tilt rack serves as a projection limiting stop. Swing up, to remove amplifer.

Tape deck slides into its niche, needs no fastening. Make cutout carefully, for a snug fit.

TV DINNER TRAY

BY ARTHUR KENNEDY

Secure in a pine and plywood holder, a TV dinner is easy to hold on your lap. Make an underframe of ¾"-by-1" pine and a top of ¼" plywood. Cut out the center of the top to

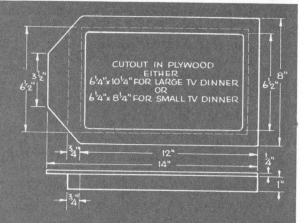

CUTOUT IN PLYWOOD
EITHER
6¼"x10¼" FOR LARGE TV DINNER
OR
6¼"x 8¼" FOR SMALL TV DINNER

3½"
6½"
8"
6½"
¾"
12"
14"
¼"
1"
¾"

accommodate either large or small TV-dinner trays. Before making the cutout, measure the tray your favorite TV dinners come in. Nail ¼" plywood over the bottom of the frame so the holder sits firmly on your lap. Sand and oil, or shellac, the holder. A similar frame can hold a dish for buffet suppers.

206

MOD MINI-CANDELABRA

BY DAVID WARREN

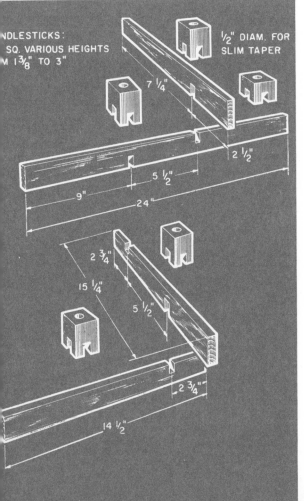

NDLESTICKS:
SQ. VARIOUS HEIGHTS
M 1⅜" TO 3"

½" DIAM. FOR SLIM TAPER

7¼"

2½"

5½"

9"

24"

2¾"

15¼"

5½"

2¾"

14½"

Miniature candelabra takes five slim candles. The three candle holders at joints add rigidity to design when glued in place.

Scraps of fine cabinet wood are too valuable to throw away, too bothersome to keep around. I designed this miniature candelabra just to use a few such scraps of rosewood cluttering up my shop.

The sketch shows the dimensions for the piece I built, but you can easily modify the design to make use of any scraps you have on hand. Assembly is easy but make a full-size layout on paper as a guide to assure squareness during glue-up. Use epoxy at the egg-crate joints; it won't shrink and can fill in any voids if the joints fit loosely. Finish? An oil or penetrating resin gives rosewood, or any cabinet wood, a deep natural glow.

NO ATTIC?
SHELVES WILL
DO THE JOB

BY FRANK GREENWALD

Modern architecture gives us a new approach to an old idea—building large shelves in a basement to store bulky items usually stacked in an attic. Called the module concept, it means that a structure of any size can be built based on a small basic unit, or module. Once you have this, you can add as many identical units as you need. Applying this concept, I built shelves that are easy to take apart, move, and enlarge—all from two types of material cut to very few different sizes.

The only materials you'll need are 12' lengths of one-inch pine board—preferably knotfree—and 1/8" tempered hardboard. Rip the pine into 1½" strips. You'll cut all pieces—shelf frames and posts—from this one size. Assemble the frames with glue, securing them with six-penny finishing nails. Use glue and brads to fasten the hardboard shelf top.

Post height depends on available head room. For uniformity, lay out one post, then use it for a pattern. Make sure the shelves fit tightly in the notches.

The hardboard flanges should be snug in the post grooves. They also are held with glue and brads.

If space permits, it's easier to bolt the finished unit together on its side.

Shelf system of pine and tempered hardboard is modular in construction—it can be easily disassembled and moved, and new sections can be added. Each shelf of this 84-cu.-ft unit holds 300 pounds.

Support posts and shelf sections are held together with stove bolts. This unit has shelves 16" deep, 24" high, but you can alter dimensions to suit your needs. Allow a 6" space at the bottom.

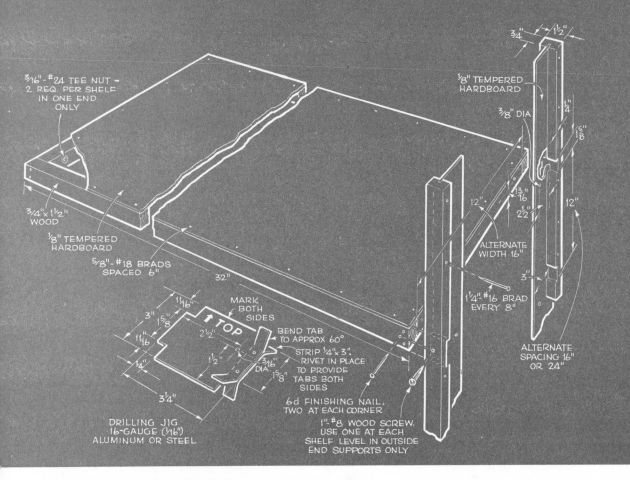

3/16"-#24 TEE NUT -
2 REQ. PER SHELF
IN ONE END
ONLY

3/4" x 1/2"
WOOD

1/8" TEMPERED
HARDBOARD

5/8"-#18 BRADS
SPACED 6"

32"

1/8" TEMPERED
HARDBOARD

3/8" DIA

1"
1/4

5/8"

12"

13"
16

2 1/2"

ALTERNATE
WIDTH 16"

1 1/4"-#16 BRAD
EVERY 8"

12"

3"

ALTERNATE
SPACING 16"
OR 24"

3/4"

1 1/2"

1 1/16"

3"

1 5/8"

1 1/16"

1/4"

3 3/4"

MARK
BOTH
SIDES

TOP

2 1/2"

1/2"

3/16"
DIA.

1 5/8"

BEND TAB
TO APPROX 60°

STRIP 1/4" x 3".
RIVET IN PLACE
TO PROVIDE
TABS BOTH
SIDES

6d FINISHING NAIL.
TWO AT EACH CORNER

1"-#8 WOOD SCREW.
USE ONE AT EACH
SHELF LEVEL IN OUTSIDE
END SUPPORTS ONLY

DRILLING JIG
16-GAUGE (1/16")
ALUMINUM OR STEEL

Metal-drilling jig ensures uniform bolt-hole location. For drilling shelves (below, left), align the projecting tongue with corner. The two ears straddle edges of shelf frame. Use same jig for drilling hardboard post flanges (below, right), with tongue in shelf notch and ears against hardboard. "Top" notation, on both sides of jig, shows its correct position for drilling both posts and shelves.

Final assembly requires only a screwdriver. Stove bolts and nuts fasten shelves to end posts; bolts and T nuts hold remaining shelves and posts. Reinforce end post joints with wood screws as in drawing.

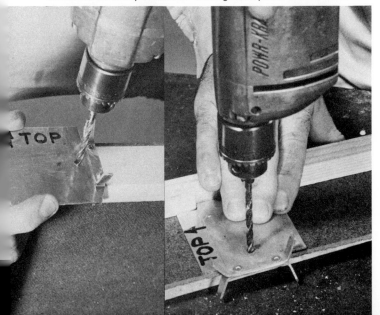

TABLETOP WITH RECESSED TILE PATTERN, BASED ON POSSIBLE MATH DISCOVERY

BY ARTHUR EARLE

You never know what wonders you may come up with when you set out to create a project. I was recently playing with a batch of one-inch-square ceramic tiles, trying to devise an interesting pattern for a tabletop insert. I innocently arranged six tiles to enclose a hexagon.

When I placed six more between the outer corners of the first six, I saw I'd formed equiangular triangles between them. Filling in with six of another color, I established radial paths which I continued out for several courses. Then I saw that the spaces between these paths left room for one additional tile in each course, so that each ring of tile increased by six. It suddenly struck me that if I continued to the sixtieth course, *that* ring would contain 360 tiles. (Continued on page 212)

Set into a coffee table, design is both decorative and useful, providing a built-in hot pad.

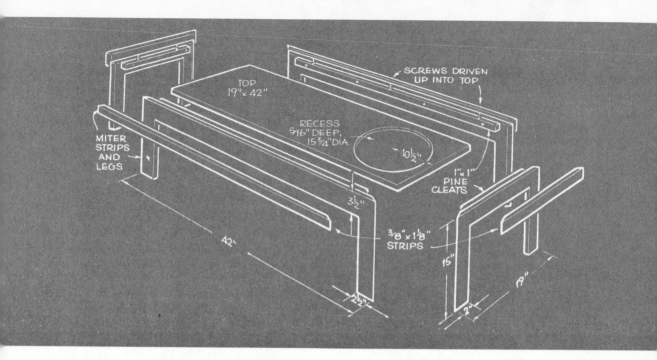

TOP
19" x 42"

SCREWS DRIVEN
UP INTO TOP

RECESS
5/16" DEEP,
15 3/4" DIA

10 1/2"

MITER
STRIPS
AND
LEGS

1" x 1"
PINE
CLEATS

3 1/2"

3/8" x 1 1/8"
STRIPS

42"

25"

2"

15"

19"

To rout out recess to take tiles, loop coat-hanger wire around nail tapped at center, then fasten other end to router frame, creating a 7⅞" radius from nail to outer edge of router bit. Swing router full circle, then remove nail and hand-guide router to cut out wood inside circle. Depth of cut should leave only rounded edges of tiles above tabletop when assembly is dropped in.

To demonstrate a project application of the author's design, POPULAR SCIENCE built the coffee table of ¾"-inch teak plywood shown on opposite page. We simplified construction by cutting each leg-and-apron unit in one piece, mitering the mating edges. The top panel merely sets on this assembly, flush at all sides, and is anchored by means of pine cleats drilled and attached to the inside faces of the aprons before they are assembled. The joint line and the exposed plies of the top are masked with mitered strips of solid teak, flush with the top surface. If you prefer to avoid purchasing this solid stock, buy a pine strip at the lumberyard, miter it to frame the top, and lacquer or enamel it black before gluing and bradding it in place. If you add such a feature strip, you can also paint the edges and inside corners of the legs black and avoid the job of veneer-taping these edges. We applied two coats

of satin urethane varnish before grouting the tiles. This finish gives the look of oiled teak, but offers the greater protection necessary for a coffee table. It also permits you to wipe off excess grout.

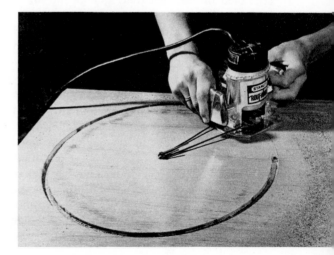

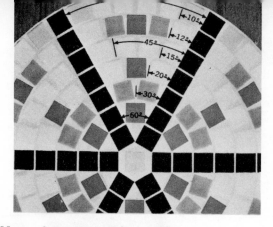

Many degrees can be read directly from the tiles

Any segment between black radials gives the direct degree readings shown. The base line of each tile represents a decreasing number of degrees in each course outward, beginning with 60 for the inner course of red tile. Each tile in the seventh course then measures 10. (This method, which shifts the segment one course outward, is easier than reading from the actual center, which would put the 10-degree tile in the sixth course, for an actual count of 36 tiles in that ring.)

Additional degrees can be read via addition or subtraction; for example, 2° is the angle between 12° and 10° readings. The colors are purely arbitrary, but the placement here creates a good design and points up some major readings. The pattern creates itself when you start with six tiles set corner to corner to enclose a hexagon, then add six more to form equiangular spaces between the first six.

With mounting excitement, I realized I'd stumbled on the fact that squares (arranged without the aid of a compass or even a straightedge) could divide a circle into 360 parts. I further saw that I'd created a design that can literally be read — like a protractor — as shown in the photo-diagram.

I think I've made an important new math discovery — as well as an attractive tile pattern that will give any project a special significance.

It's hard to believe in this day of advanced math that nobody's sure why we divide a circle into 360 degrees, though all the rules of trigonometry are based on that division. All we know is that over 5,000 years ago, astronomer-priests of Babylon declared: The circle has 360 parts. It stuck. Yet 4,000 years later,

the great Elizabethan cartographers could not readily make that division. This had led some modern scholars to doubt that the Babylonians themselves knew how. The tile pattern shown may well dispel such doubts at last, for the Babylonians were great users of tile and may easily have experienced a serendipity just like mine! The implications of the design extend beyond math and offer new solutions to questions that have puzzled scientists for centuries.

Map makers and mariners traditionally use the 32-point compass. It is easily constructed by repeatedly bisecting angles. This leads to 256 divisions. The next step would produce 512. But the tile pattern pictured here divides the circle into Babylonian degrees. Perhaps the Babylonians discovered this — even before they knew how to bisect an angle.

Calendar short. The Babylonian calendar had only 360 days. This fact has led to the conjecture that the Babylonians decided there should be 360 equal divisions in a circle because they thought there were 360 days in the solar cycle. But a farmer could not persist in such a belief for very many years, and an astronomer would know better in one. Nor does the lunar cycle lead to a year of 360 days. Twelve cycles of lunar phase change take 354 days; a complete solar cycle takes 365.25 days.

Man's methods of measuring the passage of time are completely arbitrary. Despite the fact that a solar calendar is in some ways very convenient, it is by no means essential. There is really no reason to suppose that the Babylonian 360-day calendar intended to measure the solar year, any more than there is to suppose that our months of 31, 30, 28, and occasionally 29 days attempt to measure the lunar phases.

The Babylonian calendar was divided into 12 periods of 30 days each. We can safely assume that these divisions were not intended to correspond to the moon's phases, because they quite obviously do not. If the year began with a full moon, 360 days later the moon would be in the last quarter, six days past the twelfth full moon. (The Egyptians compensated for this by adding five days to create our present calendar year.)

If the Babylonian calendar was not intended to mark time in terms of the sun or of the moon, perhaps there was another reason for choosing these divisions of time. Perhaps the Babylonian was so impressed with the *discovery* that there are 360 parts in a circle that he made his calendar correspond. Rather than the solar year or the lunar year, time may have been calculated in terms of the *circular* year, which, in this case, happens to be a rather good compromise.

Reading the message. The pattern's first course contains six tiles. The second course has twice as many as the first, the third course three times, the fourth four times—the number of tiles in a course (C) is always six times the number of the radial (R). C = 2πR, and in Babylon π = 3, exactly.

As we've noted, the 60th course will contain 360 tiles. The 59th course has 354, matching the lunar year. A 61st course would have 366, only a fraction over the number of days in a solar year.

The first course divides the circle into six parts, the second divides it into 12 parts, the third into 18, and so on. Or we may say, each tile in the first course fills one-sixth of a circle, each tile in the second fills one-twelfth of a circle—$1/6$, $1/12$, $1/18$, $1/24$, $1/30$, $1/36$—clumsy enough with our so-called Arabic notation. For a Babylonian (using a mark, ▼, for one, and a mark, ◄, for 10, made by pressing a reed stylus into moist clay), such fractions were much too cumbersome.

The Babylonian simplified the writing of fractions by devising systems in which the parts had names. Instead of writing fractions he could then write whole numbers, multiples of the fractional unit. We still use this system, writing 1 foot, instead of $1/3$ yard; 1 inch, in-

stead of $1/12$ foot; 1 ounce, instead of $1/16$ pound. The method is easy to apply to weights and linear measure. The number of sub-units chosen is completely arbitrary.

The circle poses a special case. Before a practical system can be devised, the circle must be divided into equal parts. The tile pattern performs that essential task. Then the problem becomes one of representing the fractions as whole numbers. To do this we must find what we would call the lowest common denominator, a number into which 6, 12, 18, 24, 30, and 36 will divide evenly.

The number is 360.

Each tile in the first course represents 60 parts. Each tile in the second represents 30 parts. In the third course, each tile is 20 parts; in the fourth, 15; in the fifth, 12; and in the sixth, 10 parts. In the 60th course each tile fills one part, or one degree—the "part name" in this instance.

Why call them degrees? Our word comes from the Latin, but its meaning traces back to the Babylonian. In Latin *de* means by, and *gradus* means step. From this root we get degree, and also degrade, the essential meaning of which is "to make smaller." Both relate to the pattern's pyramid (with a curving base) whose sides go down in steps that get smaller and smaller. There is one of these between each pair of radials.

Once the pattern has been analyzed, it becomes of immediate practical value. The Babylonian astronomer could hinge two sticks together, sight an angle—between the sun and the horizon, for instance—lay the sticks on the tiles and read the angles. He could work from the center of the hexagon or use the junction of two radials as the focal point and the straight side of one radial as a base line. When he did this, everything shifted outward one course, as in our photo-diagram.

Even if the pattern is crudely constructed the message can be clearly read. By doing it over again more carefully, extremely accurate

Asbestos disk, beneath tiles in table recess, provides further insulation between wood and hot objects, makes handy backing on which to mount tile. Scratch a deep 15½″ circle in ⅛″-thick asbestos board, using stick with two nails driven through, 7¾″ apart. Lay board over rough-cut plywood disk of same diameter and tap with rubber mallet to break board around score line. Rasp the rough edges.

Position tiles on pattern laid out on disk with compass and ruler, applying gob of one-hour epoxy cement to back of each tile. Slow-setting cement allows adjustment with pencil tip as design progresses. Tiles are square, not tapered. Therefore, don't try to align edges with the radius lines. When the cement is set, the tile-disk assembly is glued into the tabletop recess before the grouting procedure is started.

measurements can be obtained, superior in accuracy to any sighting device available to the Babylonian, and for many years thereafter.

One last intriguing fact: In the fourth course there are 24 tiles. The total number of tiles in a four-course pattern is 60. No better reason has yet been found to explain why the Babylonian divided the day into 24 hours and each hour into 60 minutes, setting the pattern for all of us.

As math history or archeology, this is all strictly speculative, and I am only a widely read amateur. To my knowledge, no such tile design has ever been unearthed in a Babylonian dig. But the pattern may well have been the guarded property of the priesthood, and not commonly reproduced. The best I can claim is that I'm dealing in probabilities. And what other tile pattern harbors such wisdom within its beauty?

New grouting materials ease job of filling spaces between tile for a smooth table top. Window squeegee forces the grout into joints as it scrapes excess from face of tile. For added contrast, the grout is tinted medium gray with dry carbon black.

For the table project shown, one-inch ceramic tiles were used — which actually measure a remarkably standard ¹⁵/₁₆-inch square. The same design would be valid in a much larger size — as for a circular patio, using tiles 4¼-inches square. If you wished to carry the design out to the 60th course, you'd need 10,980 tiles.

BUILD YOURSELF THE DELTA DESK

BY KEN ISAACS

Here's another variation on traditional furniture design. It's one of the small-scale furniture forms that I developed while working on the larger principles of my Matrix Idea and Living Structures. It brings to the long-popular drop-leaf desk a body shape that is a knife-edge prism in glowing color, set on a stand.

The swing-out lamp is ideally positioned for writing, yet tucks down and inside, like a swan's head under its wing, when the leaf is

Named for the Greek letter formed by its triangular end (below), Isaacs' Delta desk is a companion piece to the "I" table described on pages 191-194 of this book, and utilizes the cube chair detailed there. Overhead view (above) shows neat, rational work layout of fold-away light, typewriter, and reference books. Drop leaf is supported on enameled steel angles. Between them is trough for storing pencils, envelopes.

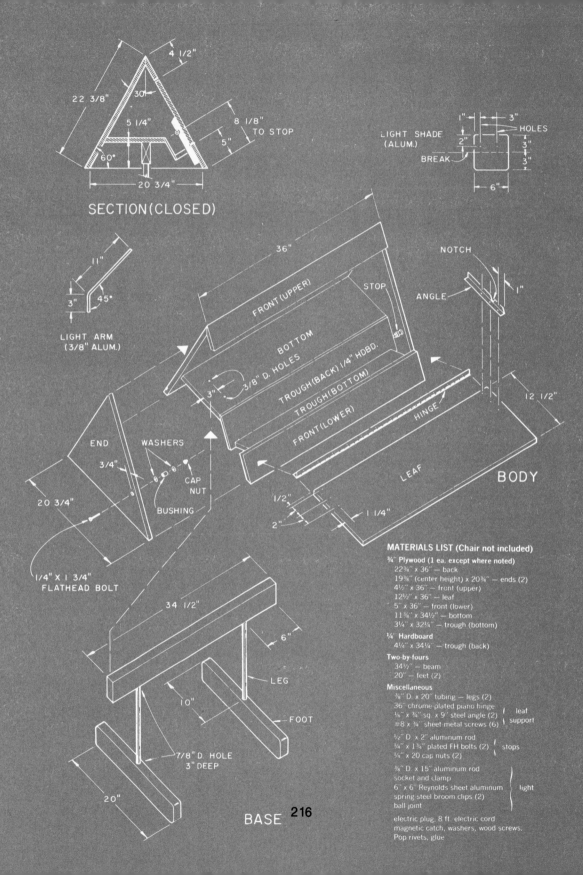

SECTION(CLOSED)

4 1/2"
30°
22 3/8"
5 1/4"
8 1/8"
TO STOP
5"
60°
20 3/4"

LIGHT SHADE
(ALUM.)
1"
3"
HOLES
2"
3"
BREAK
3"
6"

11"
3"
45°

LIGHT ARM
(3/8" ALUM.)

36"
STOP
NOTCH
FRONT(UPPER)
ANGLE
1"
BOTTOM
3/8" D. HOLES
3"
TROUGH(BACK) 1/4" HDBD.
TROUGH(BOTTOM)
FRONT(LOWER)
HINGE
12 1/2"

END
WASHERS
3/4"
CAP
NUT
BUSHING
20 3/4"
LEAF
BODY
1/2"
1 1/4"
2"

1/4" X 1 3/4"
FLATHEAD BOLT

34 1/2"
6"
LEG
10"
FOOT
7/8" D. HOLE
3" DEEP
20"

BASE 216

MATERIALS LIST (Chair not included)

¾" Plywood (1 ea. except where noted)
22⅜" x 36" — back
19⅜" (center height) x 20¾" — ends (2)
4½" x 36" — front (upper)
12½" x 36" — leaf
5" x 36" — front (lower)
11⅜" x 34½" — bottom
3¼" x 32¼" — trough (bottom)

¼" Hardboard
4¼" x 34¼" — trough (back)

Two-by-fours
34½" — beam
20" — feet (2)

Miscellaneous
⅜" D. x 20" tubing — legs (2)
36" chrome-plated piano hinge
⅛" x ¾" sq. x 9" steel angle (2) } leaf
#8 x ¾" sheet-metal screws (6) } support

½" D. x 2" aluminum rod
¼" x 1¾" plated FH bolts (2) } stops
¼" x 20 cap nuts (2)

⅜" D. x 15" aluminum rod
socket and clamp
6" x 6" Reynolds sheet aluminum } light
spring-steel broom clips (2)
ball joint

electric plug, 8 ft. electric cord
magnetic catch, washers, wood screws,
Pop rivets, glue

Clean lines when desk is closed make it a piece of modern sculpture. Leg tubing can be cut to bring leaf to best writing or typing height for any chair.

Leaf-support bracket is steel angle attached with three bolts and shimmed up with washers so leaf is level when bracket is against stop as shown in photo above; note that bracket pivots down into slot at end of trough. Below, shade is unclipped from bulb for purpose of demonstration.

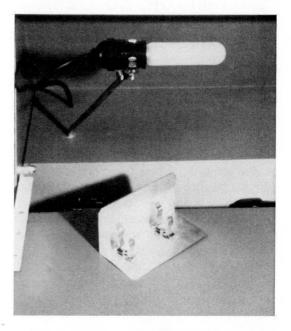

closed. The whole unit is a piece of useful sculpture.

Cut the ends first, after making sure your layout is accurate. These are the keys to the body assembly. When cutting the back and upper front pieces, set your saw to assure a tight top joint. Assemble these body pieces with glue and wood screws, then add the lower front.

Cut the beam for a snug fit between the body ends and drill the leg sockets in it and in the feet, making sure your bit is vertical. Sockets should provide a tight fit for the tubing, but you can pin the ends with a nail, if necessary. Attach dome glides to the bottom of the feet.

Screw the trough back to the angled front edge of the bottom, then glue and screw this assembly to the top of the beam.

Insert the leg tubes in the foot sockets and slip the beam onto the top ends. If all checks out, cut the trough bottom and fasten with glue and screws to the back of the lower front. Fit the leaf and attach the piano hinge to the top edge of the lower front. Join the two assemblies with glue and screws.

Cut and notch the steel angles and screw them to the leaf, shimming with washers as shown. The angle specified will support a light portable typewriter. If you'll be using a heavier machine, go to 1"-square angle and notch the free ends to fit the stop bushing for positive indexing. (The notch shown below is to clear the stop when leaf is closed.)

To make the bushings, drill a ¼" hole through the center of the aluminum rod, then cut it in half and square the ends with a file. Locate the holes for the stop bolts carefully, checking against the action of the leaf bracket before drilling through each end panel. Countersink the holes on the outside for flat-head bolts. Assembly screws, too, should all be set below surface, covered with wood putty.

The body gets an enamel undercoat, then a rolled color finish of semigloss enamel. The feet can be given a natural finish—clear sealer and wax. The angle brackets and leg tubes (unless chrome plated) can be sprayed with metal primer and a contrasting color.

The light bulb shown is a 40-watt showcase type. Broom clips are Pop-riveted to shade.

WALL-MOUNTED DESK

BY C. WAYNE CLOSE

A study desk like this is bound to please any youngster. The drawers, shelves, and perforated backboard offer plenty of storage and display space. The writing surface is exceptionally rigid; it's a scrap piece from a 1¾" solid-core birch-faced door.

We planned the desk to make use of a door cutout, banding the exposed edge with veneer. Lumberyards and cabinet shops that prepare flush doors for glass openings often sell such cutouts reasonably. Otherwise you could laminate two ¾" sheets.

The sides, shelves, and drawers were made from fir plywood since we planned to enamel everything but the writing surface. If you prefer a natural finish, better use a hardwood plywood or solid hardwood.

Rabbet the back inside edges of the sides for the perforated hardboard that forms the back. Set the board in about ⅛" past flush to allow for the hook-on fixtures.

The one-by-two at the top acts as a stiffener, and 2½" screws are driven through it into the wall studs. To mount the desk, screw a ¾"-by-1½" ledger on the wall to support the bottom of the desk.

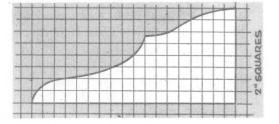

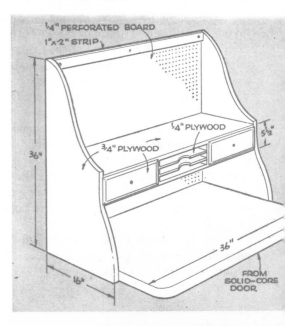

¼" PERFORATED BOARD
1"x2" STRIP
¼" PLYWOOD
¾" PLYWOOD
36"
5½"
36"
16"
FROM SOLID-CORE DOOR

218

PHOTO COASTERS

BY ROBERT WORTHAM

Make this set of man-sized coasters and you'll protect your furniture while you display your favorite photos. For storage, the entire set stacks neatly inside a five-inch cube that doubles as a contemporary accent piece.

Both coasters and cube are made from clear half-inch pine. Use lap joints at cube corners, and assemble with glue. Rout the bottom of the cube ¼″ by ¼″ for a floating look.

After assembly, spray cube and coasters with two coats of black paint. Paint dry? Next, trim your photos to size, then soak them in water and blot dry. Brush white glue on the backs of the prints and press them firmly in place. Let dry overnight, then spray coasters with two coats of varnish to protect them against damage from liquids.

Set of ten coasters stacks neatly inside a five-inch cube for storage. Both coasters and cube display favorite photos.

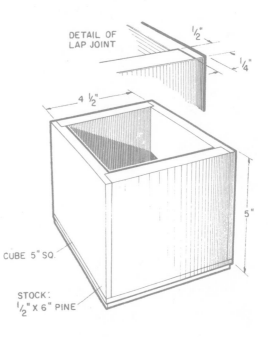

DETAIL OF LAP JOINT

½″

¼″

4 ½″

5″

CUBE 5″ SQ.

STOCK: ½″ x 6″ PINE

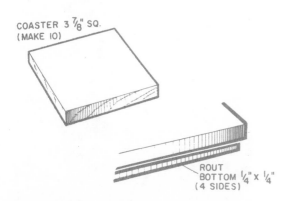

COASTER 3 ⅞″ SQ. (MAKE 10)

ROUT BOTTOM ¼″ x ¼″ (4 SIDES)

STORAGE WALL FOR A FAMILY ROOM

BY FRANK L. GREENWALD

Do you store your card tables, folding chairs, games, and other things you use for entertainment all around the house—in the attic, basement, and various closets? Why not build a special storage cabinet across the end of your family room, and have everything handy where you use it? Here's one that takes only a nine-inch strip of floor from the room's width or length.

It's removable front panels hide card tables and chairs. The center section has a foldout desk for doing household bookkeeping, or holding a projector. The cabinet top is handy for stacking magazines or serving snacks; the shelves for books.

The storage unit shown is located between a wall and a staircase. For different length walls, you can make the sections larger or smaller or add more cabinets. Minimum cabinet sizes for card tables and folding chairs are noted in the blueprint. Where one or both ends are exposed, cover the end frames with paneling, and cover the joints with corner bead.

Random-plank-type ¼″ Weldwood prefinished plywood was used, but prefinished hardboard paneling such as Masonite Royalcote would do. Plan the door joints to fall at the

Lift-out doors open up to give you easy access to the chairs and tables you use for entertainment.

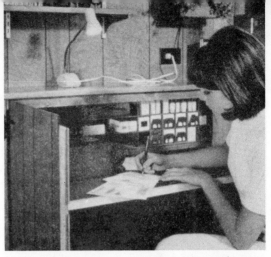

Folding desk sets up in seconds to give work space for household bookkeeping or letter writing.

panel grooves wherever possible. The varying distances between panel grooves make possible many door widths.

The basic framing is ¾″-by-1½″ strips, ripped from one-by-twelve clear pine. Cut all uprights, crosspieces, and stringers first, and then assemble the bulkhead frames using the uprights and crosspieces. Put white glue on all joints, and blunt the points of the 6d finishing nails to avoid splitting. Fasten the stringer to the frames in the same way. Set frame against wall and level it before nailing it to the studs. A few nails through the rear stringers anchor it.

Build the door frames using the opening as a guide. Next, cut the plywood covering. Use a fine-tooth saw and cut in the center of the grooves. Size all panels to cover the top and bottom stringers. On the hinged doors, cut off the bottom 1½″ and fasten these pieces to the bottom stringer.

Attach the door panels to the door frames using ¾″ #18 brads and white glue. Complete the lift-out doors by adding the interlocking plywood pieces to the lower stringer and door frame. This aligns and hinges the door, yet lets you lift it out easily. Hold them in place with bullet catches in the upper edge.

The outer door panels for the desk section are attached and the doors hinged in place before the inner panels are put on. Twist the doors to fit the opening before attaching the inner panel.

Make the desk leaf 1½″ longer than the distance between the inner faces of the doors when they are at right angles to the front of the storage unit. Cut the leaf at the fold point before cutting it to length.

Fasten the two desk-leaf pieces with a continuous hinge; then fasten the long end to the right door with two 4″ T hinges. Drill two holes in the left end to slip over nails driven into the crosspiece.

Build the interior of the desk compartment to suit your needs. An easy-to-build pigeonhole divider is shown in the blueprint on the preceding two pages.

If you use prefinished paneling to build the storage wall, you're practically done. Just stain and finish the trim to match.

Finish up the job by putting shelves on the wall over the storage unit. An easy way to do this is to use Stanley Flaire aluminum shelf standards and brackets, and Decor prefinished shelves. The brackets come in five colors.

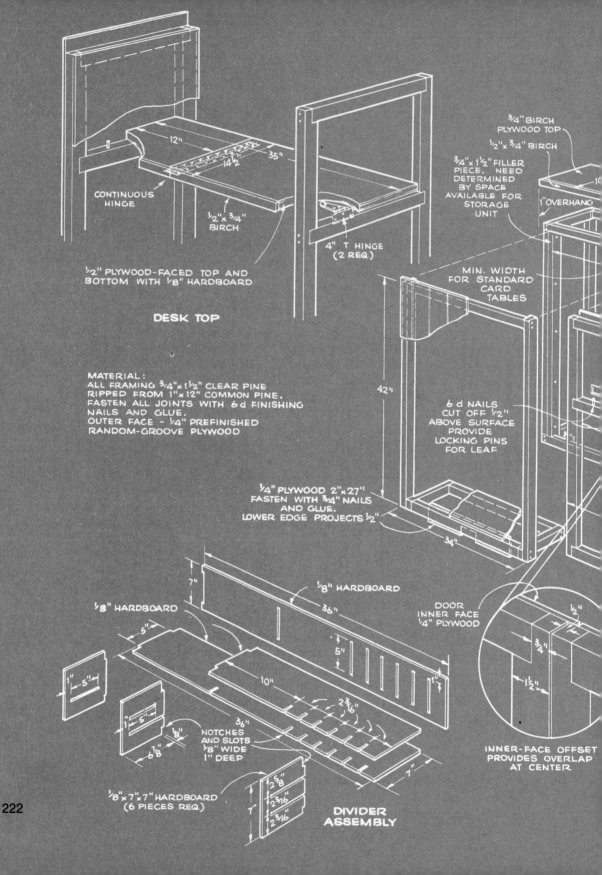

12"

35"

14½"

CONTINUOUS
HINGE

½" x ¾"
BIRCH

4" T HINGE
(2 REQ.)

¾" BIRCH
PLYWOOD TOP

½" x ¾" BIRCH

¾" x 1½" FILLER
PIECE. NEED
DETERMINED
BY SPACE
AVAILABLE FOR
STORAGE
UNIT

1" OVERHANG

½" PLYWOOD-FACED TOP AND
BOTTOM WITH ⅛" HARDBOARD

DESK TOP

MIN. WIDTH
FOR STANDARD
CARD
TABLES

MATERIAL:
ALL FRAMING ¾" x 1½" CLEAR PINE
RIPPED FROM 1" x 12" COMMON PINE.
FASTEN ALL JOINTS WITH 6 d FINISHING
NAILS AND GLUE.
OUTER FACE - ¼" PREFINISHED
RANDOM-GROOVE PLYWOOD

42"

6 d NAILS
CUT OFF ½"
ABOVE SURFACE
PROVIDE
LOCKING PINS
FOR LEAF

¼" PLYWOOD 2" x 27"
FASTEN WITH ¾" NAILS
AND GLUE.
LOWER EDGE PROJECTS ½"

34"

7"

⅛" HARDBOARD

⅛" HARDBOARD

36"

DOOR
INNER FACE
¼" PLYWOOD

½"

¾"

5"

5"

5"

1"

1"

10"

1½"

2³⁄₁₆"

1"

5"

1"

5"

⅛"

6⅞"

NOTCHES
AND SLOTS
⅛" WIDE
1" DEEP

36"

7"

INNER-FACE OFFSET
PROVIDES OVERLAP
AT CENTER

⅛" x 7" x 7" HARDBOARD
(6 PIECES REQ.)

2⅝"

2³⁄₁₆"

2³⁄₁₆"

2³⁄₁₆"

7"

**DIVIDER
ASSEMBLY**

222

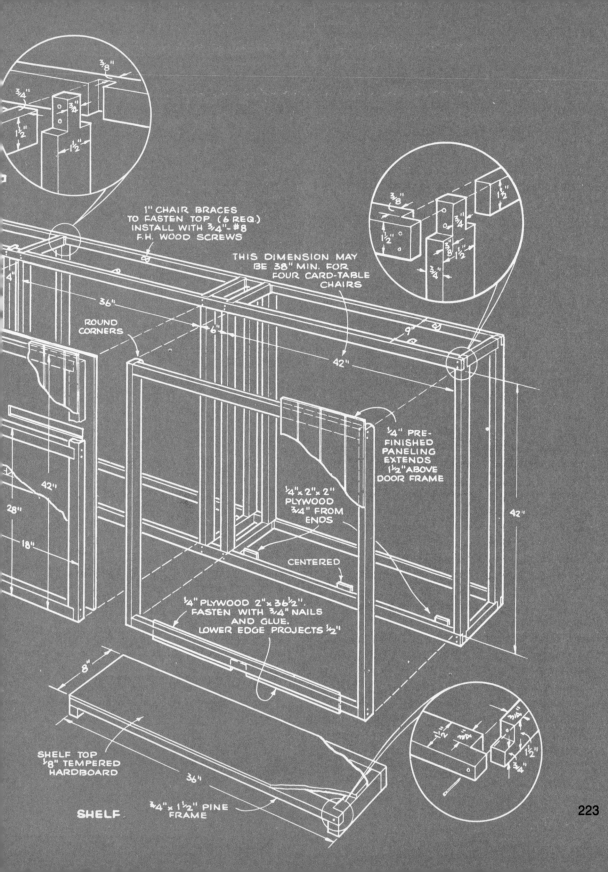

1" CHAIR BRACES
TO FASTEN TOP (6 REQ.)
INSTALL WITH ¾"-#8
F.H. WOOD SCREWS

THIS DIMENSION MAY
BE 38" MIN. FOR
FOUR CARD-TABLE
CHAIRS

ROUND
CORNERS

36"

4"

6"

42"

9"

¼" PRE-
FINISHED
PANELING
EXTENDS
1½" ABOVE
DOOR FRAME

¼" × 2" × 2"
PLYWOOD
¾" FROM
ENDS

42"

28"

18"

42"

CENTERED

¼" PLYWOOD 2" × 36½".
FASTEN WITH ¾" NAILS
AND GLUE.
LOWER EDGE PROJECTS ½"

8"

SHELF TOP
⅛" TEMPERED
HARDBOARD

36"

SHELF

¾" × 1½" PINE
FRAME

223

NONSKID CUTTING BOARD HAS OWN SHARPENER

BY HARRY WALTON

Scraps of hardwood flooring, often to be had for the asking at building sites, make a handsome, serviceable board for cutting meats or chopping vegetables.

Cut and square four pieces to identical length. Plane or saw off the tongue of one piece and the grooved edge of another. Apply water-resistant glue to the other edges and clamp up the four pieces as shown. Put a piece of paper, preferably wax paper, on each side to keep pieces from sticking to the clamp boards.

Trim both tongues and grooves off the two crosspieces (the feet). Holding them against the ends of the glued-up section, and flush with its top, drill and counterbore for 1½" wood screws. Assemble with glue all along the joint.

When the glue has set, sand or scrape off any glue or paper that stick to the top, leaving a smooth, flat cutting surface. Tap the feet for a 1½" suction cup inside each corner as shown. If you haven't an 8-32 tap, make starting holes with a No. 29 or 30 drill. Then hammer an oiled 8-32 steel bolt in slightly, and screw it ½" in to cut threads in the wood. Remove bolt, and screw in suction cups to an even depth.

Finish the board all over by swabbing on several coats of hot vegetable cooking oil. Mount a knife sharpener under the board.

Built-in knife sharpener fastened to the underside of the cutting board is handy when you want it. Suction cups keep the board from slipping on even the slickest counter surface.

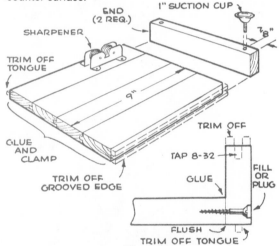

Use this clamping arrangement to glue up the pieces of flooring. Use waterproof glue and wedge the joints tight between blocks screwed to a board. Top clamping prevents buckling.

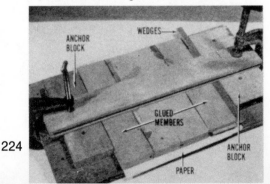

224

AN EARLY AMERICAN HUTCH

BY W. LUXENBURG

Something both decorative and useful: That's what our ancestors liked, and it's why an Early American hutch is as popular today as when Washington crossed the Delaware.

More often than not, it's made of maple, as here. But other hardwoods—birch or cherry, and even a softwood such as white pine—yield a fine piece of furniture.

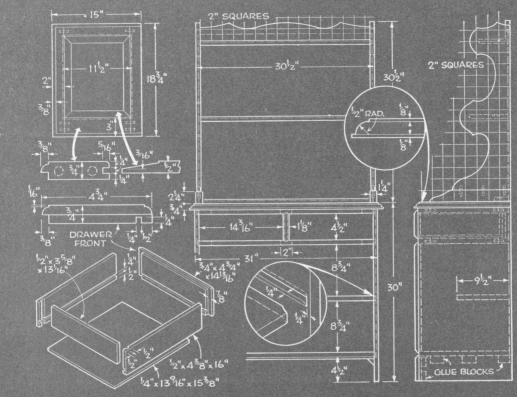

Start with the base. Cut the top, sides, bottom shelf, and drawer-slide framing. Using a dado head on your power saw, cut dadoes in the sides to receive all shelving and the drawer-slide stretchers. Note that dadoes are stopped 1/4″ short of the front so the joints will appear flush. Assemble the drawer-slide parts with dowels and glue; everything else mentioned so far, with glue. Once you have this much in clamps, nail up through the bottom shelf and top slide frame into the sides. This will give the base sufficient stability until the plywood back and the bottom glue blocks are added. When these *are* added, the base will become sturdy as a rock. Before you nail on back, cut middle shelf and glue it in place. Note that the back is rabbeted into the sides.

Finishing touches for the base include the drawers, doors, and bottom filler. Drawers are of standard construction with maple fronts, 1/2″ pine sides and 1/4″ plywood bottoms. Two sides and the front are grooved to receive the bottom, while the sides are grooved vertically to take the back.

A shaping head on your power saw will come in handy for making the doors (see section drawing) and for molding the drawer fronts. Rails and stiles are assembled with dowels and glue. Leave 1/8″ clearance on the top, bottom, and sides of the doors (and 1/8″ overall around the drawers).

Now start on the upper half. Measure and cut dadoes for shelves in the sides before doing the curved work. The curves are most easily cut on a band saw. Sides are mounted to the feet with dowels and glue, and the feet are fastened to the top of the base from underneath, with wood screws. Before putting up the shelves, groove-out plate slots. Do the same in the plate strip that fits between the base top and the back. Plywood back is rabbeted into sides, as with base, and your last major part to assemble is the scrolled top panel.

Finish by spraying a sealer coat over an oil stain, followed by a few coats of lacquer. Sand between coats, and after last coat use steel wool lightly, followed by coat of wax.

A CLOSET ORGANIZER

BY RICHARD C. SICKLER

Solution to closet clutter anywhere in the house can be a slide-in cabinet. This one was built of 3/4″ Philippine-mahogany plywood, just tall enough to slide under lower shelf 62″ from floor. Cabinet is 3″ less than closet depth of 24″; total width is 21 1/2″, leaving usable space on either side of it in 36″-wide closet. In closet shown (below), sliding doors in grooved tracks were installed in front of shelves above cabinet.

61⅞"

4¼"

7½"

21"

21¾"

21½"

Partitions were placed in some of the drawers for convenient storage. Notice the egg-crate assembly. Note that the drawer fronts—flush on three sides—have a ¾" lip on the top edge.

Support frames, recessed ¾", act as stops for the drawer fronts. Back is not needed if cabinet goes against wall. Glides were installed on bottom.

Both plywood sides for cabinet were dadoed to take shelf supports at same time. Sides were then placed on the floor and the oak drawer supports were all mounted with glue and 2¼"-#8 f.h. screws.

Bottom and top members held the sides of the cabinet while the front and rear drawer supports were being installed. Supports were half-lapped and mounted with glue and ⅝" f.h. screws.

FOOTSTOOL FROM ABE LINCOLN'S HOME

BY DAVID WARREN

What started out to be a family camping trip to the Lincoln shrines in Illinois ended in my happening upon a piece of furniture that belonged to Abraham Lincoln—this cane footstool. It caught my attention immediately as an easy piece to copy.

During the trip home, while the children chattered about the cabins at New Salem and their riverboat trip on the Sangamon, I mused about the fun I'd have working with walnut and learning to cane while producing a copy

of the footstool we had seen—and had been permitted to measure—in Lincoln's Springfield home.

It meets all the requirements of a good footstool: lightweight but strong, functional but attractive. The cane gives it a light, airy appearance; the leg design insures strength and durability. All the material necessary for the project can be purchases from mail-order supply houses such as Craftsman Wood Service Co., 2727 S. Mary St., Chicago 60647.

Making the stool. There is a charm in the slight imperfections that creep into almost every handcrafted article. Measurements of the original stool disclosed that the legs varied slightly in diameter, the ends differed in width $1/16''$, and the oval top was in fact asymmetrical.

Start by cutting the four top pieces and planing them to $15/16''$ thick. Dowel and glue them into a rectangle. Only the inside dimensions of the rectangle need to be accurate.

While the top is drying, turn the four legs. Sand all turnings completely before removing from the lathe. Mark and bore each stretcher hole.

Lincoln bought his Springfield home for $1,500, in 1844, from the pastor who married him and Mary Todd. Now restored by the state, it houses many authenticated Lincoln belongings, such as the footstool from which the one in the photo at right was copied.

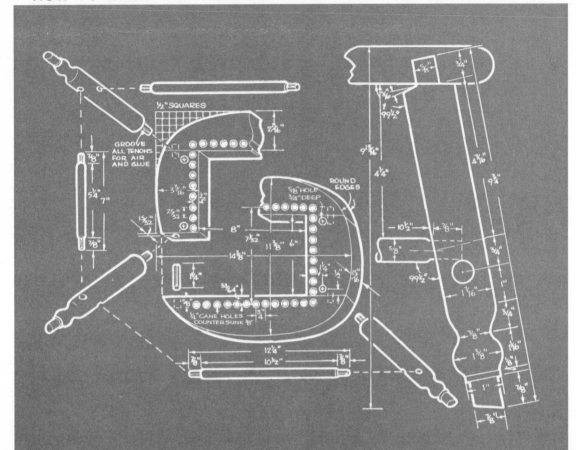

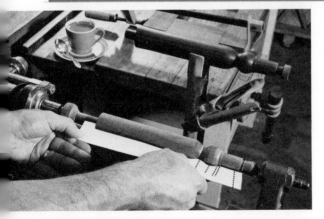

1 To turn the four identical legs, prop the first turning behind the lathe as a model for turning the other three. By checking frequently with a cardboard template, the job becomes easy.

2 Shop-built V block centered under the bit holds leg while you bore tenon holes. Insert scrap stock in first hole as a reference to insure boring second hole exactly 90 degrees from first.

3 To get equal leg splay, tilt drill-press table 13 degrees. Tape paper to table, and place work under bit. Lower quill so bit presses on center point marked for leg hole. Lock quill in this position. Pivot work until inside edges are 45 degrees to table edge and mark paper. Clamp work on guideline and drill ⅝″ hole in this and opposite corners. Make similar line for other two holes.

4 To lay out the top, prepare a template on cardboard folded into quarters. A light-colored pencil (white or pink, for example) shows up well on walnut and is easy to follow when cutting perimeter.

5 Trestle is square when diagonal measurements are equal. (Note that caning holes are drilled before final assembly.) With glue dry, a disk sander finishes feet to the proper length and angle.

Next, bore the four leg tenon holes in the underside of the top. The photos show how to set up the drill press. Mark the ¼" cane holes on the top and bore them. (Note that the spacing varies on sides and ends.) To finish, countersink each hole ⅛" on the underside.

Assemble the legs and top, and check the length of the stretchers in case your stool varies from the plan. Then turn the stretchers. The ½" tenons on the original were hand-carved for a drive fit. Whether made by hand or with power, gouge a small groove along the tenons to permit all glue and air to escape from the hole.

Lay out and cut the top's outside contour. After rounding the top edge with a spoke-shave or block plane (do end grains first), finish-sand the piece. Since final assembly locks the stool together, make a test assembly.

The finish. The original shows neither wear nor distress marks. The principal signs of age are the craze marks in the varnish. To give the stool a finish that would take scuffing from shoes, I filled the open-grain walnut and applied satin-finish polyurethane varnish to all the wood surfaces.

Caning the top. Experts say a small rectangle such as this is the simplest caning job you can tackle. After doing it, I agree. The photo sequence gives the steps.

To start, select a long strand and snip the end to a point. Next, soak it for about 10 minutes in a solution of three tablespoonfuls of glycerine, mixed with two cups of water. Two tricks I learned: (1) have another strand soaking while you work; and (2) to keep dampened cane pliable overnight, store it in a plastic bag.

Keep the smooth, rounded side of the cane up and prevent the strands from twisting, particularly as you weave on the underside and through the holes. A final hint: Don't overtighten the cane in the first four steps—just pull it snug.

HOW TO DO THE CANING PART OF THE PROJECT

1 Make pegs from 4" lengths of ¼" dowel pointed in a pencil sharpener. You will also need an awl, scissors, glycerine, water. After soaking cane, start weaving by inserting 4" through hole A and secure with a peg. Pass strand to the right, insert through hole B, pull taut, and bring up through hole C. Repeat back and forth till all holes are filled. Coil the excess cane at the end for a later step.

2 Put 4″ of cane down in hole 1, peg, and bring strand toward you. Insert into hole 2, pull taut, and bring up through hole 3. Continue weaving this way until all holes are filled as in Step. 1.

3 This step is simply a repeat of the Step 1 weaving, but the strands of cane are kept to the side of those strung initially. Cane must be kept moistened. Text gives the solution to use.

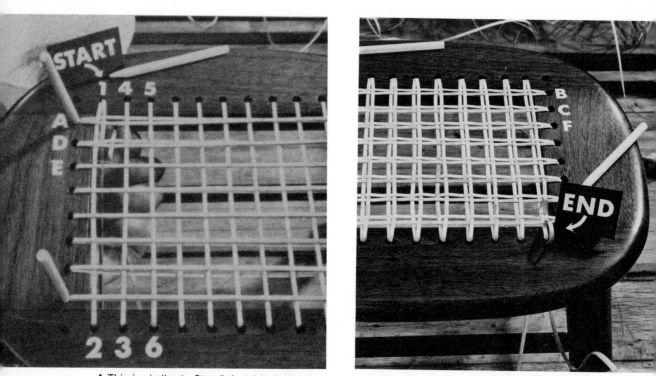

4 This is similar to Step 2, but this time cane is woven *under* Step 1 and *over* Step 3 strands (under the strands below, over the strands on top). After weaving first four strands, pull entire length through. Here again, strands are kept to the side of cane previously woven in Step 2. To arrange the cane into neat squares, simply squeeze the strands together with your thumb and index finger.

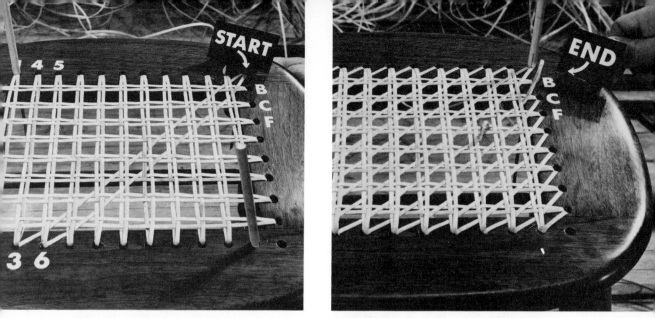

5 Care is needed here. Woven diagonally, the strand passes over the cane placed in Steps 1 and 3 and under those strung in Steps 2 and 4. Starting at the upper right-hand corner, weave over two, under two, across the panel. At the opposite corner, insert strand into hole 6, pull it taut, and bring it up through hole 3. Using the same method, you now weave back to the starting point.

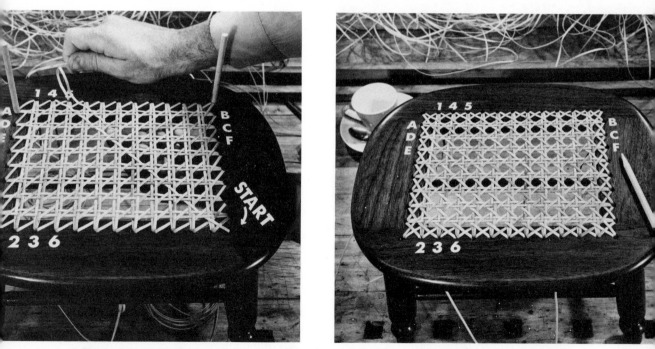

6 This is the opposite of the previous step. Strand runs under Steps 1 and 3 strands, and over those of Steps 2 and 4. Additionally, it runs over and under the strand woven in Step 5. After completing the caning operation, dampen the panel thoroughly and arrange the octagonal holes uniformly, using a peg. To keep the panel from becoming stiff, wipe it occasionally with a damp cloth.

233

7 In binding, one strand on top serves as a border; a longer strand under the seat passes up each hole and back down into the same hole to form a binding-holding loop. Repeat the process around the cane perimeter, securing the continuous piece of binding at each hole. Keep loops taut so cane doesn't slide back. When back at start, tuck last ½" of strand under starting end (below).

8 Flop the stool and, after dampening the loose ends, tie each with a half-hitch knot. Pull knot taut and trim. As cane dries it stretches and tightens.

WHAT YOU CAN MAKE WITH COUNTER-TOP CUTOUTS

There's treasure—in project material—in just about any woodworking shop in your town: the stack of cutouts left over when sinks were installed in counter tops. They come in a variety of sizes and shapes, and at bargain rates.

These cutouts can give you a head start on all kinds of projects. The top is already finished—a durable plastic laminate is bonded to a backing of ¾" plywood or particle board (usually of slightly less thickness). Your main job is finishing off the edges.

You'll find cutouts most suitable for use where you want the same qualities you have in a counter top—a surface that's waterproof and resistant to burns and scratches. If your project is for your kitchen, you may find a cutout that matches your counter top. Take your ruler along to be sure you get a cutout big enough for the item you're planning.

In most cabinet shops, cutouts are made with a router and template. This means the corners will be rounded, the edges true. Since the outside perimeter is square, it's a snap to cut the piece to size on a bench or radial saw. A combination blade cuts the material fine, but if you own a carbide-tipped blade, use it. Plastic laminate will not ruin an ordinary blade, but it will dull it.

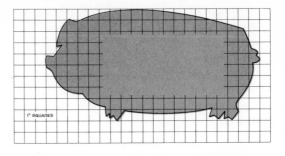

These pieces of wood covered with plastic laminate started as counter-top cutouts (photo above), left-overs from a local cabinet shop. They're inexpensive and they give you a head start on all kinds of projects, a few of which are shown below.

PORKER CUTTING BOARD

Porker cutting board can be made in 30 minutes (left-over material makes a cheese server). Draw the design on the back of the cutout. Cut with a saber saw, using a fine-tooth metal-cutting blade to prevent surface chips. Sand the edge smooth, apply wood tape with waterproof glue, and, when dry, rub with salad oil. Attach two eye hooks to hang the board.

Screws turned into the underside should not measure more than $5/8''$. You can use screws that come with factory-made legs; the plate takes up about $1/8''$, so they won't come through the top.

Finishing the edges. If you want to stick to a natural wood finish, one of the simplest is wood tape, held on with waterproof glue. Outside corner guard, with one side ripped narrower than the other, works fine, too. This is particularly good on trays; the vertical off-set keeps objects from sliding off. If you want a flush top, use lattice.

There is also molded wood trim, and shelf edge (plain or striated). Both are attached with brads and glue. Veneer can always be used and, if you have some decent plywood scrap kicking around the shop, you can make your own.

Nonwood edges. Snap-on molding is the most commonly used, but for rounded shapes (like the pedestal table), the type you screw on is best. Plastic-laminate self-edge makes a good-looking finish but is limited to straight edges and large-radius bends. And finally, if you plan to paint the edges, they must be filled, sanded, and sealed first.

You can use your favorite finishing method on any of the projects shown except the cheese server and the cutting board. Because they contact food, rub the wood surfaces with salad oil.

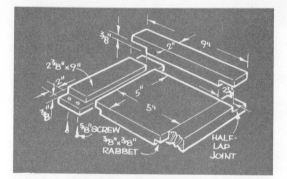

CHEESE TRAY

A walnut surround (or walnut plywood with the edges taped) cradles the cheese-holding cutout. The four walnut pieces are glued and screwed together. Rabbet the cutout on two sides and hold it in place with screws only. Then the insert can be changed, if desired. To finish, rub the wood with salad oil.

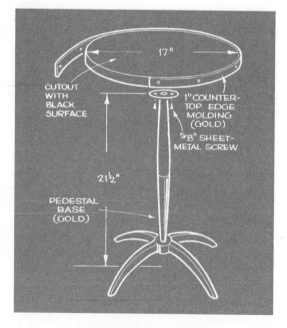

PEDESTAL TABLE

Handsome, yet simple, this table began with an attractive black circular cutout and was completed with legs and metal edge molding (gold colored) from Sears. To attach molding, tack end in place and bring the strip around until you're back at start. Cut molding with hacksaw.

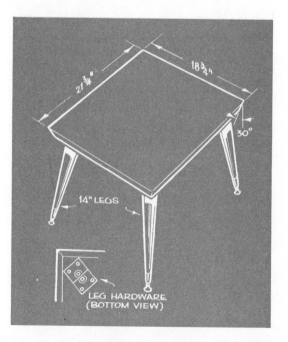

COFFEE TABLE

Top for coffee table was cut to size with saw blade set at 30 degrees. Edges were finished with flexible wood tape. A wood molding or plastic laminate could be substituted, if desired. Factory-made legs are available in several styles. They screw into hardware installed under the top.

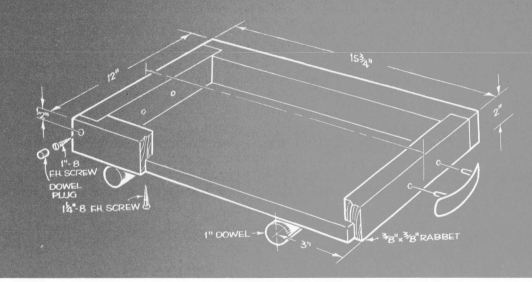

FLOWER-POT HOLDER

All sides of frame are rabbeted on bottom edges to receive the cutout. Attach it with waterproof glue and screws. Fasten the 1″ dowel "legs" with countersunk 1¼″ flathead screws. Frame shown is made of oak, with Renaissance handles by Amerock. For contrast, walnut dowel plugs were used at the corners. Wood was finished with two coats of shellac. For outdoor use, finish with exterior varnish.

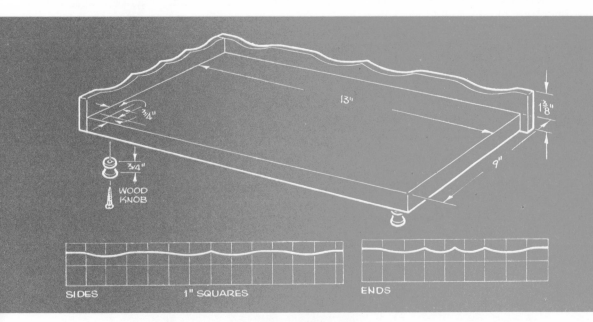

CANAPÉ TRAY

To keep weight of tray as low as possible use a cutout made of plywood rather than particle board. Sides are ½″ pine attached with glue and well-set four-penny finishing nails. To prevent wood-knob legs from scratching table tops, glue felt under each one. The tray shown was finished with oil stain. Corners and nail holes were antiqued with burnt umber. Two coats of lacquer finished the job.

PARTICLEBOARD
COFFEE TABLE

BY R. J. DE CRISTOFORO

To build this table, cut all parts to overall size first, then set up on the table saw to cut the rabbets in top frame and leg pieces. Use a dado assembly or the two-pass technique with a conventional blade to make the rabbets. Assemble the frame pieces on the top slab, using plenty of glue and 4d finishing nails.

Assemble the legs the same way, but switch to 2d nails. Pilot holes may simplify the driving of nails into the $3/8''$ slabs. Set all nails and fill holes with neutral-tone wood dough. Attach leg-mounting blocks to underside of top. Legs are secured with dowels through these blocks so they can be detached for moving and storage. (The hollow legs make a fine family "safe.")

To finish, use the pad sanding, putty filling, pad sanding, sealing procedure. I topped off with Old Master's "Creative Finish" in dubonnet red, followed with McCloskey "Heirloom" finish, light sanding, and wax.

TECHNIQUES FOR WORKING WITH PARTICLEBOARD

When you saw particleboard, remember that there's no directional grain, so forget about crosscutting and ripping; the blade you use for one does for the other. Particleboard is quite easy to cut and—surprisingly—does not

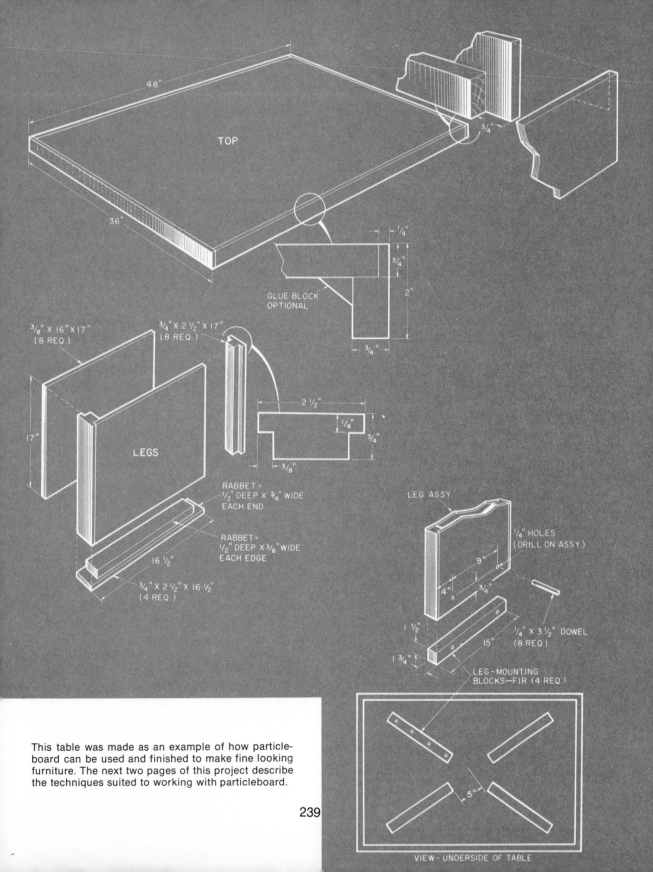

48"

TOP

36"

3/4"

GLUE BLOCK
OPTIONAL

1/4"

3/4"

2"

3/4"

3/8" X 16" X 17"
(8 REQ.)

3/4" X 2 1/2" X 17"
(8 REQ.)

17"

LEGS

RABBET=
1/2" DEEP X 3/4" WIDE
EACH END

RABBET=
1/2" DEEP X 3/8" WIDE
EACH EDGE

2 1/2"

1/4"

3/4"

3/8"

16 1/2"

3/4" X 2 1/2" X 16 1/2"
(4 REQ.)

LEG ASSY.

1/4" HOLES
(DRILL ON ASSY.)

9"

4"

3/4"

1 1/2"

1 3/4"

15"

1/4" X 3 1/2" DOWEL
(8 REQ.)

LEG-MOUNTING
BLOCKS—FIR (4 REQ.)

5"

This table was made as an example of how particleboard can be used and finished to make fine looking
furniture. The next two pages of this project describe
the techniques suited to working with particleboard.

239

VIEW - UNDERSIDE OF TABLE

No special techniques are required to saw particle-board, whether you're using saber saw (left) or table saw (right), band or jig saw. Adhesive in particleboard is abrasive, causing tool blades to dull faster than they would on various woods, hard or soft. For big projects, go to carbide-tipped tools.

chip easily on kerf lines. This must be due to the excellent particle bond.

It is abrasive, so extensive work calls for carbide-tipped tools. Just "to see," I used a heavy-gauge, conventional crosscut blade to do all the cutting required for our sample coffee table project. I'm sure a sensitive gauge would prove the teeth to be duller than they would be after a similar amount of cut.ing in pine, but, the point is, the blade did the whole job well. If it's your desire to build five of those tables or do a comparable amount of sawing, then by all means, go to carbide.

Sawing throws out stingy little gritty particles, nowhere near as soft as regular sawdust. So, wear goggles for sawing and sanding.

I suggest no changes in procedures or blades when doing saber, band, or jig sawing. Be aware of regular criteria in blade choice in relation to cut quality. Hollow-ground or taper-ground blades with many teeth produce the smoothest edges. Blades with few teeth and lots of set cut faster. The latter is the way to go if you plan to cut a bit outside the line and finish up by sanding.

Particleboard does not have a "good" side, so when considering what side of the work should be up when sawing, merely decide which surface will be exposed after assembly. This is smart because on a table-saw cut there's bound to be a bit more chipping on the bottom of the kerf than there will be at the top.

Drilling. Here, it's wise to pay maximum attention to backing up the work. This will eliminate (or at least minimize) chipping on breakthrough, a common problem when working with particleboard. This applies more to spade bits and twist drills than to fly cutters and hole saws, but it's good shop practice to keep positive contact between work and backup even if it involves clamping.

With all hole-formers, stay within the speeds and feed pressures you should use with regular lumber. Don't be over-cautious with feed or you'll do nothing more than burnish the work and dull the tool. Good speed and feed combinations provide for *steady cutting*.

Routing and shaping. Any edge you can rout or shape on wood can be accomplished on particleboard. Here, carbide-tipped cutters definitely do a better job. But regardless of the shape and smoothness of the cut, you still must do some filling to subdue the pitted porous surface you expose.

Edge treatments. Edges can be hidden by joint design and by any of the numerous methods used on plywood. This includes banding with self-adhesive wood tapes, edging or bulking with a nonrelated material such as natural wood, finishing with wood molding or T molding, etc.

Two systems I use are the waterfall edge

240

and the application of a thin surface veneer cut from the particleboard itself.

To veneer edges, work with a hollow-ground or carbide-tipped blade and organize the saw for ripping. Set blade projection a bit higher than the thickness of the stock you wish to edge—set blade-to-fence distance so the "cut-off" will be the thickness of the veneer you want.

It's okay to see how thin you can cut, but anything up to $1/16''$ is acceptable. The pass is made with the stock on edge. To stick on the homemade veneer, work with conventional glue or, better yet, with special veneer cement.

Particleboard edges, no matter how smooth the cut, are more porous than the faces and need special attention under stain or paint. My preference for a filler is a product like Duratite's Water Putty. You mix it with water and have some control over consistency. Thus you can concoct a thin coating for surfaces; a paste-like coating for edges. After it dries, you sand it smooth and the particleboard is ready for finishing.

Fastening. Nails alone are seldom satisfactory, but used as reinforcement for a good blue joint, they are acceptable. Set them the usual way, but drive them only a minimum depth below the surface. Fill the holes with a natural-tone wood dough.

Screws (preferably sheet-metal screws

Routing and shaping are best done with carbide-tipped tools. But no matter how smooth the cut, you'll have to use filler to smooth out pits. And always wear goggles—particleboard chips are sharp.

when not objectionable) provide more strength, but don't neglect conventional drilling of pilot and shank holes. In fact, the pilot hole should be as deep as the screw is long. When possible, use a longer screw (not necessarily a *fatter* one) than you would use under similar conditions in lumber and always put a drop of glue in the hole before you drive the screw.

A good idea is to go through a fastening procedure on scrap before you assemble the project. Then you can decide whether to go up or down with screw or nail sizes. Incidentally, should you get hung-up when driving nails into the edge of particleboard especially $3/8''$ or $1/2''$ stock), drill pilot holes first. Keep such holes at minimum size and dip the nail in glue before you drive it.

Sanding and finishing. It's not likely that you'll ever have to do more than pad-sand with #220 paper; #120 at the most. But the effects are easily judged if you sand some scrap along with the project; then test-finish before you commit yourself.

For a good paint job, it's best to go through the Water Putty application already described and to follow with a good pad-sanding. For a

Holes are no problem—hole saws, fly cutters, spade bits, twist drills all work well. If any precautions are required they're in area of tight backups to minimize chipping when cutter breaks through.

clear finish you can skip the surface filling. Particleboard does have tiny pit marks but they won't show under a clear finish, and can be effective under paint when you want a distressed look.

I like the idea of applying a coat of sealer to particleboard just after sanding, regardless of the final finish. Put the sealer on everywhere—outside, inside, and under.

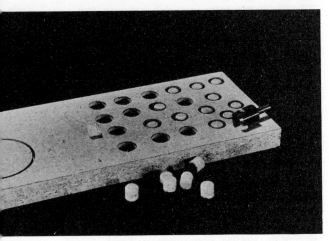

Plugs can be cut standard fashion. This brings up a good fastening trick. Use screws, conceal them with plugs—a technique similar to plugging with wood. But try to make counterboring fairly shallow.

Typical edge treatments include wood molding, self-adhesive edge banding, home-made T molding, particleboard veneer you cut in the shop. Veneer treatment produces an edge that matches the surfaces exactly, since veneer is of the same material.

HOME HOBBY CENTER

BY CHARLES E. RHINE

Whatever your hobby is—modelmaking, handicrafts, electronics—this bench is a perfect center for your activities. It's crammed with ideas taken from several types of industrial benches. Every inch of it serves to make your hobby more fun. There's plenty of room for storing tools and supplies, and lots of working space. And that unusual stool lets

242

you relax. Both pieces were designed by A. M. Warkaske, Editor of Rockwell's magazine, *Flying Chips*.

The bench has two work surfaces—one at stand-up height, one at sitting height. (The high-low stool lets you sit at either one.) The top lid of the bench closes level to make a large work surface. Or flip down the hinged endpieces, and the lid slopes forward to make a drafting board for designing new projects. Open the lid and there's a low-level bench top at chair height.

Building it: First make the drawers and the two drawer compartments. Dado end panels and glue the drawer slides in place. Build the frame for the bench top in two sections and join them with a hardwood spline. Screw the hardboard surface to the bench top so it can be easily replaced when worn. Use a ⅜" mortising bit to make the holes for the bench pins. To make the bench so it can be disassembled for easy moving, use screws to attach the bench top, the back panel, and the kneehole panel. Attach shelf cleats for back compartment before putting back panel on. Most of hobby center is ¾" plywood.

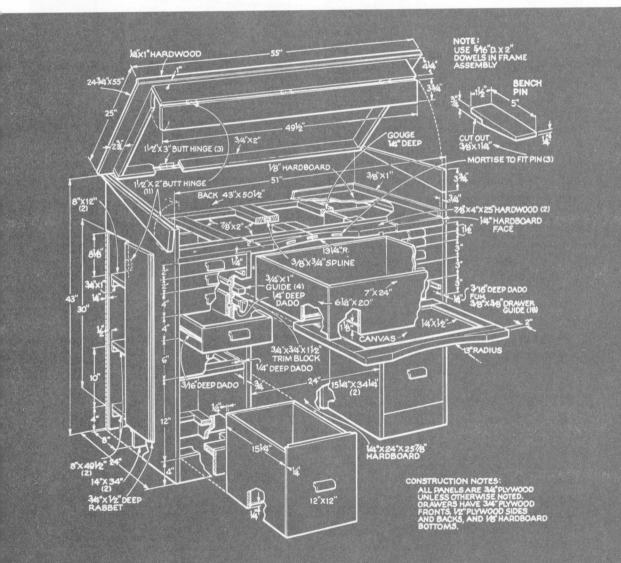

Roomy drafting board is made by flipping down the hinged endpieces to let the top slope forward. Keep drawing instruments handy in shallow top drawers.

A large drawer right under the center of the bench top makes a handy trash bin. Line it with sheet metal to make it easy to clean out. You pull the drawer out and clear the work surface with a quick sweep of a brush.

Mortises in the front of the bench top are for bench pins. Plug in a bench pin to get a handy surface for working with small parts. The jeweler's apron slides out below the trash drawer. This is a shallow drawer with a canvas bottom. You pull it out when working with small parts like those used in modelmaking. If a little screw is dropped, it's caught in the apron. You don't have to get down on your hands and knees and search the floor.

The drawers—13 of them—are made in six different sizes to fit practically any need. At the bottom of each tier is a large file drawer.

The storage space at the back of the bench can be reached by doors at either end. It holds materials up to 8″ across and 4′ long. Also, when the top lid is in closed position there is an 8″ space above the regular workbench top. This is a fine place for freshly glued, painted, or semiassembled projects to be left safe and out of the dust.

The hobby center is made mostly from ¾″ plywood. Construction details are given in the drawing. Assemble it with finish nails and glue. Set the nails and fill holes with putty. Sand all surfaces, blunting corners, and give it two coats of penetrating resin sealer.

There's plenty of storage space at the back of the bench to put long things such as dowels or lumber. There's storage space between the two tops, too.

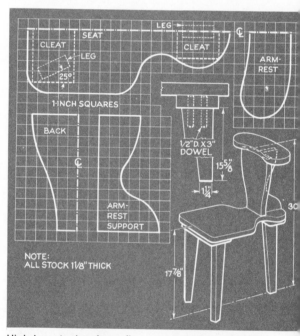

High-low stool makes a fine accessory for your hobby center. Or build it by itself to use around the kitchen. It goes together with dowels and glue.

CHILD'S SLEEP-PLAY UNIT—WITH PLAIN METAL SHELVING AND HARDBOARD

BY ROBERT MANGURIAN

With a quick and inexpensive construction system that uses steel shelving and hardboard, you can create a "total environment" for your child's room—or for your own den.

Children's rooms have always suffered from two problems: The bed, a single-purpose piece of furniture, occupies a large portion of the usually cramped floor area. And the child's clothes and toys generally clutter the remaining space, resulting in a constant battle with parents over "cleaning up the mess."

The design approach I've employed here resulted from a study of my own child's activities—playing with toys and games, reading, drawing, building things, sleeping, and keeping track of his clothes and other belongings.

My conclusion: Since the primary place for most of these activities is the floor, an effort should be made to free this valuable space. This objective—coupled with the fact that children, for the first 12 years, can comfortably occupy two levels in rooms with ceiling heights designed for adults—led to the concept of the Child's Living Machine shown here.

In only six sq. ft. It's a multipurpose unit that provides for all the functions of standard children's furniture while occupying only six square feet of floor space. The usual area required by children's furniture is 40 sq. ft.—about a third of the total area of a small bedroom. My raised sleeping platform (reached by a movable ladder) frees the floor space; supporting shelf units, accessible from both floor and bed levels, provide storage and all additional functions.

Clothing is stored at bed level and hung on the outside panels by means of standard perfboard hooks. Toys, blocks, dolls, and sports equipment are contained in the hole and slot bins. A fold-up desk-table is used whenever

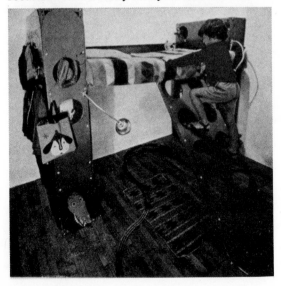

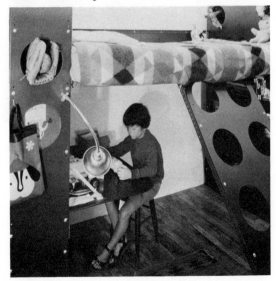

Underbunk study area has drop-leaf desk that folds up for extra play space. Adjustable open shelf is used for book storage.

Slots and holes at opposite end of bunk provide variety of storage and display bins for toys and small clothing items like sox.

Divider sections are angled across author's living room. Shelves at rear store bulky household items.

a raised work surface is needed. A fold-up sloped surface is a backrest for floor-sitting and an easel for drawing and painting.

The storage bins are designed to solve the clutter problem. Children don't take naturally to drawers, but they'll develop the habit of organized neatness if you provide them with ample bins and open shelves that keep things accessible and in sight.

Design responds to needs. My Living Machine is fully responsive to a child's growth and changing needs. The mattress platform is adjustable for head clearance, and the fold-up desk can be raised at six-inch increments to adjust to the child's growth. The sketches show the Living Machine in alternate assemblies, either of which can be placed in a room in several positions. Where possible, it's best

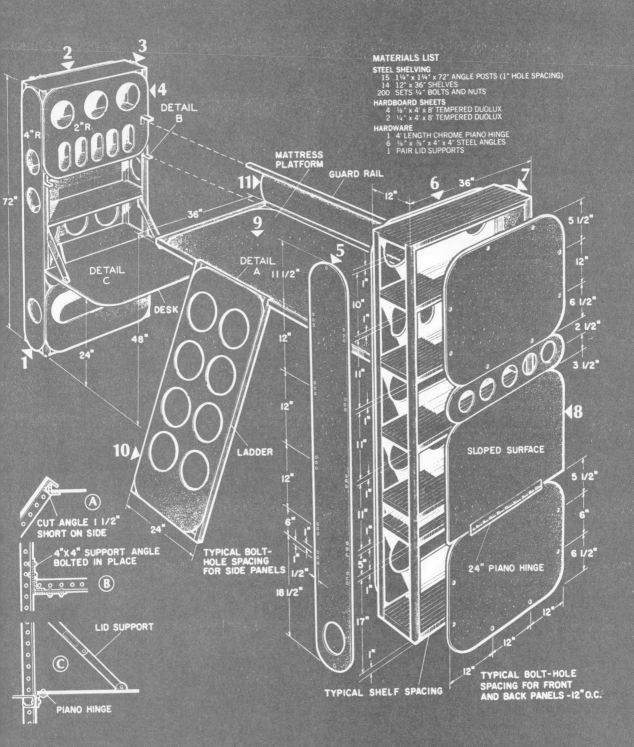

MATERIALS LIST

STEEL SHELVING
15 1¼" x 1¼" x 72" ANGLE POSTS (1" HOLE SPACING)
14 12" x 36" SHELVES
200 SETS ¼" BOLTS AND NUTS

HARDBOARD SHEETS
4 ⅛" x 4' x 8' TEMPERED DUOLUX
2 ¼" x 4' x 8' TEMPERED DUOLUX

HARDWARE
1 4' LENGTH CHROME PIANO HINGE
6 ⅛" x ⅜" x 4" x 4" STEEL ANGLES
1 PAIR LID SUPPORTS

2

3

4

DETAIL
B

4"R

2"R

72"

DETAIL
C

1

24"

48"

DESK

MATTRESS
PLATFORM

GUARD RAIL

11

36"

9

DETAIL
A   11 1/2"

5

10

LADDER

24"

12"

6

36"

7

12"

5 1/2"

12"

6 1/2"

2 1/2"

3 1/2"

8

SLOPED SURFACE

10"

11"

12"

11"

6"

5"

1/2"

18 1/2"

17"

1"

5 1/2"

6"

6 1/2"

24" PIANO HINGE

12"

12"

12"

TYPICAL BOLT-
HOLE SPACING
FOR SIDE PANELS

TYPICAL SHELF SPACING

TYPICAL BOLT-HOLE
SPACING FOR FRONT
AND BACK PANELS - 12" O.C.

A
CUT ANGLE 1 1/2"
SHORT ON SIDE

4"X4" SUPPORT ANGLE
BOLTED IN PLACE

B

LID SUPPORT

C

PIANO HINGE

247

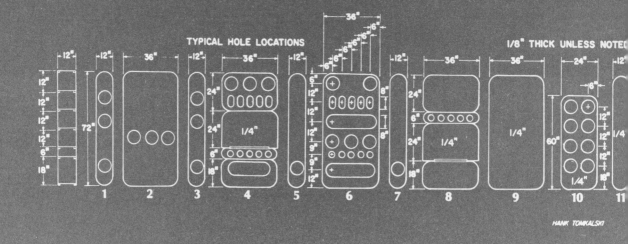

TYPICAL HOLE LOCATIONS

1/8" THICK UNLESS NOTED

1 2 3 4 5 6 7 8 9 10 11

HANK TOMKALSKI

to keep the unit away from walls to allow access from all sides. Many other configurations are possible—additional storage units, bunk beds for a shared room, and storage walls to divide floor space. You simply "customize" your own units from the various options shown in the silhouette sketches.

The system utilizes mass-produced steel office shelving for the structural elements and shelves, plus hardboard panels to replace the usual steel braces and provide facing.

The shelving is standard throughout the U.S. and outlets can be found in the yellow pages under "shelving." Shelf and post units are prepainted with baked enamel. Shelves vary in size. For the Living Machine I chose 12" x 36" shelving with 6' posts, to conform with mattress size and make best use of 4' x 8' hardboard sheets. If your child's storage needs are more extensive (and space permits) use 18" x 42" shelves instead. The posts should be 1¼" x 1¼" angle with one-inch hole spacing to conform to the dimensions on our plans.

For the facing panels, I chose Masonite Tempered Duolux because of its surface strength, ease of cutting and sanding, double-sided smoothness and excellent painting

Knocked down for moving to new home (above), sleep/play components stack in small space and are quickly reassembled at new site (below) by passing bolts through Masonite facing, angles, and shelf flanges. Predrilled holes in Masonite permit simple space adjustment.

248

properties. Some of the panels should be perfboard to provide a flexible hanging arrangement. The 12" side panels are bolted to the frame at the same time the shelves are assembled, so that each bolt does double duty. Three holes are provided at bolt locations for later adjustments in shelf spacing. The 36" front and back panels are bolted to the frame with extra holes for securing to the shelves.

Cutting the hardboard. Straight edges can be gang-cut with a portable circular saw; curves and hole cutouts are best made with a saber saw.

Drill the bolt holes by using a shelving post as a template. Same-size panels can be clamped together and drilled at one time. Sand all edges, giving special attention to the holes.

To paint the hardboard, I used metallic automotive acrylic enamel, sprayed on for childproof toughness and high gloss. You could paint the panels two different colors—one on each side—for decorative effect.

Cut the angle posts to the correct lengths with a hacksaw and file all cut edges and corners smooth. After assembly, place the mattress (I used a 4"-thick urethane foam pad) on the platform and add additional accessories, such as the gooseneck lamps.

Other uses of the system. For a divider partition, fasten storage units together at top and bottom with steel plates, or with angles spread to a degree determined by setting the units in the room at the desired angle to one another. For a flexible arrangement, join sections with hinges, instead. You'll be able to change the zig-zag.

The units can, of course, also be set against an existing wall for household storage. Use solid back panels here—full height or in combinations of between-shelf heights.

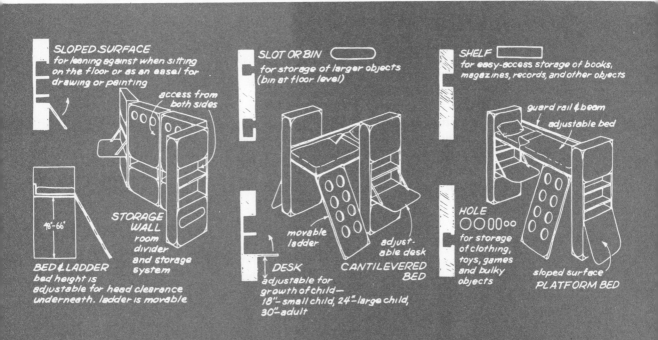

SLOPED SURFACE
for leaning against when sitting on the floor or as an easel for drawing or painting

access from both sides

BED & LADDER
bed height is adjustable for head clearance underneath. ladder is movable

STORAGE WALL
room divider and storage system

SLOT OR BIN
for storage of larger objects (bin at floor level)

movable ladder

DESK
adjustable for growth of child—18"- small child, 24"- large child, 30"- adult

adjustable desk

CANTILEVERED BED

SHELF
for easy-access storage of books, magazines, records, and other objects

guard rail & beam

adjustable bed

HOLE
for storage of clothing, toys, games and bulky objects

sloped surface
PLATFORM BED

A TRIO OF STURDY STACK TABLES

BY HARRY SHERMAN

A trio of stack tables I saw in a furniture store sent me home with a resolve to make my own set. As it turned out, I saved money, and I ended up with sturdier tables than those in the store.

The tops are plastic-laminate sink cutouts (a local cabinet shop will often sell you these at low cost). Birch 1-by-3 (36'), 2½" screws (21), and glue complete my materials list.

The drawing and accompanying table show the dimensions I used. All the spreaders and top edging pieces are made from ⅞" strips ripped from the birch, and routed half-round. All legs are 3" wide at the tops. Starting two inches down from the top they taper to 1½" at the bottom. All rails are 2" wide.

Join legs, rails, and spreaders, and glue and screw the unit in place—three screws through the back rail, and a pair through each side rail.

The finish is up to you. I used rubbed varnish, but a careful multicoat enamel job—sanded lightly between coats—gives you a nice oriental-style finish.

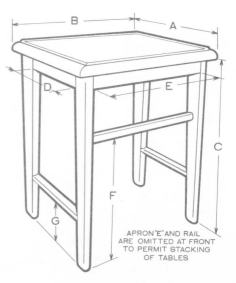

APRON "E" AND RAIL ARE OMITTED AT FRONT TO PERMIT STACKING OF TABLES

Dimension	large	medium	small
A	15¼"	13"	11¼"
B	19¼"	15"	11¾"
C	24"	23"	22"
D	9¾"	7¾"	6⅜"
E	17¼"	13⅜"	10⅛"
F	6"	6"	6"
G	15¼"	14¼"	13¼"

CANDLESTICK PLATE HOLDER

Copied from a Colonial original, this candlestick plate holder can be hung on a wall or set on a flat surface. It's adjustable for plates up to 11″ in diameter.

Use white pine ³/₈″ thick for base, upright, and brace. Draw the patterns on a grid of

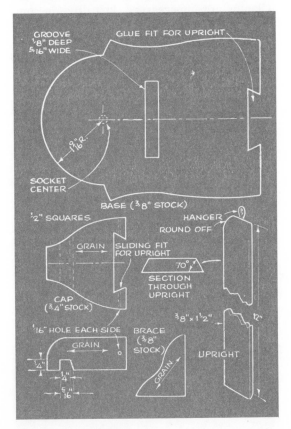

squares and saw out the parts. You can make the plate groove by lowering the base onto a circular saw set to cut ⅛″ deep, or by chiseling it out by hand.

Rip the upright at 70 degrees along both edges. Cut the dovetail notch in the base to a close fit for the upright. Glue it and the brace in place without nails.

The socket may be taken from an old candlestick or from a dime-store one. Mount it with a countersunk screw or, if it has a threaded shank, screw this directly into the base. After sliding the cap down over the plate, push decorative tacks through the two holes to lock it.

The Colonists used polished metal plates in the holder as reflectors, but a fine china plate will do, too.

DESKS YOU CAN SIZE TO SUIT YOUR HOME

BY R. J. DE CRISTOFORO

Build desks by the foot? Sure, why not? That idea occurred to me as I began designing a desk for my two boys who share the same room. The system is based on four elements—a stack of drawers, an open bookcase, a pencil drawer, and a top. Combine them as you wish to solve your own desk problem. Add bookcases and make it a 20-footer. Put doors on one of them to make a cabinet. Style

another as a housing for TV or hi-fi equipment.

Think of the bases—drawers and bookcase—as separate units and build as many of each as you wish. When they're finished, fasten them to the underside of the desk top with small angle irons and screws. Being underneath, the angle irons are hidden, yet easily removed for disassembly.

To build the drawer units, first make up the sides and rout dadoes for the drawer divider frames. Next, cut the 3/4"-by-2"-by-15 1/4" plywood strips that form the dividers and assemble them with glue and corrugated fasteners. These assemblies must be square, so use a large carpenter's square as a guide during assembly.

After completing the drawer divider frames, coat the dadoes in the drawer-unit sides with white glue and press the dividers into place. Clamps are unnecessary. Just drive in some 1/2" finishing nails.

Next, add the top board and baseboard. Coat the mating surfaces with white glue and

DART GAME

Make your desk long or short simply by building the right base units— bookcases and stacks of drawers made mainly of ¾" plywood. Finished desk comes apart for moving or base-unit rearrangement.

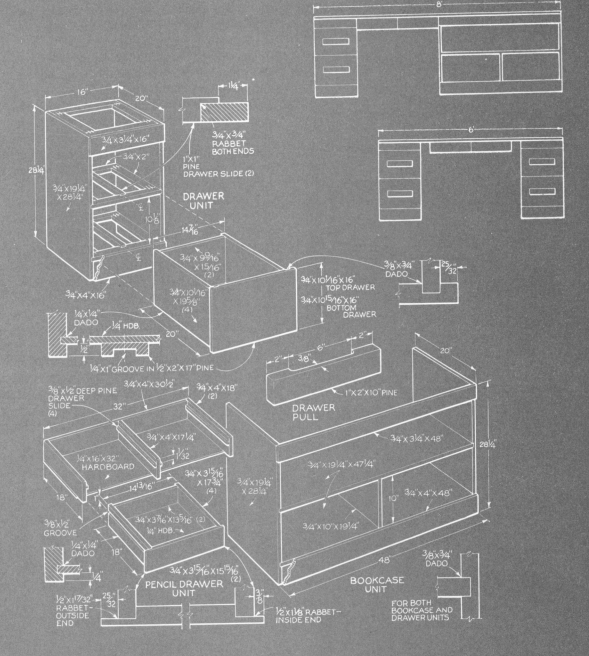
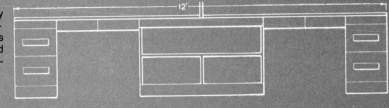

Drawers are roomy—13" wide, 18" long, 8⅝" deep. Beveling of drawer tops and bottoms, top board, and top of baseboard is optional.

Bookcase is 4' wide and vertical clearance between shelves is 10". If you prefer a cabinet instead of open shelves, add doors.

Desk top is ¾" plywood with plastic overlay. Similarly covered desk-top divider establishes center boundary of 12' desk used by two boys.

secure with finishing nails. At this point the case should be sturdy enough for the fitting of drawers.

Make the drawer fronts first, putting dadoes in them for the sides and bottom, checking for fit as you do so. Then cut the sides and bottom, assemble the pieces, and hold them together by hand for a final check to see if the drawer fits. The drawer slides and guides are the most critical components. Make sure they're perfectly aligned before fastening them permanently.

To build the bookcase, make the sides first, then the shelves. Assemble them, and cut and add the other three parts.

To make a pencil drawer, start with the case, then cut the pieces for the drawer, checking them for fit in the case before final assembly. The bottom of the case is intentionally less than the full case depth to provide a finger grip for opening drawers.

The amount of material required depends upon the length of the desk you'll build, plus your choice of base units. Decide these factors. Then, before ordering materials, work out a cutting pattern. I got my 12' desk, including the 22"-by-12' top, out of three 4'-by-8' panels of ¾" plywood, one 4'-by-4' panel of ¼" hardboard, and an odd piece of ¼" hardboard from which I cut pencil-drawer bottoms.

The desk top is as simple as you want to make it. I made and covered mine by applying plastic sheet with contact cement. You can order yours already covered.

I let the top sheet of plastic overlap the banding and dressed up the joint by smoothing the top edge with a file. If you do likewise, attack from above. Hold the file at a 10-to-20-degree angle and—to avoid chipping—cut only on the downstroke.

The drawer-unit and bookcase finish? I filled exposed edges and nail holes, gave the pieces a sanding and dusting, then applied a coat of resin-type sealer. I again sanded after the sealer dried, then applied an undercoat and top coat of paint.

254

ROTATING BOOKSHELF

BY HARRY WALTON

Useful on a student's desk or in a book-lover's den, this lazy susan holds a 2' length of books in a space about 14" square. It turns at a touch.

Either ⅜" or ½" plywood may be used for the bottom board and partitions. A handhold is cut in one, and both are slotted for a half-lap joint. Use glue and screws to fasten the partitions to the bottom. Sand the underside

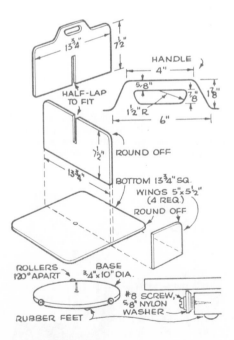

of the bottom smooth and shellac it to resist roller wear. The small wings may be of ¼" plywood, attached with glue and brads.

Cut the circular base from ⅝" or ¾" stock. Three ⅜" faucet washers (⅝" o.d.) on the edge extend at least 1/16" above the top surface. Mount them with wood screws and metal washers so they spin freely. The rotating shelf pivots on a 1½"-10 wood screw as its weight rides the rollers.

CORNER-HUNG BAR

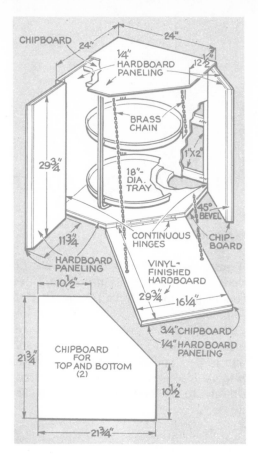

A new type of lazy Susan brings drinks and glasses to your fingertips in this space-saving bar. It's a Roll-a-Shelf, with two metal shelves that rotate on rollers attached to three standards placed around the rim. Tassell Industires, Grand Rapids, Mich., makes it.

The bar is constructed of one-by-two clear pine covered with wood-grained hardboard such as Masonite Royalcote. Butt-join, glue, and use metal fasteners at the corners of the frame. Miter the edges of the doors so they'll fit flush with the let-down shelf. Trim exposed edges with hardboard strips. For the doors, use 30" continuous hinges; for the drop shelf, a 15" hinge. Attach one-by-two strips horizontally under the bar, one on each wall. They'll support the weight while screws hold the bar flush to the walls.

This bar fits snugly into a corner, an unobtrusive cabinet when closed. The center panel drops down to become a holding and mixing shelf, and lazy Susan metal shelves hold glasses and bottles.

AN EASY CHAIR JUST FOR YOURSELF

BY R. J. DE CRISTOFORO

It's a lucky fellow who can buy an easy chair that gives comforting support to each tired muscle. Chairs, unlike shoes, aren't made to match individual shapes, widths, and lengths. But you no longer have to put up with a chair that doesn't bend in the same places you do. Here's an easy chair that supports your body in all the right places and puts you in your most relaxing pose, no matter

Spent a lifetime sitting in chairs that don't fit your frame? Do it no more. Whatever length your body and legs are, here's a chair that fits you.

how long or short you are. It's a chair for you alone. You can't buy it; you have to build it. Here's how you custom-design it:

Your personal easy chair must be built to fit the three basic dimensions of your own body. These are: (A) head to hip, (B) hip to knee, (C) knee to foot, as shown in the drawing of the man in the blueprint.

Also, an easy chair built just for yourself should curve the same way your body does when you're in your favorite resting position. If you're not sure what this position is, you can find out by using a three-piece template like the one in the photo below showing a dummy in various poses. The three pieces of the template are made to the A, B, and C dimensions described above and are joined

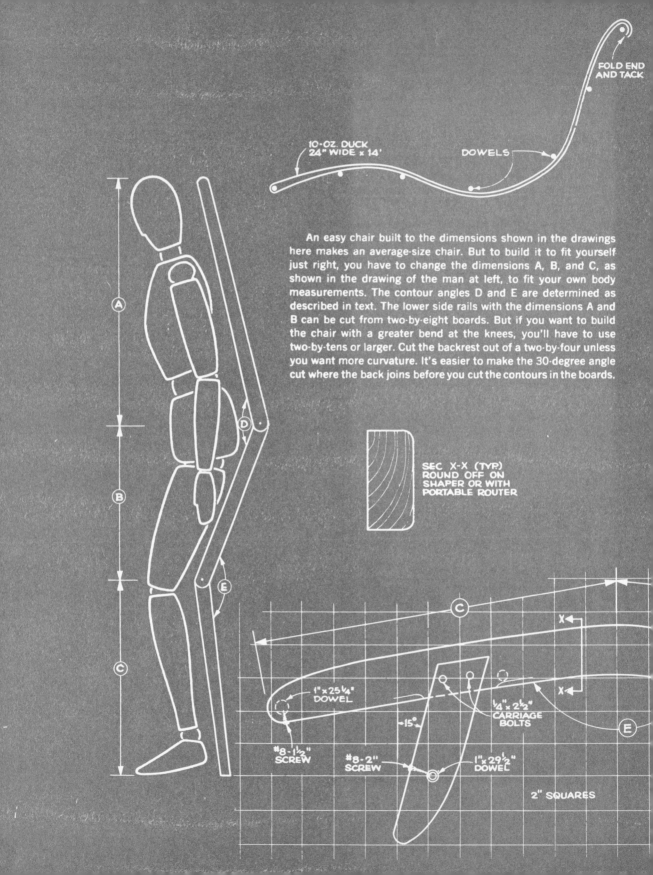

FOLD END
AND TACK

10-OZ. DUCK
24" WIDE x 14'

DOWELS

An easy chair built to the dimensions shown in the drawings here makes an average-size chair. But to build it to fit yourself just right, you have to change the dimensions A, B, and C, as shown in the drawing of the man at left, to fit your own body measurements. The contour angles D and E are determined as described in text. The lower side rails with the dimensions A and B can be cut from two-by-eight boards. But if you want to build the chair with a greater bend at the knees, you'll have to use two-by-tens or larger. Cut the backrest out of a two-by-four unless you want more curvature. It's easier to make the 30-degree angle cut where the back joins before you cut the contours in the boards.

SEC X-X (TYP)
ROUND OFF ON
SHAPER OR WITH
PORTABLE ROUTER

Ⓐ

Ⓑ

Ⓒ

Ⓓ

Ⓔ

Ⓒ

X

X

1" x 25¼"
DOWEL

¼" x 2½"
CARRIAGE
BOLTS

15°

Ⓔ

#8-1½"
SCREW

#8-2"
SCREW

1" x 29½"
DOWEL

2" SQUARES

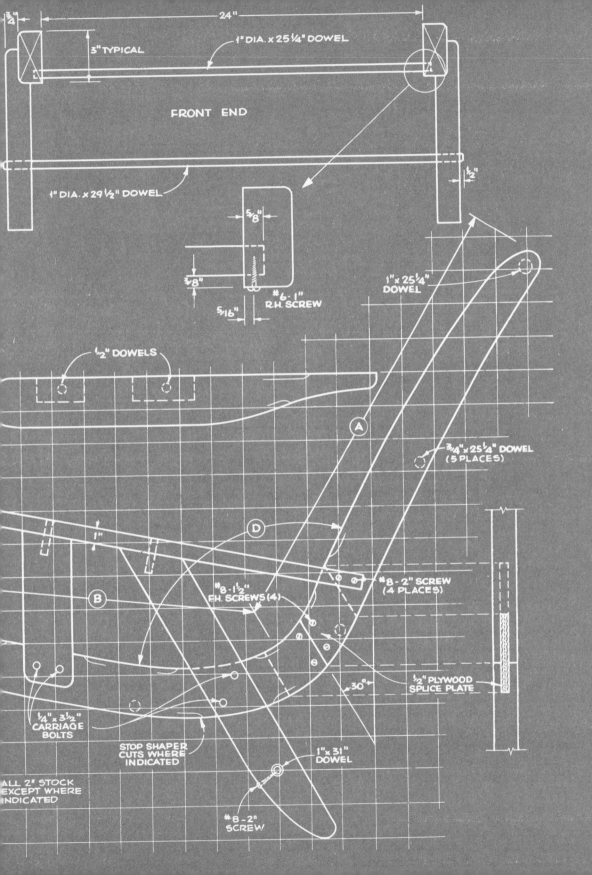

3/4"

24"

3" TYPICAL

1" DIA. x 25 1/4" DOWEL

FRONT END

1" DIA. x 29 1/2" DOWEL

1/2"

5/8"

3/8"

5/16"

#6-1"
R.H. SCREW

1" x 25 1/4"
DOWEL

1/2" DOWELS

A

3/4" x 25 1/4" DOWEL
(5 PLACES)

D

1"

#8-1 1/2"
F.H. SCREWS (4)

#8 - 2" SCREW
(4 PLACES)

B

1/2" PLYWOOD
SPLICE PLATE

30°

1/4" x 3 1/2"
CARRIAGE
BOLTS

STOP SHAPER
CUTS WHERE
INDICATED

1" x 31"
DOWEL

ALL 2" STOCK
EXCEPT WHERE
INDICATED

#8 - 2"
SCREW

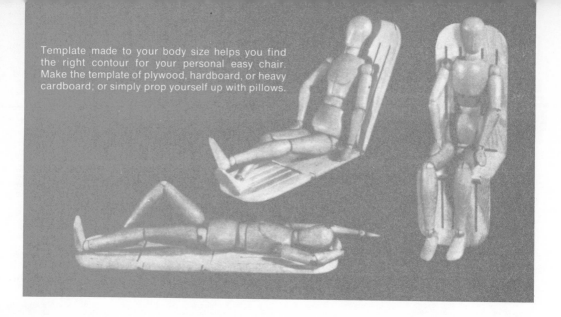

Template made to your body size helps you find the right contour for your personal easy chair. Make the template of plywood, hardboard, or heavy cardboard; or simply prop yourself up with pillows.

with hinges, strips of rubber, or heavy cloth. Prop up your template in various positions and lie down on it. Keep testing positions until you find the one that's most comfortable. Then measure the angles D and E (see blueprint).

Now you're ready to start building. You can simply transfer your dimensions to the blueprint, or if your lengths and bends differ greatly from those in the blueprint, you can redraw the plans to scale on graph paper. Either way, the construction details as shown in the blueprint will be the same; only the three dimensions (A,B,C,) and two angles (D,E) change. You'll just have to adjust the curvature between the three planes to suit yourself.

You can use any wood you want. A good grade of pine was used in the chair shown above, but redwood, mahogany, or other wood to match your decor would do as well.

The sides of the chair are made of 2"-thick stock joined with a ½"-thick plywood splice plate. Cut the 30-degree angle where the bottom and back pieces join, and cut the grooves for the splice plate before you saw the contour.

You have a choice between assembling the side pieces first and then cutting the full contour, or cutting the contours on the individual pieces, then assembling. It's easier to cut smaller pieces, but you'll probably be more accurate if you assemble the pieces first, then cut the contours. At any rate, tack the pieces for each side together and cut them both at once with a saber saw, bandsaw, or jigsaw. After cutting, sand all edges smooth.

To make the chair look less bulky, it's a good idea to round off the outside edges, limiting the cuts to those areas indicated on the blueprint. You can do this job fast on a shaper or a portable router, less easily with a rasp and sandpaper.

Drill the holes for the dowel stretchers, remembering that the two extreme ones are 1" in diameter while the other five are ¾". Drill all the holes ⅝" deep. Chamfer the ends of the dowels and assemble both sides and all the dowels at one time. Apply glue to the dowel ends and the holes, and hold the assembly together with bar clamps. Make sure assembly remains in alignment while glue sets.

The arms, arm supports, and rear legs are assembled as a unit before being attached to the sides. Don't predrill the holes for the dowels that pass through the arm. Instead, make the assembly with glue and a couple of finishing nails, then drill down through the arm and insert the dowels. Cut the dowels just a bit longer than necessary and sand them flush after the glue sets.

Shape the front legs, then clamp them to the frame to determine the angle and size of the rabbet. Clamp the legs together to drill the through holes for the 1″ dowel stretchers.

Final assembly. I found the best system is to attach the front legs first. Then place the frame on a level surface and block up the back end to the right height. Clamp the leg assemblies lightly in place and fidoodle with them until they are correctly aligned. Then drill for the bolts and the arm screws.

Finish the wood parts, applying penetrating resin, varnish, shellac—whatever your preference—before you add the ducking. Next, put on the pad and plop down for an enjoyable rest.

A standard 6′ lounge pad will fit in most cases. If your easy chair is a bit longer than 6′ you can possibly get by just by adding a pillow to the top end of the pad. Another possibility: Use a combination of smaller pads to make up the right length. But if you have a really oddball-size chair, you'll have to buy a slab of foam rubber the right length and put a cover on it.

Bolt ends are covered with rubber bumpers to avoid snagging the pad. Or they can be cut off and filed smooth. Additional screws driven in from the inside of the frame will reinforce the splice joint.

Leg-and-arm assembly is surface-mounted. Carriage bolts were used to permit disassembly, but heavy wood screws (driven from the inside surface of the side pieces) and glue may be used instead.

Ducking is put on after the wood is finished. It need not be pulled drum-tight. If the dimensions of your easy chair vary from those in the blueprint, you'll have to measure the length you need.

Front legs are rabbeted at the top and attached to the side frame with carriage bolts. Clamp the legs to the side frame to determine the angle of the rabbet cut. Round all edges on both sides of legs.

SAW BOOKENDS

BY GENE FLORIDAY

Here's a set of bookends for office, den, or shop that's sure to draw quizzical glances and raised eyebrows. An old saw, or one of the inexpensive imported models, along with some shop scrap is all you need for the project. To keep the blade from rusting, spray it with clear lacquer. Assemble with glue and screws (from the back). Finish the wood parts with stain and semigloss varnish.

After cutting the wood to shape, drill the holes for the saw holding screws (on the side that will be facing the wall) and kerf the uprights with a hacksaw. Cut the handsaw in two, insert in the slots and drill the holes to accept the screws.

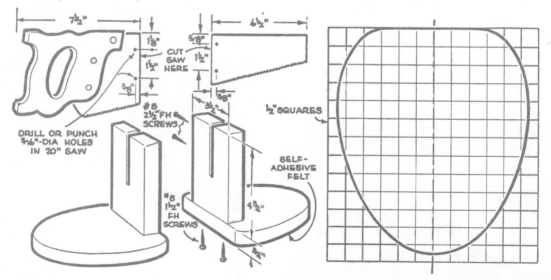

DRY-SINK RECIPE HOLDER

BY HARRY WALTON

A copy of a piece of colonial furniture, this miniature is made of crate wood to look authentic—even to the knots. Stock can be thinned to $3/16''$ with a sander or planer attached in the drill press; scale-size wood is available at hobby shops. Cut front and sides with grain vertical, dry-sink section with grain horizontal. Simulate planks by scribing with a scratch awl. Assemble with glue and brads, keeping inside dimensions to accommodate standard file cards. Stain and shellac. Cut and bend hardware from thin sheet metal, paint black. Mount false door with escutcheon pins.

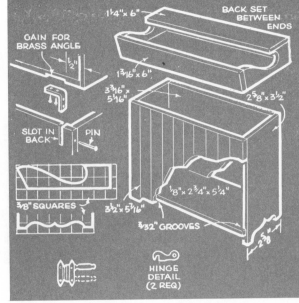

263

CARVING BOARD

This well-and-tree carving board adds to the pleasure of carving by letting you bring the roast to the table in appropriately elegant style. You'll need a router to make it (if you don't have one, try a tool-rental outfit). Once you've constructed the template, you'll be able to turn out enough boards in a weekend to fill a big part of your Christmas gift list.

Jigsaw the router template from ¼" hardboard. Cut around the contour of the center section first, and save the trimmed-off piece for the template's outer section. Saw the guide slots slightly undersize and file to the exact size of the ¼" router-bit shank.

Cut the hold-down lugs and stand-offs from scrap hardboard and glue them in place. Be sure stand-offs are under each of the four screws in the center section, and that there is clearance around the slots for the ⅝" half-round router bit used to make the grooves.

Make the carving board from a 14"-by-17" piece of ¾" hardwood. Walnut was used here. If you use a glued-up board, keep the joint off center, and see that dowels are not in a spot where they'll be exposed by the board's routed design.

Make trial cuts on scrap pine or plywood.

The board in use below was made with a router and the template shown at far right on opposite page. Using the template, any number of carving boards can be made quickly.

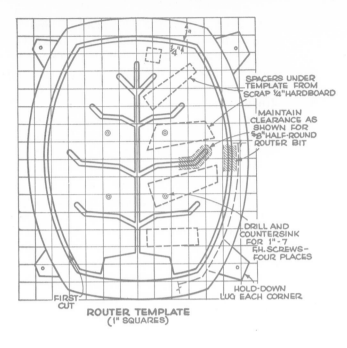

SPACERS UNDER TEMPLATE FROM SCRAP ¼" HARDBOARD

MAINTAIN CLEARANCE AS SHOWN FOR ⅝" HALF-ROUND ROUTER BIT

DRILL AND COUNTERSINK FOR 1"-7 F.H. SCREWS— FOUR PLACES

HOLD-DOWN LUG EACH CORNER

FIRST CUT

ROUTER TEMPLATE
(1" SQUARES)

PARTIAL SECTION COMPLETED BOARD

Screw the center section of the template to the stock with four #7 flathead screws. Carefully locate the outer template, using the router-bit shank as a guide. After routing, mark the outside edges and remove the template. Saw the outside edges, sand, and finish with a molding router bit around the edge. Finish-sand the entire board.

Use $3/16''$ stainless-steel rod for the meat-holding spikes. Point them with a file while they're chucked in a lathe or drill press. Bore out the four screw holes and glue the spikes in place.

Wipe the wood with hot salad oil for a finish that can be readily restored.

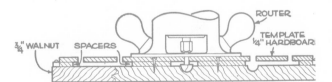

ROUTER

TEMPLATE ¼" HARDBOARD

¾" WALNUT   SPACERS

FANCY PARSONS TABLE

BY JACKSON HAND

The modern simplicity of the Parsons table (named for the famous design school where it originated—not for a village preacher) can be combined with the classic elegance of patterned paneling to create a unique piece of furniture. You won't believe how easy it is to make.

The paneling is called Marvelour. Made by Marlite, it is a hardboard with an actual flocked surface. It's intended as a wall panel, and comes in Marlite's standard 16"-by-8' planks. Once I'd run my fingers over that felt-like surface and studied the striking "brocade" pattern, I realized the panel would make a fine prefinished "veneer" for simply-constructed plywood furniture.

Marvelour is made by imprinting a pattern of adhesive on the hardboard surface; flocking is dusted over this, sticking only to the adhesive. For solid backgrounds, they spread adhesive all over the board, then overprint the raised pattern in a matching or contrasting color.

Marlite originally market-tested many panel patterns, but they've announced that they'll actually produce only four versions:

- Red pattern on red ground.
- Blue pattern on light-blue ground.
- Gold pattern on white ground.
- Gold stripes on white ground.

Unless you can find a dealer with some of the original market-test supply, you can't duplicate my table. But a striking variation might be a top of red-on-red with blue-on-blue for the aprons and legs.

Before you start veneering furniture with a flocked panel, you want to know how durable the surface will be under household abuse. I checked this out by pouring catsup on a sample and letting it dry. Next morning I washed off the catsup with soap and water; no visible damage. Later, though, I found one problem. If a heavy object rests on the table top for any length of time, it imprints. This will disappear after a while, but if you'll be using your table in a way that will produce nuisance imprints, just put a sheet of clear Plexiglas over the top. The sheen of the textured surface shows through, and the acrylic sheet is at least as easy to maintain as a lacquered or varnished finish.

A still simpler (and less expensive) solution is to skip the flocked surfacing on the top and

The generous top—protected by a sheet of Plexiglas—makes an ideal coffee table.

266

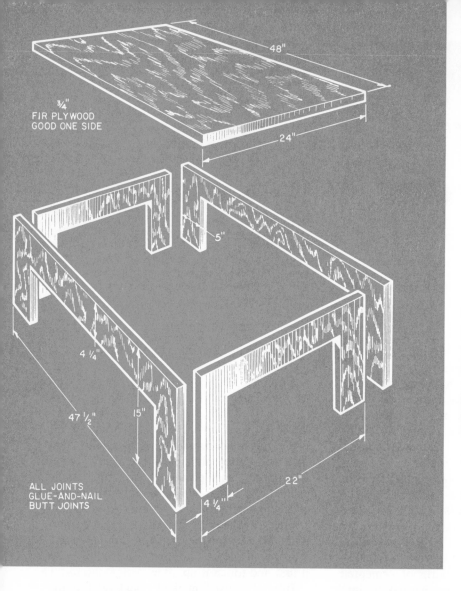

3/4"
FIR PLYWOOD
GOOD ONE SIDE

48"

24"

5"

4 1/4"

47 1/2"

15"

22"

ALL JOINTS
GLUE-AND-NAIL
BUTT JOINTS

4 1/4"

Variety of patterns and colors was market-tested before Marlite settled on production of four types listed in the text.

Match the Marlite by taking a sample to a custom-mix paint store, for enameling the back and edges of the leg assembly.

merely paint this a color to match your choice of apron pattern. You'll need such an enamel (a quality semigloss is best) to paint the edges and the inside faces of the legs, anyway.

Actual construction. It couldn't be simpler: Buy a 4-by-6 sheet of 3/4" fir plywood, good one side (A-C). Cut out the five rectangles involved, to dimensions shown. Note that the top projects 1/4" beyond the base on all sides to mask the upper edge of the facing panels. If you paint the top, as suggested above, simply

bring the paint down over these exposed edges. If you apply a flocked panel to the top, as I did, paint these edges *after* the facing is on, so you coat the hardboard edge at the same time. With the 1/4" Marvelour laminated to all surfaces, you'll have a table measuring 24"-by-48", 16" high, with all faces flush-mating—the hallmark of the Parsons design. If you modify dimensions, be certain to accommodate the basic module of the flocked pattern you've chosen.

Glue and nail the ends between the sides,

267

Everything you need: two types of flocked panel and (on the plywood assembly) glue, paint, contact cement, water putty, hammer, finishing nails, plane, and saber saw.

Contact-cement trick takes two sheets of paper, overlapped to prevent contact of glued surfaces. When facing is positioned, open slit between papers and strike with fist.

then add the top. Now's the time to fill all voids in the plywood edges with water putty and sand them smooth. In adding the facing panels, apply to legs and aprons first. Marvelour comes in standard 16"-wide wall planks, so you'll need two mating pieces for ends, three for each side. Trim them so there's about ¾" space at each corner.

Brush contact cement on the outer faces of the plywood assembly and on the back of the cut-to-fit hardboard pieces. Let it dry. Lap sheets of paper (newspaper is okay) on the work area, as shown above right. Position the hardboard, and slip one of the sheets of paper back to reveal a narrow strip of cemented surface. Then hammer the hardboard into contact with your fist, moving down the slot. This locks the cemented surfaces together so that you can slip out both sheets of paper and, knowing that the hardboard is in perfect position, complete the contact by striking with your fist all over the surface.

Since Marlite planks have special tongue and groove edges, the next piece will be self-positioning, but you establish contact with the same method.

The final step. Cap each corner with two strips of ¼"-thick wood, painted a matching color. You butt these right against the Marlite edges to conceal and protect them from traffic around the table. The strips can be applied with the same contact cement. An alternate corner treatment: Use standard pine corner-mold trim, available at any lumber yard. Apply with white glue and brads—but paint it first and touch it up after.

If you've used flocked panel on the top surface, cut your Plexiglas cover to size and plane and sand the edges smooth. You can let it lie loose (the size gives it sufficient weight for this) or anchor it with an oval-head screw through each corner. And that's it—a unique piece of furniture.

FRAME CLOCK

BY JOHN WOODWARD

A quick job of facelifting can turn an ordinary wall clock into a bold classic design that makes a fine gift, or a keepsake for your own use.

The supplies you'll need to make a frame clock are few and easy to get. Start with a square electric clock—one with a good face. I used a GE #1425G, about $5 in department stores. Next, pick out a bold picture frame molding. At a fabric store pick up a piece of velvet or felt large enough to cover the clock face. Finally, get a strip of decorative gold trim from a drapery shop. About 14 inches should do. Got everything together? Follow the step-by-step photos for assembly.

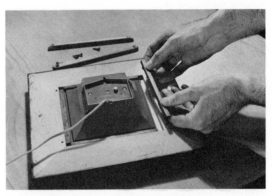

Measure frame molding along edge of clock, miter cut to size and assemble. Clock here has a square crystal. Remove and replace it later.

Make shims of pine to fill spaces between clock edges and frame recess, if necessary. Then secure the clock snugly with two wood strips.

Cut velvet or felt to cover outer portion of clock face, glue fabric in place. Make circular cut carefully with sharp scissors.

Measure gold trim to make complete circle around the clock face. Fasten in place with beads of white glue. Replace crystal.

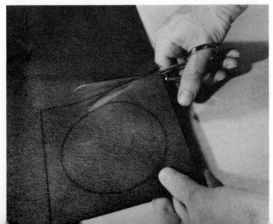

ADD A MODERN VANITY TO YOUR BATH

BY HANK CLARK

Want a modern bathroom vanity? Install it yourself—and save a wad. The job's mostly simple carpentering.

Change the counter length to suit your space if you can't use exactly the size shown here. But you'll usually find that the other two major dimensions—the height and depth (from the wall)—are what you want.

Buy the lavatory before you start. Turn it upside down on the piece that will become your counter top, mark around it, and make the cutout with a saber saw. The rest is like making a box with two sides, a front, and a bottom. No back is needed since the pipes enter there.

After sides, front, and bottom are glued (use waterproof) and screwed together, lay out the door on the front panel and make the cutout, again with a saber saw. The saw kerf clears away enough wood to let you edge the door and the opening with the vinyl or other covering that you choose for the vanity. Cover the door edges before you surface its front.

Applying the surfacing material over the plywood was a simple matter. We used a flexible Goodyear vinyl (Conolite) and found that it turns a ¾" radius nicely. Set this into adhesive applied with a notched spreader. When you form the covering around a radius,

apply pressure on both sides of the bend to get a smooth turning. Wipe off adhesive at once.

Before setting the bowl into the counter, apply caulking to the base of the fixtures and set them into the bowl openings. Secure the fixtures with nuts turned up underneath. It's also best to caulk the drainpipe into the sink before setting it.

You can reach through the door to angle securing screws up into the counter top after setting the bowl and fastening it with clips.

When you have placed the cabinet against the wall, you may want to call a plumber to make the connections. However, there's no reason you can't do it yourself if you've ever worked with copper tubing.

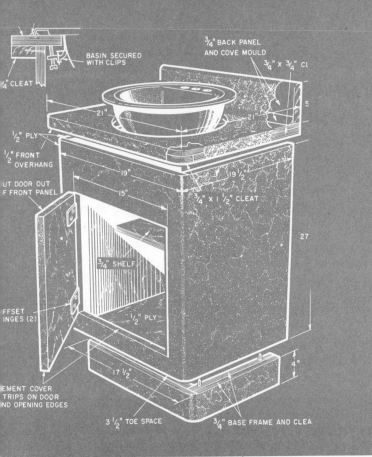

Wrap flexible surfacing material around entire cabinet after rounding corners and applying mastic with notched trowel. Let the mastic set, then cut out door opening.

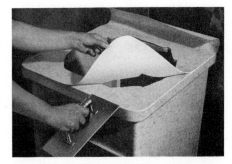

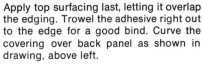

Apply top surfacing last, letting it overlap the edging. Trowel the adhesive right out to the edge for a good bind. Curve the covering over back panel as shown in drawing, above left.

Edge the top panel with a continuous strip of covering. A Surform and sanding block can be used to smooth off covering edge for a neat meeting of edge and top surfacing.

Set the bowl into a bead of caulking inside its edge as shown here for water-tight seal. Then lift off entire top panel, turn over, and fasten the bowl to its under surface with clips.

SNACK BAR FOR THE KITCHEN

BY THOMAS B. SHEARER

This is a snack bar, a room divider, and a storage cabinet all in one. The dining side has just enough room for two to breakfast or grab a snack. Install a telephone on the wall and it's a convenient planning center. The other side has a handy storage cabinet.

The frame is made entirely of ³/₄″ plywood. The snack shelf is covered with a white plastic laminate such as Formica, and the top is surfaced with ¹/₄″ white translucent glass. The cabinet doors are ¹/₄″ perforated hardboard and slide on stock door tracks.

Assemble it with finish nails and glue. Set the nails and fill the holes with putty. Build up the outside edge of the snack shelf on the underside with an additional strip of ³/₄″ plywood to take a 1¹/₂″-wide edging of the plastic. Use contact cement to attach the plastic and the glass top. Give the plywood surfaces a coat of sealer and finish with enamel, or wood stain and wax, to match the woodwork of adjacent rooms.

In addition to frontside function as snack bar, this project provides a handy storage cabinet in the rear portion. For details on construction, see drawing at the top of the next page.

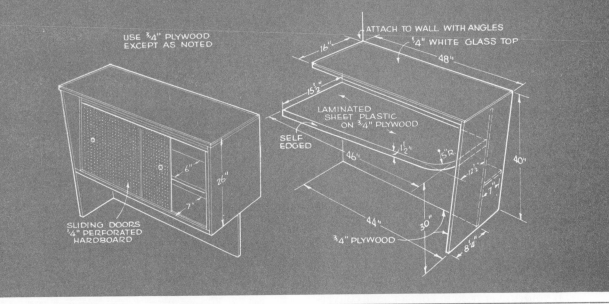

USE ³⁄₄" PLYWOOD
EXCEPT AS NOTED

SLIDING DOORS
¹⁄₄" PERFORATED
HARDBOARD

6"

26"

7"

ATTACH TO WALL WITH ANGLES

¹⁄₄" WHITE GLASS TOP

16"

48"

15½"

LAMINATED
SHEET PLASTIC
ON ³⁄₄" PLYWOOD

SELF
EDGED

46"

1½"

5"R

12½"

1"

40"

44"

30"

³⁄₄" PLYWOOD

8¼"

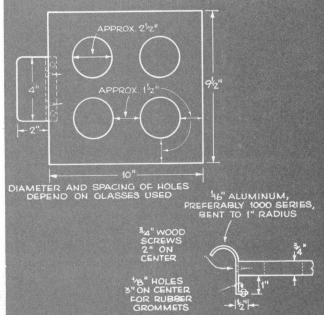

BEVERAGE SERVER

Here's an attractive server that is spillproof. This one holds four glasses, but size can be varied. Tapered glasses wedge into holes cut in a hardwood board. The holes should be sized so that the glasses extend down about an inch below the base. The holes can be made with a fly cutter in a drill press, or jig-sawed after first drilling a small hole for the blade.

Curve the aluminum handles by bending them around a piece of pipe. The handles should extend 1½" below the bottom of the tray so glasses are held above the resting surface. Rubber grommets prevent marring furniture.

For a handcrafted look, peen the handles; and for a tough, alcohol-resistant finish, coat the wood with a tough penetrating resin varnish.

APPROX. 2½"

APPROX. 1½"

9½"

4"

2"

10"

DIAMETER AND SPACING OF HOLES
DEPEND ON GLASSES USED

¹⁄₁₆" ALUMINUM,
PREFERABLY 1000 SERIES,
BENT TO 1" RADIUS

³⁄₄" WOOD
SCREWS
2" ON
CENTER

¹⁄₈" HOLES
3" ON CENTER
FOR RUBBER
GROMMETS

³⁄₄"

1"

½"

273

FIVE-DOOR PHONE BOOTH FOR YOUR FAMILY ROOM

BY A. J. HAND

If you've ever tried to hold a phone conversation over the sound of a rousing game of Ping-Pong, you know what our family-room phone booth is for. Step inside the carpet-lined booth, close the twin cafe doors, and you're suddenly in a private world of your own.

Industrial designer Gary Gerber created the phone booth out of five doors—the twin cafe doors plus three stock flush doors that form the H-shaped structure itself. Take a look around back of the booth and you'll find a handy bonus—a compact wardrobe with plenty of space to store jackets, boots, and hats.

How to make it. To start, fasten the three flush doors together using four 3" T braces and white glue. Then add the rear shelf to make the assembly rigid.

The carpet lining comes next. You'll need three pieces: one 36" by 80", and two 24" by 80". The type with foam-rubber backing is the easiest to apply. (Another alternative? Self-stick carpet tiles.) Apply carpet with ordinary carpet cement; this is easiest if you lay the booth on its side while you work.

Now before that cement sets completely, measure up from the bottoms of the door panels to find the position of the triangular

Sound-absorbing carpet lining and twin cafe doors cut family-room decibels to minimum inside booth. Phone directories go on the triangular shelf.

shelf and seat. Take a sharp knife and cut away the carpet where the blocking for the seat and shelf goes. Clean off any remaining cement, then glue and nail the blocking in place, and install the seat and shelf.

Trim both 3' cafe doors to 17¼" wide and mount. Add coat hooks around back. Pick an accent color from the carpet and use a matching enamel to paint shelves and seat, the cafe doors, and flush-door edges. Finally apply a natural finish to the flush doors. When it's dry, step inside, dial your neighbor, and ask him over for a game of Ping-Pong.

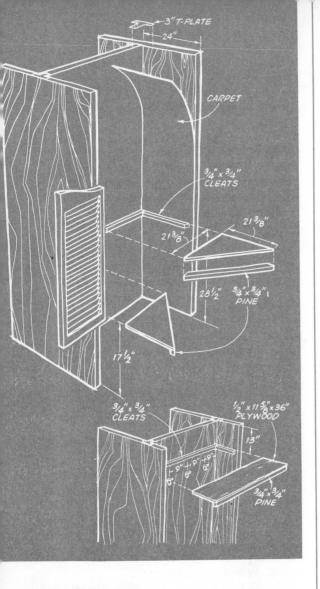

MAGAZINE RACK

BY EARL J. ROBERTS

You can keep all your magazines conveniently corralled in one spot if you build this cage-like rack. Make a cardboard pattern of the top and use it to cut top and bottom to size. (Note: Only the top gets the two oval slots.) After rounding the edges, clamp the two pieces together, as shown in the sketch. Drill through the bottom and halfway through the top for the dowels. Assemble the rack with glue; clamp until dry. Construction is faster and easier if you finish all parts before assembly. Use walnut stain and two coats of lacquer.

Bonus in back of booth is a wardrobe for storage of outdoor clothing. Five-door booth is made of three 36"-by-80" flush doors combined with two 3' louvered cafe doors.

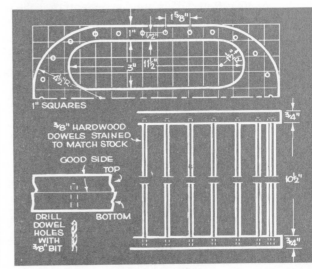

HOME-SHOW STAND SETS UP FAST, STORES FLAT

BY ROSARIO CAPOTOSTO

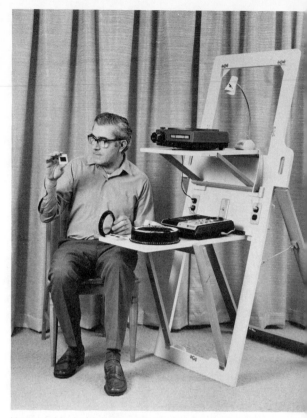

Upper table is high enough for eye-level, distortion-free projection. Lower shelf is editing table, holds tape player, extra slide magazines and other items.

When you want to show home movies or slides, this stand sets up quickly. When the show is over, it folds flat to slip against a closet wall. You make the stand from one 30″-by-69″ sheet of fir plywood.

The upper table, or folding shelf, is 44″ from the floor, a height that permits straight-ahead, distortion-free projection at average sitting-height eye level—even over the heads of kids. The lower table, at 27½″, has multiple usage: It will support a tape player for a synched slide narration or movie music; it also provides you with a work surface for slide or film assembly, editing, and other chores. Both levels are conveniently reached from a sitting position.

For added convenience, a power cord is built in to supply current to twin outlets. A single-pole, double-throw switch activates either outlet so that a table, floor, or work lamp plugged into one side will shut off when the current is switched to the equipment outlet. Various switching arrangements are possible. Work out the one best suited to your needs.

Select plywood with two good sides. Use a plywood-cutting blade for smooth cuts. To make the inside cuts with ease and accuracy, make a saw guide by nailing a ¾″-by-4″-by-42″ straight board to a piece ¾″-by-2″-by-50″. This high-walled rip guide insures that the

saw base will be held true and square to the work at the start of the cut.

Clamp or tack-nail the guide to the work. Rest the toe of the saw base on the panel with the rear raised up so the blade is off the work. Tape back the blade guard—and exercise *great care*. With power on, press down on the saw so the blade makes contact with the wood. When the base is all the way down, push the saw forward and continue the cut up to the intersection. The circular saw will leave a small radius uncut on the underside of the board due to the curved profile of its cut. Complete the cut flush to the corner with a saber or hand saw.

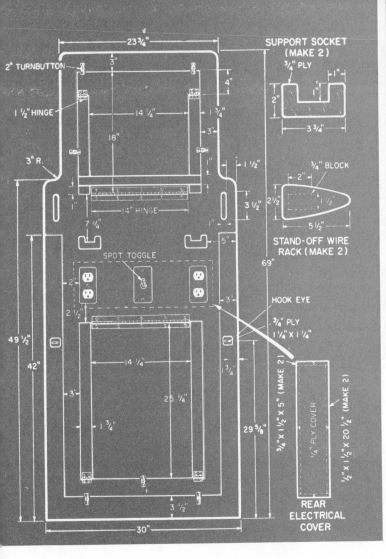

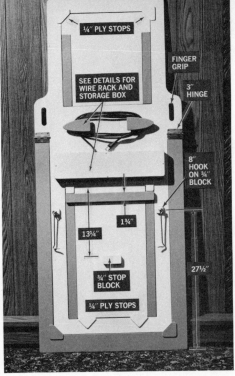

Stand folds flat—to little more thickness than the ¾" plywood from which it's made. The rear view when folded is seen above, with layout and assembly data. Front view is shown below. Use dimensions in drawing at left to lay out front of the stand. Cuts are made with circular saw.

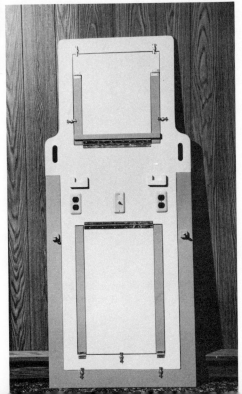

As each piece is removed, mark it with the mating piece. After sanding, reassemble the sections in their original positions and attach the hardware. Keep in mind that the locations of the table-support cleats, and especially the large hooks and eyes, are critical if the tables are to be level. The dimensions given above for the location of the hook should give a leg-to-leg spread of the stand (at floor level) of 29″. Use hinges that have little or no play at the pivot.

For a neat job, paint all the parts before you assemble them (two tones will add interest).

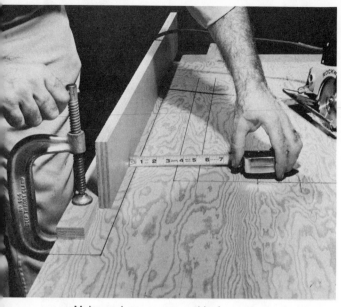

Make and use a saw guide for accuracy in internal cuts. Measure distance between edge of the base and the blade. Double-check alignment of guide. Make all internal cuts with kerf centered on the lines.

Place cardboard shims in saw kerf to center hinging parts accurately as you install hinges. An alternate: Install the hinges before you make crosscuts, so parts are kept in exact location while cutting.

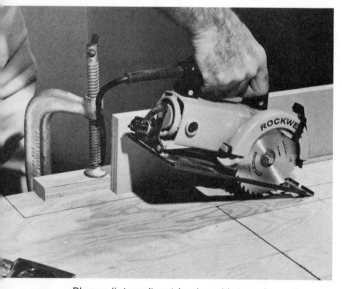

Plunge (internal) cut begins with toe of saw base on work, blade guard taped back, and blade raised off wood. Switch on power, lever blade into wood.

Lay out panel following dimensions at top of page. Remember that each inside part will be used in place from which it's removed. There's almost no waste.

REFRIGERATOR SHELF

BY JOHN WOODWARD

Food at the back of the bottom shelf of a refrigerator is hard to reach. The solution? A rotating shelf that slides out.

Make a base of two-by-twos to fit the refrigerator. Mount aluminum flanges at the rear and connect them to the refrigerator shelf supports to keep the tray from tipping down when you slide it out.

Cut the circular shelf from ½" waterproof plywood. Cover with white Formica and circle it with white plastic weather-stripping, lapped ¼" above the top to keep items from sliding off. Paint all wooden parts with white enamel.

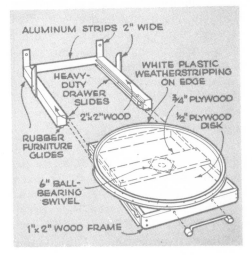

ALUMINUM STRIPS 2" WIDE

WHITE PLASTIC WEATHERSTRIPPING ON EDGE

HEAVY-DUTY DRAWER SLIDES

¾" PLYWOOD

½" PLYWOOD DISK

2"x 2" WOOD

RUBBER FURNITURE GLIDES

6" BALL-BEARING SWIVEL

1"x 2" WOOD FRAME

279

A STORAGE WALL —TWO ROOMS FROM ONE

**It's a privacy partition . . .
wardrobe . . . bookshelf . . .
closets for linen and storage**

BY LOUIS HOCHMAN

If you're making do with a less-than-ideal older home, you may have a problem similar to mine: rooms awkwardly joined by wide openings that may originally have had French doors—or a long, narrow room that could function better as two.

When I partitioned such a space in our home, I designed a two-faced functional wall that gave us handsome library shelves on one side and a bedroom wardrobe on the other.

As a bonus, I included several compartments for cumbersome items such as card and snack tables and projection screens.

The swing-down false front below the bookcase is faced with sheet brick but you could substitute any prefinished paneling of your choice. I built the entire case of ¾″ plywood, finishing off the exposed edges with veneer tape (1-by-10 lumber could be used instead). The wardrobe assembly that stands back-to-back with the bookcase is framed of 2-by-2s (plus 1-by-2s) and covered with ¼″ panels; any prefinished wall paneling could be used for the exposed facing, with ordinary good-one-side ¼″ plywood for the back.

Bookcase backing. Note that this rear panel does double duty as the back of the bookcase, so you'll want to place the good side toward the shelves. Note also the back panel is doubled at one side to create a pocket for the sliding pass-through door. The latter hangs

Big opening (below) connected the study and bedroom in the old floorplan. New built-in is shown above and at far right from both sides.

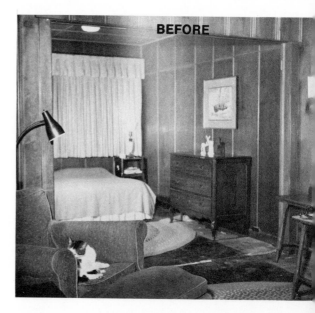

BEFORE

AFTER AFTER

from a standard track, available from any builder's supply or home center, mounted at the back of the bookcase before framing the wardrobe. (See Section "X".) I used a sturdy L-shaped bracket of $3/4''$ lumber; if your bookcase goes all the way to the ceiling (instead of butting up beneath a door opening, like mine) you'd just build this bracket into the rear of the bookcase. I bought a louvered door ($1\frac{1}{8}''$-by-$25''$-by-$80''$) for better air circulation.

Space your bookshelves to match the various heights of your books. My middle shelf, for example, has a clear height of $10\frac{1}{2}''$ for conventional books, while the upper and lower shelves offer heights of $12\frac{1}{4}''$ and $13\frac{1}{2}''$ for taller volumes.

That brick-faced door on the compartment shown pivots on "open-end" hinges I adapted from ordinary hangers for window screens. They make the door fully detachable, for access to large "dead-storage" items. Just bend the female portions to a steeper angle, as

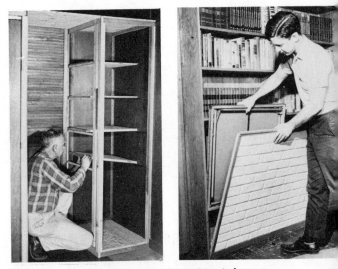

Both sides of wall have storage compartments for general household use. Linen closet (left) has big plywood shelves. Card table stores in bookcase.

281

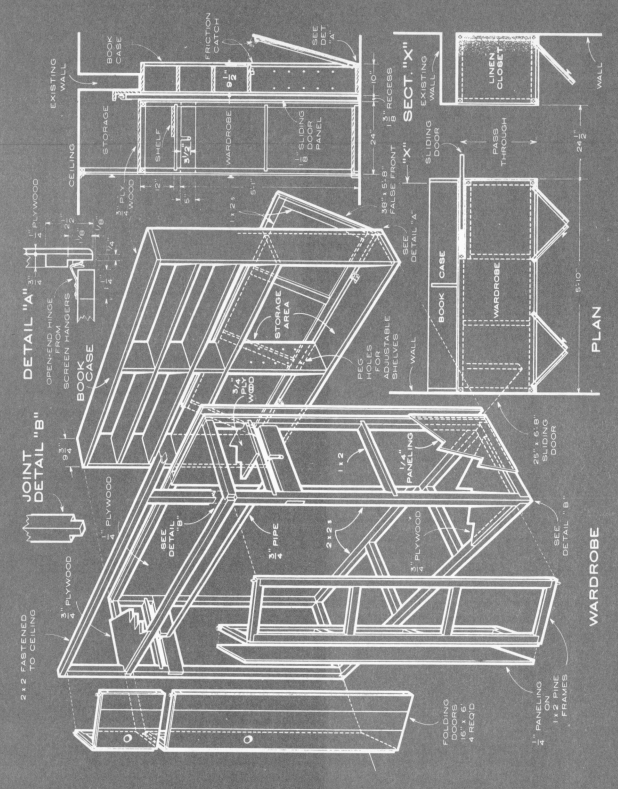

JOINT DETAIL "B"

DETAIL "A"

OPEN-END HINGE FROM SCREEN HANGERS

BOOK CASE

2 x 2 FASTENED TO CEILING

¾" PLYWOOD

¼" PLYWOOD

9¾"

3"

2½"

¼" PLYWOOD

1¼"

⅛"

¼"

1½"

BOOK CASE

EXISTING WALL

STORAGE

CEILING

SHELF

3½"

3 PLY ¼ WOOD

12"

5"

WARDROBE

⅛"

FRICTION CATCH

9½"

SEE DET "A"

SLIDING DOOR PANEL

5'-1"

38" x 5'-8" FALSE FRONT

24"

10"

1 ¾" RECESS

SEE DETAIL "A"

SECT. "X"

"X"

LINEN CLOSET

WALL

EXISTING WALL

SLIDING DOOR

PASS THROUGH

WALL

BOOK CASE

WARDROBE

24½"

5'-10"

PLAN

25" x 6'-8" SLIDING DOOR

SEE DETAIL "B"

¾" PLYWOOD

STORAGE AREA

PEG HOLES FOR ADJUSTABLE SHELVES

1 x 2 s

¾ PLY WOOD

SEE DETAIL "B"

¾" PIPE

1 x 2

¼" PANELING

2 x 2 s

¾" PLYWOOD

¼" PANELING ON 1 x 2 PINE FRAMES

FOLDING DOORS 16" x 6' 4 REQ'D

WARDROBE

282

shown in Detail "A", and mount them in a rabbet cut along the bottom rail of the frame. Though the rest of the frame is of 1-by-2s, I used a 1-by-3 here.

Wardrobe framing. On the opposite side of the bookcase, I stole enough bedroom floorspace to build the wardrobe-linen closet floor to ceiling and wall to wall, broken only by the 2'-wide door opening. The 2-by-2 framing is simple. First, lay out the floor section (or sections, in my case). Then add the uprights and the rails. A wardrobe height of 76" (from room floor to top shelf) gives adequate space for hanging clothes plus 12" of shelf height directly above the clothes pole for hats, boxes, and small luggage. For an unsupported pole of this length, I recommend galvanized water pipe.

The doors are made by cementing prefinished paneling to 1-by-2 frames. The number and size of them depends, of course, on the dimensions of your wardrobe. Four 16-inchers, hinged in pairs from the inside, did my job.

Since the doors fold against one another

when opened, the backs are never exposed; there's no need to recess the hinges or panel the rear of the frames. The hardware I used (Acme Fold-Aside) is typical; it has a track at both top and bottom, so both top and bottom edges of each door panel must be drilled to take a pivot pin or roller guide.

Upper doors. Although I could have managed with less hardware for the short upper doors, I installed the same system. A 2-by-2 on the ceiling provides a means for mounting the top track. One extra pair of short doors (not shown in sketches) takes care of the overhead section above the doorway and linen closet.

As seen in a photo, it's much easier to build shelves into the linencloset frame *before paneling the side.*

To complete the project, I ripped leftover paneling into strips and contact-cemented these to all exposed framing—taking care to match the grain and groove patterns.

Now I'm making my family nervous by looking around for other rooms to divide and conquer.

Simple drilling jig, made from scrap and clamped to framed-panel doors, aligned with opposite sides, assures uniform location of holes for mounting hardware and keeps bit at right angles to edge of door. After drilling, remove jig and attach pivot pin (second photo). Bracket for folding-door pivot is mounted to ¾" plywood floor of wardrobe (third photo). Top channel for doors is screwed to bottom edge of rail above wardrobe opening. Ceiling of wardrobe (also ¾" plywood) extends across pass-through and linen closet; compartment above it has its own folding doors.

MODULAR PLANTER

BY BILL COYLE

This eye-catching planter with the modular design is for anyone whose favorite house plants deserve a nicer stage for doing their act. Since the individual modules are not permanently fastened together, they can be shifted easily around to suit different room layouts. Whether you assemble them in a corner, under a window, or use them as a room divider, the choice of more than a dozen combinations is yours.

Building the planter is a cinch—strictly a one-weekend project for any home woodworker. The one power tool required is a radial-arm or a table saw, for cutting the miters.

Materials are also minimal. A complete list includes about 24′ of 1-by-10 pine, 6′ of 1-by-8, a length of ⅛″ dowel, a handful of 1¼″ finishing nails, white glue, wood putty, stain, and varnish.

The sketch shows dimensions. Here's the procedure I recommend for making your planter: Start by cutting the side panels for all five modules. First, cut the parts to length, then rip the miters.

Getting it together. Before assembling the modules, nail and glue the support cleats in place. To assemble, apply glue to mitered edges and clamp with corner clamps. Then reinforce the joints with finishing nails. I predrilled the nail holes to prevent splitting.

Note that when the finished units are arranged, the small floating units are supported by dowel pins projecting about ¾″ from the

Planter can go together in a straight line or it can fit a corner. Three floor modules are of different heights to give you extra flexibility in arrangement.

284

sides of the floor units. On any side that may require these dowel supports, drill two 1/8" holes 10" up from the bottom, and about 5' apart on center. Then cut a 1½" length of dowel for each hole.

The number of sides you prepare with dowel supports depends on the planter arrangement you plan to use. But by preparing three sides of each floor unit you'll have the option of any of a dozen or so possible combinations.

Finally, don't glue the dowels in place. Those not in use can then be hidden by pushing them in flush with the planter surface.

When the carpentry work is done, you're ready to finish the planter. Apply wood putty to the nail holes. Sand all the corners and outer surfaces. Make sure you remove all plane marks and glue smears; they'll show up under the stain.

Now for the stain. The choice of stain is up to you, but it's best to stay away from the mahogany stains, especially those in the red range. They don't look natural on pine. You're better off with one of the antique-pine stains, the kind that gives new white wood an aged look.

Whichever you use, apply it according to the manufacturer's instructions. And don't

Floating modules slip in between floor units and rest on dowel-pin supports. Cleats of 1" stock hold the plant carriers. Sketch at right gives assembly details.

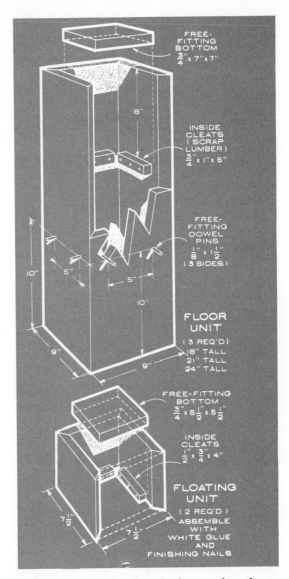

forget to stain the dowel pins so that those not in use will blend in with the surface finish when pushed in flush.

When the stain is dry, finish up with at least two coats of varnish, sanding between coats. Finish the planters inside as well as out to protect the wood against moisture and to prevent warping. Exposed end grain—always a problem on stained wood—was dealt with by brushing on black enamel, which provided a nice accent.

285

HEADBOARD FOR NIGHT OWLS

BY JOHN WOODWARD

Here's a dream headboard for those who like to read or write in comfort during bed-time hours. Twin doors behind you open to place at your fingertips all the reading matter and writing materials you might want. There's even space for a small radio, glasses and a high-intensity lamp on one of the doors.

The frame consists of one-by-four pine stock. All other wood materials can be $1/2''$ or $5/8''$ plywood, hardwood-surfaced for those panels that will show. Thin embossed wood molding was used around edges of the shelves to retain items placed there.

As seen in the drawing, the one-by-four frame was doubled at the floor and hardware

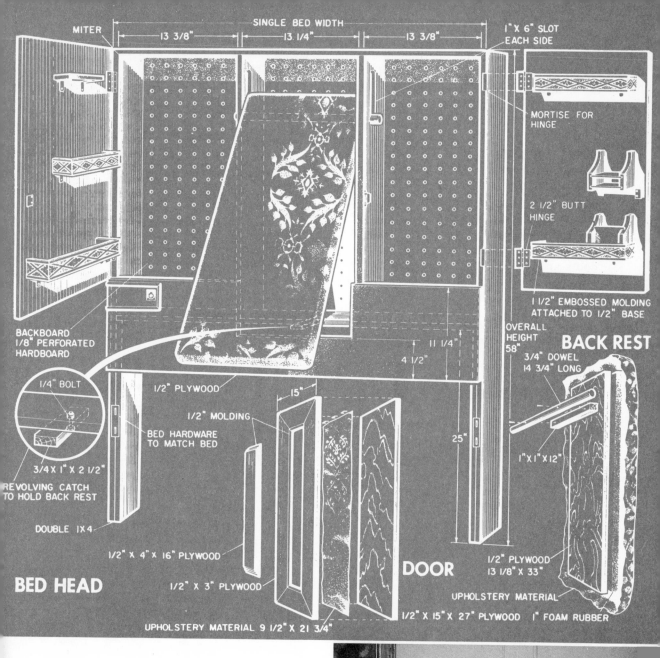

SINGLE BED WIDTH

MITER

13 3/8" · 13 1/4" · 13 3/8"

1" X 6" SLOT EACH SIDE

MORTISE FOR HINGE

2 1/2" BUTT HINGE

1 1/2" EMBOSSED MOLDING ATTACHED TO 1/2" BASE

OVERALL HEIGHT 58"

BACK REST

3/4" DOWEL 14 3/4" LONG

1" X 1" X 12"

BACKBOARD 1/8" PERFORATED HARDBOARD

11 1/4"

4 1/2"

1/2" PLYWOOD

1/4" BOLT

1/2" MOLDING

BED HARDWARE TO MATCH BED

15"

25"

3/4 X 1" X 2 1/2"

REVOLVING CATCH TO HOLD BACK REST

DOUBLE 1X4

1/2" X 4" X 16" PLYWOOD

1/2" X 3" PLYWOOD

DOOR

1/2" PLYWOOD 13 1/8" X 33"

UPHOLSTERY MATERIAL

BED HEAD

UPHOLSTERY MATERIAL 9 1/2" X 21 3/4"

1/2" X 15" X 27" PLYWOOD   1" FOAM RUBBER

During the day, the headboard is an ornamental piece of furniture (photo on opposite page), giving no hint of the many work and reading advantages it offers a nonsleeper (see right) at night.

was installed to take the side rails of a conventional single bed. This attachment could be omitted, of course, and the entire headboard fastened to the wall with lag screws. Then you would simply place the regular bed in front of it.

Pieces of quality upholstery material were stapled inside the door framing. Mitered molding around the inner edges of the frame pieces covers the staples and edges of the fabric. Matching fabric went on the face of the backrest.

Antique white paint was applied to the doors and shelf moldings, and matching off-white enamel to the frame and the lower facing. Brass pulls finish off the two doors.

A foam-padded backrest tilts out at a convenient angle as a ½″ dowel across its top slides down in the retaining slots on each side. Adjust the backrest to suit your own comfort. A pivoting latch on bottom frame cross-piece keeps backrest in its up position.

Convenient shelves are attached inside doors with small brass angles. Arrange and dimension the shelves to suit your requirements. The retaining shelves have ½″ plywood bottoms, surrounded with 1½″ embossed wood moldings.

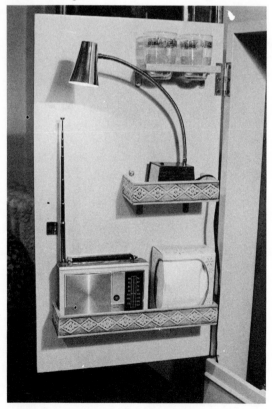

each end that hold it for eye-level selection without letting it swing down enough to spill the contents. Match the tray length (and finish) to your cabinets; compartmentalize it to take the spices you normally keep on hand. A simple catch or hook holds the tray closed. Full counter space is then usable and the rack is virtually unseen.

UNDER CABINET SPICE RACK

BY JERRY VAN DYKE

My wife likes to keep a variety of spices handy, and she prefers to leave them in their original containers, since these are usually better dispensers than those standardized spice-rack units. But storing these odd-shaped little cans and jars in a cupboard proved impractical. In digging through them for the spice needed, she usually sent others cascading onto the counter below.

So I designed this shallow pull-down tray that snugs up under the cabinets. It's hinged along the rear edge, with folding supports at

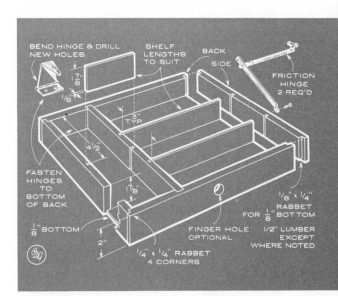

STORE-ALL TABLE WITH HIGH-STYLE HINGES

BY AL LEES
Designed by Gary Gerber

A well-designed cocktail or coffee table should do more than provide a place to rest refreshment. It should corral the clutter of your living room or den by offering tuck-away storage compartments. But this function calls for multiple hinges, and the project would bristle with barrels, pins, and exposed screws if you used conventional hardware. For this reason, Homecraft's designer cabinet hinges were used by Gary Gerber in creating a storage table that could take its place in any living room. The hinges have no visible pivots or screws to mar their richly sculptured patterns. They're easily back-mounted on standard $\frac{3}{8}''$-lip doors by drilling two holes through the panel to take protruding screw sockets. An abbreviated hinge base, completing the exclusive integral-pin construction, is blind-mounted to the doorframe.

(If the Sculptura line isn't available at local stores, write for a brochure from Gries Reproducer Co., 400 Beechwood Ave., New Rochelle, N.Y. 10802.)

Construction of our table is deliberately simple. We chose mahogany-faced plywood (with matching veneer tape) and Baroque-pattern hinges and pulls in silver finish.

We cut cabinet parts to the sizes shown (except doors, which we fitted last) and did all grooving prior to assembly. If you don't own a dado head, cut the grooves with repeat passes on a table or radial-arm saw, and clean up with a chisel.

Richly sculptured designer hinges are mounted on cabinet doors with hinge-base on door frame.

Doors on cabinet backs cover top half of area with shelf, allowing open space for magazines below.

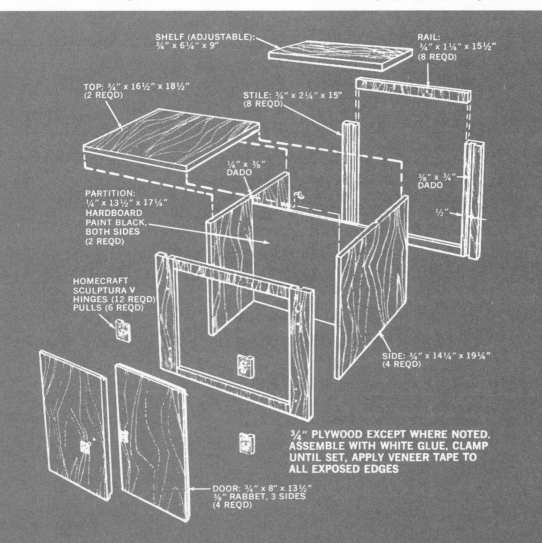

SHELF (ADJUSTABLE): ¾" x 6¼" x 9"

RAIL: ¾" x 1¼" x 15½" (8 REQD)

TOP: ¾" x 16½" x 18½" (2 REQD)

STILE: ¾" x 2¼" x 15" (8 REQD)

¼" x ⅜" DADO

⅜" x ¾" DADO

½"

PARTITION: ¼" x 13½" x 17¼" HARDBOARD PAINT BLACK, BOTH SIDES (2 REQD)

HOMECRAFT SCULPTURA V HINGES (12 REQD) PULLS (6 REQD)

SIDE: ¾" x 14¼" x 19¼" (4 REQD)

¾" PLYWOOD EXCEPT WHERE NOTED. ASSEMBLE WITH WHITE GLUE, CLAMP UNTIL SET, APPLY VENEER TAPE TO ALL EXPOSED EDGES

DOOR: ¾" x 8" x 13½" ⅜" RABBET, 3 SIDES (4 REQD)

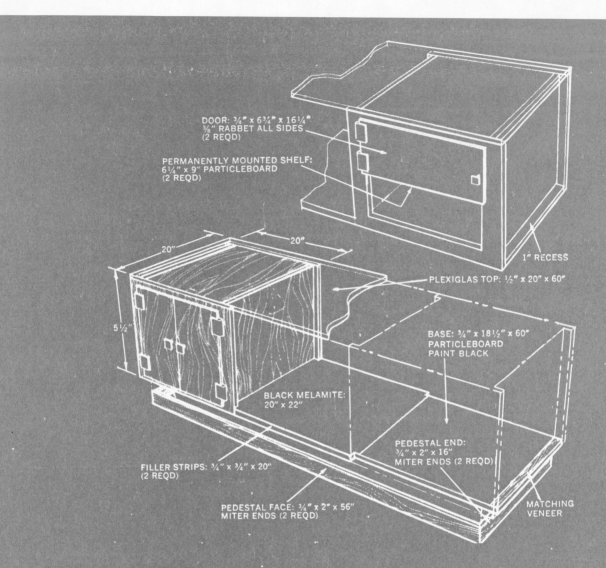

DOOR: ¾" x 6¾" x 16¼"
⅜" RABBET ALL SIDES
(2 REQD)

PERMANENTLY MOUNTED SHELF:
6¼" x 9" PARTICLEBOARD
(2 REQD)

1" RECESS

20"

20"

5½"

PLEXIGLAS TOP: ½" x 20" x 60"

BASE: ¾" x 18½" x 60"
PARTICLEBOARD
PAINT BLACK

BLACK MELAMITE:
20" x 22"

PEDESTAL END:
¾" x 2" x 16"
MITER ENDS (2 REQD)

FILLER STRIPS: ¾" x ¾" x 20"
(2 REQD)

MATCHING
VENEER

PEDESTAL FACE: ¾" x 2" x 56"
MITER ENDS (2 REQD)

MATERIALS LIST

¾" Hardwood Plywood
2 Pedestal end: 2" x 16"
2 Pedestal face: 2" x 56"
4 Side: 14¼" x 19¼"
8 Frame stile: 2¼" x 15"
8 Frame rail: 1¼" x 15½"
2 Top: 16½" x 18½"
4 Front door: 8" x 13½"

2 Rear door: 6¾" x 16¼"
¾" Particleboard
1 Base: 18½" x 60"
2 Attached shelf: 6¼" x 9"
¼" Hardboard
2 Partition: 13½" x 17¼"
½" Plexiglas
1 Top: 20" x 60"

Two cabinet shells are identical. Assemble face frames, then glue side panels into precut dadoes. Slip hardboard partition into ¼″ grooves in sides.

Exposed plywood edges are masked with matching veneer tape after assembly. Let glue set, trim flush with sharp knife.

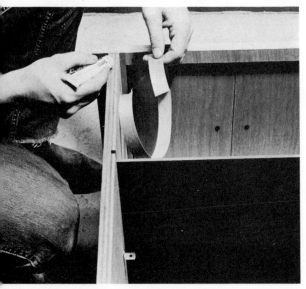

Screw the 2″ pedestal to the particleboard base before attaching the cabinet assemblies. Apply filler strips to both edges of the base, between these cabinets, to bring the open center section to full 20″ width. These strips will be hidden by veneer tape on their sides and by the black plastic laminate used to face the exposed center recess.

This laminate is applied with contact cement, as on a countertop. For fitting ease, apply the laminate before the cabinets are anchored.

The acrylic top (which could be plate glass, if easier to find) is held in place by its weight alone.

Hinges come in five designs, with matching pulls at left. Clockwise from bottom center: Baroque, Fleur-de-Lis, Contempora, Basketweave, Florentine.

BEHIND-DOOR PANTRY

BY DON KIRK

In today's overcrowded homes, it's a bonus if you can utilize space you didn't know you had. Does your kitchen door open against a corner? If so, what possible use is that wall space—scarcely deeper than the jamb trim? It was going to waste in our kitchen, yet we were short of food cupboards. So I tucked in this canned-goods rack, the same width as the door panel.

The fact that the rack is only one can (or bottle) deep is a plus—you can inventory your stock at a glance. Details I'm proud of:

• That open shelf creates a recess at doorknob height so the door still opens fully.

• Since no protruding pulls were possible I used touch-type latches.

• No need for a space-stealing back panel— screw the rack directly against the wall with cleats or metal angles.

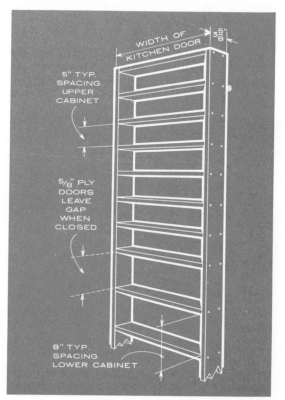

LIST OF MANUFACTURERS
AND SUPPLY SOURCES

Alta Industries
3015 N.W. Industrial
Portland, Oregon 97210

The Armor Company
Box 290
Deer Park, New York 11729

Armstrong Cork Company
1010 Concord Street
Lancaster, Pennsylvania 17604

Buckingham-Virginia Slate Corporation
1103 East Main Street
Richmond, Virginia

Albert Constantine and Sons, Incorporated
2050 Eastchester Road
Bronx, New York 10461

Craftsman Wood Service Company
2727 South Mary Street
Chicago, Illinois 60608

Decor Corporation
Division of Vanguard Industries, Incorporated
10607 Chester Road
Cincinnati, Ohio 45215

Dremel Manufacturing Company
Dept. 350
Racine, Wisconsin 53406

E.I. DuPont De Nemours, & Company
Building Products Division
Wilmington, Delaware 19898

Edmund Scientific Company
Barrington, New Jersey 08007

Georgia-Pacific Corporation
900 S.W. Fifth Avenue
Portland, Oregon 97204

The Goodyear Tire and Rubber Company
P.O. Box 9023
Akron, Ohio 44305

Grant Pulley and Hardware Company
High Street
West Nyack, New York 10994

Gries Reproducer Company
400 Beechwood Avenue
New Rochelle, New York 10800

Heli-Coil Corporation
Shelter Rock Lane
Danbury, Connecticut

Horton Brasses
Box 95, Brooks Hill Road
Cromwell, Connecticut 06416

Knape and Vogt Company
2700 Oak Industrial Drive
Grand Rapids, Michigan 49505

McClosky Varnish Company
7600 State Road
Philadelphia, Pennsylvania 19136

Masonite Corporation
Dept. TR-10
Box 777
Chicago, Illinois 60690

National Lock
Division of Keystone Consolidated
Industries, Incorporated
1902 7th. Street
Rockford, Illinois 61101

Period Furniture Hardware Company
123 Charles Street
Boston, Massachusetts 02114

Reynolds Metals Company
P.O. Box 27003-ZA
Richmond, Virginia 23261

Sear, Roebuck and Company, Incorporated
925 S. Homan Avenue
Chicago, Illinois 60624

Simon's Hardware Incorporated
421 Third Avenue
New York, New York 10016

The Stanley Works
New Britain, Connecticut 06050

Steel Rule Die Manufacturing Company
53 Toledo Street
Farmingdale, New York 11735

Tassell Industries, Incorporated
435 Lake Michigan Drive, N.W.
Grand Rapids, Michigan 49504

U.S. Plywood
777 Third Avenue
New York, New York 10017

Watco-Dennis Corporation
1756 ssnd.
Santa Monica, California 90414

Weller Industries
Division of Cooper Industries, Incorporated
100 Wellco Road
Easton, Pennsylvania 18042

INDEX

Abbeduto, Patrick, 136
Abbott, Jim, 168-172
Allphin, Willard, 138-140

Bars:
   corner-hung, 256
   -desk-bench, 198-200
   snack, 272-273
Beall, Jerrold R., 180-185
Benches:
   bench-desk-bar, 198-200
   phone, 138-140
   sailmaker's, 178-180
Bend-by-kerfing method, 127-129
Benrey, Ronald, 131
Bogash, J. F., 172
Book rack for desk, 165
Bookcase, knockdown puzzle, 147
Bookends, saw, 262

Bookshelves, 48
   coffee table, 107-110
   rotating, 255
Brothers, W. P., 167
Bucher, Carlton G., 107-110
Buffets:
   slate-topped, 70-71
   with woven panels, 178-185
Burke, Howell M., Jr., 198-200

Cabinets:
   gun, locking, 104-105
   projection, swivel-top, 80-83
   shallow, 49-50
   storage, 137
Candelabra, mod mini, 207
Candlestand, Shaker-style, 196-197
Candlestick plate holder, 251
Caning, 58, 231-234

Capotosoto, John, 118, 123
Capotosto, Rosario, 19-22, 61-65, 106, 148-154, 173-176, 276-278
Carving board, well-and-tree, 264-265
  See also Cutting boards; Slicing platform
Centerpiece, double-duty, 34
Chairs:
  cube, 191-195
  easy, custom-built, 257-261
  multipurpose, 126-130
  open-space frame module, 186-187, 189-190
  outdoor-indoor, 113-117
  reclining, 55-59
Chinese Domestic Furniture (Ecke), 132
Clark, Hank, 270-271
Clement, J. W., 195
Clock frame, 269
Close, C. Wayne, 218
Coat rack, 61-65
Coffee mug house, 72
Cotton, Thomas W., 80-83
Couch, double, 124-125
Counter-top cutouts, 234-237
Coyle, Bill, 284-285
Cristoforo, R. J. de, 84-87, 126-130, 252-254, 257-261
Cutting boards:
  from counter-top cutout, 235-236
  nonskid, 224
  See also Carving board, well-and-tree; Slicing platform

Davis, Chester, 6-10
Desk caddy, 18
Desks:
  Air Force Academy, 74-79
  -bench-bar, 198-200
  custom-built, 252
  delta, 215-218
  easy-to-build, 168-172
  provincial-style, 6-10
  trestle, western-style, and bench, 73
  wall-mounted, 218
Directory holders, 60
Distressing wood, 89, 178

Doll crib, Early-American, 103
Donegan, Robert E., 34

Earle, Arthur, 210-214
Ecke, Gustav, 132
Eymann, William, 126-130

Furniture Antiques Found in Virginia (Lynch), 94

Gerber, Gary, 274, 290-293
Gilmore, Bob, 146
Glowka, A., 47
Graves, John, 11
Greenwald, Frank, 39-46, 208-209, 220-223
Guest room, 148-154

Half-lapping, 162-163
Hampers:
  dual purpose, 146
  log, 140
Hand, A. J., 274-275
Hand, Jackson, 266-268
Hawkins, W. J., 98
Headboard, 286-288
Hedin, R. S., 137
Hobby bench-desk-bar, 198-200
Hobby center, 242-244
Hochman, Louis, 280-283
Home-show stand, 276-278
Huff, Darrell, 1-3, 124-125
Huston, H. V., 201-206
Hutch, Early-American, 225-227

Indoor-outdoor furniture, 113-117
Inlaying, 95
Isaacs, Ken, 141-146, 148-154, 186-190, 194-195, 215-218

Jig, 61-62, 173-176
Johnstone, James B., 33

Kanelba, George S., 36-38
Kennedy, Arthur, 206
Kerfing, 127-129
Kirk, Don, 294

Kitchen towel holder, 110
Koren, Sergey, 165

Lamps:
  aquarium, 161-165
  telescoping wood rings, 19-22
Lathing, 19-22, 102, 159-160, 197
Lees, Al, 138-140, 148-154, 290-293
Luggage rack, 185
Luxemburg, W., 225-227
Lynch, E. Carlyle, 94

McCafferty, Phil, 88-92
Magazine rack, 275
Make-up stand, 125
Mangurian, Robert, 245-249
Microdorm, 141-146
Mitering, 204
Moldings, 6, 45, 49-50, 235

Oliver, Rich, 147
Ottomans:
  contemporary, 98
  outdoor-indoor, 113-117
Outdoor-indoor furniture, 113-117

Pantry, behind-door, 294
Payne, Jack, 176-177
Peninsula, movable, 4-5
Philips, Mack, 51-54
Phone booth, for family room, 274-275
Photocoasters, 219
Picture frame, classic, 35
Planters:
  hutch-style, 12-13
  mobile, 111
  modular, 284-285

Rabbeting, 169, 238
Recipe holder, dry-sink, 263
Reppert, John E., 12-13
Rexrode, L. O., 93
Rhine, Charles E., 242-244
Riedel, John, 140
Roberts, Earl J., 275
Rutherford, Donald, 70-71

Schultz, R. E., 27-31
Sculpting, 53-54
Servers:
  beverage, 273
  Corian-topped, classic style, 88-92
Settees:
  outdoor-indoor, 113-117
  Shaker, 99-102
Shearer, Thomas B., 49-50, 272-273
Shelves:
  adjustable wall system, 36-38
  air-conditioner, 123
  balcony, 93
  basement, 208-209
  bookshelves, 48, 107, 255
  box, 33
  coffee table bookshelf, 107-110
  crawl space, 47
  movable, 112
  refrigerator, 279
  storage wall, 280-283
Sherman, Harry, 250
Shoe rack, 167
Sickler, Richard C., 14-18, 113-117
Sleeping unit, child's, 245-249
Slicing platform, 54
  See also Carving board, well-and-tree;
    Cutting boards
Spice racks:
  space-saving, 136
  under cabinet, 289
Stools:
  Abe Lincoln footstool, 228-234
  multipurpose, 126, 127, 130
Storage grid, 186-187, 189-190
Storage walls:
  family room, 220-223
  two-faced, 280-283

Tabletop, recessed tile pattern, 210-214
Tables:
  aquarium, 161-165
  buffet or dining, 27-31
  Chinese, 132-136
  coffee:
    bookshelf, 107-110

Tables (*continued*)
    glass-topped, 131
    marble-topped, 39-46
    music center, 201-206
    particle board, 238-242
  dining:
    drop-leaf, 172
    marble, 1-3
  end, sculptured, 51-54
  floating, 11
  game:
    flip-top, 118-123
    seven-in-one, 14-18
  "I," 191-195
  Parsons, fancy, 266-268
  party, 61-65
  pedestal, from counter-top cutout, 236
  Pembroke, 94-97
  rocker, 66-69
  slaw-board, 176-177
  stack, 250
  store-all, 290-293
  tile, Spanish-style, 84-87
  tilt-top, 155-160
  typewriter, 32
Taggart, Frank, 55-59

Tiling, 84-87, 210-214
Trays:
  grooming, 38
  TV dinner, 206
Treves, Ralph, 185
"Turniture," all-in-one, 23-26
Typewriter stand, 194

Van Dyke, Jerry, 289
Vanity, 270-271
  corner, 166-167

Walker, Lester, 23-26, 61-65, 66-69, 126-130, 173-176
Walton, Harry, 255
Wardrobes:
  child's, 106
  storage wall, 280-283
Warkaske, A. M., 243
Warren, David, 99-102, 132-136, 155-160, 196-197, 207
Weathering wood, 89
Weed, R. W., 112
Woodward, John, 32, 269, 279, 286
Wortham, Robert, 125, 219